Principles of Supply Chain Risk Management and Banks

How Supply Chain Resilience in a Digital Age Helps Banks Navigate Through Extreme Events

Pascal vander Straeten

Value4Risk LLC Dallas

Value4Risk

Published by Value4Risk LLC, Prosper, Texas

ISBN: 9781734184105

For general information on our other products and services or for technical support, please contact our Customer Care Department at info@value4risk.com.

ACKNOWLEDGEMENTS

This book project began in the Spring of 2016. I was already in my fourth year since I had established VALUE4RISK, a consulting and research company focused in business resilience. During those years, and also based on my prior 25 years of experience as a senior bank executive in risk management, I noticed that not much had been written on business resilience for banking organization. I have been very much interested in extreme risk management, and how it can affect the strategic planning and governance of a bank.

In the scope of this quest for a better comprehension of extreme risk management for the banking industry, I wanted to scout the corporate sector and see how companies that operate in extreme environments cope with extreme conditions. Currently, within the banking industry, most of the knowledge concepts about extreme events are either too much tainted by the traditional risk management methods that attempt to predict the future occurrence and severity of an extreme event using quantitative models. Or, otherwise, the knowledge tools are too much geared on Big Data in trying to map all possible scenarios and hazards that have taken place in the past, and that could affect companies in the future.

Organizations need to be proactive to ensure that they are ready to handle any risky situations that can interfere with their operations. The concept behind the book, therefore, focuses on making a bank agile, resistant, resilient and be able to recover quickly when an extreme event takes place rather than predicting times when the firm is likely to encounter risks and reacting when the events turn up. A resilient business model is not just about being to resist the impact of an extreme event, but also how fast the firm can recover from the impact of an extreme event.

The exciting feature of this book is the fact that the concept of supply chain management that is going to be used in this study to address business resiliency has been borrowed from the nonbanking world. Indeed, supply chain risk management is used in the manufacturing world and could be applicable to the banking industry for example whereby it would endeavor an integrated risk management approach of a front-to-back processing for all banking activities to manage both everyday as well as exceptional risks along the supply chain.

This book will enable banks and researchers to understand how supply chain risk management is very different from traditional risk management because it will show that extreme risks will be addressed through the prism of stakeholder relationships, customer relation management, and business resiliency rather than using probability theories. Therefore, this book will focus much more on the governance, business processes, qualitative methods, and risk mitigation techniques surrounding supply risk management than on the quantitative approaches, such as using as distributions of probabilities.

Over recent years, I have received numerous constructive comments on my notes from several pundits, such as university professors, entrepreneurs, and government officials as well as former colleagues. I am deeply thankful to them. This has not only helped me improve successive versions of the compendium but also given me an in-depth opportunity to learn how different organizations and professionals think about the issues presented here.

The latitude of the proposed research is multi-disciplinary and will draw upon the disciplines of business administration, management theory (including strategic planning), change management, business resiliency, and of course risk management. As a result of the integration of different disciplines, plus the research methodology, the research is expected to develop a generic model of supply chain risk management for the banking industry. The study should aid these institutions to improve their effectiveness and efficiency when facing extreme risk events. It will contribute to the risk management discipline by providing a qualitative risk tool aimed at making banks more resilient.

It goes without saying that all opinions and faults found here are my own.

Dallas, Texas, October 2019

"At the wonderful science museum in Barcelona, I saw an exhibit that beautifully illustrated "chaos." A nonlinear version of a pendulum was set up so that the visitor could hold the bob and start out in a chosen position and with a chosen velocity. One could then watch the subsequent motion, which was also recorded with a pen on a sheet of paper. The visitor was then invited to seize the bob again and try to imitate exactly the previous initial position and velocity. No matter how carefully that was done, the subsequent motion was quite different from what it was the first time ... I asked the museum director what the two men were doing who were standing in a corner watching us. He replied, "Oh, those are two Dutchmen waiting to take away the `chaos.'" Apparently, the exhibit was about to be dismantled and taken to Amsterdam. But I have wondered ever since whether the services of those two Dutchmen would not be in great demand across the globe, by organizations that wanted their chaos taken away."

Murray Gell-Mann, author of The Quark and the Jaguar

About the Author

Pascal vander Straeten has a passion for financial risk management and geopolitics, and, over the years, he has specialized in the risk management of extreme events, institutional banking, and capital markets activities as well as corporate finance, with a particular focus on initiating and enhancing efficiencies in relation to risk processes that focus on proactive risk management and economic capital savings.

Pascal has already published two books:

- In August 2017, Pascal published "Tail Risk Management: Building a Resilient Financial Business in a Volatile World". That book was selected to become the object of an in-depth Ph.D. research.
- In April 2018 he published a second book "An Overture to Geofinance: Global Finance, Geopolitics, and the Wielding of Power: Theory and Praxis". This book was awarded being one of the best independent non-fiction books by Kirkus Reviews for 2018.

He has more than twenty-five years of professional experience in the risk management of commercial banks, with assignments in Australia, Belgium, France,

Germany, Italy, Luxembourg, Spain, the United Kingdom, and the United States. Most recently, he ran the credit-risk management of the financial market activities of a large global commercial bank.

Currently managing his own financial- and political-risk advisory and research firm (Value4Risk), he aims to assist businesses and financial organizations in weathering extreme (tail) risk events as well as in creating a risk-aware corporate culture with business resiliency. He has a proven track record of setting up, building, and expanding risk-management frameworks and processes.

His expertise includes day-to-day management of large credit-risk and underwriting departments, designing and executing risk policies, regulatory-change management, developing and implementing training modules in relation to enterprise risk management as well as financial and political tail-risk management, and developing risk-mapping, early-warning, and reverse stress-testing tools.

Academically speaking, Pascal holds two masters (cf. a Master of Applied Economics from the Universiteit Antwerpen and an Executive MBA from the University of Washington). Additionally, he also obtained a postgraduate degree in International Politics from the Université Catholique de Louvain. Last but not least, he is currently doing a Ph.D. with the University of Leicester.

Table of Contents

List of Main Abbreviations

ATM: automated teller machine

B2B: Business-to-Business

BPM: Business performance management

Brexit: Withdrawal of the United Kingdom from the European Union

CB: Consumer business

CCP: Central counterparty clearing

CDM: Cash deposit machine

CDS: Credit default swap

CFPB: Consumer Finance Protection Bureau

CIT: Cash in transit

CPG: Consumer packaged goods (institutions)

COSO: Committee of Sponsoring Organizations of the Treadway Commission

DoD: Department of Defense

ERM: Enterprise risk management

FHLB: Federal Home Loan Bank

FI: Financial institutions

FinTech: Financial technology

FX: Foreign exchange

GDP: Gross domestic product

GDPR: General Data Protection Regulation (EU regulation)

GFC: Global financial crisis

Grexit: Withdrawal of Greece from the European Union

IIF: Institute of International Finance

IoT: Internet of things

ISM: Institute for Supply Management

ISO: International Standards Organization

ISP: Independent service providers

IT: Information Technology

KM: Knowledge management

KPI: Key performance indicators

KYC: Know your customer

KYV: Know your vendor

OCC: Office of the Comptroller of the Currency

ORM: Operational risk management

P&L: Profit & loss

PCI-DSS: Payment Card Industry Data Security Standard

PI: performance impact for the node

REI: risk exposure index

ROA: Return on asset

S&OP: Sales and operations planning

SARS: Severe acute respiratory syndrome

SCM: Supply chain management

SCOR: Supply chain operations reference model

SCRAM: Supply chain resilience assessment and management tool

SLA: Service level agreement

SSAE: Statement on Standards for Attestation Engagements

SSC: Service supply chain

STP: straight-through-processing

TPRM: Third party risk management

TTR: Time to recovery

List of Figures

To the love of my life and best friend, Barbara, without whose support
I would not have been able to reach my goals.

Preliminary Remark - Research Methodology

While supply chain management has risen to great prominence in recent year, there is hardly any research on related developments that are applicable to the banking industry, and concomitantly there are hardly any development in related research methodologies. Yet, as supply chains cover more than one organization, one central issue is how to collect and analyze data along the whole or relevant part of a supply chain.

Within the 17 sections a wide array of research material has been assembled bringing together a rich selection of theoretical and practical examples of how supply chain risk management is applied within the corporate industry and could be implemented within the banking world. The book relies on papers about theoretical implications as well as papers on a range of key topics, such as resilience, systemic risk, operational risk, and sustainability. It is my hope that this book will be of great interest to both practitioners and scholars alike in the area of supply chain management and banking, but also to adjacent fields, such as operational and extreme risk management.

The analysis of this book is based on both primary and secondary data. First part of this book, theoretical framework and evolution of SCM evolved from secondary data sources, particularly online databases, books, journals, conference papers, etc. On the other hand, the 2nd part of this book is furnished based on the analysis of literature, past theoretical frameworks, interviews with stakeholders.

In essence, I conducted a literature review by combining topics, such as supply chain risk management, banks, resilience, sustainability, business model, operational risk, extreme risk, process management. and governance. I researched the criteria and instruments used in supply chain risk management within the corporate world, and see how I could transpose them to the banking industry. I endeavored to be as much as possible market oriented in order to propose best practices that could be readily applicable to the banking industry.

The primary data were based on interviews I had with senior executives from several banking institutions as well as corporate organizations that practice supply chain risk management on a daily basis, such as, logistics, distribution, and manufacturing (assembling). I held one-on-one sessions with these professionals after submitting them a list of questions pertaining to the application of supply chain risk principles to their operating activities.

The book consists of seventeen sections that map a road toward a gradual understanding of how supply chain risk management is relevant to the banking industry. In the first three sections I go over the theoretical framework revolving around resilience, supply chain management, and supply chain risk management; these three sections are the building blocks of this book.

In section four and five I trace the application of supply chain risk management, first in the servicing industry and, then, in the banking industry. In section six and seven I discuss the various parties involved in a supply chain, with a focus not only on third parties but also on first and second parties. The latter parties are typically involved in the flows of data and money that stream within an organization. I will also talk (section eight) about the phenomenon of service level agreements between these various parties. In the ninth section I postulate about the concept of value chain and how it differs from a supply chain within a banking organization. Indeed, given the proximity and the complementarity of the concepts used, it is necessary to clarify these before undergoing an in-depth study of the origins of the competitiveness and the essential activities of the chain.

In the following sections (cf. ten and eleven) I introduce the concept of resilience and how supply chain risk management are paramount for an organization to achieve sustainability and agility in terms of business model. In section twelve, I broach the subject of working capital in symbiose with supply chain risk management. Indeed, while many are aware of the opportunity that supply chain management represents for reducing transportation costs, it is not obvious to the lion share of banks that this is also a component of working capital management.

Section thirteen embraces the world of technology by introducing it to the realm of digital banking and how the latter impacts supply chain risk management. As such, over the past couple of decades, the explosive growth of the Internet has made it much easier for organizations to transact with each other around the world. It is therefore to also talk about the connectivity and universal reach of the Internet, and how it has enabled organizations to integrate and better coordinate all their various processes.

The fourteenth section creates a parallel between operational risk management and supply chain risk management, and notably in terms of business performance management as the latter supports organization wide integration and collaboration via workflow.

Section fifteen aims at helping executives within a banking organization to build a case for a wide adoption of the notion of supply chain risk management beyond the traditional realm of procurement. Often, given that executives who understand the need still struggle to create the business case and get approval for the appropriate levels of investment, the section proposes a practical five-step approach based on best practices. Section sixteen builds a business case pleading for banks to adopt supply chain risk management to cover the entire networks of supply chains from back-to-front. In the final section I enumerate a couple of final thoughts on the applicability of supply chain risk management within a banking organization.

It is also key to note that this book has found inspiration and grounds for further research through many other books that have equally addressed the topic of supply chain risk management. Therefore, the author has attempted to consolidate these existing essays on supply chain risk management and bring their findings to the attention of organizations active in the banking industry. For the sake of academic accountability, the author has, as much as he could, referenced each and every work he consulted or cited. as exhaustively as he could. Additionally, the author attempted to make the book as illuminating as possible. Therefore, the book addresses both concepts primarily in general terms as well as provides concrete examples of how the ideas it covers can be implemented in practice. Illustrative graphs were added to the research attempting to make it a more useful tool for those looking to make risk management decisions.

A last but not trivial remark: you will notice that in several passages of this book, several concepts and statements are being repeated. It's on purpose, and the reason is twofold:

- Repeat for clarity: Like it or not, many readers skim. No matter how clearly concepts are expressed the first time, these words may literally not have been seen. Content needs to cut through a reader's dense fog of information clutter, chronic interruption, and recurring fantasies about such things as supply chain, risk management, resilience, analytics, and sustainability. And since many concepts are important, they are worth repeating. It is especially important to repeat calls to action.

- Repeat for certainty: Do not assume readers got it the first time or that they still remember it. Since this book contains some powerful or important ideas, the audience is being hit with them more than once. Whether the concepts are being spoken to new readers or old hands, it makes sense to repeat key messages every few chapters or so. The more you repeat a concept, the deeper and richer the thinking gets each time the concept is revisited.

INTRODUCTION

As soon as a bank places the customer at the center of its delivery strategy, that bank has to follow the peculiar business dynamics that influence and shape the client's business decisions. Almost any business decision has an impact on the supply chain, and in a globalized world, supply chain collaboration is one of the most highly prioritized corporate objectives.

Financial market players - be it financial institutions (banks, insurance companies, asset managers, brokers) or prudential authorities - could learn a lot from how the corporate world is coping with the risk management of disruptive events.

In the corporate world, they call this Supply Chain (Risk) Management, and while there is a somewhat equivalent concept labeled as financial supply chain management within the banking world, the latter merely revolves around the payments side of trade, from the moment a purchase order is submitted to the time of settlement and everything in between.

In the corporate world - from a definition perspective - Supply Chain Management (SCM) is described as the management of the flow of goods and services that includes the movement and storage of raw materials, work-in-process inventory, and finished goods from point-of-origin to point-of-consumption. In essence, SCM draws heavily from the areas of operations management, logistics, procurement, and information technology, and strives for an integrated approach.

Interestingly enough, within the financial services industry, nothing comparable exists because when one thinks about it, the granting of a loan is the essence of a banking activity as it is through these lending activities that banks generate revenues (yes, nowadays, banks also generate massive revenues from non-lending activities) as the primary root of banking is transforming money, namely collecting deposits and lending them to the economy (be it households, firms, and governments).

However, banks do not have an integrated approach in managing the different phases to deliver an end-product/service to a customer and where they view, for example, the lending process as a supply chain. Yes, they have a B2B paperless computer driven lending process in the case of a mortgage loan where the consumer can purchase or refinance a home without ever signing or handling a piece of paper.

And, they do not have a streamlined, fully integrated chain of supply of services that involves back office, middle office, risk management, business developers, finance, and IT being part of one chain. All these departments work in silo with, yes, bridges between themselves, but without really thinking about their service as being part of an integrated chain.

In other words, what is missing is the risk management of front-to-back processing for all banking activities. Some banking areas have adopted this train of thought such as Treasury or Trade Finance, but traditional activities such as corporate banking, retail banking or institutional banking still operate in silo architectures and lack integrity of operations.

IGURE 1: FLOW CHART LETTER OF CREDIT

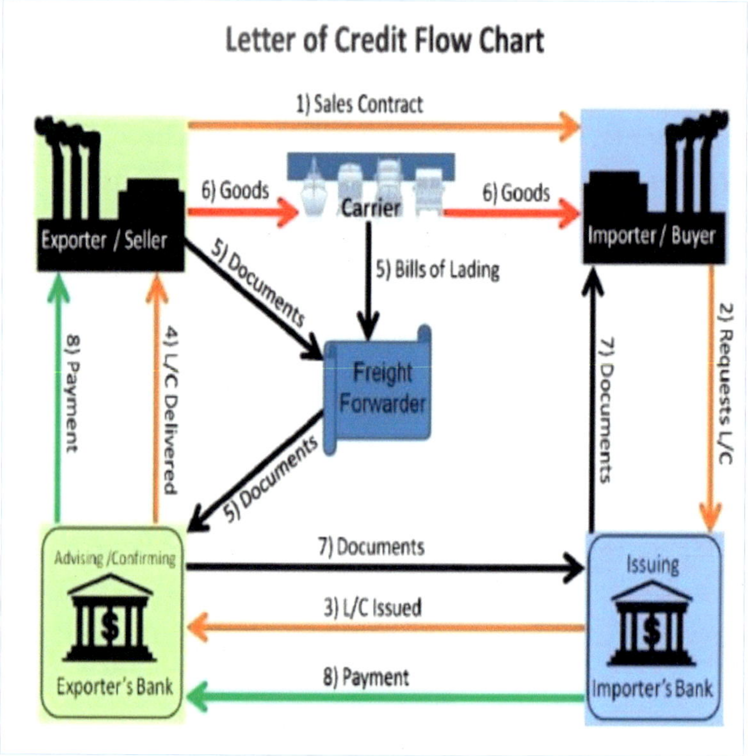

Source: The Balance, 2018

In an ideal world, the workflow of the sales desk should be integrated with the middle office, risk management, back office (cf. about settlement and confirmation), accounting, reporting, and inquiries. A simple proof of this segregation is the mere existence of difference IT architectures and software programs for each of those activities lacking efficient bridges among these areas of operations.

Going back to the corporate world, traditional methods for managing supply chain risk rely on knowing the likelihood of occurrence and the magnitude of impact for every potential event that could materially disrupt a firm's operations. For frequent supply-chain disruptions—poor supplier performance, forecast errors, transportation breakdowns, for example—those methods work very well, using historical data to quantify the level of risk.

However, it is a different story for low-probability, high-impact events—mega-disasters like Hurricane Katrina in 2005, viral epidemics like the 2003 SARS outbreak, or major outages due to unforeseen events such as factory fires and political upheavals. Because historical data on these rare events are limited or nonexistent, their risk is hard to quantify using traditional models. As a result, many companies do not adequately prepare for them.

That can have disastrous consequences when catastrophes do strike and can force even operationally savvy companies to scramble after the fact—think of

Hitachi and Mitsubishi following the 2011 Fukushima earthquake and tsunami.

Instead of designing a risk model that focuses on determining the probability that any specific risk will occur, it is more appropriate to center on the description of the supply chain that puts the emphasis on the impact of potential failures at points along the supply chain (such as the shuttering of a supplier's factory or a flood at a distribution center), rather than again the cause of the disruption. This type of assessment removes the necessity to establish the probability that any specific risk will take place; a logical approach given that the mitigation strategies for disruption are equally effective regardless of what caused it.

Using this approach, companies can quantify what the financial and operational impact would be if a critical supplier's facility were out of commission for, say, two weeks—whatever the reason. The computerized model can be updated easily and quickly, which is crucial since supply chains are in a continual state of flux.

A central characteristic of this approach is time to recovery (TTR), namely the time it would take for a particular node (such as a supplier facility, a distribution center, or a transportation hub) to be restored to full functionality after a disruption. TTR values are determined by examining the historical experience and surveying the firm's buyers or suppliers.

To conduct the analysis, the approach removes one node at a time from the supply network for the duration of the TTR. It then determines the supply chain response that would minimize the performance impact of the disruption at that node—for instance, drawing down inventory, shifting production, expediting transportation, or reallocating resources. Based on the optimal response, it generates a financial or operational performance impact (PI) for the node. A company can choose different measures of PI: lost units of production, revenue, or profit margin, for instance.

The approach analyzes all nodes in the network, assigning a PI to each. The node with the largest PI (in lost sales, for instance, or lost units of production) is assigned a risk exposure index (REI) score of 1.0. All other nodes' REI scores are indexed relative to this value (a node whose disruption would cause the least impact receives a value close to zero). The indexed scores allow the firm to identify at a glance the nodes that should get the most attention from risk managers.

This approach provides several benefits. It:

- Identifies hidden exposures. The approach helps managers identify which nodes in the network create the highest risk exposure—often highlighting previously hidden or overlooked areas of high risk. It also allows the firm to compare the costs and benefits of various alternatives for mitigating the impact.

- Avoids the need for predictions about rare events. The approach determines the optimal response to any disruption that might occur within the supply network, regardless of the cause. Rather than trying to quantify the likelihood that a low-probability, high-risk event will strike, firms can focus on identifying the most significant exposures and putting in place risk-management strategies to mitigate them.

- Reveals supply chain dependencies and bottlenecks. Companies can also use the analyzes to make inventory and sourcing decisions that increase the robustness of the network. This includes taking into account the likely scramble among rival companies to lock in alternative sources if a supplier's disruption affects several firms. Such cross-firm effects of a crisis are often overlooked. Contracts with backup suppliers can be negotiated to give a company priority over others should a disruption with the primary supplier occur, which would decrease time to recovery and financial impact.

- Promotes discussion and learning. In the course of analyzing the supply chain in this way, managers engage in discussions with suppliers and internal groups about acceptable levels of TTR for critical facilities and share insights about best-practice processes to reduce recovery time. As a result, the impact of disruptions is minimized.

This approach could also be transposed to the financial services industry, and its way on how to risk manage extreme events with a low probability but high severity.

In practice, for a bank, one could map out the supply chain (front-to-back) process that involves the provision of a loan to a household or business entity or the settlement of payment, and look at how external events could disrupt the provision of this service to the end-customer.

FIGURE 2: MAPPING APPROVAL PROCESS LOAN

STEP 1: Complete Loan Application					
STEP 2: Processing (collecting, analyzing, and verifying)					
Order/ check credit report or rating report	Oder/ Check appraisal or collateral/ asset report	Order/ check background (compliance, KYC)	Order/ Check Miscellaneous docs		
STEP 3: Underwriting (interpretation and thorough analysis of information in loan package)					
Analyze creditworthiness	Analyze collateral/ asset	Define loan conditions			
STEP 4: Decision-taking, and if Approved, Closing and Funding					
Order Loan Docs	Docs signed and verification signature	Follow up docs returned	Final Conditions	Funds requested	Title or lien recorded (if it is a secured transaction)

These events could involve the lack of funding due to dry out of the interbank market or a lack of confidence from fixed income investors; the occurrence of a system defect that would prevent the bank from closing the deal (cf. physical disruptions would be covered by operational risk management); the default of a swap counterparty involved in the transaction; exacerbated

FX movements or a sovereign crisis affecting international payments, for example.

The risk management of disruptive events is partially covered by operational risk management. Indeed, operational risk can be created by a broad range of different external events ranging from power failures to floods or earthquakes to terrorist attacks. Similarly, operational risk can arise due to internal events such as the potential for failures or inadequacies in any of the bank's processes and systems (e.g., its IT, risk management or human resources management processes and systems), or those of its outsourced service providers.

Operational risk arising from human resources management may refer to a range of issues such as mismanaged or poorly trained employees; the potential of employees for negligence, willful misconduct; conflict of interests; fraud; rogue trading; and so on. Therefore, the emergence of mistrust, failure to communicate, low morale and cynicism among staff members, as well as increased turnover of staff, should be regarded as indicative for a potential increase in operational risk.

However, financial events are not covered by operational risk management, such as a market crash, the spill-over effects of the bankruptcy of a systemically important financial institution, the impact of a Grexit or Brexit, a very hard landing of the Chinese economy, a military confrontation between the West and Russia in central Europe, the take-over of Saudi Arabia by ISIS, an escalating conflict between China and the Philippines, for example. All these events will, in one way or the other, from a supply chain management perspective, also disrupt the provisions of financial services to the end-customer.

Therefore, it is highly useful to map the process that allows a description of the front-to-back process concerning payments, lending, investments, for example, and look at how a disruption would impact one of the nodes alongside the supply chain for each of those financial activities, and how long it would take for the system to recover its senses, i.e. re-conduct the business as a going concern to the benefit of the customers.

It is common knowledge that R.K. Oliver and M.D. Weber, two consultants in the field of logistics, introduced the concept of Supply Chain Management (SCM) in literature at the beginning of the 1980s (Felea & Albăstroiu, 2013). Although, the study conducted in the area of collaboration and integration of various functional units started long before the term SCM was introduced. In literature, these academic efforts could be described in various domains, such as marketing, logistics, management research, organizational theory, operational research, through focused theoretical contributions, such as: collaboration and cooperation; bullwhip effect in production-distribution systems; channel searching; inventory location and control; and hierarchical production planning.

Practitioners' concern and scholars' interest concerning supply chain management have gradually grown over the last forty years when companies found that they can no longer compete effectively when they operate in silo not in partnership with their suppliers or other stakeholders in the supply chain, and saw the advantages of collaborative partnerships within and beyond their organization. Applicability of SCM has been thoroughly studied in various application fields during since the early 2000s, and many definitions of supply chain management have been suggested in the literature.

Notwithstanding the popularity of SCM in business and academic environments, there is considerable ambiguity about its meaning because, as postulated by Habib (2010), some researchers defined SCM in operational terms involving the flux of raw materials and products, while other theorists claimed it as a management philosophy, while others described it in terms of a management process, or as an integrated system. SCM is, on the one hand, a type of management philosophy, and on the other hand, a form of integrated system. Such confusion indicates the necessity to study the processes related to SCM more thoroughly to define the notion with precision.

Over the past ten years, risk management has grown to become an ever-larger part of the operating model of banking institutions as prudential authorities enhance scrutiny, clients raise expectations, and technology advances at a fast pace. Managing third-party risk is particularly challenging, exerting enormous pressure on banking institutions to account for how other organizations utilize and shield their data, and manage sustainable operations, especially for critical services.

Within this realm, it is essential for banking institutions not to be inhibited by the requirements of supply chain risk management (supply chain risk management) but instead, view that this role can be a vital enabler. Effective supply chain risk management is not primarily about keeping regulators on the right side of the organization — it is an opportunity to generate business value while concomitantly managing risk now and for the years to come. Strategic and efficient supply chain risk management functions will cut down operating costs but also create the foundation for deeper, trustworthy relationships with clients that will yield a healthy competitive advantage in the future.

The quest for effective customer relationship management (CRM) most likely embodies the Holy Grail of supply chain risk management, given that genuine CRM necessitates the integration of applications as diverse as marketing, customer profitability analysis, demographics, desktop underwriting, credit rating, and contact center management systems.

The more the various parties involved in this supply chain comprehend themselves as partners and prime movers in a traditional supply chain, the more readily they can embrace and take advantage of the lessons that other organizations have experienced about the complexity and arduous job of integrating the supply chain. The credit card and mortgage origination businesses highlight some instructive illustrations and key take-away lessons that can be applied to many other sub-sectors of the industry.

Given that supply chain management within the banking industry has mostly been focusing on the external supply chain, namely a chain of data or services provided by external suppliers involving contractors, vendors, and consultants, for example, an organization's performance would be strengthened by the management of the relations with those external suppliers. However, in opposition to the manufacturing and logistics industries that have also been paying attention to internal supply chains, not much academic research has been conducted about the internal supply chain within the banking industry. The purpose of this book is to remedy such phenomenon and present research on the topic of, amongst others, internal supply chain risk management, and to come up with a set of instruments that maps the supply chain networks (both internal and external) as a way for enhancing the resilience of a banking organization.

SECTION I: THEORETICAL FRAMEWORK ON RESILIENCE

CONCEPTS ON UNCERTAINTY, RESILIENCE & THRIVING

Resilience has been an evolving notion and is distinct from traditional risk management. For the last fifty years, risk analysis tools have played a significant role in corporate decision making, particularly when combined with financial models. In practice, risk management entails analyzing all possible outcomes of a process or project, then weighing the potential benefits against the potential risks of the investment.

Nowadays, the leading approach to enterprise risk management is driven by the Committee of Sponsoring Organizations of the Treadway Commission (COSO 2004). In many applications, risks can be measured based on historical data, but analyzing risks requires hypotheses based on personal information.

Resilience is described as the ability of a system to survive, adapt, and grow in the face of turbulent change (Fiksel, 2006). Business systems have to face technological progress, political turbulence, financial risk, and ever-increasing prudential pressures, highlighting the fact that organizational growth does not proceed smoothly. Resilience is an aspect of complex systems such as firms, towns, or other social ecosystems. Systems evolve through cycles of accumulation, growth, crisis, and rebirth, and even self-organize into more desirable and new configurations.

The entire organization needs to play a role in maintaining and creating supply chain resilience. A resilient supply chain can win-over disruptions and continually adapt itself to satisfy the changing needs and expectations of its shareholders, clients, and other stakeholders.

The traditional metric to manage uncertainty is risk management, which is particularly challenging when threats cannot be predicted. Deliberate threats such as riots, terrorism, vandalism, and cyber theft can even adapt to new security measures. Concomitantly, organizations are accepting broader responsibility for the social, political, and environmental impacts of their supply chains.

All corporations rely on their suppliers to keep smooth operations and their clients for recurrent revenue. Therefore, a resilient firm is truly only as resilient as its supply chain. Jack Welch, the former CEO of GE, wrote in an HBR segment (Tichy and Charan, 1989) that resilience should be on every manager's must-have list because anyone who is really in the game messes up at some point. He concludes that "the most successful people in any job always own their failures, learn from them, regroup and then start again with renewed speed, vigor, and conviction." Learning, anticipating, reacting, and identifying are all at the core of resilience.

A critical step in the risk management process is risk assessment based on the assessed likelihood of an event and the calculated severity if the event takes place. The greatest weakness of risk management is its incapacity to adequately quantify low-probability, high-severity events.

Additionally, the traditional risk assessment approach cannot cope with unforeseeable events. The notion of supply chain resilience can bridge these gaps and supplement existing risk management programs, thus allowing for a supply chain to survive and bounce back from unforeseen disruptions, and thereby yield competitive advantage.

Genesis of Resilience Studies

Resiliency theory has been researched across many scientific disciplines and domains, illustrated by, for instance, the fact that resiliency is defined in the area of psychology as the ability to bounce back and withstand hardship by repairing oneself. Below are a couple of other illustrative examples of how resilience applies to the various fields of science (Ledesma, 2014 and Rutter, 1979):

- Human development: resiliency is defined as the ability to withstand or successfully cope with adversity.
- Developmental psychopathology: it refers to the ability to cope with challenges and threats while maintaining an internal and integrated sense of self.
- Psychiatry: it is psychological and biological strengths humans use to master change successfully.
- Medicine, as the ability to recognize pain, acknowledge its purpose, tolerate it for a while until things begin to normalize.
- Nursing: it is the ability to regenerate power to respond to the internal or external environment for survival, growth, or development.
- Epidemiology: it refers to the ability to survive stress and to rise above disadvantage.
- Change management, it is viewed as the ability to demonstrate both strength and flexibility during

the change process, while displaying minimal dysfunctional behavior.

- Social sciences: resilience is the ability to recover from adverse life experiences and become stronger while overcoming them.

THEORIES OF RESILIENCE

Resilience comes from the word 'resiliens' in Latin, which means the elastic or pliant quality of a substance. Masten (2005) describes resilience as a class of events characterized by favorable outcomes notwithstanding severe threats to the adjustment of development.

Resilience is described as the ability to bounce back from frustration, adversity, and misfortune, and is essential for any leader wanting to operate effectively (Ledesma, 2014). The literature shows that there is a direct correlation between the stress of the leader's job and its ability to preserve resilience in the face of protracted exposure to adversity.

- Rutter (1987), a psychiatric risk researcher, defines the term as being used to describe the positive tone of individual differences in organizations or people's response to adversity and stress. Janas (2002) came up with the term 'resilience' as the capacity to bounce back from frustration, adversity, and misfortune.

- Ledesma (2014) in "Conceptual Frameworks and Research Models on Resilience in Leadership" postulates about resilience that "survival, bouncing back, and thriving are notions associated with resilience, and describe the phase at which an organization or individual may be during or after coping with adversity".
- Perry (2002) defines resilience as the ability to face stressors without significant adverse disruption in operating. In developmental literature, resilience is typically debated in terms of protective psychological risk parameters that help with the development of positive outcomes and sound personality characteristics.

Resilience is also utilized interchangeably with adaptation and adjustment, positive coping, and persistence. In essence, resilience researchers postulate that resilience is focused on the understanding of individual variations in response to threats. While some organizations fall prey to adversity and stress, other institutions survive and respond adequately to the challenges that come with the hazards of life and conducting business.

Models of Resilience

Several academics have used different terms for the three resilience models that essentially describe the same mechanisms for the impact of stress on quality adaptation. These models include the compensatory model, the challenge model, and the protective factor of immunity versus vulnerability model (Ledesma, 2014):

1. The compensatory model apprehends resilience as a factor that neutralizes exposures to risk. Risk factors and compensatory factors independently contribute to the prediction outcome.
2. The challenge model indicates that a risk factor provided it is not too extreme, can enhance a person's adaptation. In essence, the experience prepares the individual for the next challenge.
3. In the protective factor model of resilience, there is an interaction between protection and risk factors, which restricts the probability of an adverse outcome and moderates the effect of exposure to risk. This model of resilience is derived from developmental literature and systems theory. It indicates that these protective factors foster favorable outcomes and healthy personality characteristics despite unfavorable or aversive life circumstances. The protective

> factors identified included emotional management skills, intrapersonal reflective skills, academic and job skills, ability to restore self- esteem, planning skills, life skills, and problem-solving skills.

In Werner and Smith's (2001) study, four central characteristics emerged for the young adults labeled resilient: an active approach toward problem-solving, a tendency to perceive experiences in a positive light even when they were suffering, the ability to gain other people's positive attention, and a strong reliance on faith to maintain a positive life view.

Organizational Resilience

Organizational resiliency refers to an organization's capacity to foster an environment that enhances the career resiliency of its employees. An organization committed to developing resilient employees will (Ledesma, 2014) "foster openness in communication, encouragement of individual contributions for personal growth, risk-taking all with the promise of employee recognition and rewards. Resilient organizations structure, and restructure themselves to attain a mission, support the optimal development of shared decision-making".

They also provide feedback, set goals, and have intelligence-gathering mechanisms (Nishikawa, 2006). They employ people who react quickly and efficiently to change and perceive experiences constructively, ensuring adequate external resources, expand decision-making boundaries, develop the ability to create solutions on the spot, and develop a tolerance for uncertainty.

In the context of resilience and leadership development, protective factors that raise a leader's chance of winning-over adversity must be taken into account. The literature indicates the significance of external support systems and the relevance of confiding and supportive relationships that are typical for resilient individuals. These relationships shield the individual against the effects of stressful events, and, therefore, should warrant considerable attention by organizations aiming to develop resilient leaders (Ledesma, 2014).

Howard and Irving (2013) found that leadership development is gained and shaped through active engagement in hardship or obstacle. They argue that by overcoming obstacles, a person builds a competency to deal with and bounce back from adversity successfully. This implies that organizations have an invaluable impact on building their employees' resilience capacity through leadership training while strengthening the resilience of the overall organization.

Because a key factor in building a leader's capacity for resilience is to ensure a social network of support in times of need, the standard practice of how organizations grow them should be reevaluated. Leaders should be able to have access to trusted peers, mentors, and colleagues and time to reflect and partner-up with professional peers and mentors. They should also be given transformational development opportunities that require less social isolation and greater opportunities for partnerships - all aspects that are essential when hiring and retaining resilient leaders.

Thus, it is paramount for organizations to commit themselves to fostering the resiliency of both the employee and the organization as a whole. While very little research currently exists on the topic of organizational resiliency, the recent surge of studies on thriving and hardship dictate a necessity for a more exhaustive understanding of how resilience can be fostered within organizations.

The overwhelming advantage for the organization that fosters resilience and thriving in its workplace is a more highly motivated workforce (O'Leary, 1998). As a result, there is a mutually favorable outcome for both the employees and the organization.

THRIVING

The term "thriving" refers to a, organizations or person's capacity to proceed beyond his or her first level of operating, and to function and grow notwithstanding ongoing exposure to stressful experiences. The prevailing literature indicates some factors that characterize thriving and resilience.

These parameters encompass hardiness, positive self-esteem, solid coping skills, self-efficacy, a sense of coherence, optimism, adaptability, robust social resources, low fear of failure, risk-taking, determination, a high tolerance of uncertainty and perseverance (Ledesma, 2014). Organizations thrive when they surpass and transcend their prior level of functioning, recoup and even accelerate their upward psychological trajectory. They also seem to have mentally and emotionally benefited from their suffering. And, because of their exposure to crisis situations and how they have trained the staff for coping with stress, organizations seem to begin to flourish.

These various models of resilience and thriving bring to the foreground the role of adaptation in enduring and overcoming crisis situations. Thriving can provide a useful framework for the integration of various concepts (such as coping, self-efficacy, and support, for example) used to explain adaptive response to challenges. The modern literature on thriving suggests that people will respond to thriving in three different ways when confronted by a challenge: They may (Ledesma, 2014):

- survive the incident,
- recover from the incident, and
- thrive as a result of enduring the hardship.

Subsequently, survivors (i.e., organizations) are able to continue to operate, although it may be in an impaired state. Recovery indicates a return to baseline where individuals return to their former level of operation. However, thriving yields a transformation that consists of a cognitive shift in response to a stress situation. A person may reset priorities and have a stronger sense of self. Usually, thriving is the result of a traumatizing event where a person's sense of meaning, purpose, or identity is in jeopardy.

Recent studies in resilience have started to look at the concept of "thriving" whereby thriving emerged from a scientific study on vulnerability and coping paradigms. Thriving is grounded on an individual's positive transformation resulting from the experience of adversity (Nishikawa, 2006). The study of thriving and its application to the field of science, psychology, and medicine can "enhance the understanding of health and provide essential opportunities for prevention and intervention" (Ickovics & Park, 1998, p. 237).

Although thriving has received attention in the fields of social and behavioral psychology primarily in the last decade, the belief that "people are capable of transmuting traumatic experiences to gain wisdom, personal growth, positive personality changes, or more meaningful and productive lives has been a central theme in centuries of literature, poetry, and personal narratives" (Saakvitne, Tennen, & Affleck, 1998, p. 281). As indicated above, thriving has prompted the field to explore perspectives in the hope of seeking an answer to why some people thrive following adversity and others do not. Besides, Patterson and Kelleher (2005) state that "thriving is largely determined by a person's resilience capacity".

They explain that three energy sources—personal values, personal energy, and personal efficacy—account for resilience ability and help fuel an individual's response to adversity. In essence, as an individual learns from adversity, his or her resilience capacity is broadened through strengthening these three energy sources, which, in turn, provide more fuel for the person to cope with the future. Consequently, one becomes more capable and better prepared to address the next crisis.

Patterson and Kelleher (2005) define a resilience cycle that may be adopted by people coping with adversity. The researchers claim that even the most resilient persons experience a rollercoaster effect as they navigate through the aftershocks of the traumatic experience. A four-cycle phase to resilience is defined and includes a deteriorating phase, an adapting phase, a recovery phase, and a growing phase (Nishikawa, 2006). Resilience capacity, for the most part, largely conditions where in the cycle, the individual finds him(her)self.

As such, if a person is unable to adjust to his/her challenging experience, he/she will most likely sink into a dysfunctional level and will be unable to cope or survive the adversity. However, some may adapt but not fully recover, thus reaching the survival level. Then, there will be those who can reach the recovery phase and will return to the status quo (Ledesma, 2014)[1]. Ickovics and Park (1998, p. 239) state that "Understanding the process of thriving can have crucial implications for prevention and intervention for those who face the challenges associated with illness, injury, upheaval, and personal or social adversity of many kinds". Organizations can develop its staff for such interventions with an eye toward reinforcing the overall health and well-being, rather than fostering a return to baseline of the status quo.

[1] However, a small minority of individuals, those who are thrivers, will reach the growing phase and achieve a strengthened resilience level. This growing phase is referred to as thriving.

SECTION II: THEORY SUPPLY CHAIN MGMT

BACKGROUND

During the last decade researchers typically focused on supply chain management (SCM) issues in organizations active in manufacturing and logistics. Research objectives have now widened and may include adding value, reducing cost, or slashing response time in various parties involved in the manufacturing supply chain (Habib, 2014). However, very few studies were attempted in financial organizations, and banking institutions in particular.

SCM provides for-profit organizations assistance when competing in a dynamic international market. The goal of SCM is to acknowledge activities across and within organizations with the aim to deliver better customer value and foster a stronger resilience. Given that banking organizations are equally for-profit organizations that operate on a global scale, there is no reason why SCM should not apply to them as well. The goal is to provide the organization added value by creating money and making these monies available for productive outcomes.

An integrated banking supply chain would involve the coordination and information being shared up and down the process among all stakeholders involved (Habib, 2011). With technology facilitating data flow, a coordinated supply chain can be determined to meet the planning, strategic, and operational objectives of the banking institutions. It also means creating feasible and effective partnerships both inside and outside the banking organization. SCM is needed for various reasons (Habib, 2014): improving operations, better outsourcing, raising profits, enhancing customer satisfaction, generating quality outcomes, tackling competitive pressures, increasing globalization, boosting the importance of E-commerce, and growing complexity of supply chains.

Supply chains are relatively easy to define for manufacturing industries, where each participant in the chain receives inputs from a set of suppliers, processes those inputs, and delivers them to a different set of customers. With banks, one of the main suppliers of process inputs is clients themselves, who provide their minds, bodies, knowledge, or belongings as inputs to the service processes (Habib, 2011).

Evolution of Supply Chain Management

Before the 1950s, logistics was debated in military terms, and it had to do with the procurement, maintenance, and transportation of military assets, materials, and personnel. The research and practice of logistics and physical distribution emerged later, namely in the 1960s and 1970s. The logistics era before 1950 has been characterized as the "hibernation years", when logistics was not considered a strategic function. Right after the wat (1950s) changes took place that could be classified as a first transformation. The relevance of logistics increased considerably when physical distribution management in manufacturing companies was acknowledged as a distinct organizational function. The SCM concept was coined forty years ago by management consultants in logistics. In those days the supply chain must have been viewed as a single entity and that strategic decision-making at the top level was needed to manage the chain in its original formulation (Habib, 2014). This perspective was shared with logisticians as well as theorists in marketing.

Ever since its introduction in the early 1980s SCM has become one of the most widely used concepts within management studies. Numerous journals in customer management, distribution, integration, marketing, manufacturing, and transportation, for example, published articles on SCM. The evolution of SCM persisted into the 1990s due to fierce global competition, and there was also a revolutionary shift within the management literature itself (Lambert and Cooper, 2000): "One of the most significant changes in the paradigm of modern business management is that individual businesses no longer compete as solely autonomous entities, but rather as supply chains. Business management has entered the era of inter-network competition, and the ultimate success of a single business will depend on management's ability to integrate the company's intricate network of business relationships."

Supply Chain – Terminology

In general, a supply chain is made of a large number of partners including customers, distributors, manufacturers, and suppliers. The supply chain involves some other components such as materials, resources, and activities within each partner. Thus, managing a supply chain requires an approach where components are integrated at the primary level and implemented in systems capable of supporting such integration. As such, one needs to understand the various components involved, relationships between these components, and the level of integrations and integration of individual networks across business processes (Chandra and Kumar, 2000).

Materials, activities (operations), resources, and suppliers are four main components involved in a business process within the manufacturing environment. If the business process and related strategies are associated with the supply of raw materials, the supplier becomes an additional component (Samaranayake, 2005). If the business process involves a customer at any stage, the customer can be considered as one of the components for planning and execution. For example, make-to-order strategy is initiated with a customer order.

Therefore, the customer is a component in the associated structure under this strategy. Other components such as warehouses, delivery activities, and resources involved in distribution networks, can also become a part of the business process. Each component can be represented by an icon or a symbol in a structure with all the relationships between components using appropriate precedence.

SUPPLY CHAIN – DEFINITIONS

Contemporary literature provides a litany of definitions for the notion of "supply chain" and the terminology is thus well rooted throughout scholar works, as illustrated by these standard definitions (cf. for the sake of neutrality these definitions have been ranked in alphabetical order):

- Ayers (2001 p. 4) suggest that a supply chain is: "Life cycle processes comprising physical information, financial, and knowledge flows whose purpose is to satisfy end-user requirements with products and services from multiple linked suppliers". According to this definition, the supply chain encompasses processes that cover a broad range of activities including sourcing, manufacturing, transporting, and selling physical products & services. And he continues (Ayers, 2001): "Life cycle refers to both the market life cycle and the usage life cycle, and these are not the same for durable goods and services. Therefore, product support after the sale becomes a key supply chain component." An integrated supply chain model can generally consist of three interrelated flows: informational flows (website linkages or electronic data exchange), material flows (which has itself three different phases (purchasing, transformation, and distribution), and the financial flow (which includes both the payment to subcontractors and suppliers for the merchandises and services as well as the payment by the client to the retailer for the final product) (Waller, 2003). The physical distribution is a vital component of supply chains, and financial and information components are as crucial as physical flows in many supply chains. Also, one needs to underscore the role of knowledge inputs into supply chain processes. For instance, the supply chain process for new products necessitates close coordination of intellectual inputs (cf. the research and design) with physical inputs (cf. prototypes and components, for example).

- Căescu and Dumitru (2011): Any product sold on the consumer goods market, in its evolution from commodity to finished products, undergoes a series of successive intermediations on the B2B market (. For instance, in the case where an end-consumer buys a bottle of soda with a soda manufacturer, he/she does not buy the bottle directly from the producer itself, but rather from a distributor (i.e., an intermediary, such as supermarket or local grocery store, and the product becomes the object of several intermediations or transactions on the B2B market on the circuit that goes from manufacturer – wholesaler – retailer – final consumer.

- Chen and Paulraj (2004) stated that "a typical supply chain is a network of materials, information, and services processing links with the characteristics of supply, transformation, and demand".
- Chopra and Meindl (2007, p.3) state that "a supply chain consists of all parties involved, directly or indirectly, in fulfilling a customer request. Within each firm, such as a manufacturer, the supply chain covers all functions involved in receiving and filling a customer request. These functions include, but are not restricted to, new product development, marketing, operations, distribution, finance, and customer service".
- Lambert, Stock and Ellram (1998): Other describe a supply chain as the alignment of organizations that deliver goods or services to markets and their clients. The supply chain encompasses producer, suppliers, transporters, distributors, warehouses, wholesalers, retailers, other intermediaries, and even customers themselves.

- Mentzer et al. (2001, p. 4) herald a supply chain as "a set of three or more entities (organizations or individuals) directly involved in the upstream and downstream flows of products, services, finances, or information from a source to a customer" with three variations of supply chain complexity:
  i. A "direct supply chain": the direct supply chain consists of a central organization, its suppliers and customers;
  ii. An extended supply chain: this 'long' supply chain encompasses suppliers of the immediate supplier, and customers of the immediate customer; and
  iii. An "ultimate supply chain": a supply chain that includes all organizations that are involved in all flows of products, services, finance, and information from the ultimate suppliers to the ultimate customers. Also, the ultimate supply chain encompasses functional intermediaries such as market research firms, financial and logistics services providers.
- Moise (2008, p.198): The flows direction in the supply chain is not only forward, from the first supplier to the final customer. Goods can flow

back up the supply chain for different reasons such as service or repair, remanufacturing, recycling or disposal. The reverse chain can play an essential role in areas, such as customer satisfaction, environmental protection, and recycling. Reverse logistics is a range of competencies or programs focused on moving products in the reverse direction in the supply chain (i.e., from consumer to producer), and related activities may consist of recycling, handling product returns, reuse of materials, refurbishing, waste disposal, or remanufacturing.

- Seifbarghy and Gilkalayeh (2012): A supply chain may also have multiple linked suppliers There are a large number of different configurations for the supply chain. Some are very short and simple, such as "a small grocery buying vegetables directly from the farmer, and the others are long and complicated, like a fish cannery that source from fishermen, and sell the products through a retail network. Increasingly more companies coordinate in both upstream and downstream echelons in a supply network the material and information flow among different suppliers, manufacturers, and distributors".

- Thomas and Griffin (1996): The typical supply chain is characterized by three traditional stages: procurement, production, and distribution. Each one of these phases may be characterized by its location throughout several facilities in different regions around the world. An illustration of this is the automotive industry with assembly plants located in various whereby the supply of different components is set on a global stage.

SUPPLY CHAIN MANAGEMENT - TERMINOLOGY

Bearing in mind previous set of definitions, one could describe a supply chain as a chain consisting of all the activities and process associated with the flow of products and data from the commodity phase to the end-consumer of the product/service.

The integration of activities and processes among the members of the supply chain is traditionally labeled as Supply Chain Management (Handfield and Nichols, 2003). Moreover, the domain of Supply Chain Management (SCM) was erected (Russel and Taylor, 2009) to manage the flow of data, goods, and services across a network of clients, firms, and supply chain partners, and ever since its establishment as a management concept some forty years ago, supply chain management has been the object of significant modifications and adjustments.

Many scholars attribute the foundations of SCM to the way how the logistics function evolved over the last decades, and several consider that logistics and SCM are synonyms. Indeed, a scholar, such as Waters (2008, p. 38), states that "Logistics - or supply chain management - is the function responsible for the transport and storage of materials on their journey from original suppliers, through intermediate operations, and to final customers".

Now, even though SCM is embedded with logistics management activities, there is however a distinction between the notion of supply chain management and the traditional concept of logistics:

- Supply chain management reckons not only all the traditional logistics but also includes activities such as finance, marketing, customer service, and new product development (Hugos, 2006).
    - Ballou, Gilbert and Mukherjee (2000) herald three aspects of SCM:

  - Intra-functional dimension (regarding the management of processes and activities within logistics as a function of the organization);
  - Inter-functional coordination (refers to the coordination of activities (about specific functions) between the functional areas of the organization);
  - Inter-organizational coordination (concerning the coordination of the chain of activities taking place between legally distinctive organizations, in compliance with the product flow).
- On the other hand, Larsson and Halldorsson (2004) pinpoint four conceptual approaches on SCM in comparison to logistics, namely a traditionalist, re-labeling, unionist, and intersected approach:
  - The traditionalist school views SCM as a part of logistics, along the lines of external or inter-organizational logistics.

  - The re-labeling perspective simply renames logistics: what was logistics is now SCM.
  - According to the unionist view, logistics is a part of SCM, limiting logistics to one of many business processes or areas (Felea and Albastroiu, 2013).
  - The intersection perspective shows that SCM is a broad strategy that cuts across many if not all business areas where logistics covers the operational decisions; SCM is related with a strategic decision, and tactical decisions fall to the intersection.
- Logistics is the management function responsible for all the flows of materials within the scope of a single organization, while SCM posits a broader perspective of the movement through all related stakeholders that characterize the supply chain.

SUPPLY CHAIN MANAGEMENT - DEFINITIONS

Thereby, over the past 30 years, Supply Chain Management (SCM) as a management function has been studied by various practitioners and researchers alike.

Below is a non-exhaustive synthesis of the conceptual evolution regarding supply chain management through several notions and definitions of SCM from its inception until today (cf. for the sake of neutrality those definitions have been ranked in alphabetical order):

- APICS - Association for Operations Management: SCM refers to „the design, planning, execution, control, and monitoring of supply chain activities to create net value, building a competitive infrastructure, synchronizing supply with demand, and measuring performance globally."
- Bowersox, Closs and Cooper (2002): "Supply chain (sometimes called the value chain or demand chain) management consists of firms collaborating to leverage strategic positioning and to improve operating efficiency. For each firm involved, the supply chain relationship reflects a strategic choice. A supply chain strategy is a channel arrangement based on acknowledged dependency and relationship management. Supply chain operations require managerial processes that span across functional areas within individual firms, and link trading partners and customers across organizational boundaries."

- Bozarth and Handfield (2008): "Supply Chain Management is the active management of supply chain activities and relationships in order to maximize customer value and achieve sustainable competitive advantage."
- Chartered Institute of Purchasing & Supply: SCM is „the management of all activities aimed at satisfying the end-consumer, as such it covers almost all activity within the organization; it includes several key success factors that include a clear procurement strategy, effective control systems, and development of expertise".
- CIO (business unit of International Data Group) Dictionary, compiled by T. Wailgum and B. Worthen (2008) expresses the essence of SCM concept, defining the term in this way: „the combination of art and science that goes into improving the way a company finds the raw components it needs to make a product/service, and deliver it to customers."
- Global Supply Chain Forum (GSCF): it states that SCM is a new business model necessary for an organization's success, and everyone in the organization needs to be involved. According to the GSCF definition, after Lambert, Cooper and Pagh (1998, p.1): „Supply Chain Management is

the integration of key business processes from end-user through original suppliers that provides products, services, and information that add value for customers and stakeholders."

- Krajewski, Ritzman, and Malhotra (2007): "Supply Chain Management consists of developing a strategy to organize, control, and motivate the resources involved in the flow of services and materials within the supply chain."
- Logistics & Supply Chain Management Society: SCM refers to „a business strategy to improve shareholder and customer value by optimizing the flow of products, services and related information from the source to the end-customer, and encompasses the processes of creating and fulfilling the market's demand for goods and services. It is a set of business processes engaged in a common goal of satisfying the end-customer."
- Oliver and Webber (1982): "Supply chain management (SCM) is the process of planning, implementing, and controlling the operations of the supply chain with the purpose to satisfy customer requirements as efficiently as possible. Supply chain management spans all movement and storage of raw materials, work-in-process

inventory, and finished goods from point-of-origin to point-of-consumption."

- Simchi-Levi, Kaminsky and Simchi-Levi (2008): "Supply Chain Management is a set of approaches utilized to integrate suppliers efficiently, manufacturers, warehouses, and stores, so that merchandise is produced and distributed at the right quantity, to the right locations, and at the right time, in order to minimize system-wide costs while satisfying service level requirements."
- Sweeney (2007): "Supply Chain Management is the systemic, strategic coordination of the traditional business function and tactics across these business functions within a particular company, and across businesses within the supply chain, for the purpose of improving the long-term performance of the individual companies and the supply chain as a whole."
- Tan, Kannan and Handfield (1998): "Supply chain management encompasses materials/supply management from the supply of basic raw materials to final product (and possible recycling and re-use). Supply chain management focuses on how firms utilize their

suppliers' processes, technology, and capability to enhance competitive advantage."

- Wisner, Tan, and Leong (2012): "Supply chain management is the integration of trading partners' key business processes from initial raw material extraction to the final or end-customer, including all intermediate processing, transportation, and storage activities, and final sale to the end-product customer."

This full spectrum of definitions for supply chain management (SCM) illustrates the holistic approach to the operation of the organization, and for theorists SCM is a melting pot of various fields, with influences from transportation, logistics, operations management, marketing, distribution, as well as information technology (IT) and purchasing.

In most theoretical approaches, SCM seems to be defined as:

- On one hand, as a term that involves integrating and coordinating all the activities involved in delivering a good or a service (i.e., including activities regarding supply of spare parts and raw materials, manufacturing, assembly, and tracking processes, inventory and warehousing, order management and entry, distribution across all channels, delivery to the client, and the data analytics required to monitor all of these).

- On the other hand, practitioners usually focus in their definitions on various supply chain management targets, such as embedment the activities across and within organizations in such a way as to generate value to clients, increasing customer satisfaction, determine improving operations, increasing profits, reducing cost, reducing response time in various activities involved in the supply, manufacturing and delivering chain, tackling competitive pressures, better exploitation of the opportunities of globalization (Felea and Albastroiu, 2013).

Bearing in mind the main criteria for describing supply chain management the practitioners' concepts are drawn mainly from the point of view of the management activities and objectives.

THE FOUR MAJOR CRITERIA OF SUPPLY CHAIN MANAGEMENT

Analysis of SCM literature reveals that there are many perspectives on supply chain management, but academic textbooks and researchers in the field of logistics and supply chain management typically adopt the Council of Supply Chain Management Professionals (CSCMP) definition, namely: "Supply Chain Management encompasses the planning and management of all activities involved in sourcing and procurement, conversion, and all logistics management activities." (CSCMP, 2012)

Analyzing these definitions, several key concepts and derived concepts used to explain the term SCM can be identified (Felea and Albăstroiu, 2013):

- the key concepts are the following: business function, business processes, collaboration, controlling, coordination customer requirements, customer value, competitive advantage, costs, planning, implementing, integration, logistics activities, managerial processes, manufacturers, motivating, movement, organizing, processing, point-of-origin, performance, point-of consumption, storage, suppliers, stores relationship, service level, transportation, and warehouses;
- the derived concepts are the following: at the right time, efficiently, finished goods, inventory, long term operations, raw materials, right quantity, sharing data, systemic, strategic,

sustainable, to the right locations, and working process.

The study of definitions, key and derived terms resulted in the identification of four major criteria: management activities; logistics activities, objective, and components. Within each criterion the most significant key and derived concepts have been regrouped (Felea and Albāstroiu, 2013):

- Management activities:
  - Key terms: controlling, implementing, motivating, organizing, and planning,
  - Derived concepts: efficiency, goods, and services; SCM consists of controlling efficiently of all the activities involved in the flux of merchandises and services from the initial supplier to the end-client, including planning, organizing, implementing, and motivating.
- Logistics activities:
  - Key terms: processing, storage, and transportation.
  - Derived concepts: finished goods, raw materials, and work-in-process inventory; SCM includes transportation, processing, and storage of raw materials, work-in-

process inventory, and finished goods from the initial extraction stage to the final customer.

- Objectives:
    - Key terms: competitive advantage, customer requirements, relationships, trust, and value.
    - Derived concepts: long term and sustainable; SCM includes some value-added processes designed to achieve sustainable competitive advantage, build trust among the supply chain partners, establish long term relationships, and to satisfy customer requirements.
- Components:
    - Key terms: manufacturers, stores, suppliers, and warehouses.
    - Derived concepts: products and services; SCM encompasses manufacturers, suppliers, stores, warehouses, and other stakeholders that are involved in the movement of services and products from the point-of-origin to the point-of-consumption.

The Objectives and Goals Of Supply Chain Management

The responsibility of a supply chain director is to monitor the flow of materials from the source all the way to the end-customer. The remit sounds straightforward, but the implementation is far from easy illustrated by the fact that the limiting factors on materials and data flow across any supply chain make the job daunting, and occasionally close to impossible (Trudgian, 2018).

Supply chains are facing a plethora of potential disruptions, from supply decoupling points through to client SLAs (i.e., service level agreements), and every logistics movement in between. Organizations typically focus on their supply chains when they are interested in the following issues (Krištofík, 2010, and Gerald, 2016):

- Gaining visibility over all the processes involved in the financial supply chain.
- Enhancing efficiencies throughout the entire chain.
- Cutting costs throughout the chain.
- Releasing working capital by getting a better understanding of where funds are required.

- Embracing a collaborative method towards other stakeholders in the chain.

Supply chain management is integral to conducting a business in order to improve customer service, cut operating costs, and boost the company's financial position. The objectives of supply chain management are collaborative efficiency, long-term stability, optimized logistics, product portfolio management, and quality improvement.

To fuel a company's efficiency and productivity, as well as the overall bottom line of the P&L of the organization, it is key to focus on supply chain management, or SCM. Supply chain management is a collaborative approach to moving the goods or services from a company to the end-consumers. The above-mentioned objectives of supply chain management assist firms in gaining a competitive edge in the marketplace and creating a supply chain that is as resilient and profitable as possible (Giorgio, 2018).

A supply chain is the interconnected patchwork of organizations, individuals, activities, resources, systems, and technologies involved in the conception and sale of a product or service. An organization 's supply chain starts with the sale and delivery of the commodities necessary for production, and finishes with the delivery of the product or service to the end-consumer.

Because SCM encompasses so many stages, it allows organizations to look at each phase of the process to make sure its leaders focus on efficiencies, and are not losing value. The result is obtaining a better product or service delivered to the end-consumer more effectively.

Supply chain management can become increasingly crucial to an organization as global markets and networks expand. Through supply chain management, organizations can boost customer service, reduce operating costs, and improve a company's financial position.

Supply chain management can also have a more significant global impact, such as restricting energy consumption and reducing air pollution, not to mention assisting in the distribution of merchandises in a crisis situation. Below are the five objectives that any supply chain manager should be compelled to achieve (Trudgian, 2018):

- Product portfolio management: This first goal may surprise the casual observer. However, taking an active in monitoring what products are utilized and sold by a business is a pillar for improved supply chain control. Nearly every organization has a product portfolio that mirrors the Pareto principle (cf. where 20% of the products generate 80% of revenue), or more importantly for the supply chain manager, 20% of the revenue is generated by only 80% of products. In other words, there's always a large number of products the supply chain has to take into account with that, in practice, bring nearly no added value to the business. For the supply chain, these products are synonymous to obsolescence risk and are slow moving, which in turn fills up valuable warehouse space, constrains working capital, and raises operating costs. If an organization does not have an effective approach to manage its product portfolio, then the supply chain manager needs to take the initiative and create a more effective portfolio management.

- Working on quality improvement: Bear in mind that delivering consumers the best value is an objective that transcends both the organization and its stakeholders in the supply chain. The more deeply connected an organization is with those stakeholders, the more likely it is to boost the overall quality of the consumer experience.

Retailers, as the most straightforward link between consumers and goods, are the ones who often collect feedback and complaints about product quality. Therefore, in a collaborative supply chain, organizations should create a system for those retailers to share these customer feedbacks to the company and other stakeholders in the supply chain. This precious feedback allows an organization to address any problems or defects, and to zoom on constant improvement of products. This creates a win for all those involved in the supply chain because consumers recognize and appreciate value.

- Optimized transportation and logistics: a key component of supply chain management is addressing transportation and logistics within a company. In an independent business environment, each company is responsible for its role in ordering, shipping and transporting goods, but costs are high and timing is unfortunate. With supply chain management, the vendor or buyer, can plan optimized transportation and logistics activities with the vendors and buyers the organization works with. Orders are automated between a reseller and a vendor, and vendors quickly pull, ship and transmit orders to buyers for clear communication.

- Working to ensure efficiency: managing inventory, transportation, and logistics can be complicated and costly for a company if it does not have an effective SCM system. When manufacturers, wholesalers and retailers collaborate on a supply chain system, it is easier for a company and its partners to ensure efficiency. For example, the company could share inventory data with its supplier, and vice versa. This allows for fast replenishment of inventory to meet customer demand. That efficiency in getting goods to the right place at the right time minimizes inventory costs, and meets customer demand.
- Maintaining long-term stability: By forming strong trusting supply chain relationships and working toward best practices in distribution, a company can aim for long-term stability. Collaborative planning, coordination and distribution activities spread the risks of business decisions across multiple companies. As an organization, and those it works with look for improvement opportunities, a common result is a stabilization within its industry. Shared

interests in meeting customer needs also cause the organization and other companies within the supply chain to communicate about optimizing distribution systems.

SECTION III: THEORY SUPPLY CHAIN RISK MGMT

INTRODUCTION

The swift globalization of supply chains has made them vulnerable to chaotic disturbances, such as economic unrest, demand fluctuations, geopolitical tensions, or natural or man-made disasters with potentially damaging long- and short-term impacts on the organization (Wieland & Wallenburg, 2012).

Generally speaking, organizations require resilient supply chains to mitigate the adverse effects of disruptions on revenues, costs, and customers. Not surprisingly, understanding and effectively managing supply chain risk is a key capability for building and maintaining resilient supply chains (Brindley,2004, p.80).

Risk management in the supply chain has become increasingly important as companies both large and small seek to extend their global reach. Enterprises entering new markets often need to form new supplier relationships, engage with state-owned entities, and adapt to local laws and culture. The resulting complexity in the supply chain can mask a wide range of financial, regulatory, and legal risks.

In this context, it's not surprising that supply chain waste and disruptions arising from fraud and abuse have become more common. A recent Deloitte Touche Tohmatsu Limited survey (2016) found that 85% of surveyed global supply chains had experienced at least one disruption in the past 12 months.

Fortunately, proactive risk management in the supply chain has shown to be a cost-effective approach. Companies that indicated that they proactively manage supply chain risk spend 50% less to manage supplier disruptions than companies that stated that they aren't proactive.

DIFFERENCES SUPPLY CHAIN MGMT AND SUPPLY CHAIN RISK MGMT

As your organization makes strategic choices, such as expanding geographic reach and taking on the related risks, you need to effectively manage risk from beginning to end. This mindset can help your organization gain competitive advantage, maintain your brand's reputation, and ultimately, use an understanding of risk to drive performance.

Truly understanding the supply chain requires stringent processes and capabilities for supply chain data analytics. Many organizations are using data analytics to look at not just financial transaction information, but also other more operational details to really understand where their potential risks lie. Indeed, the complexity of today's environment has made the use of supply chain data analytics critical for identifying supply chain waste, fraud, billing anomalies, and risk patterns.

Supply chain risk management corresponds to an execution of strategies to address both recurrent and non-recurrent risks along the supply chain based on continuous risk assessment with the objective of reducing vulnerability and ensuring continuity.

In other words, supply chain risk management is to apply risk management process tools, with partners in a supply chain or on your own, to deal with risks and uncertainties caused by, or affecting, logistics-related activities or resources in the supply chain.

Supply chain risk management involves cash-flow management to ensure profitability (e.g. Faisal et al., 2007) and to save costs (Manuj and Mentzer, 2008). From a business continuity perspective, supply chain risk management aims at managing exposure to serious business disruptions arising from risk within and outside the supply chain.

In this sense, supply chain risk management aims to build the capability to reduce vulnerability and ensure business continuity. When a firm is better able to manage risks than the competition, it can lead to an improved market position. Thus, supply chain risk management aims not only to reduce costs and vulnerability but also to ensure profitability, business continuity, and potentially longer-term growth. Supply chain risk management aims at reducing supply-chain vulnerability via a coordinated holistic approach, involving all supply-chain stakeholders, which identifies and analyzes the risk of failure points within the supply chain. Risks to the supply chain range from unpredictable natural threats to counterfeit products, and reach across quality, security, to resiliency and product integrity.

Mitigation plans to manage these risks can involve logistics, cybersecurity, finance and risk management disciplines; the ultimate goal being to ensure supply chain continuity in the event of a scenario which otherwise would have interrupted normal business and so profitability. Sometimes, it's possible for supply chain logistics techniques such as supply-chain optimization to prejudice contingency planning which would otherwise reduce the overall risk level for that particular supply chain. It is also becoming more common among businesses especially manufacturers to employ a supplier quality management software, which integrates all phases of the supply-chain cycle. This approach is shown to increase transparency, reduce overhead costs, and improve operational efficiency. However, supply chain risk management is a multi-faceted concept. As a result, different perspectives could be defined, with either an emphasis on the pathway and objectives of supply chain risk management or with a focus on the various supply chain risk management stages. As such, a holistic view is recommended that would incorporate not only the different stages of supply chain risk management, but also the objectives and the pathway to supply chain risk management.

Such holistic approach would call for a new, comprehensive definition that is:

- internally consistent, so supply chain risk management can reflect both the nature of risk management and supply chain management, providing researchers from different fields with a common understanding of supply chain risk management; and,

- externally consistent with the aim to solving real business problems.

As such, such holistic definition of supply chain risk management would be:

> The identification, assessment, treatment, and monitoring of supply chain risks, with the aid of the internal implementation of tools, techniques and strategies and of external coordination and collaboration with supply chain members so as to reduce vulnerability and ensure continuity coupled with profitability, leading to competitive advantage.

This definition reflects the full supply chain risk management process, the pathway to supply chain risk management, and the objectives of supply chain risk management. It is a holistic definition that denotes the positive outcome of managing negative forms of supply chain risks, eventually resulting in competitive advantage, and it offers a conceptualization that integrates objectives-based, process- based, and outcome-based thinking into one exhaustive framework. The conceptual framework helps understand the objectives of supply chain risk management that motivate a firm to select and implement strategies in the supply chain risk management process while also investigating how internal and external pathways influence supply chain risk management practices and their outcomes from a holistic viewpoint.

APPLICATION ISO APPROACH TO SUPPLY CHAIN RISK MANAGEMENT

Risk management is the identification, evaluation, and prioritization of risks (defined in ISO 31000[2] as the effect of uncertainty on objectives) followed by coordinated and economical application of resources to minimize, monitor, and control the probability or impact of unfortunate events or to maximize the realization of opportunities (Hubbard, 2009, p. 46).

1. Risk identification aims to discover all relevant risks and recognize future uncertainties to

---

[2] ISO 31000 is a family of standards relating to risk management codified by the International Organization for Standardization. The purpose of ISO 31000:2018 is to provide principles and generic guidelines on risk management. ISO 31000 seeks to provide a universally recognized paradigm for practitioners and companies employing risk management processes to replace the myriad of existing standards, methodologies and paradigms that differed between industries, subject matters and regions.

manage them proactively. This stage is critical to the success of managing supply chain risks – only by identifying a risk can any risk management activity be triggered. This implies an early judgement is needed in risk identification to decide whether a risk is relevant and thus should be further assessed or mitigated. Hence, risk identification needs to follow a comprehensive approach to identifying all potential supply chain threats and vulnerabilities. And, risk prioritization helps organizations identify the most significant risks. High priority might be given to risks that have a high degree of impact or that can be mitigated immediately. Developing and implementing risk treatment actions involves considerable investment, and it is unlikely that a company will be able to deal with all possible risks. Risk prioritization therefore helps decide which risk types to develop actions against, allowing a firm to manage its limited risk treatment resources.

2. Risk evaluation: effective supply chain risk management requires a comprehensive yet rapid and cost-efficient assessment of supply chain risks. Risk can be assessed using data (if available) or expert judgement and scenarios.

This means risk assessment can be formal or informal and quantitative or qualitative. Risk assessment is inherently subjective as each analyst has his/her own concept of what constitutes a risk and of the nature of upstream/downstream relationships. Tsai et al. (2008) concluded that combining objective data and subjective perception might result in a more robust construction of risks, which in turn would improve the effectiveness of risk prediction and assessment. In assessing risk, the following factors should be considered.

3. With respect to risk prioritization, there are several terms for the types of risk treatment actions available, influenced by the business context under study.
    - Risk acceptance: there are no standard guidelines to determine how much risk an organization should accept. The acceptable level is context-dependent and may be linked, for example, to risk propensity, i.e. the willingness of a person or organization to engage in risky behaviors and accept uncertain outcomes in decision-making. But willingness to accept a risk does not mean the risk has

to be ignored. It should continue to be tracked to ensure the accepted consequences do not escalate. If the consequences exceed a certain threshold, organizations need to consider how to avoid, transfer, share, or mitigate the risk.

- Risk avoidance: risk avoidance seeks to eliminate the types of events that could trigger a risk. For example, a company could discontinue specific products, suppliers, or geographical markets if supply is unreliable. Thus, the company is removing the root cause of the risk.
- Risk transfer: it indicates that responsibility is assigned to another party. For example, business disruption risks can be transferred through business interruption insurance. Risk transfer however appears more appropriate for disruption risks with a small probability and high impact, e.g. natural disasters and terrorist attacks, than for operational risks with a high probability and low impact.
- Risk sharing involves another party sharing some or all risks. From the

buyer's perspective, risk can be shared usually through contracts with clauses that account for potential changes in associated risks and relationship development. Suppliers, for example, would pre-order to share inventory risk in the presence of financial constraints or increase capacity when orders are guaranteed by their customers. Similar to risk transfer, risk sharing seems appropriate for dealing with risks that have a low probability and high impact in order to reduce the associated costs and increase customer service levels.

- Risk mitigation seeks to actively reduce risk to an acceptable level. It applies both to the reduction of the probability of a risk event and to the consequences. Mitigation strategies are typically suitable for operational risks with a high probability and low impact. The selection of a risk mitigation strategy also depends on the risk type and the organization's budget; and organizations should carefully evaluate the acceptance, avoidance, sharing, and transfer options before selecting a mitigation strategy. As risks are often interconnected, alleviating one risk type might aggravate and/or mitigate another (positive vs. negative dependence); hence, mitigation strategies should be employed with minimal contradiction and with particular attention to those risks that have negative dependences.

BEST PRACTICES SUPPLY CHAIN RISK MANAGEMENT

The following ten supply chain risk management practices can be applied simultaneously to an organization or the elements of an organization. The practices are:

1. Assure sustainment activities and processes. The sustainment process begins when a system becomes operational and ends when it enters the disposal process. This includes system maintenance, upgrade, patching, parts replacement and other activities that keep the system operational. Any change to the system or process can introduce opportunities for subversion throughout the supply chain.
2. Establish and maintain the provenance of elements, processes, tools and data. All system

elements originate somewhere and may be changed throughout their existence. The record of element origin along with the history of, the changes to and the record of who made those changes is called "provenance." Acquirers, integrators and suppliers should maintain the provenance of elements under their control to understand where the elements have been, the change history and who might have had an opportunity to change them.

3. Limit access and exposure within the supply chain. Elements that traverse the supply chain are subject to access by a variety of actors. It is critical to limit such access to only as much as necessary for those actors to perform their roles and to monitor that access for supply chain impact.
4. Manage disposal and final disposition activities throughout the system or element life cycle. Elements, information and data can be disposed of at any time across the system and element life cycle. For example, disposal can occur during research and development, design, prototyping or operations/maintenance.
5. Perform continuous integrator review. Continuous integrator review is an essential

practice used to determine that defensive measures have been deployed. Its purpose is to validate compliance with requirements, establish that the organization behaves in a predictable manner under stress and detect and classify weaknesses and vulnerabilities of elements, and processes.

6. Perform supply chain risk management awareness and training. A strong supply chain risk mitigation strategy cannot be put in place without significant attention given to training personnel on supply chain policy, procedures and applicable management, operational and technical controls and practices.
7. Share information within strict limits. Acquirers, integrators and suppliers need to share data and information. Content to be shared among acquirers, integrators and suppliers may include information about the use of elements, users, acquirer, integrator or supplier organizations as well as information regarding issues that have been identified or raised regarding specific elements. Information should be protected according to mutually agreed-upon practices.
8. Strengthen delivery mechanisms. Delivery, including inventory management, is an essential

function within the supply chain, which has a great potential for being compromised. In today's environment, delivery can be physical such as hardware or logical such as software modules and patches.

9. Uniquely identify supply chain elements, processes and actors. Knowing who and what is in an enterprise's supply chain is critical to gain visibility into what is happening within it, as well as monitoring and identifying high-risk events and activities. Without reasonable visibility and traceability into the supply chain, it is impossible to understand and therefore manage risk and to reduce the likelihood of an adverse event.
10. Use defensive design for systems, elements and processes. The use of design concepts is a common approach to delivering robustness in security, quality, safety, diversity and many other disciplines that can aid in achieving supply chain risk management. Design techniques apply to supply chain elements, element processes, information, systems and organizational processes throughout the system. Element processes include creation, testing, manufacturing, delivery and sustainment of the element throughout its life. Organizational and

business processes include issuing requirements for acquiring, supplying and using supply chain elements.

SECTION IV: SUPPLY CHAIN MGMT SERVICING INDUSTRY

BACKGROUND

Supply chain management is a very popular management function and can be best depicted as how an organization manages the flow of procedures so that their goods or services can move from the point of commodities, then stored, and dispatched or delivered to the end-customers. Everything that takes place in between constitutes what is colloquially called as supply chain management. Historically, supply chain management has gotten numerous modifications and overhauls along the past decades, including using 'The Internet of Things' to its benefit. But all of these have enabled the processes used to manage the supply chain to become more efficient and effective. SCM will encompass the research, designing, planning, execution and control of that process, and eventually every single process that is involved in establishing and maintaining the flux going will be included as well. This, regardless of whether overseen on a local, regional, or global scale, will necessitate sound optimization and logistic strategies. Providing an effective supply chain management can be a service offered by organizations ensuring that they can get the most out of the process and boost their revenues. Other than being beneficial to products, strategic supply chain management can also be advantageous in the service industry. If one considers, that a supply chain will implement strategies that will cut down spending, enhance quality and timely delivery of the service, along with an outcome of boosted profitability (Kiger, 2016). If the quality is boosted in the input, then it will also be apparent in the service itself, which will result to more clients acknowledging the quality and buying the service.

Discrepancies Manufacturing and Servicing Industry

As for supply chains for the services industry, they hold numerous distinctions from the supply chain of manufacturing of goods and products. Although they both have inputs, in the manufacturing industry and the service industry there must be labor completed to process everything required to give the end consumer what they need or want. Besides doing internal labor, they will both expect suppliers to carry out various roles to help obtain the outcome. There is one primary difference, and it lies in the costs of assembling industry that include transporting, storing and controlling a physical material. By and large, the service industry will incorporate the control of data and systems administration (Abilla, 2010). This will change the capital ventures substantially in physical gear and apparatus that the manufacturing industry will have, instead of a software and hardware framework. Logistics for the manufacturing industry will include moving objects from one place to another, and, of course, taking into consideration the cost based on weight and size. In the service industry, this will not have any consequence at all, since it does not care about moving around physical objects, yet rather moving data round.

FIGURE 3: SUPPLY CHAIN FOR MANUFACTURING COMPANY

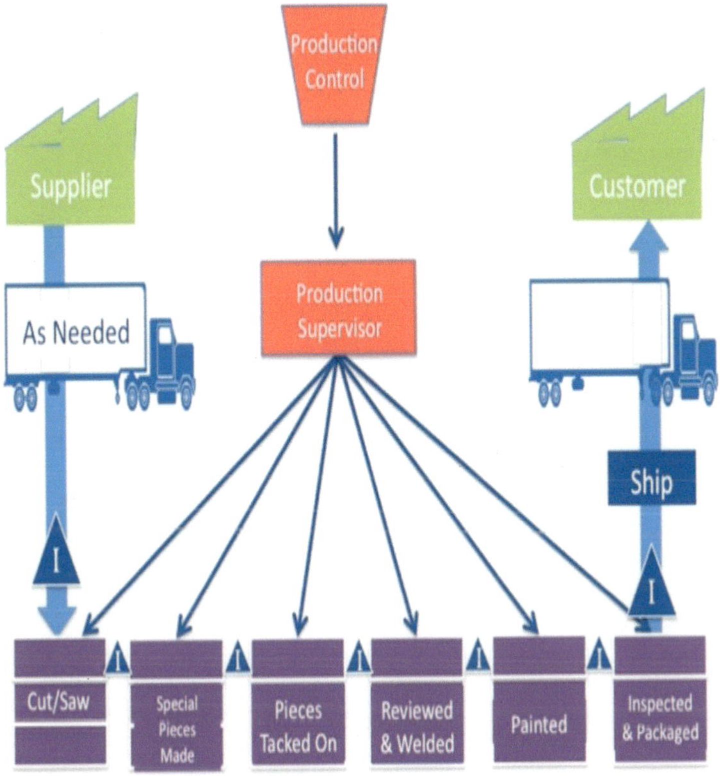

Source: Griffin&Co, 2018

This will not require the same needs as moving around products, yet instead finding the best channels to distribute the data. In this way, on the manufacturing side of things, it is fundamental to locate the best rates for transportation, containers or distribution centers to cut costs, while the service industry finds approaches to redesign their servers and boost invested labor and diminish costs.

FIGURE 4: SUPPLY CHAIN OF A MARKETING AGENCY

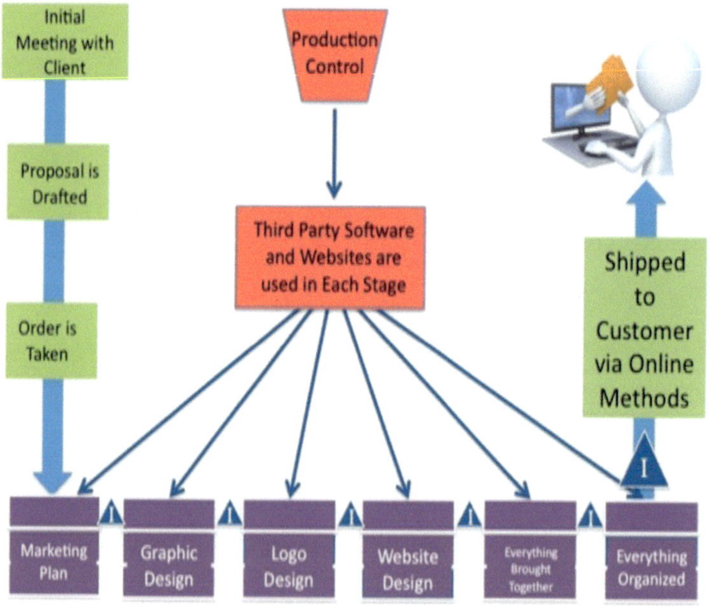

Source: Griffin&Co, 2018

The final result in the manufacturing industry is when commodities have been totally changed into the state in which the end client will buy it. This physical product is what will be given and delivered to the client and will be the proof of what was once transformed from crude materials.

This will require a spot to fabricate it, to assemble it, to store it and a process of shipping to take it to the location where it will be sold. In the service industry, the service provided will be a completed task or delivered knowhow (Abdou & Kathawala, 2003). There will be no physical evidence of the exchange but a few docs. When the transactions are completed in either industry, the objective is to have a happy client who is eager to pay for the end product or service.

The enhancement process in the assembling industry and the service industry varies since in the manufacturing industry it will include mostly expanding the speed of conveyance, which Amazon is an excellent example of, and cutting costs (Taylor, 2010). They will require to analyze different techniques that can and will allow these two things to happen like understanding bottlenecks, inventory stocks running dry, or innovations as far as manipulating materials.

With respect to the service industry, optimization will be at its core in its systems administrations capacities and the data stream. The partnerships built by a service company will decide how the organization can turn out to be increasingly viable and decrease costs. Bottlenecks can likewise take place in this industry, same as the assembling one, yet here there will be data bottlenecks brought about by an excessive number of endorsements or superfluous methodology. The aim for both industries will be the same, which is to get the end result at a lower cost and delivery time.

The service sector is the new driver of today's business environment as well as of the structures of the present economies. The service industry has boosted rapidly because of the financial globalization process, making its contribution to economic growth is increasingly apparent (Liu et al., 2017). The significance of the services' business sector expanded significantly as a main impetus of GDP especially in developed countries. The GDP share of the services sector in developed countries presents nearly 66% of total GDP, while in emerging economies, service businesses generate almost 50% of GDP which highlights the potential effect of a successfully overseen service supply chain (SSC) (Baltacioglu et al., 2007).

As already alluded to, the end-goal of any organization is a satisfied client. The process of obtaining, locating, and transporting the inputs required to do this is the core function of supply chain management.

Supply chain design in the manufacturing industry necessitates a great deal of focus on the physical product and a broader supplier base, while service firms typically have little need for physical inputs other than office supplies, and often work with a much smaller group of suppliers. Below are the building blocks of a typical supply chain (Tan, 2002; Millsap, 2012; Elgazzar & Elzarka, 2017):

- Logistics: Traditional manufacturing supply chain management centers around logistics as far as moving physical material starting from one location to the next area. The size and weight of products being transported and the distance from the provider to the manufacturing facility can play a noteworthy role in the cost of the product. In service organizations, especially in the financial sectors, these aspects are immaterial on the grounds that no product is moving with the exception of maybe a couple of sheets of paper. While the manufacturing industry endeavors to arrange for better delivery rates and fill containers with products to cut down cost per unit, the service industry upgrades servers and puts in new programming to speed the stream of communication, in this manner diminishing the labor costs required to manufacture a finished product.

- Inputs: Both the service and the manufacturing industries require a contribution (input) of labor to finish the handling necessary to fulfill their promise to the end client. Furthermore, companies in the two industries require contributions from suppliers of various kinds. At long last, both industries require capital investment in hardware that enables their representatives to do their work. The key contrast is that the greater the cost of manufacturing labor is involved in procuring, shipping and controlling physical material, while practically all service industry labor is used on controlling data and establishing partnerships. In light of this difference, capital investments in apparatus and gear are typically a lot higher in the manufacturing industry.
- Optimization: In a manufacturing organization, improvement of the supply chain is accomplished fundamentally by improving the

rate of shipping and cutting costs. Organizations work to diminish physical bottlenecks and inventory, and arrange better pricing on crude materials. The essential method to speed production is to locate a quicker way to move or control the components. The key drivers of optimization in a service model are partnerships and data stream. By building partnerships with organizations whose strengths supplement its own, a corporation can decrease costs. By taking out virtual bottlenecks brought about by duplicate endorsement loops or other elusive delays, a service company can understand a similar objective as the manufacturing company: a lower-cost finished product, shipped to the client all the more rapidly.

- Finished Goods: Traditionally, a finished good is an item that has been totally changed from a commodity structure to a structure that is prepared to pitch to the client. It's a physical unit that has been assembled, tried and packaged, and is presently sitting on a rack at a distribution center or a store, prepared to be sold. In the service industry, a 'finished good' equals a closed file. The loan has been booked, the home sale has closed, or the class has been finished, leaving no physical proof aside a couple of sheets of paper. Be that as it may, the objective of either finished product is a client who is happy with the product or service she paid for.

Notwithstanding the rapid development of the service sector and the critical significance of managing this sector, service supply chain management is still immature in literature.

In contrast to the manufacturing industry, there is a noteworthy absence of comprehension of the notion of SSC and the implementation of its practices in addition to the lack of studies that focused on how to model, oversee, establish measurement items and evaluate the performance of SSC.

The changing of SSCs' structure from a linear to network form makes the assessment of the functioning of the entire supply chain more entangled, which necessitates monitoring a growing volume of data to choose the proper performance indicators (Leończuk, 2016).

Contrary to the manufacturing sector, the supply chains in a service industry cannot be standardized as they vary and lack standard features (Ellram et al., 2004).

The absence of a standard unified SCC management framework is viewed as one of the main challenges that affect the viability and efficiency of SSC management practices (Zhang and Chen, 2015).

In addition, the immaterial nature of services makes it hard to apply a number of logistics activities to service supply chains and requires a lot of integration and close collaboration with both suppliers and clients so as to gain the synergy advantage of collaboration operation in the supply chain (Baltacioglu et al., 2007).

Supply Chain Frameworks For Services Industry

Any organization requires a well-defined supply chain. As the service industry develops in significance, so does the need for structures, performance metrics and strategies for this type of industry activity.

The level of responsiveness and efficiency that the manufacturing segment has seen because of the development and study of supply chain management methods over the last twenty years must now be translated to the service industry.

The change from an industrial based economy to a service-based economy has been taking place in the developed countries over the last 20 years. The service industry keeps on growing and is rapidly becoming the leading industry activity in the economy.

Of the Dow Jones Industrial Average index stocks, close to 60% are in the service sector (CNN Money, 2019), with three of those organizations (out of thirty that composes the DJI) – Microsoft, Intel and IBM – among the world's most competitive operations in the service sector.

The ever-advancing, new information technologies are one of the main reasons behind this economic transformation in the US from manufacturing to services. The significance of these services cannot be overstated; because these service industries depend heavily on information technology, they are also 'vectors' of technical progress. The service sector in the Dow Jones Industrial Average consists of the technological sector, consumer services, and other (banks, insurance, real estate, and other financial services. While trade, transportation and utilities lead the list as the largest service industry employers (CSI), professional and business services, education and health and leisure and hospitality are also very crucial to the contribution of the services to the Gross Domestic Product (GDP). For the United States, these services are not just for the use of US residents alone either. In 2017 in the US, private services exports were in excess of $734 billion, with a trade surplus of over $250 billion (Commission, Recent Trends in U.S. Services Trade, 2018). This trend has grown in virtually every segment of the US services industry.

One alarming metric though, is often overlooked. Although the professional and business services segment contributed about 19-20 to the GDP in both 2016 and 2017 (Commission, Recent Trends in U.S. Services Trade, 2018), there has been an increasing trend of offshoring these services in particular to reduce labor costs (for example, to India and the Philippines). The largest area of this is seen in high-skilled jobs such as architecture, engineering, law and more recently, medical diagnostic services (Commission, Recent Trends in U.S. Services Trade, 2018). There are conflicting opinions as to whether or not this trend allows for a focus on core competencies (Wolfl, 2004), or merely the desire to reduce labor costs. Some feel that offshoring these services will, in the long run, boost productivity growth in the domestic economy by enhancing the economy of the consumer while others feel that it merely devalues the wages of the often highly educated service worker (Gorg, Geishecker, & Krieger-Boden, 2011).

The significance of service firms to the economy is crucial; however, improvement is needed to bring the service industry to the level of efficiency and responsiveness that the manufacturing sector has grown accustomed. Particularly since this sector relies heavily on its customer base, new paradigms, frameworks, and performance measures specifically designed for the service industry are necessary to ensure this growing trend.

EXISTING SUPPLY CHAIN PROCESSES IN THE SERVICE INDUSTRY

Just as the focus of attention on building world-class supply chains (SCs) and partnerships in manufacturing started in the latter part of the previous century, the attention needs to turn now on the supply chains within the service sector. Numerous interrogations need to be given answers to determine if existing models of structures, performance metrics, network design and implementation apply to the service industry. Building a foundation for the supply chain in these service-type industries is crucial to the execution of the activities within this sector (Ping & Jia, 2010).

A comprehension of the external environment is vital to any organization so as to take into consideration positive customer loyalty. While goods-producing firms will in general depend on nonexclusive SC models, for instance, the SCOR model (Supply Chain Operations Reference Model) or Porter's Value Chain model (Porter, 1985), the focal point is typically centered around profit with some level of quality and service. In any case, the service industry incorporates both not-for-profit as well as for-profit firms. And, within those for-profit firms, the level of human-interaction within those services and the reliance on person-to-person interaction on the overall success of the firm is very divergent. Accordingly, the question is raised: Is a conventional supply chain model relevant for all service industries or is it explicit to the service industry? The relevance of developing foundational models of SCs for the service industry is an imminent task and next to no research has been completed to date on that subject. As evidence of this pressing need, one can take a gander at the efficiency observed on both sides of the Atlantic and also in NE Asia. In 2018, the service sector generated some 80% of the GDP in the US (The World Factbook, 2018).

However, that percentage is due to approximately 80% of the population being employed in that industry, while services in countries such as India contribute a little over 55% to the GDP and employ just 33% of the population (compared to 45% of employment in China in 2017 and 52% of GDP) (Statista). Notwithstanding the fact that the proportion of GDP generated by the service industry has somewhat stabilized around 75-80% from a decade ago in the United States, it is excessively high in comparison to other countries. Consequently, a solid base of modeling the SCs in these industries must be investigated to accommodate for future development and a higher degree of efficiency and quality.

In May 2019, the Institute for Supply Management (ISM) reported that not only does the service sector report strong growth over the last ten years, recruitment in this sector has equally been strong (ISM, 2019). One can assume that this is, at least partially, due to more focus in this area in terms of the management and execution of service systems (Homan, 2012).

The decrease in the GDP contribution to employment percentage may be an indicator of this; however, literature remains sparse on definitions regarding both frameworks and performance measures. (Elgazzar & Elzarka, 2017) One can assume that, through more increased focus in this area of service supply chains, the productivity, capabilities and performance of them can only increase as those of traditional supply chains of the previous few decades. Undoubtedly, the primary defining distinction between a manufacturing and service company is that human labor is the core building block of the latter, while a physical product is that of the former. The attributes that characterize each of these then, also differ. Numerous researchers debate about the definition of these characteristics:

> Fisk et al., 1996) contend that the four noteworthy features that distinct a service-oriented industry from a physical goods-driven industry are immateriality, inseparability of manufacturing and consumption, perishability, and heterogeneity.
>
> Others, such as Pride and Ferrel (2003), claim that there are six fundamental characterizing attributes: the previously-enumerated four plus the attribute of being client-based relationships as well as the need for direct customer contact.
>
> While some may postulate that goods industries also embrace these last two, it is the service industry that is dependent on these characteristics as an inherent part of their service. In addition to immateriality, perishability, and heterogeneity Baltacioglu et al.

(2007) also argue that simultaneity is another critical piece of a service framework.

Service systems are also distinct from manufacturing systems by their processes. As an illustration, Sengupta et al. argue that the decisions are extremely centralized in a physical goods driven industry with much standardization in terms of policies and procedures and very little variation, while in a service system, the degree of variation is consequential due to the fact human aspect of local decision-making (Sengupta, Heiser, & Cook, 2006).

Disparity between a manufacturing and services supply chain (Ellram, Tate, and Billington, 2007):

Area	Service industry supply chain	Manufacturing systems supply chain
Production System	Pull (initiated by customer demand)	Push (sell from inventory)
Logistics System	Customized to customer need	Uniform, mass approach
Finished Goods Inventory	Kept at low level	Tightly controlled
Suppliers	Must be responsive	Responsiveness not critical
Customer relations	Critical to overall success	Often at a low level

Irrespective of what the characteristics may be, most scholars concur that a service is an implementation of an activity, instead of a tangible item. Above table outlines some major differences in the attributes of a manufacturing goods-driven supply chain versus a service-oriented industry supply chain. Traditionally, goods industries are push systems, with companies keeping high levels of inventory for commodities and finished goods. The suppliers in a service-oriented industry oftentimes ARE the "products" and, accordingly, need to be receptive to the aspirations of the clients. Frequently these types of industries have to face their customers and hence the relations among them are vital. In this manner, the metrics by which a service firm will gauge itself must be unmistakable from a manufacturing company.

Taxonomy of Architectures

One of the major sanctioning aspects of supply chain management is that the corporate vision is client-focused and able to foster change all through the organization as well as among its external linkages. The objective of the SC architecture is to design process and functions that are embedded across the SC to generate a competitive edge with a differentiation between process-centered and performance measure-centered frameworks. (Elgazzar & Elzarka, 2017)

Performance Measured Structures

A performance measurement system can be described as the set of metrics used to assess both the efficiency and viability of activities (Neely, et al., 2000). The lion share of goods-producing organizations defines their performance metrics in terms of reliability, quality, delivery speed, flexibility, and cost. While the definitions of each of these metrics differ and are often opaque the literature on performance measures in goods-producing industries is vast.

FIGURE 5: SUPPLY CHAIN PERFORMANCES MEASUREMENT

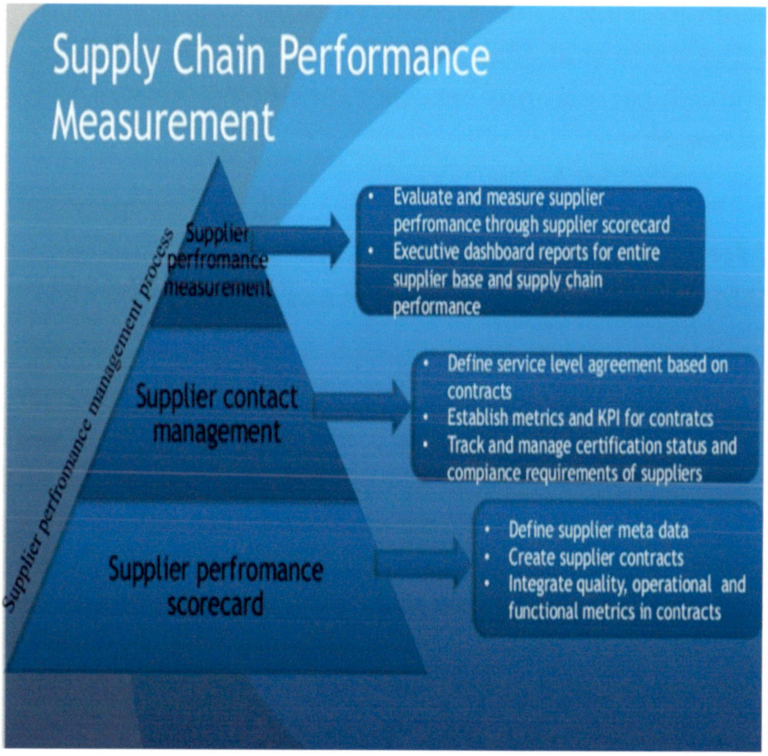

Source: Shurrab, 2013

Nonetheless, one regular theme is that an organization chooses to quantify what is most relevant to the success of the business. Some researchers have decided to describe broadly the variables that will advance the most accomplishments in a service-driven organization. So as to understand SC practices in both services and manufacturing, a major research study was performed by Sengupta et al. (Sengupta, Heiser, & Cook, 2006) to establish correlations between specific SC metrics and strategies.

The authors concentrated on the performance metrics of service SCs and the contrasts among those and the manufacturing industries as the basis to elect the vital elements for progress.

> A discrimination is made between financial and operational performance. The latter is credited apparent consumer loyalty. The former identifies with profit and loss metrics in comparison to its market contenders. Results demonstrate that these distinctions between services and manufacturing: data sharing and degree of customization (in contrast to rival companies) is much more vital to operational excellence in the service-oriented sector, and putting

strategic relevance on the distribution network can significantly impact financial performance.

Yet, higher expenses for customization is linked to lower profitability given that the service-oriented industries are unable to achieve a premium price in opposition to their peers in manufacturing. A competitive edge can be obtained by focusing the full-service delivery system around three aspects: configuration, resources, and the flux of the processes. Each one of these three areas have five related crucial activities, namely: simplicity of the processes, best practices, a unified vision, connection and visibility within the organization, and visibility. SC strategy for services is based on three aspects: responsiveness to the market, efficiency of process, and quality of service.

Process-Centered Structures

Most of the writings on SC frameworks for the service sector stem from the adaptation of an existing, established framework into this service industry.

The growth in the service sector is linked to the growth in service purchasing and that there is little control over this system, thus yielding to a lack of supply chain management frameworks. A process model is best applied to the service industry and thus develop a seven-step process model including: information flow, capacity and skills management, demand management, supplier relationship management, customer relationship management, service delivery management and cash flow.

Knowledge Management

Knowledge management (KM) is focused on the creation, storage, dissemination, and utilization of organizational knowledge.

Knowledge management could likewise be characterized as a set of processes that transpose data into valuable knowledge. The organizational components which formulate knowledge management are human resources practices, technology, organizational structure and culture (Plessis, 2007). As per Nissen (1999) the core capabilities of knowledge-based systems can be subdivided into five domains: knowledge formalization, problem-solving application, knowledge capture, knowledge organization, and knowledge distribution. Nissen further postulates that each capability necessitates a specific approach or technology. Knowledge management is a vital feature towards achieving supply chain performance, as organizations need to own and disseminate expertise about various aspects of the process.

FIGURE 6: KNOWLEDGE MANAGEMENT & SUPPLY CHAIN

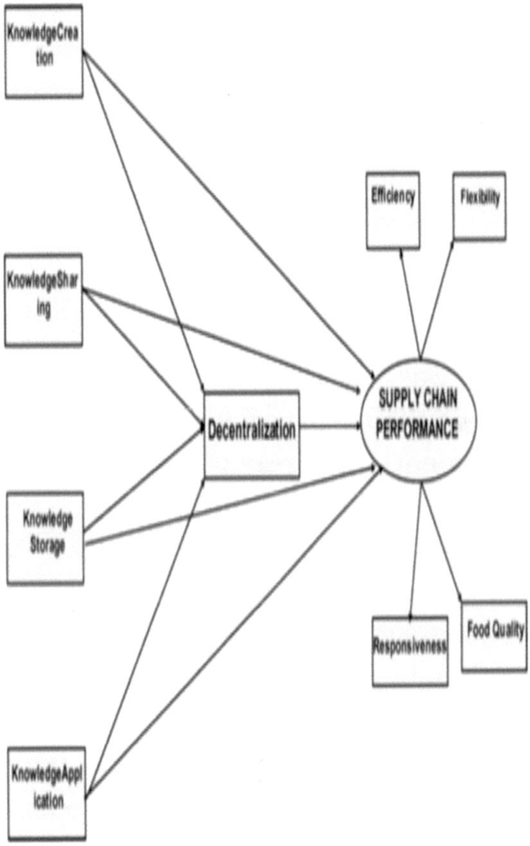

Source: Dost, et al., 2018

Knowledge management can eliminate trivial or duplicated steps in the manufacturing process and enhance communication that would yield lower expenses. Supply chain stakeholders would gain from quick learning by gaining insights of another's learning curve with specific procedures or processes. This would result in better customer perceptions and higher quality of the brand offering.

INFORMATION FLOW MANAGEMENT

Data stream is described as a flow that connects the different members in the chain. It is viewed as a vital practice of service supply chain management which provides support and allows for other processes and procedures in the SC, such as defining the scope of the work, demand planning, feedback on the performance, and the skills necessary from fellow service providers. Given that data stream is considered as paramount for integration in a strategic alliance (Zhou and Benton, 2007), supplying the right amount of relevant data to the appropriate person at the right moment has become crucial for reinforcing partnerships between SC members as well as facilitating a more viable supply chain management (Mukaddes et al., 2010). The graph below highlights a fully integrated supply chain (f. ex. with Capstone Logistics) that relies on information stream between the various stakeholders.

FIGURE 7: DATA MANAGEMENT & SUPPLY CHAIN

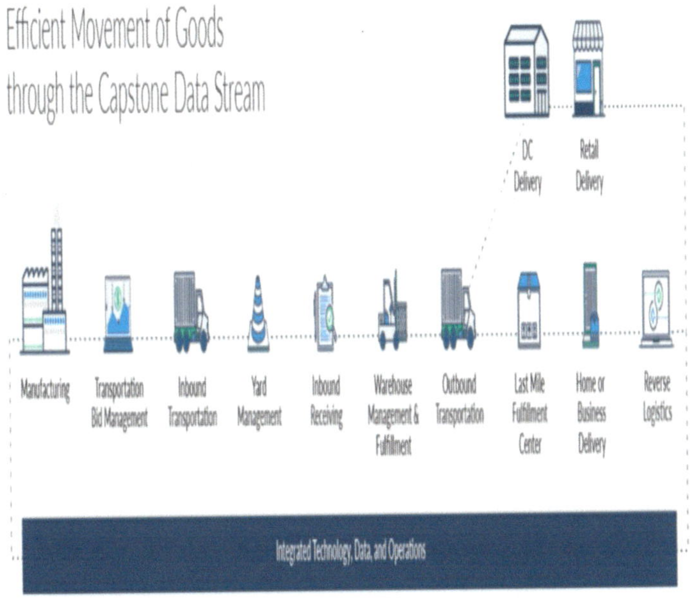

Source: Capstone Logistics

Modern studies pinpoint the relevance of data sharing between stakeholders to deliver clients who are downstream more adequately and effectively. Also, it has become clear that data stream management is emerging as a vital process connecting other processes in a way allowing more prominent responsiveness at every step of all these processes. Additionally, data stream can strengthen SRM and CRM by enabling the most productive and efficient flow of data between SC stakeholders.

Capacity and Skills Management

As services are intrinsically elusive, capacity management within the service industry alludes to the processes, the organization, the staff, and the assets required to satisfy the client's expectations. To put it differently, capacity revolves around the company's resources to fulfill the client's needs. As for skills management which essentially centers around on the company's staff, suppliers of services can distinct themselves from one another by acquiring and retaining qualified staff. Skilled labor is crucial to the service industry as it is labor intensive. Be that as it may, skills and capacity management is challenging to cope with, nevertheless assessed.

FIGURE 8: SKILLS MANAGEMENT & SUPPLY CHAIN

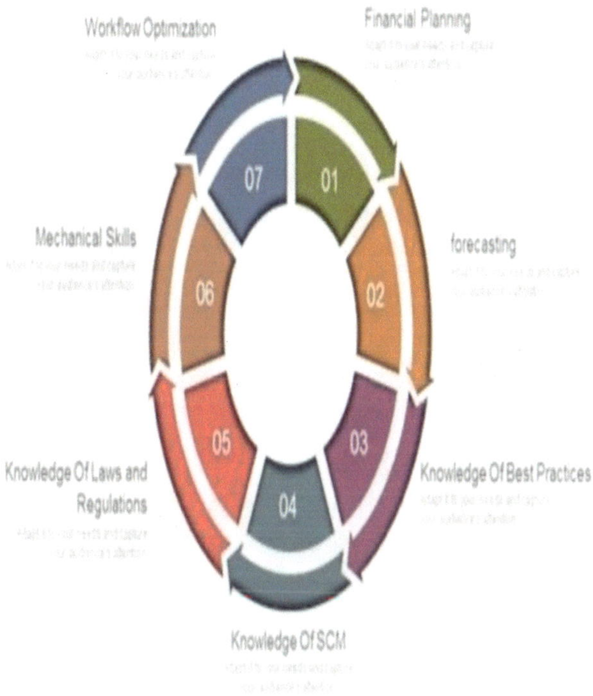

Source: Logistics Bureau, 2016

Subsequently, various scholars have attempted to come up with reliable and valid metrics to quantify skills and capacity performance in the service industry. Metrics included the adequacy of physical assets to satisfy the service demand, customer service and waiting time, and flexibility in fulfilling clients' expectations.

Demand Management

Demand management is characterized as the balancing act whereby clients' necessities are weighted against supply chain capacities with the aim to decrease fluctuation and uncertainty, and increment flexibility. In comparison to the manufacturing industry, managing demand for SSC entails extra challenges.

The intangible aspect of a service renders it difficult to stockpile services to cushion against fluctuating demand levels causing for increased levels of demand uncertainty in SSC (Johnson and Mena, 2008). Hence, demand management in SCC necessitates full comprehension of existing capabilities and workloads available on top of unambiguous identification of potential to absorb extra work through recruitment and overtime (Ellram et al., 2004).

FIGURE 9: DEMAND DRIVEN SUPPLY CHAIN

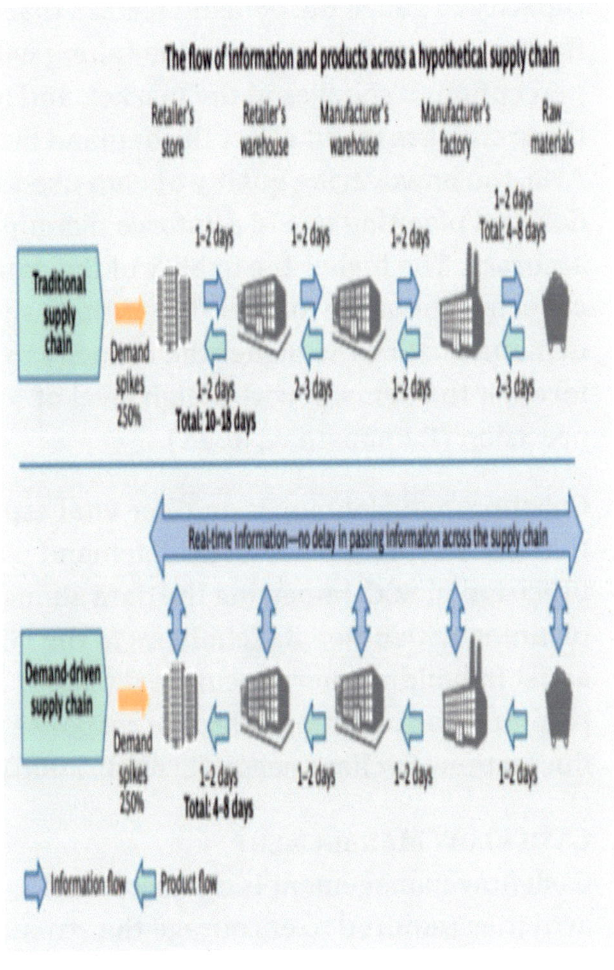

Source: Arkieva, 2018

The demand planning accuracy relies on the capacity to gauge the demand factors that fluctuate from service to another along with the perception of changes in the market, and how these changes might affect the demand factors. Also, the unwavering quality of data used for demand planning would reinforce planning accuracy. The higher the quality of the data collected about the market fluctuations and demand factors, the higher the capacity to forecast the demand with a high level of precision (Ramanathan, 2011).

Collaborative planning is another vital aspect that can strengthen the level of demand planning precision in SCC. Imparting the data about planning with other stakeholders in the SC can assist in building more accurate demand planning and adopting a flexible response to fluctuations in client needs (Li et al., 2006).

Cash Flow Management

Cash flow management is characterized as activities required to encourage the stream of funds across the supply chain, including paying suppliers and internal transfers as well as invoicing customers. A firm's cash flow is profoundly embedded with its supply chain which requires an approach based on collaboration the SC to bring down the total payment cycle time, and subsequently enhance the general financial viability of the SC.

Having a mutual vision among the supply chain (SC) stakeholders warrants trustworthy and predictable cash flows across the entire SC, and this is viewed as the most important challenge facing SC cash flows management (More and Basu, 2012).

Cash to cash cycle practice is viewed as the vital performance metric of supply chain cash flows management. The cash to cash cycle illustrates the value of net cash flows yielded across the SC, beginning with the incoming material and service activities with suppliers, followed by manufacturing activities, and lastly to the outcoming sales operations with clients (Chen, 2011).

FIGURE 10: CASH TO CASH CYCLE IN SUPPLY CHAIN

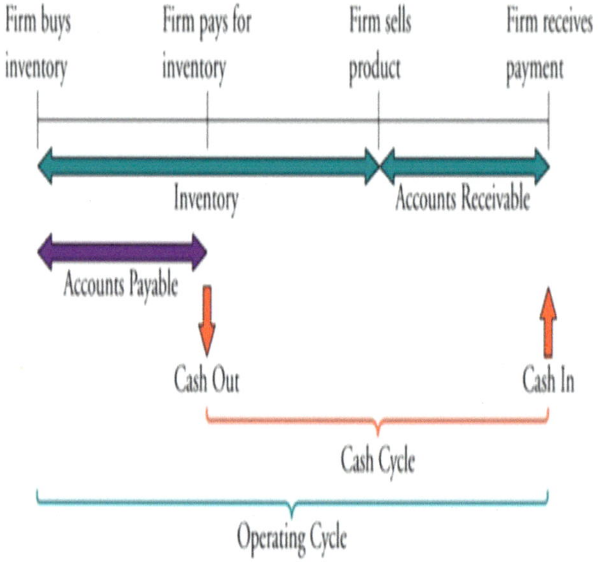

Source: Mayer, 2012

The cash to cash cycle time measures the average time required to transform cash invested into commodities into cash gathered from clients by quantifying the number of days that payables are not paid (days of credit), the number of days that inventory stays dormant (days sales in inventory), and the number of days that receivables are gathered (average collection time). Additionally, data analytics applications can assume a vital role in strengthening cash flows management by automating the payment procedure and controlling the cash flow control system.

Risk Management

Supply chain risk management supply chain risk management is the identification of potential causes of hazard and implementation of suitable strategies through an integrated approach among supply chain partners, to decrease supply chain vulnerability. Supply chain risk has equally been characterized as any hazard to the data, product, and material flow from unique providers to the conveyance of the end-product. Various vital trends caused for the increased relevance of supply chain risk management, specifically lean and agile operations, outsourcing, higher customer expectations, volatility and variability of demand, increased terrorist threats, and natural disasters. The process of risk management has been lately acknowledged as a prerequisite process in the supply chain, particularly in the service industry as services have long life cycles and are complex, which are two aspects that cause for higher risk exposure. There is no doubt that risk-adjusted SCs can permute into better competitive advantage and stronger financial performance.

FIGURE 11: RISK MANAGEMENT IN SUPPLY CHAINS

Source: Lu & Xia, 2014

Organizations that include the supply chain risk management process into their activities can gain from achieving better planning, mapping hazards before events take place and generate a crisis situation, improved financial performance as a result of uninterrupted operations, and prioritization and allocation of resources. Typically, the supply chain risk management process revolves around three core dimensions: risks mapping, risks analysis and the determination of adequate responses (Waters, 2007).

CUSTOMER RELATIONSHIP MANAGEMENT (CRM)

In order for an organization to be successful, a happy client is a vital prerequisite. As a result of globalization, clients are all over the world and organizations cope with the challenge of making sure that these clients are well catered and retained. As Gunasekaran et al. (2004) stated "without a contented customer, the supply chain strategy cannot be deemed effective".

FIGURE 12: CUSTOMER RELATIONSHIP MANAGEMENT AND SUPPLY CHAINS

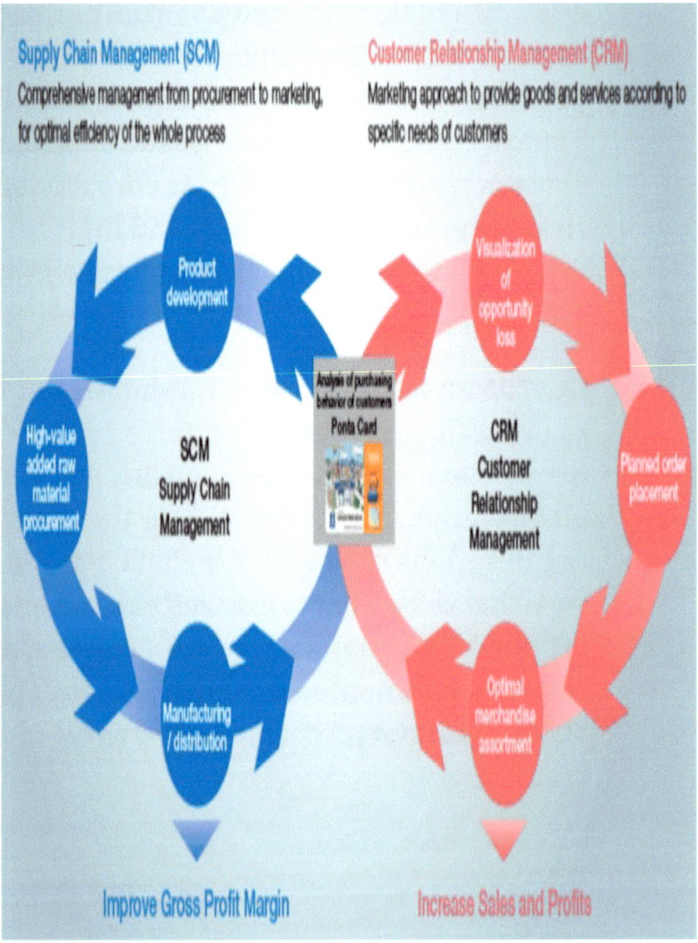

Source: Lawson, 2019

Subsequently, SC metrics that focus on strengthening the relationship between companies and customers must be flagged. Payne and Frow (2005) defined customer relationship management (CRM) as "a strategic approach that is concerned with creating improved shareholder value through the development of appropriate relationships with key customers and customer segments". And, connecting CRM with SC processes strengthens solid performance and raises shareholder value. Quantifying CRM performance is a daunting assignment, and this is mainly due to the fact that CRM processes are intermingled with other types of functions within.

Supplier Relationship Management (SRM)

Suppliers play an essential role in modern supply chains and directly affect the failure or success of supply chain networks. Since most of supply chains rely on outsourcing, it is vital to establishing robust relationships with suppliers. SRM can be described as "a process where customers and suppliers develop and maintain a close and long-term relationship as partners.

FIGURE 13: SUPPLIER RELATIONSHIP AND SUPPLY MANAGEMENT

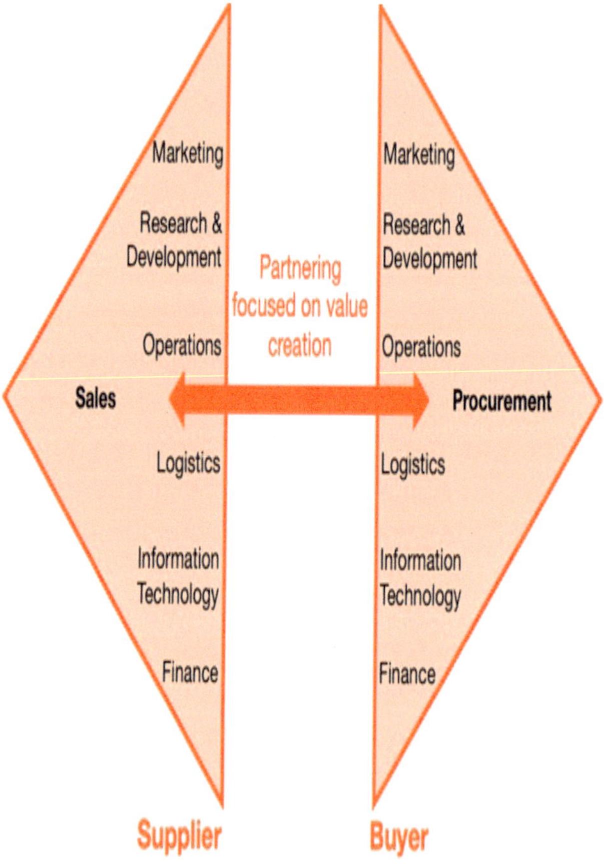

<u>Source</u>: Verweij & Peek, 2013

SRM is composed of five key elements: coordination, cooperation, commitment, information sharing and feedback. These fundamental elements which reflect the collaboration in planning, forecasting and replenishment activities have a positive impact on strengthening supply chain relations in addition to facilitating the information flow across the supply chain" (Cassivi, 2006).

SERVICE DELIVERY MANAGEMENT

Service delivery management is characterized as "making promises to the customer, enabling service providers (internal or external) to meet those promises and meeting the promises. Service delivery management process includes three main activities, namely: define a customer order, create a network to deliver the order and enable the network to deliver the order" (Johnson and Mena, 2008). Nonetheless, engaging a service delivery system requires the steady infrastructure (job design, aptitudes, etc.) and frameworks (facilities, assets, etc.) along with the process for supplying a service. The process design plays a fundamental role in the service delivery systems. A well-thought design can add to the overall competitiveness of the service company by means of the supply of top-quality service while preserving process efficiency (Frei and Harker, 1996). Service design should concentrate on facilitating the execution of service delivery processes in an adequate manner that warrant the delivery of the suitable service's result (Mohr and Bitner, 1995).

FIGURE 14: SERVICE DELIVERY IN SUPPLY CHAINS

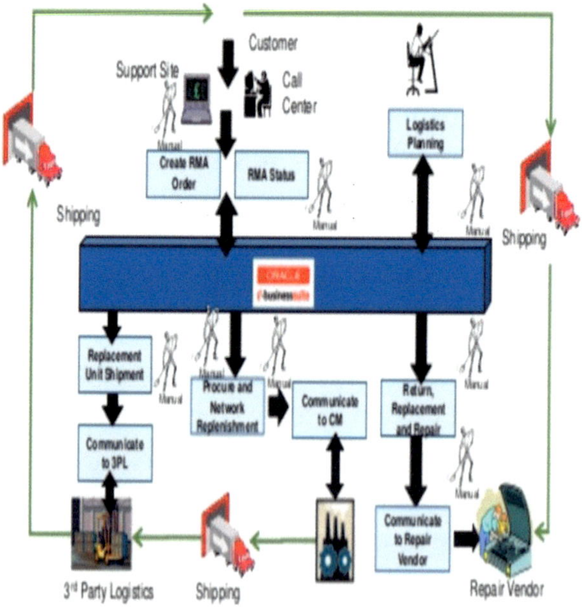

Source: Brown & Lepeak, 2017

Order fulfillment and customer service management can be described as two vital supply chain management processes. The fulfillment of the client order process effectively necessitates mutualizing the updated data about the client order status with vital supply chain stakeholders. Besides, the client service management process should be reinforced by an interactive communication platform with the client in order to supply him with the perquisite real-time data on promised service availability and delivery dates.

Take-Away Message

Despite the fact that the service industry has become increasingly important as the principal impetus of the structures of today's economic systems, research reveals the absence of a holistic coordinated structure in relation to service supply chain management.

Much research has been conducted on SC management and operations, and even though they vary in their scope, the lion share of them acknowledge that SC activities and processes include: sourcing, sales, transportation, marketing, and manufacturing. In this way, if the 'product' is an event, at that point some of these customary SC activities, specifically, transportation and production, are not part of the traditional definition.

New paradigms need to be made as to accommodate the prevalence of the services and their contribution to the GDP. Much work should be done in order to make sure that these service industries are operating at an efficient level. The attention paid to SC management over the last three decades which has allowed organizations to grow from the starting point of functional independence to inter-organizational integration, as suggested by Stevens (Stevens, 1989).

The last stage, suggested by Hewitt (Hewitt, 1994) integrates intra-company and intercompany management. This last stage is the epitome of an ideal supply chain management for manufacturing industries. What is now required is the transposition of that optimization to the services sectors.

SECTION V: SUPPLY CHAIN RISK MGMT W/ BANKS

INTRODUCTION

The theories of supply chain risk management and supply chain resilience were examined concerning the use of qualitative risk tools to help the banking industry (and in particular the U.S. Global Systemically Important Banks (G-SIBs)) become more resilient when facing tail events.

This study aims to provide insights on what the concepts of supply chain risk management and supply chain resilience entail and how they could be applicable to G-SIBs. Effective supply chain risk management and supply chain resilience are essential to a successful business. However, whereas the concept of supply chain risk management is cause-oriented, it needs to be combined with the concept of supply chain resilience, which aims to ensure that the supply chain can bounce back from risks irrespective of their cause. Acknowledging that banks also operate as supply chains, and understanding the banks' vulnerability to supply chain risk – both up and down the chain – will help banking executives to spot the weakest links in the chain. In today's interconnected and globalized world revolving around lean supply chains and cost-cutting, there is, alas, little spare capacity in the supply chains.

Highly integrated, complex, cross-border and multi-agency delivery modes mean that very few banking organizations have a clear understanding on the depth of their supply chains. supply chain risk management and supply chain resilience are therefore important risk mitigation techniques to optimize supply chains in the long term, and hence assist banks in building more resilient business models. Moreover, alas, today's operational risk management within banks does not embrace nor comprehend that notion of supply chain risk management and supply chain resilience. Further studies are required to understand the application of the theories of supply chain risk management and supply chain resilience to the G-SIBs and to evaluate the present-day challenges posed by the implementation of the theories of supply chain risk management and supply chain resilience as qualitative risk tools for managing the effects of tail risks.

The last thirty years have been aberrant for risk managers working in the banking industry as a myriad of financial disasters have been affecting the banking industry and financial markets as a whole. Notwithstanding new and advanced mathematical models to calculate the probability and severity of a sequence of risk events that might affect banks, not to mention a string of new harsh regulatory provisions, many banking executives continue to feel that the business models of their banks remain vulnerable to the rise of emerging risks.

Indeed, albeit the lion share of the U.S. banks is nowadays in compliance with the prudential regulations (Gray & Jopson, 2018), virtually all of these rules (not to mention internal functions within the bank) ignore a series of emerging risks, amongst which supply chain risk. Also, a recent survey by EY and co-sponsored by the IIF (Jackson & Schlich, 2013) shows that banking executives remain wary about the range of risks facing the industry in the short and long term. Broader technological, geopolitical, economic, social and environmental concerns are regarded as materially menacing further underpinned by signs of increased global regulatory fragmentation. As a result, competition among financial actors is becoming acuter notwithstanding banks' balance sheets that are deemed to show for it. In other words, as a result of increased financialization of the economy, globalization, and interconnectedness, banking executives feel that the banks' business models are insufficiently inclusive failing to take into account a range of emerging risk factors.

CONTEXT OF SUPPLY CHAIN RISK MANAGEMENT

One way to better understand the risk environment into which banks need to operate is through the theories of supply chain risk management and supply chain resilience. In essence, a banking organization can be viewed as supply chain due to the myriad of actors that interfere in the delivery of services to the banks' clients. And, these actors can be either internal (cf. different departments within the bank (IT, back-office, front office, middle office, risk management, etc.)) or external (third-party vendors and contractors).

However, when the words 'supply chain' and 'supply chain risk management' come to mind, casual observers will typically associate these concepts with the world of manufacturing, logistics, and resources, and not immediately with the realm of banking. Indeed, in the corporate world the definition for the concept of supply chain risk management is (Felea & Albāstroiu, 2013) "the risk management of the flow of goods and services that includes the movement and storage of raw materials, work-in-process inventory, and finished goods from the point of origin to the point of consumption." In essence, supply chain risk management draws heavily from the areas of operations management, logistics, procurement, and information technology, and strives for an integrated approach. With the exception when the media talks about cyber-attacks affecting the infrastructure of financial organizations or the growing importance of software vendors supplying financial organizations, interestingly enough, within the financial services industry nothing comparable to an integrated supply chain (risk management) exists (Camerinelli, 2017). In the corporate world, traditional methods for managing supply chain risk rely on (Simchi-Levi et al., 2014) "knowing the likelihood of occurrence and the magnitude of impact for every potential event that could materially disrupt a firm's operations. For common supply chain disruptions —poor supplier performance, forecast errors, transportation breakdowns, and so on—those methods work very well, using historical data to quantify the level of risk".

However, it is a different story altogether for low-probability, high-severity events such as the 2007-2008 GFC, Hurricane Katrina in 2005, the 2003 SARS outbreak, or significant outages due to unforeseen events such as geopolitical upheavals. Since historical data on these exceptional episodes are scarce or even nonexistent, their risk is hard to measure utilizing conventional mathematical models. As a result, many organizations do not adequately prepare for them. That can have disastrous consequences when calamities do strike and can compel even operationally savvy organizations to scramble after the fact (Simchi-Levi, 2015). To address this challenge, in addition to investing resources in designing a mathematical model that focuses on determining the likelihood that any specific risk will take place, it is equally appropriate to center on the description of the supply chain. This would put the onus on analyzing the impact of potential failures at points along the supply chain (cf. such as the impact of a sudden default of a swap counterparty during the closing of a loan), rather than again the cause of the disruption (Simchi-Levi, 2013). This type of analysis removes the requirement to determine the probability that any specific risk will occur - a savvy approach since the mitigation strategies for disruption are equally valid regardless of what caused it.

Application of the concept of 'supply chain' to banks

As such, one interesting angle to adopt a fresh perspective (Kim et al., 2016) is by looking at how leading consumer business (CB) organizations efficiently move goods through their supply chains, and apply it to the banking world.

Indeed, transposing this concept to today's banks (cf. be it commercial or investment banks), one can readily associate cash as goods, whereby banks can apply proven CB strategies to reduce excess inventory, lower handling, and processing costs, improve operating efficiency and optimize their network of ATMs.

FIGURE 15: BANK AS USER OF SUPPLY CHAIN MANAGEMENT

The Bank as User for SCM

4 Flows:

1. Material.	Money (Cash)	Banks are the solvency meter in societies. House of trust for several parties.
2. Capital.	Investments	Private Investments. Public Financial Needs.
3. Information.	Economic - Financial	Economic information to protect outside. Financial information to improve inside. Other Specific information (Legal, HR, ..etc.)
4. Man power	Employees	

2 Ends:

1. Suppliers.	Depositors
2. Customers.	Investors

Source: QNB

Indeed, when you think about it, the granting of a loan, for instance, is the essence of a banking activity as it is through these lending activities those banks generate revenues. And, this is the primary root of banking, namely transforming money by collecting deposits and in turn lending them to the economy (cf. be it households, businesses, and governments). However, banks do not have an integrated approach (Jackson & Davis, 2015) in managing the different phases to deliver an end-product/service to a customer failing to view, for example, the lending process as an integrated supply chain from the front to end.

Yes, they have a B2B paperless computer driven lending process in the case of a mortgage loan where the consumer can purchase or refinance a home without ever signing or handling a piece of paper. But, the life cycle of a loan goes much further than merely an online application (cf. infra: Example of (absence) of an integrated supply chain within a bank). Again, banks do not have a streamlined fully integrated chain of supply of services that involve back office, middle office, risk management, business developers, finance, IT, etc. (Davis, 2017). All these departments work in a silo with, yes, bridges between themselves, but without really thinking about their service as being part of an integrated chain.

In other words, what is missing is the risk management of front-to-back processing for all banking activities. Granted, some banking areas have adopted this train of thought such as Treasury or Trade Finance, but these are more the exception than the rule. Traditional activities such as corporate banking, retail banking, and institutional banking still operate in silo architectures and lack integrity of operations, making them not only quite onerous (and hence inefficient), but, even worse, exposing them to potential disruptions. In an ideal world, the workflow of the sales desk should, through technology platforms, be integrated with the middle office, risk management, back office (in relation to settlement and confirmation), accounting, reporting, and inquiries (Davis, 2017). A simple proof of this segregation is the mere existence of different (and not always compatible) IT architectures and software tools for each of those activities causing an absence of effective bridges among these areas of operations.

The closest thing that banks have to supply chain risk management is maybe operational risk management, and more specifically Business Continuity Management; but that does not suffice. The first step for banks to comprehend and embrace this concept of supply chain risk management (and supply chain resilience) is acknowledging that the various business lines within banking organizations also operate as supply chains. The next step, similar to what happens in the manufacturing world, is the understanding of the banks' exposure to supply chain risk – both up and down the stream, thereby helping to identify the weakest links.

In today's globalized and interconnected world that keeps on stubbornly focusing on concepts of 'lean' and 'cost-cutting,' there is alas little spare capacity in the supply chains. Complex, multi-stakeholder, outsourced and even cross-border delivery schedules mean that few banks (and businesses overall) can claim accurate visibility to any significant depth in the supply chains of their various business lines. supply chain risk management and supply chain resilience are therefore essential risk mitigation approaches that should underpin any decision to optimize supply chains in the long run, and hence help build more resilient banking business models.

Alas, today's operational risk management within banks does not embrace nor comprehend that view of supply chain risk management. More critically, if banks were to manage their cash supply chain more effectively, they would also be able to improve resiliency and better position themselves to compete in the marketplace (Kim et al., 2016).

However, this approach within banks is still in its infancy. Also, banks like many other corporates outsource a growing number of their activities, hence relying on third parties to deliver specific services to internal or external stakeholders. In other words, the risks in a supply chain are critical because of increasing outsourcing, off-shoring, product variety, lean 'production', and supply chain security issues (Blos et al., 2012).

Moreover, organizations are at a higher risk of system failure because of the massive interdependency throughout the global supply chains. Due to those facts, resilience is becoming the primary concern of any banking organization, and supply chain risk management can be one of the tools to achieve this resilience.

Mapping Of A Supply Chain In A Bank

As a reminder, in commerce, supply-chain management (SCM), the management of the flow of goods and services, involves the movement and storage of raw materials, of work-in-process inventory, and of finished goods from point of origin to point of consumption.

Interconnected or interlinked networks, channels and node businesses combine in the provision of products and services required by end customers in a supply chain. Some of the processes in banking service supply chain are similar to a goods supply chain. The context of these processes, however, is different in services:

FIGURE 16: CONTEXT SUPPLY CHAIN

Demand Management	• Due to lack of buffer inventory it is difficult to manage uncertain demand for services. • Understand the capacity available and current workload. • Possibilities of additional workload by hiring part time or by doing overtime.
Customer Relationship Management	• Customer segmentation & monitoring relationship by understanding customer needs and changing behavior of customers.
Supplier Relationship Management	• Identification of requirements with clear specifications. • Select suppliers & provide clear scope of work and statement of work. • Negotiate & sign contracts with appropriate service level agreements to avoid in uncertainty from supply side.
Service Delivery Management	• Meeting customer's expectations through statement of work or SLA. • Enabling service providers to meet promises by monitoring SLA compliance and payment terms.

Order Process Management	• Order processing function in which service organizations get orders from customers. • Check status of orders, communicate the status to customers, actual filling the orders & make orders available to the customers. • Order processing span over intersection of other functions of supply chain management to perform sub processes like order preparation, transmittal, entry, filling and status reporting.

Service supply chain deals with flow of information, capacity (incl. materials and employees), and cash:

- Information flow: it deals in sharing information among service supply chain entities on service level agreements, scope of work, required skills of service provider, feedback, and payment related terms.
- Capacity flow: it deals in managing capacity in the form of material and human resources. Service companies manage capacity flow by investing in assets, recruiting quality staff, and recruiting appropriate staff.
- Cash flow: it deals in the flow of funds governed by payment terms based on the performance

towards agreed goals. But, determining appropriate timing and payment is a challenging issue in services.

The service supply chain is the network of suppliers, service providers, consumers and other supporting units that performs the functions of transaction of resources required to produce services, transformation of these resources into supporting and core services, and the delivery of these services to customers.

Service level agreements (SLAs): forms of contracts agreed between service provider and the customer or client. SLAs are important for managing the relationship between service supply chain partners, and mostly prevail in Business-to-Business services.

An SLA defines the nature of the goods or services and the level of quality to be provided. It helps in development and formalization of service provider client relationship. It is comprised of following components:

- Service specification, such as key dimensions of performance such as response time, reliability, availability, accuracy, and setting the ways to measure performance of each dimension to reduce the likelihood of disagreements at a later date about performance. Also, set mutually agreed target for each dimension. It should be based on the service provider's cost and capability and client requirement regarding ultimate users (internal and external customers of clients). Lastly, define clearly the who is responsible for measuring each dimension.

- Routinized relationship: it deals in the day to day operation of agreement by devising and implementing a mechanism for reporting performance against standards at agreed regular intervals, and setting out procedures to handle the situations of failures against standards. These failures should be taken as opportunities for service provider and client to work together to solve problems.
- Developmental relationship, whereby one needs to:
  - Appreciate the role of SLAs to develop a long-term relationship by
  - Arranging routine discussion of the measures and targets.
  - Share ideas for improvement of standards and relationship.
  - Reviewing the measures and standards regularly.

So, we can summarize some features of service supply chain as presented below:

- Human labor is a significant component of the value delivery process
- Involvement of human component leads to greater variations and uncertainties
- in service output and lesser standardization in service processes.
- Service supply chain is bi-directional – i.e., the customer also acts as a supplier (customer-supplier duality).
- Efficiencies are measured through management of capacities, information and cash flow, flexibility of resources and service performance.
- Service capacity serves as the substitute for inventory. Operational agility is achieved through strategic use of capacity.

DEFINITION SUPPLY CHAIN RISK MANAGEMENT & RESILIENCE

A definition by Wieland and Wallenburg (2012) about supply chain risk management yields the following: supply chain risk management is "the implementation of strategies to manage both every day and exceptional risks along the supply chain based on continuous risk assessment with the objective of reducing vulnerability and ensuring continuity." To put it differently, supply chain risk management is to apply risk management process tools, with either external partners in a supply chain or the bank's own internal service providers, to deal with risks and uncertainties caused by, or affecting, service delivery-related activities or resources in the supply chain (Brindley, 2004).

With supply chain risk management, through a coordinated, holistic approach, all supply chain stakeholders (both internal and external) identify and analyze the risk of failure points within the supply chain (Trowbridge, 2017). Typical risks that might affect the supply chain oscillate from unpredictable cataclysmic threats to cyber-attacks and fraud, third party failures, and reach across quality, security, to resiliency and product integrity. Supply chain risk management is cause-oriented as it typically involves four processes: identification, assessment, controlling, and monitoring of supply chain risks (Wieland & Wallenburg, 2012).

Though, as a result of the increasing complexity of many supply chains and their environments, these processes might not suffice to warrant that for all eventualities a contingency plan exists.

That is why supply chain risk management needs to be combined with the concept of supply chain resilience (Christopher & Peck, 2004), as the latter which aims to ensure that the supply chain can bounce back from risks irrespective of their cause.

Supply chain resilience is, therefore (Ponomarov & Holcomb, 2009) "The adaptive capability of the supply chain to prepare for unexpected events, respond to disruptions, and recover from them by maintaining continuity of operations (Caddick & Buchanan, 2011) at the desired level of connectedness and control over structure and function". Similar to the typical methodology for quantifying risk, supply chain risk can be defined as a function of the probability of an event's occurrence and its severity.

The main disadvantage of applying this approach to measure supply chain risk is that it necessitates quantifying the occurrence or probability of many different event types for n number of supply chain locations (which can be tens of locations in a large banking organization). In that respect, an interesting metric to measure supply chain resilience is what is called Time-To-Recover. TTR is the time it takes an organization to restore 100% of operational output following a significant supply chain disruption.

The determination of TTR assumes that the facility is virtually unusable due to a significant event, and would need substantial reconstruction and re-sourcing used in banking operations. As such, financial market players - be it financial institutions (banks, insurance companies, asset managers, brokers) and/or prudential authorities - could learn a lot from how the corporate world is coping with the risk management of disruptive events (yes, we have operational risk management but that only covers part of the problem).

The top supply chain vulnerabilities of banks are (Jackson &Davis, 2015):

FIGURE 17: SUPPLY CHAIN VULNERABILITIES BANKS

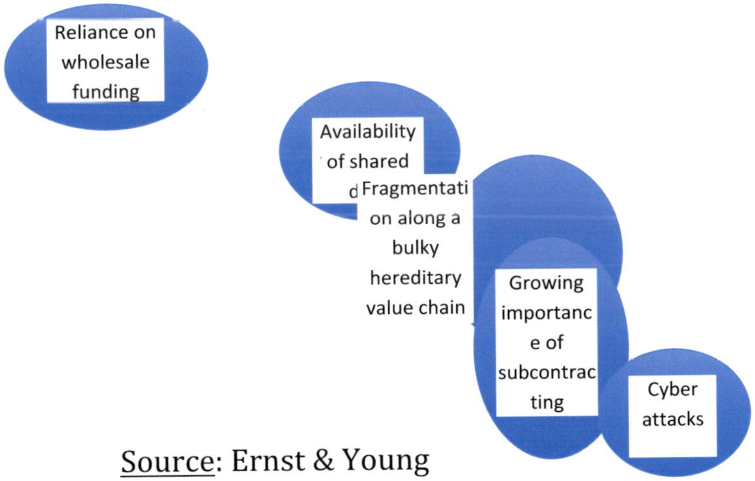

Source: Ernst & Young

The reliance on wholesale funding affects mostly the smaller banks that need to rely on brokered deposits to support loan growth, while concomitantly larger commercial banks have reduced their dependency on short-term borrowings (i.e., these short-term borrowings typically include federal funds and securities sold under agreements to repurchase, commercial paper as well as other borrowings from FHLB and other market participants). While before the GFC they typically represented 25-30% of total liabilities, nowadays they have fallen to 10-15% (which is still meaningful in absolute numbers when considering a bank with close to one trillion of USD in assets). Other vulnerabilities affecting the supply chain of banks are the increasing reliance on subcontractors (causing a third-party risk), the lack of inter-compatibility between databases from different departments (look at the reconciliation efforts that are necessary every quarter as well as by year end between finance and risk management, for example).

WHY SUPPLY CHAIN RISK MANAGEMENT & RESILIENCE

The objectives of supply chain risk management and supply chain resilience for banks and the benefits of an integrated supply chain include:

- Ensuring 'production' (such as the origination of loans, the collection of deposits, the signing of asset management agreements in the scope of private banking, etc.) and delivery capabilities.

- The avoidance of revenue losses in case of disruptions and reduction of costs.

- The fulfillment of regulatory requirements and compliance.

- Safeguarding the corporate image and customer satisfaction.

These approaches also provide some additional benefits (vander Straeten, 2016). It:

- Identifies hidden exposures. The approach helps managers identify which nodes in the network create the most significant risk exposure—often highlighting previously hidden or overlooked areas of high risk. It also allows the firm to compare the costs and benefits of various alternatives for mitigating the impact.

- Avoids the need for predictions about rare events. The approach determines the optimal response to any disruption that might occur within the supply network, regardless of the cause. Rather than trying to quantify the likelihood that a low-probability, high-severity incident will strike, organizations can focus on identifying the critical exposures and putting in place risk mitigating strategies (Simchi-Levi et al., 2014).

- Reveals supply chain dependencies and bottlenecks. These analyzes can also help banks make better sourcing decisions that increase the resilience of the supply chain. This includes taking into account the likely struggle among competing banks to lock in alternative sources of funding (liquidity) if a liquidity provider's disruption affects several banks in the market. Such cross-firm impacts of a crisis are often underestimated. For example, also, sourcing contracts with backup vendors can be negotiated to grant a company priority over others in the event a disruption with the primary vendor would take place. Such decisions could then decrease time to recovery after the disruption and hence the financial impact for the banking organization.

- Fosters a culture of 'stakeholdership', learning, and discussion. In the scope of analyzing the supply chain in this way, managers engage in discussions with vendors as well as internal suppliers of data or services about acceptable levels of TTR for critical services and share insights about best-practice processes to reduce recovery time. These discussions are then put into stone through service level agreements. As a result, the effect of disruptions is brought to a minimum, and thus also the financial impact for the bank.

- A resilient supply chain is a competitive advantage, reduces customer perception of assumed risks and moves organizations from simple risk management to risk resilient growth (Turner, 2011). It is not just playing defense — it is also about playing offense — finding competitive advantage by shaping a supply chain resilience strategy focused on sustained performance that remains agile and fundamentally operations-focused. It is about balance.

Incentives as mentioned above should convince banks about the need to adopt and embrace these concepts of supply chain risk management and supply chain resilience. In other words, these approaches should be transposed to the banking industry, thereby not only assisting 'Risk' on the ways how it manages disruptions caused by low probability - high severity extreme events but foremost supporting the executive leadership in designing more resilient banking business models.

RECENT TRENDS IN SUPPLY CHAINS AFFECTING BANKS

Over the last several decades, supply chain networks in the corporate world have on an ongoing basis evolved to deliver speed, capacity, efficiency not to mention customer service through organizational trends such as volume consolidation, specialization, globalization, and information availability (Appel, 2012). The emphasis on relentless cost optimization has highlighted the tension between cost cuts and supply chain resilience – with the removal of traditional buffers such as excess capacity, redundancy, and safety stock.

Figure 18: Recent trends supply chains in banking

Trend	Example	Risk Impact
Globalization	Outsourcing, offshoring	Local concentrated risks become globally diffused, involving multiple actors
Specialization	Geographical concentration of production	Efficient process can be easily disrupted by localised event
Complexity	Product/network complexity	Reliance on multiple parts/players in diverse locations reduces visibility and adds latency into monitoring systems
Lean processes	Single sourcing, buffer stock reduction	While initially efficiency is improved and costs are lowered, fewer alternatives in case of disruption
Information availability	Track and Trace	Systems increasingly reliant on information flow

Source: World Economic Forum

Also, when you think about it, these developments have also affected the banking industry and shifted risk distributions. As a result, their effects have often included sharing risk more broadly around the world (cf. through the effects of the Basel Accords, for instance, or the existence of central counterparty clearing (CCP)), reducing high-frequency risks and focusing risk within individual business lines (real estate, proprietary trading, commodities, securitization, etc.).

Another common feature has been to separate risk from responsibility, twist incentives and manufacturing moral hazards – the notion that a party that is secluded from risk will behave differently from how it would act if it had taken full exposure to risk (cf. Look at how Basel III requires banks to maintain an interest in their securitizations (Sarkisyan & Casu, 2013), based on the assumption that retaining "skin in the game" induces banks to improve screening and monitoring of ~~borrowers. Examples of the~~ proposed rules requiring

[3] It includes Article 122a of the Capital Requirements Directive (CRD II) in the EU and Section 941 of the 2010 Dodd-Frank Act in the US.

'securitizers' to retain a portion of the credit risk in the assets that they securitize[3]).

As organizations, including banks, look for efficiencies and cost reduction opportunities in supply chain and delivery processes (f. ex. Online banking), they need to be aware of the potential impact on their risk profile. The increasing vulnerability of supply chains (Peck, 2006) requires a new focus on managing and mitigating risk, which extends beyond the walls of a single organization. It necessitates a much higher level of consciousness of where the risks lie.

OWNER OF SUPPLY CHAIN RISK MANAGEMENT & RESILIENCE

As already indicated previously, technology should facilitate the integration of workflows within a banking organization making it more inclusive. For instance, IT platforms should connect the workflow of the front office with the middle office AND risk management AND back office (about settlement and confirmation) AND accounting AND reporting. A simple proof of this existing segregation is the mere existence of difference IT architectures and software packages for each of those activities lacking useful bridges among these areas of operations and therefore causing bottlenecks when trying to produce reporting data that is consolidated and exhaustive.

The objective of an effective supply chain risk management program is therefore to smoothen these workflow chains connecting all the dots from front-to-end so that professional services can be rendered to the clients irrespective of the (challenging) environment into which a bank can be in (momentarily as a result of an unexpected event). In other words, leadership guidance is essential to any successful supply chain risk management program. A committed leadership not only helps identify risks well before they become the source of a disruption; additionally, such as an engaged team also provides a swift and thorough response to any incidents that might take place (SCRLC, 2011).

Ultimately, leadership, reporting, and ownership of supply chain risk should rest with operational risk management (Borghesi & Gaudenzi, 2012) and the board. Indeed, according to the two authors "operational processes represent the core business of most organizations, and therefore the proper assessment of operational and supply chain risks is critical to effective and efficient prevention and protection of an organization". However, a capable supply chain risk management steering team should be composed of leaders of not only ORM, but also of the following functions (non-exhaustive list):

- Front/ middle/ back office
- Risk management group (incl. Governance)
- Business continuity
- Enterprise risk management
- Finance (incl. Accounting, reporting)
- Logistics
- Audit
- Security
- Vendor management.

These different functions should have representation on both the executive steering team and the implementation team. Going back to the corporate world, conventional techniques for managing supply chain risk rely on knowing the probability of occurrence and the severity of impact for every potential event that could critically hamper an organization's business operations. For typical supply chain disruptions, such as poor supplier performance, forecast errors, delivery failures, etc., those techniques are robustly relying on historical data to quantify the level of risk (Simchi-Levi et al., 2014). However, it's a different story for low-probability, high-impact events—mega-disasters like Hurricane Katrina in 2005, viral epidemics like the 2003 SARS and 2014-2015 Ebola outbreaks, or significant outages due to unforeseen events such as factory fires and political upheavals. These black swans, such as the 2007-2008 GFC and the 2010 Eurozone crisis, too have affected the banking industry for instance. Because historical data on these rare events are limited or nonexistent, their risk is hard to quantify using traditional models.

As a result, many companies do not adequately prepare for them, and that can have calamitous consequences when catastrophes do strike and can force even operationally savvy companies to scramble after the fact. To address this challenge, aside from developing a financial model that focuses on determining the probability that any specific risk will occur, it is equally appropriate to center on the description of the supply chain that puts the emphasis on the impact of potential failures at points along the supply chain, rather than again the cause of the disruption. For example, the sudden lack of liquidity to fund a corporate loan or close a securitization, or the imminent default of a partnering syndicated bank in a project finance deal, or the fall-out of a swap provider. This type of analysis removes the need to determine the probability that any specific risk will occur—a valid approach since the mitigation strategies for disruption are equally valid regardless of what caused it (Simchi-Levi et al., 2014). Using this approach, banks can quantify what the financial and operational impact would be if a critical funding supply were suddenly out of commission for, say, two weeks—whatever the underlying reason in the market. Proper mapping of the supply chain is therefore crucial since supply chains are in a continual state of flux.

Example Of The Mapping Of A Supply Chain For A Bank

To illustrate how a mapping of a supply chain for a bank works, the mortgage supply chain is a very good example as it is a critical component in the business activities of any commercial bank. The supply chain refers to the operational system both for delivering mortgages to borrowers and financing those mortgages. This is not as much about policy as it is about the business practices and the institutions that allow for the provision of mortgages in the private sector. The supply chain below demonstrates that there are several stakeholders involved, internally as well as externally, at each step of the way that are interconnected. Hence, they all need to work together in order to deliver a mortgage loan on a as competitive basis as possible (cf. not just money wise, but also in terms of customer experience). It is key to look at a supply chain as an integrated value chain.

FIGURE 19: SUPPLY CHAIN MORTGAGE LOAN W/ COMMERCIAL BANK

Steps	Activity	Process	Internal stakeholders	External stakeh.
1	**Borrower outreach/ acquisition**	Preliminary pricing, offer expertise, persuade consumer.	Mortgage consultant, Front office	Broker, Housing counsel agencies
2	**Prequalification of borrower**	Obtain credit score, initial quantification, prepare & counsel, update pricing.	Loan officer, Front office	Broker
3	**Loan processing**	Obtain application, provide good faith estimate, pre-approval.	Mortgage consultant	Broker
4	**Underwriting and loan decision**	Final pricing, verify credit, property analysis, preparation loan documents.	Underwriter, Credit analyst, Appraiser, Middle Office	Underwr. contractor
5	**Closing and funding**	Sign loan documents, disburse funds, lien perfection, and document stack.	Loan officer, Finance, Back office, Middle Office	Title company

6	**Servicing & loan management**	Loan management, annual reviews.	Credit analyst, Loan portfolio manager, Appraiser, Middle office	Specialty servicer, Rating agency
7	**Monitor investment**	Loan repayment, default management, enforce guarantees, litigation, enforce representations & warranties.	Loan portfolio manager, Credit analyst, Accounting, Finance	Trustee

FINDINGS SUPPLY CHAIN FOR MORTGAGE LOAN ORIGINATION:

Currently, there is no mortgage supply chain system that actually establishes communication between the risk mitigation that happens on the front end through counseling, all the way into loan repayment, or in the worst case into default management and litigation. Another failure is that the contemporary mortgage loan supply chain is expensive as evidenced by the numerous steps and various stakeholders that need to be involved. Fortunately, advances in technology allow (or will soon) for a smoother, faster, and hence less onerous supply chain – or, in other words lower manufacturing costs. Banks also lack an integrated supply chain that is connected to a technology platform for mortgages in the way that, for example, travel companies or tax returns or car buying are connected. Such platforms, such as Quicken exists for higher credit score loans (cf. well-priced high-quality low-risk mortgage to customers); however, many loans are non-conforming, and for those no technology platforms are out on the market. These failures illustrate that banks need to start thinking about the mortgage supply chain holistically and how it could connect across internal and external stakeholder networks, but also how the supply chain can be transformed into a value chain. Banks need to redesign their lending process from end to end, allowing it to eliminate numerous handovers. For example. a bank from the Benelux (McKinsey & Company, 2018) was able to achieve about 30 percent greater efficiency. Failing to achieve an end-to-end orientation, banks will continue to face disappointing results. Attempts to improve the credit process piece by piece tend to lose customer focus, become incremental, and miss the big-picture (holistic) opportunity to deliver a fundamental step change in performance and approach. For example, banks could improve the efficiency of commercial mortgage operations by integrating loan accounting, servicing, asset management, borrower customer service and investor reporting into a single platform. This platform would include, for example, an advanced imaging and document management platform, plus internet portals for borrower customer service and investor reporting. The other advantage is that the loans would be delivered on a secure, hosted basis. There would also be an option for shared servicing thereby providing to outsource selected processing activities through, for instance, a private label arrangement, while retaining direct control of the borrower relationships and asset management responsibilities.

FIGURE 20: SUPPLY CHAIN DIGITAL ONLINE MORTGAGE LOAN W/ FINTECH

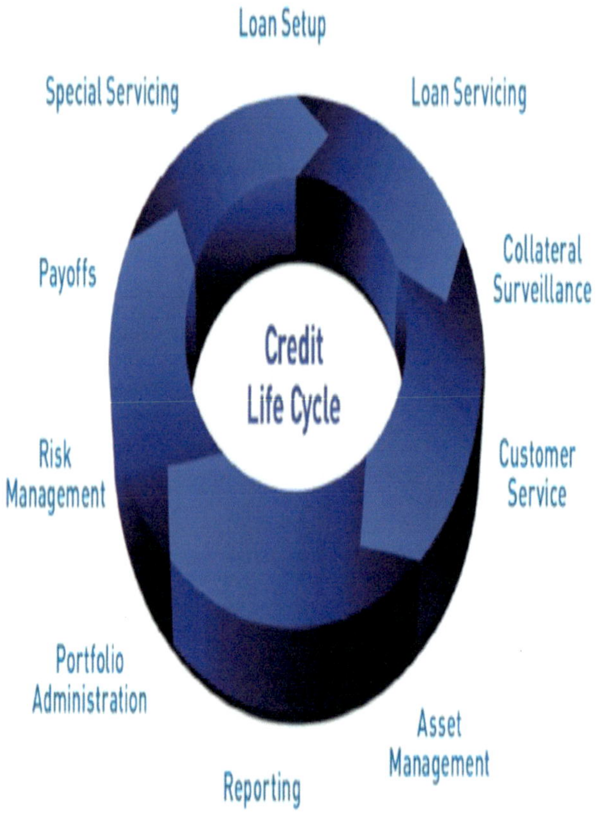

Source: SupplyChain247, 2015

CONCLUSION

Most banking organizations have operational risk management policies that can cope with localized disruptions. However, recent high-profile events have put into the limelight how risks outside the control of individual banking organizations can have unintended spillover effects that can no longer be mitigated by one banking organization alone.

Given that operational processes represent the core business of banking organizations, therefore the proper assessment of operational and supply chain risks should be viewed as critical to effective and efficient prevention and protection of an organization. And, ultimately, operational risk management should own the risk management of the supply chain. Now granted, disruptions should no longer be viewed as the 'sacred domain' only of operational risk managers, even in the realm of banks. Already, changes to governance models in the wake of the 2008 Global Financial Crisis have pushed banking organizations to review their approaches to identifying and mitigating systemic risks.

C-suite level leadership and corporate boards are ought to increasingly understand and being held accountable for the many aspects of organizational risk, including supply chain risk management.

And, while regulators have not been stepping up their game cf. regulatory scrutiny prioritizes reporting and not risk measurement nor comprehensive and dedicated risk management programs in relation to the supply chain), banking executives should not be complacent either and instead be proactive.

The geopolitical, macroeconomic and systemic implications of regulating in a complex banking environment necessitate new approaches to mitigating risks that might affect the supply chain. Systemic risks within supply chains of banks (and other corporate organizations) are characterized by an unexpected trigger event and a supply chain setup that cannot absorb the shock and knock-on effects. The initial event can result in a domino effect causing massive disruption or failure across an entire industry or even region.

However, having the resiliency in place for effective response, no matter what the cause, it felt more important than forecasting of specific disruptions. While highlighting banking industry resilience in the face of recent shocks, it is critical to identify the most concerning vulnerabilities that damage the resilience of supply chains.

The goal of supply chain risk management and supply chain resilience is not to forecast what or when – but instead helping organizations (i.e., in this case, banks, also) in getting better prepared and able to timely respond in a thorough and planned manner to minimize the consequences of a disruptive event. While likely types of disruption can be identified, the precise nature of systemic disruptions to supply chains within banking organizations and their delivery modes is hard to predict.

Therefore, planning for a specific trigger event is not as important as having the inherent resiliency, flexibility and adaptability within banking organizations to be able to respond and recover regardless of the type of disruption quickly, and supply chain risk management and supply chain resilience are one of the best tools for that.

SECTION VI: THIRD-PARTY RISK MANAGEMENT

BACKGROUND

Similar to existing operationally-oriented risk management mandates, such as "know your customer" (KYC) and increasingly detailed "know your vendor" (KYV) guidelines, that have given rise to much more rigorous risk management techniques, supply chain management initiatives are progressively becoming equally important.

Concomitantly with these new regulatory mandates, large banking institutions are also becoming more receptive increasing supply chain risks through formal internal audits, legal actions, or more in-depth interpretations of existing standards and rules.

Working models from the pre-GFC era need to be "right-sized" to fit with a new market reality.

> These individuals who believe in the interminability of this environment have shown greater urgency in this strenuous right-sizing exercise. And, those who claim the prevalent market environment will return to a prior reality have embraced a more "wait and see" approach to right-sizing.

Re-framing operating models that exhibit enhanced performance and spryness at lower costs – "more-for-less" – have turned into a mantra from this wound. Additionally, among numerous other types of initiatives, the utilization of contractors and consultants has consistently grown among asset managers, banks, insurance, and brokerages.

With consensus expectations – and plentiful proof, the use of these contractors and consultants will continue its upward direction for the foreseeable future in the financial services sector – and become progressively tied to both basic as well as crucial activities.

The financial services industry today constitutes an essential backbone of the global economy. The banking sector in particular is flagged as one of the critical infrastructure sectors given that its incapacitation or destruction would debilitatingly affect homeland security, national economic security, national public health or safety, or any combination thereof.

The banking sector is, by the nature of its business, a highly intertwined industry as well. Greater interconnectivity brings about more significant cybersecurity risks due to the fact that (i) the interconnected entities are likely connected to additional entities which could also be the source of cybersecurity risk, and (ii) there are too many things to secure and monitor. Add to this the fact that third-party vendors are a widely acknowledged reality today.

Undoubtedly, these vendors have over the years come up with game-changing, innovative solutions for the banking sector. Accordingly, they assume a vital role in the proficient and gainful functioning of several banking organizations.

Be that as it may, this increased dependence on third-party vendors has also implied additional exposure to cybersecurity hazards and vulnerabilities. Prudential authorities have become progressively worried about third-party vendor risk management practices, particularly in the banking industry.

It is paramount to keep in mind that agreeing with a third-party vendor does not imply that accountability and responsibility have been contracted to third-parties as well. Based on experience, one can claim that third-party vendors frequently have disappointingly low standards with regards to cybersecurity and data protection.

While there have been several data breaches over the years where the third-party vendor was clearly at fault, more recent ones have shown that these still happen and will continue to take place, as illustrated by below examples:

- In April 2017, Scottrade Bank acknowledged a data breach that exposed the personal information of 20,000 of its customers because a third-party vendor uploaded a file to a server without adequate cybersecurity protections[4].
- In July 2017, Italian bank UniCredit had their accounts hacked through one of their third-party vendors that led to the exposure of 400,000 customer loan accounts[5].

Other major data breaches that have taken place since the early 2000s are (Armerding, 2018):

FIGURE 21: BIGGEST DATA BREACHES SINCE 2000

---

[4] http://securityaffairs.co/wordpress/57773/data-breach/scottrade-bank-data-leak.html

[5] https://www.scmagazineuk.com/unicredit-banks-third-party-leads-to-hack-on-400000-clients/article/677546/

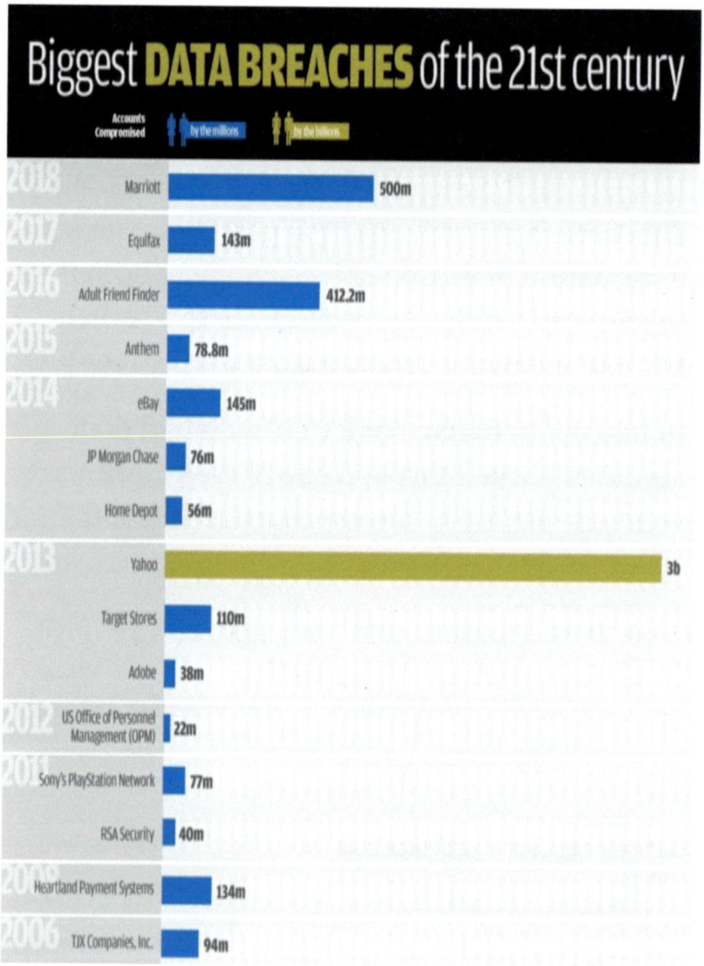

<u>Source</u>: Armerding, 2018.

These illustrations highlight that third-party vendors can frequently cause serious cybersecurity risks to outsourcing banks:

- Operational disruptions: If the data breach involved a cyber hacker, then one has more challenges to face. In such situations, one can never ascertain what the hackers have been able to obtain or how far into the network they were able to penetrate. Hackers, typically, frequently like to leave behind backdoors so that they can return later without being challenged by cybersecurity protections. This can result into significant harm to the overall operations. The situation is akin to knowing that there is an enemy already on the inside but not knowing where, when, or how hard the hacker will strike.

- Prudential issues: Banks also bear the responsibility of legal and regulatory compliance to protect consumer data and privacy. A data breach is often taken as a clear indication that the bank was likely negligent and failed in its regulatory obligations. And this results in regulatory fines and penalties that can end up being debilitating. Add to that the costs involved with digital forensic investigations and cybersecurity remediation in the aftermath of the breach and one is talking about a significant added financial burden here.

- Financial and reputational damage: The aftermath is going to be the same as a direct hacker attack on the bank. While the financial damages can be significant from regulatory penalties to lawsuits from customers, the stains on the brand and reputation will be hard to clean. Banks house customer money and that requires a customer's trust. Losing that trust can deliver a devastating blow to a bank's very business model.

Prudential authorities, such as the Office of the Comptroller of the Currency (OCC) in the United States, have already made it clear[6] that banking organizations are responsible for mitigating risks correlated with all of their third-party vendors.

Numerous banking institutions often underestimate third-party vendor hazards and under-invest in related cybersecurity protections, the investment being not just

---

[6] https://www.occ.gov/news-issuances/bulletins/2013/bulletin-2013-29.html

money but also time. And then others do realize the importance of proper third-party vendor risk management but fail to develop a robust approach towards it.

With a dedicated risk management process in place combined with the suitable investment of time, effort, and financial resources it is possible to adequately manage third-party vendor risks[7]. Below are a couple of examples of the types of control that banks should put in place (Oracle, 2015):

- Third-party vendor risk assessment: Perform a formal third-party vendor risk assessment periodically or whenever there is a significant change in either the technical infrastructure or third-party vendor composition. Annually review all the vendors one does business with. For high risk vendors make sure that one has commensurate cybersecurity controls in place. An internal or third-party assessor should

---

[7] Federal Banking institutions Examination Council (FFIEC) IT Examination Handbook InfoBase, available at http://ithandbook.ffiec.gov/it-booklets.aspx

review these controls and test them for their effectiveness periodically.

- Third-party vendor management program: Develop and maintain a comprehensive third-party vendor management program. It will go a long way in pleasing the regulators, but will also form a strong foundation for managing third-party vendor cybersecurity risks. Appoint key personnel with specific roles and responsibilities to manage vendors and associated cybersecurity risks. Allocate transparent reporting chains and accountability. Ensure that essential areas such as classifying and optimizing vendor portfolios, formalizing an appropriate plan for onboard vendors, managing transitions to support changes, and terminating relationships with vendors are in place. Also ensure that contracts, vendor performance and vendor relationships are managed well and closely monitored. Continuously improve the third-party vendor management program by reviewing it on an ongoing basis.

- Due Diligence: Due diligence should be performed on all the significant third-party vendors serving the institution. One of the main things to consider when performing due diligence is to review the vendor's financial stability and monitor it on an ongoing basis. The goal is to keep validating and reinforcing that the vendor meets the standards and stability required to provide the service or product to the bank without causing any risk to the environment or continued operations.

- Monitor continuously: Banks should continuously monitor third-party vendors. Review contracts and agreements, appoint personnel to monitor the vendors, review certification reports from the vendors, and also test banks controls that are in place precisely to address vendor connections and data flows to see how robustly they can manage risks that could potentially arise from vendors. Banking organizations need to rank periodically third-party vendor relationships by their risk profile to establish which vendors require closer monitoring. Lastly, it is a good idea to have the third-party vendors perform comprehensive security reviews of their technical infrastructures. Such reviews include deep-dive, configuration-level cybersecurity assessments that go to the nuts and bolts of every technical component that a vendor uses in its organization. Comprehensive security reviews, owing to their highly technical and deep focus, can provide a significant marker of cybersecurity health and enable confidence in the vendor's cybersecurity posture.

- Prudential requirements: Ensure that one addresses laws, regulations, and critical applicable for banking institutions. Regulators will expect that the third-party vendor risk management processes are in line with the level of risk and complexity of the institution's third-party relationships. Also ensure that one evaluates the third parties and require them to have a regulatory compliance program in place to determine if they comply with applicable laws and regulations and whether the cybersecurity posture and protection profile of the vendor aligns with that of the bank.

- Tools: Technological advancements have meant that there is a sea of data continually moving in and out of organizations. Given the challenging nature of monitoring and control in such an environment, tools can act as powerful accelerators to increase the efficiency and accuracy of third-party vendor management and also provide real-time data with analyzes. This will enable one to make more informed decisions and even provide predictive insights into trends, patterns and warning indicators.

- Fourth party risk: A fourth party is a third-party's third-party and one needs to focus on them too. One needs to know about all the critical vendors the third-party relies on. Verify how capable the third-party vendors are in monitoring their critical vendors and also review the vendor's policies and procedures in place pertaining to vendor management. Ensure that the contracts specify that the critical services that are performed by the bank's vendors cannot be further outsourced.

Managing Third-Party Risk

The tsunami of prudential scrutiny resulting from the 2007-2008 global financial crisis has now reached beyond banks to the companies that supply them. Under the broad notion that activities can be outsourced, but responsibility cannot, the Consumer Finance Protection Bureau (CFPB) and other regulators in the United States are holding banking institutions responsible not only for their actions, but also for those of their vendors and suppliers.

Thus, over the past years, a couple of U.S. banking institutions such as Capital One, Discover Card and American Express have paid n aggregated total of $525 million to settle complaints of deceptive selling and predatory behavior by their third-party suppliers[8]. Through these actions, and others, the nature of the due diligence companies are required to conduct is expanding well beyond the traditional assessments for supplier, operational, and IT security risks.

The rules have not changed entirely, but the emphasis has. Regulators are sensitive to other risks, such as strategic and reputational risks, that even smaller third parties can cause for customers, and are critical of organizations' processes for monitoring these risks.

This new regulatory thrust represents a major test for banking institutions, which typically have more than 20,000 suppliers (Krivin et al., 2013). And, sadly, banking organizations frequently have only a limited

---

8

https://www.pcisecuritystandards.org/documents/PCI_DSS_V3.0_Third_Party_Security_Assurance.pdf understanding of the ways that suppliers and vendors interact with customers. However, as they must bear the costs of suppliers' misdeeds, banking institutions now have a strong incentive to broaden and deepen the way they manage these relationships.

And there is also a business case for doing so: effective third-party management is a mainstay of good operational health and cost management. One has found that the current state of the art requires organizations to develop or improve along the following six elements[9]:

- An exhaustive inventory of all third parties with whom the organizations has a relationship. Numerous organizations find it challenging to establish this list; company-wide reviews and data algorithms to reconcile data are viable tools that can help.
- A thorough index of explicit client risks to which third parties can expose the organizations. Many institutions do not fully comprehend all the hazards their third parties run. A master risk

[9] https://www.gartner.com/technology/home.jsp

register, tied to the issues that the regulator is actively seeking, can help track them down.

- A risk-based segmentation of the supplier base. Not all providers convey the same amount of risk, and subsequently organizations need to triage their vendors better to ascertain the most effort is devoted to the greatest hazards.

- Rules-based due diligence testing. Treating every vendor in a similar fashion does not make sense, and as such, carefully designed rules can help organization concentrate their risk analysis of suppliers.

- A disciplined governance and escalation framework. At numerous organizations, third-party risk management does not have a natural owner, and thus building up one and giving that group the right decision-making powers is essential.

- Integrated technology and MIS workflow process and tools. Even though adapting current risk IT applications to third-party management is tricky, and designing a new one is even harder, a purpose-built off-the-shelf application remains the right answer for many.

Organizations that have effectively built these six components are finding that the work is yielding the expected benefits of lower risk costs; just as vital is the advantage of being able to present a coherent approach to all the key stakeholders. In the United States, the protection of consumers' interests dates back at least to the late sixties. But in the past decade, and especially since the 2007-2008 global financial crisis, all the major financial prudential authorities including the OCC (Office of the Comptroller of the Currency), the FRB (Federal Reserve Bank), and the FDIC (Federal Deposit Insurance Corporation), have taken a keener interest than ever in shielding the financial consumer from the risk of predatory behavior by third parties contracted by banks and other banking institutions[10].

The U.S. Dodd-Frank Wall Street Reform and Consumer Protection Act created the Consumer Financial Protection Bureau, an agency charged with just this kind of protection. Over the past years, the U.S. banking regulators have, for instance, issued more than $25 billion in fines and other actions against five leading mortgage servicers, in part for missteps by their

---

10 https://www.dhs.gov/sites/default/files/publications/nipp-ssp-financial-services-2015-508.pdf

suppliers, such as foreclosure law firms (Krivin et al., 2013). And, thus, an essential topic of the regulator's work to date is that while banking institutions can outsource activities, they cannot outsource their responsibility of consumer protection to third parties.

How to mitigate supply chain risk in the banking industry

Financial services companies are faced with balancing strict data privacy rules (such as, PCI-DSS and GDPR) with the growing need to leverage customer data. And with more regulations looming on the horizon, companies must continuously keep up with the latest legislation, guidelines, and best practices to keep pace with compliance. Alongside these pressing demands, financial services companies must also find ways to mitigate their supply chain risk better.

It often seems like companies are being pulled in multiple directions at once, making a holistic approach to financial services security a must. Unlike manufacturing, where the supply chain consists of moving physical objects, financial services supply chain issues revolve around information and knowledge transfer. This knowledge is most often held by the human capital of a company. Losing information, knowledge and experience to turnover and attrition is a vital risk of human capital. Others include complacency and fraud.

Risks associated with human capital can be mitigated with data and analysis tools, including emerging automated technologies, that collect and organize a company's vital information. Outsourcing provides another option to keep an information supply chain running around the clock. While these solutions will help mitigate risks, of paramount importance are adequate internal financial control and information integration to assure a financial services company runs as it should.

Financial services companies can mitigate their supply chain risk through:

- Due diligence. Companies (brokers/asset managers) that have a very long cash cycle are a more significant risk and typically a more significant investment, too (since the balance is effectively the short-term investment into them).
- Credit rating. Good credit rating (if available) signals financial health of an organization broadly. Not too much debt, so as not to constrain the cash flows; robust risk policies; plenty of liquidity if needed.

- Cash reserves. As above, these are a good indicator if a partner can invest in a new capability in crunch time, or will have the fat to last through the lean times.

It is crucial to keep in mind that risks are about opportunities as well as threats. All of this can be used as an advantage if one is customer-facing: identify the opportunity before others, pitch it upstream, and watch the partners help the company realize it.

For years, the global supply chains of corporations have been a murky business. Many companies have little knowledge of whom they are doing business with. Transparency is crucial. Better due diligence on third-party relationships improves transparency within the supply chain.

But for many corporations, conducting this due diligence efficiently and effectively is a challenge; multi-national corporations may have tens of thousands of third parties and vendors. Just conducting a simple internet search on each of these vendors would take thousands of working hours, and even they might not be fully compliant with anti-bribery and corruption legislation.

By deploying accurate, efficient, automated screening led due diligence and machine learning algorithms to speed up this process, a financial services company can reduce the cost and timeframe of conducting due diligence on a large number of third-party suppliers. Ongoing monitoring programs can automatically flag if a third-party supplier is connected to criminal activity or Politically Exposed Persons (PEPs), who pose a greater risk of corruption and bribery.

Furthermore, global databases can link information, including names and addresses, to the right persons and entities, so a corporation can verify the identities of the suppliers they are working with. This enhances transparency within the supply chain without draining a corporation's time or resources. Greater transparency then protects corporations from potential financial and reputational recriminations, and enables them to operate more efficiently.

In the age of GDPR in particular and privacy regulations in general, one of the most significant risks in the supply chain is the transfer of personal data between supplier and vendor. Compliance tools can help find data leaks before hackers do and before they turn from leaks into full-blown breaches. This is especially poignant due to the large fines produced by GDPR and the tenacity by which it is expected to be enforced.

Cyber risk is fast becoming a top priority for procurement and supply managers, particularly in financial services organizations which hand over large amounts of potentially sensitive data to third parties for processing. The protection of information that pertains to customers is of paramount importance to FinServ companies.

As was seen when Equifax – a consumer credit reporting agency – was hacked in 2017, the fallout from data breaches can be ugly. Yet procurement and supply managers cannot mitigate supply chain cyber risk alone. Mitigating supply chain cyber risk requires buyers to cooperate with experts from IT and compliance during supplier evaluation and selection. Their knowledge should feed the procurement process.

In good times, risk creates a better return on investment; in bad times, risk is to be blamed. There is not an endless supply of money; there is a real supply chain of money globally. Banks hold money, lend money, and act as a profit center, but few understand risk.

They deploy 'clever software' or algorithms to decide how much they can lend to businesses or individuals. The money might come from the savers within the bank, or even in the short term from other businesses within the bank, it might be a bank bond to support new lending, other banks, or even the central bank based on a loan.

Enter blockchain. No trade is lost, no trade can be changed. Same-day reporting and the option of seeing those smart contracts behind the trade could be a reality. The bank will know the true worth, which in turn affects the tier one capital ratio, as part of a stress test.

The lenders can feel happy about supplying overnight or ongoing support to the bank. Blockchain in a financial supply context will present an immutable truth. Cryptographically hashed transactions will allow for total transparency between banking institutions and regulators. The technology to mitigate risks in a financial institution's supply chain is ready, the question is, are the banks ready to reveal all?

To best understand how to mitigate risks, one first has to identify the most significant threats. A cyber-attack resulting in data theft and data security breaches is the number one critical potential catastrophe that keeps CIOs and IT Directors up at night. Banks, mortgage lenders, and brokerage houses are the main drivers of the financial service industry and that is why FINRA[11] exists.

One need added layers of security much like armed guards, cyclone fences, alarms, and thick steel doors. One would be amazed at how many companies are still uploading critical digital assets to a public drive or a cloud-based file share service assuming that they are protected from cyber-attacks. One wrong click on an email via cell phone and a so-called impenetrable wall is rendered to a flimsy piece of tissue paper offering no barrier to a well-planned hack.

One first step financial services companies need to take towards minimizing their vendor risk is to disconnect

[11] FINRA stands for Financial Industry Regulatory Authority and it is a non-governmental agency regulating major sectors of the financial industry, primarily stock exchanges. FINRA reports to the SEC. Having a regulatory agency making sure stock brokers play fair still does not protect data that is being transmitted over the internet. Cloud-based platforms are no help either, ultimately because their very nature means a company does not truly own their data if they are migrating it to someone else's server. What to do? Financial services companies have to treat their data like it is the gold bars locked up in Fort Knox.

from the web. Sounds radical? One may be surprised to learn that this process is well underway in some of America's largest banks and investment firms.

IT security researchers agree that roughly 80% of data breaches and malware incidents are web-borne and in some way browser-related (Filkins et al., 2016). The regular browser has become the main gateway for attacks on the local IT infrastructure of firms (not only) in the financial sector. Locally installed browsers – including those labeled "secure" by their makers – indiscriminately process all content from the web on the user's computer or mobile device. This opens the door for data exfiltration and for malicious code to infiltrate the corporate network, for example through infected vendor websites or compromised third-party business apps.

The finance sector's growing reliance on external services and third-party web apps has resulted in a steady increase of attacks exploiting the inherent security vulnerabilities of the traditional browser.

So, what are financial services company to do, remove the browser? Banks, accounting and law firms, federal and state regulators, even the nation's largest supply chain operator – the Department of Defense (DoD) – all have arrived at the same conclusion: remove the browser, remove the attack surface.

By disconnecting the browser from the local IT and moving it into the cloud, they are creating an additional layer of security, without any of the tradeoffs associated with other approaches to solving the browser crisis.

As part of mitigating supply chain risk, a large part of that comes down to IT security or cybersecurity. When it comes to managing cyber risk, one can often recommend three types of approaches. Looking at technology, processes and people to identify any gaps in IT security – then work on remediating them and updating the processes to prevent them from reappearing.

- For technology, this means conducting a vulnerability assessment to scan devices connected to the network, websites, apps, and firewall configurations.

- For the processes, one wants to make sure the IT practices are in line with industry standards so that one is unintentionally opening itself up to new risks.

- For people, invest in security awareness training so that one can enable staff to identify and avoid cyber threats like phishing, malware, and scams.

There are several security tools one can add to the business to scan emails, manage communications, and better quarantine any malicious threats if they happen to make it through.

To mitigate supply chain risks, the firm could:

- Have diversified suppliers and alternate suppliers who can replace parts of the supply chain in the event of a disruption;

- Work with businesses in various different jurisdictions; and

- Have diversified funding sources, so that parts of the supply chain can be funded appropriately while shifting them across to new jurisdictions.

The vital accounts of the company and financial structures are crucial here, and quite a bit of this repositioning is being seen as the trade war heats up. The 'siloing' of data has plagued financial services like lending for much too long, when information isn't easily shared the results are duplicated efforts, a mountain of manual data entry, a higher error rate, and a general lack of transparency.

This is why blockchain is more than just a buzzword. It has the potential to shatter silos by letting all the relevant parties access the same documents and any updates or changes to these documents at the same time, from any location or software application. It is like giving everyone access to the same file cabinet and when a change is made or transaction is completed, all the participants will be able to see it. Instead of passing information back and forth, reinventing the wheel each time, participants access the information they need when they need it.

Data analytics is a necessary part of any risk mitigation for financial companies. The financial industry is an industry of numbers both in the products it yields and the services/supplies it consumes. Risk analytics takes those numbers, analyzes them and discerns insights that indicate risk of loss and outright fraud in the services or supply chain.

Effective metrics and analysis can even provide predictive insights. Risk analytics is ideally suited to industries that produce large amounts of data like the financial industry. As with any analysis, the larger the population, the keener the insights and the better the predictive abilities. In this way, risk analytics not only alert a company when something is wrong, but they can also be utilized to highlight when something is right. These insights can then be utilized to implement efficiencies and cut costs. For financial services companies, expanding efforts to include their supply chain, minimizing supply chain risk means effective supply chain management and building resistance to ensure the whole operation works in sync in anticipation of potential challenges.

Strategies include diversifying suppliers - as over-reliance on a few major suppliers dramatically increases risks of delivery failures and reduces price negotiation vantage points - maintaining higher inventory for operations flexibility, and creating partnerships, or possibly investing in, or acquiring suppliers. Financial services companies are well versed in managing risk for all the distinct phases of the supply chain, from assessing credit risk to funding a loan, or managing loan delinquencies. But they often lack a clear picture of risk across the entire supply chain from the back office, middle office, risk management, business developers, finance, and IT.

All these departments work in silos to assess the risk of their areas of responsibility using their methods, technologies, and biases. And yet none of the processes that support the supply chain operate exclusively within a silo. Which means the most significant risks are often left undiscovered until something goes wrong, at which point mitigation options are limited and can be very costly to implement. Financial services companies can better manage supply chain risk if they close the gaps between domains and stop worry about the probability of a specific risk event occurring. It is the impact of potential failure at any point along the supply chain (such as a data center outage) that matters.

The definition of an attitude toward supply chain risk will vary widely based on industry and business unit. In manufacturing, for example, it is reasonably straightforward. What will impact your ability to make widgets for your customer base? Within financial services, however, risk impacts an organization's ability to support its customer base in more nebulous ways. Regardless of where precisely the risk sits or how it translates to the end user, supply chain risk is something that financial services organizations need to approach strategically and proactively. There are two ways they can go about this. One takes an internally-focused approach; the other focuses on risk from the outside. The former starts at the core of a business' hierarchy and organizational structure. Simply put, how do the different business units collaborate? Do they function independently with their goals and objectives, or do they build links to each other in order to deliver on broader organizational goals?

Externally, having a robust, well-fitting supplier relationship management program can give the organization insight into what risks factors may be out there. This starts with a clear segmentation model and a methodology that aids the business in determining which suppliers are critical to their operations. These providers require more internal efforts to manage, but (with the right motivation) they will also help the business innovate and develop competitive advantages. Such close relationships will prove essential when risk factors start to loom on the horizon. Critical suppliers will not hesitate to provide a heads-up. Through the length of an engagement, they will make it easy to navigate and respond to anything that might stand in the way of meeting stakeholder and customer expectations. Compared to other risk areas weather-related supply chain risks in financial services is not something that first comes to mind. This is because financial services products are mostly e-commerce/e-business and not affected much by the weather.

That said, there is some risk which is indirectly related to the financial service products. The weather-related supply chain risk for financial services is primarily a business continuity issue relating to physical and personal assets. Because of this, the risk from weather might be perceived as unimportant or inconsequential due to the e-commerce aspect of the financial business. A financial company's weather-related risk would include losing internet connectivity, physical property loss due to damage, business continuity disruptions due to loss of power, and personal assets not being able to physically get to an office or telework. All of these could potentially have the same impact as a cyber security breach which might be seen as a more obvious supply chain risk.

Financial services companies can mitigate supply chain risk by:

(i) Diversifying sources of leads with content marketing. Create valuable content that helps the target audience succeed. Nothing attracts new prospects better than providing them value for free;

(ii) Diversifying lender partnerships from the get-go. When financial markets are strong, it is much easier to create partnerships with multiple lenders. Having a single lending partner is a major risk.

Standard strategies to mitigate supply chain risk include diversifying suppliers, creating partnerships, or possibly investing in or acquiring suppliers. But one can also consider new technologies like blockchain as a very exciting alternative. Blockchain can help mitigate supply chain risks with smart contracts that will be able to manage contractual relationships with alternative suppliers, automatically dealing with supply chain issues such as interruptions in delivery and inventory maintenance, as well as monitoring movement of goods and services along with the supply chain in order to ensure smooth operations.

METHODS SUPPLY CHAIN RISK MANAGEMENT & RESILIENCE

Banks need to move from a fragmented and decentralized supply chain risk management (cf. in the best case, if they already have a description about such a supply chain) to a centralized resource management structure in order to better leverage synergies and increase the overall maturity level of an organization. Implementation of standardized roles and responsibilities, and global policies and procedures have to be supported by an extensive change management program.

One tool to manage supply chain risks efficiently is by drawing 'heat' maps showing risk-events on a matrix defining likelihood and consequence levels. This technique (SCRLC, 2011) "allows managers to see the relative likelihood and consequence of differing risks easily." To use this method effectively, it is paramount to have well-defined and consistently used criteria for the different likelihood and consequence levels.

FIGURE 22: HEAT MAP

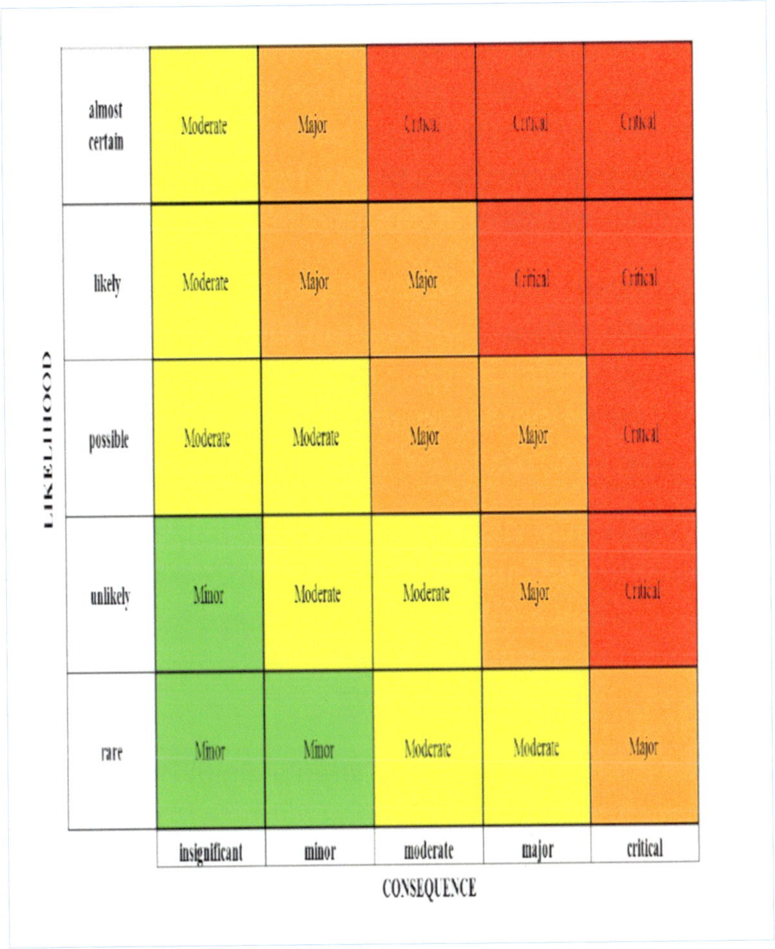

<u>Source</u>: SCRLC

The next step is for any banking organization, having prioritized its risks, determine how it may seek to address them. Once an organization understands its supply chain and has analyzed its potential risks, it can implement an effective supply chain risk management program with its partners, that is, its various internal and external suppliers of data and services.

Nowadays there are vendor companies that provide supply chain software and content product category based on combining massive third-party datasets, with graphical views into an organization's data/ service-supply base, and role-based alerting.

The ability to map risks across multiple data/ service supplier tiers and business lines in near real-time can give banks a powerful new tool to manage their supply chains far more intelligently and proactively.

TTR AND REI

A central characteristic of this supply chain risk management approach is also the notion of Time To Recovery (TTR) (Simchi-Level, 2015), namely the time it would take for a particular node in the chain (cf. such as the sudden absence of funding or a default problem with a swap provider) to be restored to full serviceability after a failure.

To conduct the analysis, the approach removes one node at a time from the supply network for the duration of the TTR. It then determines the supply chain response that would minimize the performance impact of the disruption at that node, for instance:

- relying on emergency liquidity sources,
- finding a new swap provider through the intermediation of a central clearing party,
- taking on a temporary basis a more prominent exposure on the books until the bank finds a newly participating bank in the syndication.

In other words (Sonnier, 2014), by breaking a supply chain into nodes of interaction, banking organizations "can determine the financial and operational impact of each node, and then calculate the repercussions of disruption if a node were to be out of operation for a certain period.

The model assesses costs induced by potential disruption based on the estimated Time-To-Recovery (TTR), determining the financial impact" a particular risk node might have. From the optimal response (Zsidisin et al., 2004), it generates a financial or operational performance impact (PI) for the node.

An organization can choose different measures of PI: lost units of loan production, revenue, or profit margin, for instance. The approach analyzes all nodes in the network, assigning a PI to each. The node with the most massive PI (in lost revenues, for instance, or lost units of loan production) is assigned a risk exposure index (REI) (Simchi-Levi, 2013) score of 1.0.

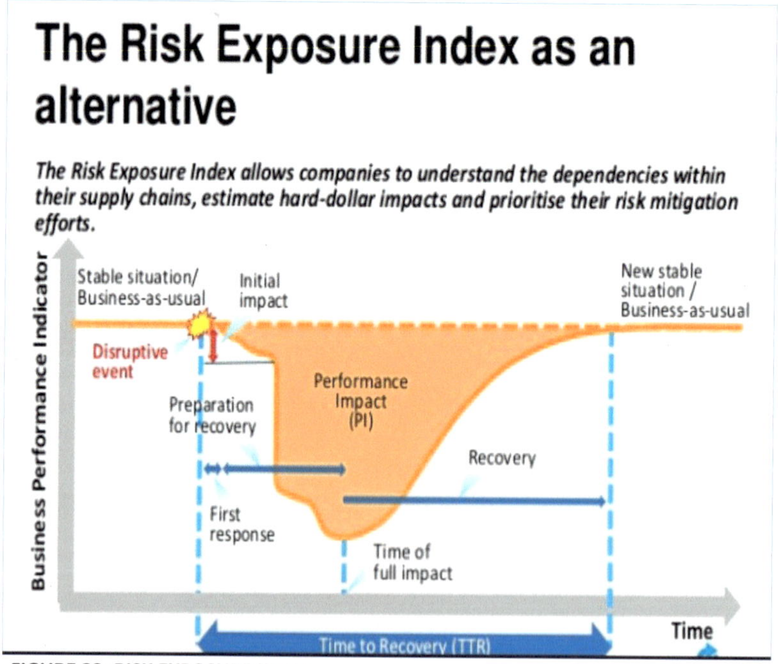

FIGURE 23: RISK EXPOSURE INDEX

Source: Danie Schoeman and SAPICS

All other nodes' REI scores are indexed relative to this value (cf. a node whose disruption would bring about the least impact gets a value close to zero) (Sonnier, 2014). The indexed scores allow the organization to identify at a glance the nodes that warrant the most attention from risk managers.

HOW TO MANAGE THIRD-PARTY RISK IN BANKING

Today's business landscape is loaded with significant pitfalls such as data loss, like cyber threats, cataclysm, and corruption that may result in supply chain disruption. Therefore, it is critical to have in place a formal risk management framework within the banking organization that:

- heralds the conduct of a thorough due diligence of new vendors,
- monitors existing third parties, and
- makes sure these contractors are following appropriate procedures failing which it will affect not only the reputation of the bank, but potentially cause a disruption of activities, and hence a loss of revenues.

While there is regulatory guidance about third-party risk management in the banking industry, the latter is still in its infancy (Park et al., 2015) with organizations deploying different methods, some less effective.

From a governance perspective, and based on a survey conducted by EY in 2018 (i.e., Global financial services third-party risk management survey: Is it time to shift the perspective of third-party risk?) there is no governance ruling that stipulates which function within the bank is the owner of responsibility for third-party risk management.

With less than 50% of the banks TPRM resides with the procurement function, and the remainder is split between IT security, operational risk, enterprise risk and business lines. However, having TPRM owned by procurement is similar to a situation where in a context of lending the front office would also be the one rating the borrower and deciding on the loan (cf. in other words, there would be a conflict of interest and a lack of impartiality and independence).

In other words, there is very little consistency in the responsibility and ownership of different functional components of TPRM, showing that organizations are unique in deploying ownership structures and operating models that reflect the structure and culture of their organizations.

While the survey shows that procurement is the most likely home for TPRM, it should instead be the responsibility of ORM. While regulators need to step up their game regarding how banks protect themselves against third-party issues (cf. regulatory scrutiny prioritizes reporting and not risk measurement nor risk management programs), banking executives should not be complacent either and instead be proactive.

FIGURE 24: THIRD PARTY RISK MANAGEMENT RESPONSIBILITY

Organizations align TPRM activities across numerous parts of the business

There is currently very little consistency in the responsibility and ownership of different functional components of TPRM, showing that organizations are unique in deploying ownership structures and operating models that reflect the structure and culture of their own organizations. However, we are seeing a consistent shift towards centralizing ownership of the TPRM function with responsibility for setting program expectations, structure, strategy and direction.

While firms have begun to centralize the main TPRM resource group, there is still little consensus for where most of these functions are executed. Organizations have been successful at centralizing in certain areas of the function, and unsuccessful in others. Organizations have successfully centralized primary responsibility for performance monitoring (87%) and exit strategy (74%) within the lines of business. Procurement is also typically responsible for notification of upcoming and expired contracts (66%) and termination of contracts (57%).

There have also been areas in which there is no consensus as to which is the responsible party, including SOCR (Service Organization Control s Reporting) report reviews, business continuity assessments and local country risk assessments.

Source: EY

EXAMPLE NON-INTEGRATED SUPPLY CHAIN W/ BANK

Below are two figures as an example of a workflow that is not interconnected. One workflow concerns a mortgage loan application (origination) highlighting that different actors at each step of the way are not indeed interconnected (FDIC, 2018):

FIGURE 25: EXAMPLE NON-INTEGRATED SUPPLY CHAIN BANK

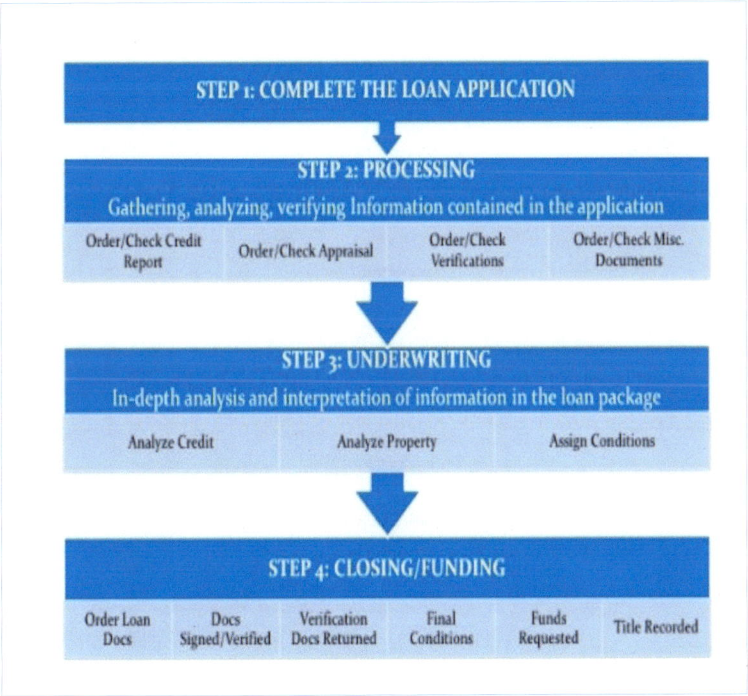

Source: FDIC

And, another workflow concerning the secondary market and servicing:

FIGURE 26: EXAMPLE WORKFLOW MORTGAGE PROCESS

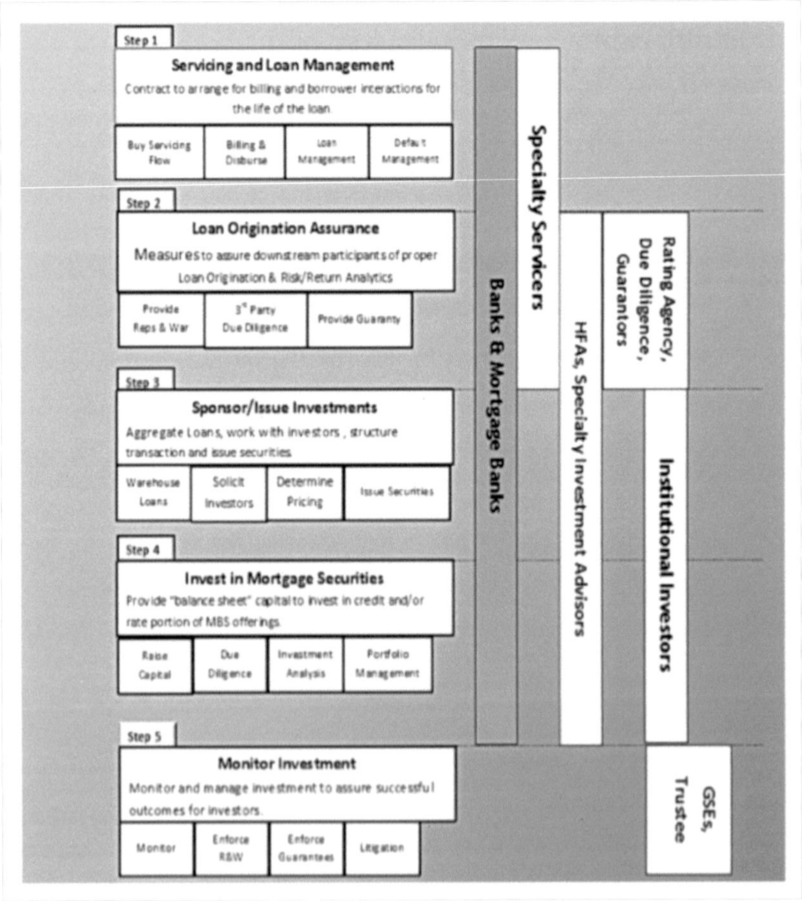

<u>Source</u>: Davis (2017)

In practice, for a bank, one could map out the supply chain (front-to-back) process that involves the provision of a loan to a household or business entity or the settlement of payment, and look at how external events could disrupt the provision of this service to the end customer.

Again, these events could involve the lack of funding due to dry out of the interbank market or a lack of confidence from fixed income investors; the occurrence of a system defect that would prevent the bank from closing the deal (cf. physical disruptions would be covered by operational risk management); the default of a swap counterparty involved in the transaction; exacerbated FX movements or a sovereign crisis affecting international payments; etc.

Now, granted, the risk management of disruptive events is partially covered by operational risk management. Indeed, operational risk can be created by a wide range of different external events ranging from power failures to floods or earthquakes to terrorist attacks. Similarly, operational risk can arise due to internal events such as the potential for failures or inadequacies in any of the bank's processes and systems (e.g. its IT, risk management or human resources management processes and systems), or those of its outsourced service providers. Operational risk arising from human resources management may refer to a range of issues such as mismanaged or poorly trained employees; the potential of employees for negligence, willful misconduct; conflict of interests; fraud; rogue trading; and so on.

Therefore, the emergence of mistrust, failure to communicate, low morale and cynicism among staff members, as well as increased turnover of staff, should be regarded as indicative for a potential increase in operational risk. However, financial events are not covered by operational risk management, such as a market crash, the spill-over effects of the bankruptcy of a systemically important financial institution, the impact of a Grexit or Brexit, a very hard landing of the Chinese economy, a trade war between the US and China, etc.

All these events will in one way or the other from a supply chain management perspective also disrupt the provisions of financial services to the end-customer. As such, it is highly useful not only to map the process that allows a description of the front-to-back process in relation to payments, lending, investments, etc., and look at how a disruption would impact one of the nodes alongside the supply chain for each of those financial activities, and how long it would take for the system to recover its senses, i.e., re-conduct the business as a going concern to the benefit of the customers. However, it is even more exciting to use today's technological developments to build IT platforms that allow for the establishment of an integrated supply chain within the bank. An excellent example of an already operational well-oiled and integrated supply chain is the one in place with a small FinTech lender (i.e., Springboard Home Loans):

FIGURE 27: EXAMPLE SUPPLY CHAIN FINTECH

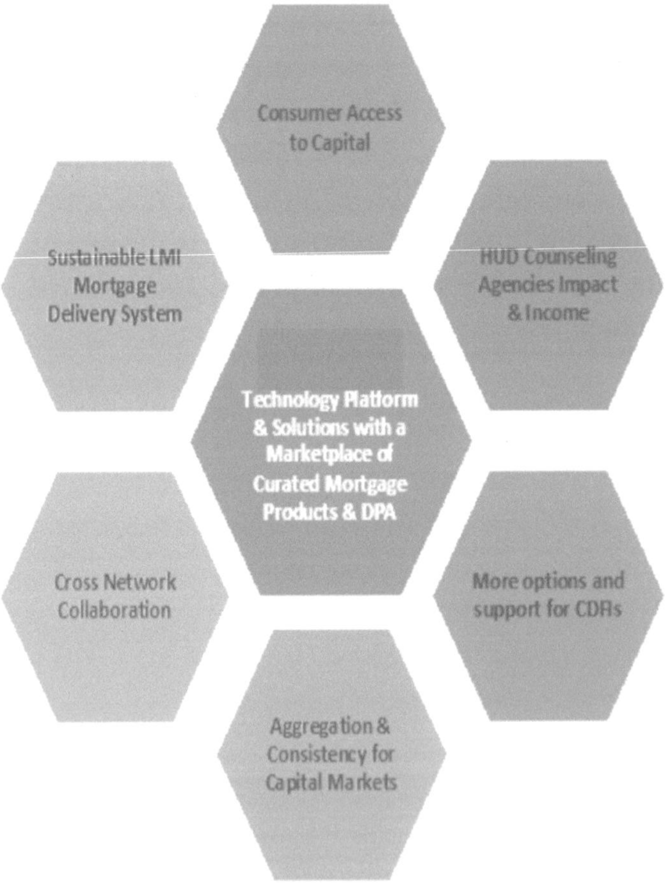

Source: Springboard CDFI

Generally speaking, by gaining a better understanding of the threats that could impact a supply chain, the latter would be able to anticipate better, react to, and recover from the unexpected (Wu & Blackhurst, 2009). And, ultimately, the bank would emerge as more resilient as a result.

Focusing on building supply chain resilience as part of a bank's risk management strategy allows the organization to transform its view of risk to create value rather than merely manage it.

SECTION VII: 1ST, 2ND, 3RD, 4TH, & 5TH PARTY RISK MGMT

DISTINCTION BETWEEN PARTIES SUPPLYING SERVICES

Various types of flows can exist between parties, namely data, services, or cash; or in other words, there can be a data supply chain network, a service supply chain, or a cash supply chain. And, by viewing a service/ data/ cash as 'inventory' moving through the prism of the bank supply chain network, it becomes apparent that banks and distribution companies face very similar challenges.

In the corporate world - from a definition perspective - supply chain management has been described as the management of the flow of goods and services that includes the movement and storage of raw materials, work-in-process inventory, and finished goods from point of origin to point of consumption. In essence, supply chain management draws heavily from the areas of operations management, logistics, procurement, and information technology, and strives for an integrated approach.

Interestingly enough, within the financial services industry, nothing comparable exists because when you think about it, the granting of a loan is the essence of a banking activity as it is through these lending activities that banks generate revenues (yes, nowadays, banks also generate massive revenues from non-lending activities) as the primary root of banking is transforming money, namely collecting deposits and lending them to the economy (be it households, firms, and governments).

But banks do not have an integrated approach in managing the different phases to deliver an end-product/service to a customer and where they view, for example, the lending process as a supply chain. Yes, they have a B2B paperless computer driven lending process in the case of a mortgage loan where the consumer is able to purchase or refinance a home without ever signing or handling a piece of paper.

However, they do not have a streamlined fully integrated chain of supply of services that involves back office, middle office, risk management, business developers, finance, and IT. All these departments work in silo with, yes, bridges between themselves, but without really thinking about their service as being part of an integrated chain.

In other words, what is missing is the risk management of a front-to-back processing for all banking activities. Granted, some banking areas have adopted this train of thought such as Treasury or Trade Finance, but traditional activities such as corporate banking, retail banking and/or institutional banking still operate in silo architectures and lack an integrity of operations:

- Information or service or cash supplied by a first party : this is the most powerful data of all, because it's the information an organization collects from either other departments within the same organization (f. ex. from the Finance Department, Risk Management, Back Office, Middle Office, Internal Audit, Front Office (Lending Officers, Financial Markets, Asset Managers, etc.). Typically, these types of information originate from the relationship and interaction the various units within the organization have with themselves , and subsequently the organization is 'working' these data to generate a proprietary data analysis (for example, an underwriting or credit score or internal rating based on information provided by Accounting which is the owner of accurate outstanding exposures). In turn, this proprietary data is supplied to another department to help it make a decision, for example.

These types of services are internally ruled by Service Level Agreements (SLA) between departments; this data exchange resulting from the SLA is viewed as the most relevant and accurate. In other words, this is information created within your institution, and it is where it all begins. Risk comes in many forms: operational, transaction, financial, credit, strategic, compliance, reputation, concentration, and cyber, among others. Every decision your institution makes has the potential to introduce risk from big picture moves like a change in strategy or a new business line to smaller details like new disclosures. First-party risk is best handled with enterprise risk management (ERM).

ERM is the unified systems, processes, culture, and approach your institution uses to manage risk. It ensures that risk management isn't a solo activity but one that links your institution's mission, vision, and values with strategy and decision making to ensure that the amount and types of risk your institution takes on is commensurate with its risk appetite. It makes sure risks are identified, measured, monitored, and mitigated.

- Information or service supplied by a second party: this is a relatively new form of data collection, and it is essentially another company's first-party data that is collected and sold to the bank by that brand in the scope of a partnership. In theory it enables brands to exchange data with each other in situations where it benefits both parties. One example might be a bank working with an insurance company to mutually benefit from each other's data sets. Most often from other brands whose data sets might compliment your organization and vice versa, as mentioned above, and usually under a pre-determined and defined agreement.

- Information or service supplied by a third party: this is most familiar type of flow of data. The information the bank can buy pre-collected from an external source; for example, a set of external ratings from Moody's/ Fitch/ Standard & Poors, or market prices (bonds, stocks, CDS, etc.) from Bloomberg or Markit. Because these data sets are sold 'off the shelf', they are by definition not unique, which of course diminishes their value and means competitors could easily access the same insight.

- Information or service supplied by a fourth party: the bank outsources functions and your vendors probably do too; a fourth-party is someone your vendor outsources to. Fourth-party vendors go by a lot of names. Some companies call them providers, while others call them strategic partners. They can provide bill pay, mobile banking, core processing, legal or other services.

  Your institution is not just responsible for what your vendor does. It is also responsible for the activities of its third-party vendors (aka fourth-party vendors). The more critical third-party vendors your vendor has, the greater the costs and risks of vendor management. There are ways to limit fourth-party vendor risk. When considering vendors, ask them about outsourcing and have them disclose their vendors so you can consider the potential cost of managing these relationships when comparing prices and risk. Due diligence on these vendors is a must. That includes everything from financials and test results to cyber security and business continuity planning.

- Information or service supplied by a fifth party: This is where things can get extra convoluted. When the bank's vendor's vendor outsources, this is a fifth-party. (It does not necessarily even stop here as that vendor can outsource to yet another vendor creating a sixth, seventh, eighth-party and beyond.) Once again, your institution is responsible for the actions these vendors take on your behalf. It's important to know about any critical third-party vendors your vendors' vendors are using to understand potential risks and to have strategies for mitigating them (cf. The SSAE 18[12] is your ally in understanding these relationships). The alternative is following

---

[12] Statement on Standards for Attestation Engagements, which is overseen by The American Institute of Certified Public Accountants (AICPA) and more specifically the Auditing Standards Board (ASB). The main purpose of SSAE 18 is to clarify certain old standards and streamline and simplify the review process. The update to this standard will also demand companies take more control and responsibility of the people they work with, primarily third-party vendors.

the chain of critical vendors, making vendor management onerous.

A Holistic View on the Entire Supply Chain

In an ideal world, the work flow of the sales desk should be integrated with the middle office, risk management, back office (in relation to settlement and confirmation), accounting, reporting and enquiries, amongst others. A simple proof of this segregation is the mere existence of difference IT architectures and software tools for each of those activities lacking efficient bridges among these areas of operations.

But, it's not unusual for departments within organizations to function independently, failing to coordinate on overlapping reporting and compliance requirements. Add in the complexities of mergers & acquisitions, multiple enterprise resource management systems, divestitures, and all the other changes to product & services catalogs, and the compliance and reporting process becomes even more challenging.

FIGURE 28: CASH SUPPLY CHAIN IN BANKING

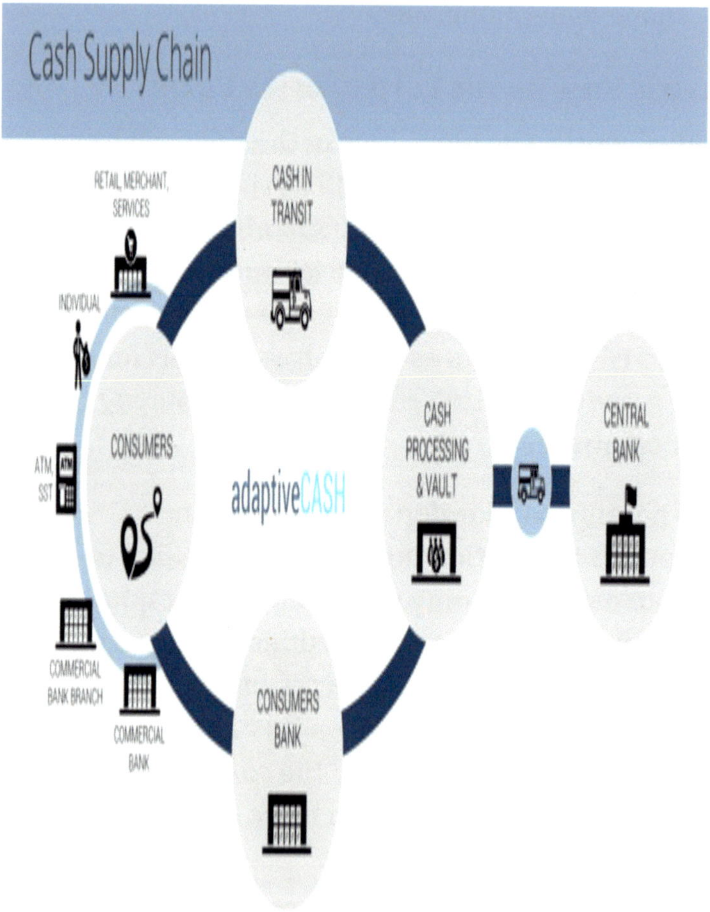

Source: Adaptive Cash, 2019

Going back to the realm of corporates, traditional methods for managing supply chain risk rely on knowing the probability of occurrence and the severity of impact for every potential event that could materially disrupt an organization's operations. For common supply-chain disruptions, such as poor supplier performance, forecast errors, and transportation breakdowns, those methods work very well, using historical data to quantify the level of risk.

But it's a different story for low-probability, high-impact events—mega disasters like the earthquake hitting Haiti in 2010, viral epidemics like the 2019 swine flu outbreak in Asia, or major outages due to unforeseen events such as floods impacting factories and geopolitical tensions.

Because historical data on these exceptional are nonexistent or limited, their risk is hard to measure using traditional risk management models. As a result, many organizations do not adequately prepare for them. That can have disastrous results when catastrophes do hit and can compel even operationally savvy organizations to scramble after the events took place —think of Toyota and Sony Chemical following the 2011 Fukushima earthquake and tsunami.

To provide a solution to this challenge, in lieu of developing a financial model that focuses on determining the likelihood that any specific risk event will take place, it is more appropriate to focus on the understanding and mapping of the supply chain that puts the onus on the effects of potential failures at points along the supply chain (such as a flood at a distribution center or the shuttering of a supplier's factory), instead of solely centering on the reason for the disruption.

This type of analysis obviates the requirement to assess the probability that any specific risk will occur—a valid approach since the mitigation strategies for a disruption are equally effective regardless of what caused it.

Using this approach, companies can quantify what the financial and operational impact would be if a critical supplier's facility were out of commission for, say, two weeks—whatever the reason.

The computerized model can be updated easily and quickly, which is crucial since supply chains are in a continual state of flux. Overall, one can identify basically several types of supply chain relationships within a financial institution.

The one that was described as first and second party whereby:

- on the one hand, an internal supply chain is feeding an internal supply chain (i.e., aka: first party (a service provided by and to the benefit of the internal data supplier), and,
- on the other hand, a second party (a service provided by one outside data supplier to the benefit of an internal party) is supplying data to an internal agent.

However, there can also be instances where an internal agent will supply data and performs a service to the benefit of an external agent, who in turn will use the compounded information to yield a service to the company

> For example, the bank will provide a third party a database will the outstanding risk exposures on a bond portfolios composed of asset backed securities; in turn this third party will analyze these portfolio data and use the analytics to deliver a particular service to the bank (for example a calculation of the actual risk appetite of the bank).

VARIOUS STAKEHOLDERS IN THE SUPPLY CHAIN

Banking is a dynamic and time-critical business sector, where information is king and knowledge is power. Methods which automate business processes and enable the minimization of risk and maximization of trading, sales and research capability, are becoming vital contributors to bottom-line efficiency.

Hence, technology alone cannot seek to deliver by itself, but in this case must be tied to an accurate model of the operating organization.

The differing needs of people's roles in the bank also dictates the type of data system that is used, which generally falls into one of three categories.

FIGURE 29: SUMMARY ROLES WITHIN BANKS AND RELATED DATA SYSTEMS

Role	Trading	Sales	Research	Risk & Administration	IT Support
Information Feeds	✓		✓		✓
Decision Support Systems	✓			✓	✓
Visual Systems	✓		✓		✓
Customer Management		✓		✓	✓
Business Operations	✓	✓	✓	✓	✓
Distribution & Infrastructure			✓	✓	✓
Development			✓	✓	✓
Business Impact	Operational	Tactical	Operational, Tactical, Strategic	Operational	Operational and Tactical

Source: Oracle, 2015

Decision support systems provide the trader, broker or corporate financier with information that will enable them to reach a decision more quickly or more accurately than the competition, or using an interpretation that is more valuable than that used by the competition, or a combination of all three.

Mapping techniques employ graphical and indexed information to be presented to the end user, to help in the interpretation of data and as an aid to decision support and to enable people to make decisions more quickly by enabling them to reach conclusions much faster from the same initial data.

Systems which allow the business to operate and run smoothly, are by far, the most important to the bank. Investment banks rely on the most up- to-the-minute on stock data, including securities prices, economic information and general news and trends.

Generally, information needs are satisfied via providing information in a variety of formats: digital and proprietary newsfeeds; paper reports and journals; corporate information databases.

By getting access to this information quickly, competitive advantage can be gained. Business operations need to be supported by administrative systems which can assist in the running of the investment bank's operations. Generally, such systems fall into a three-tier architecture: front-office, middle-office and back-office operations. Indeed, many of the leading „bulge bracket" investment and brokerage houses, are keen to leverage internet technologies and collaborate together.

Products are now available which manage the flow of transactions in a similar way (Workflow) to how the management of the flow of documents in an organization are automated. These products are beginning to be used in banks to automate dealing transactions, routing them through the back-office as necessary, which speeds up settlement and the production of accounting records, for example. The process of automating the processing of trades in the middle and back-office is referred to as straight-through-processing (STP).

A greater degree of automation in these offices reduces the total staff time spent on administration and settlement, freeing those resources for areas where greater competitive advantage can be sought, or enabling the firm to reduce its overheads.

The ultimate goal of STP is that the entire process be automated from the point at which the order is made through to final settlement, with applications only requesting human intervention in exceptional circumstances. This level of processing is not common at present, but applications are slowly getting closer to this ideal. Another example of using workflow is in the generation and distribution of market research within a banking organization:

FIGURE 30: WORK FLOW MARKET RESEARCH IN BANKING

SCM Equivalent	*What*	*How*	*Where*
'Make'	Issue / IPO, primary market products (foreign exchange, treasury products, bonds, equities, derivatives)	Analyst report, market report, exchange filing, Trading floor / system, Institutional marketing	Institutional organisation, Central Bank, National Government, Corporate organisation, Industry media
'Source'	Primary & Secondary market, client, broker, analyst, clearing bank, central bank, issuing bank, regulatory authority	Investment bank, Central bank, Institutional Fund Manager, National Government, research distribution services,	Stock Exchanges, Brokers Secondary and "after market" exchanges (e.g. 'over-the-counter' exchange traded derivatives, OTC ETD)
'Move'	Trading, Settlement, research distribution, depository account, bill presentment and payment, Swaps (FX, interest rate), Derivatives, Futures and Options products	Stock Exchanges, Electronic Communications Networks (ECNs), Clearing and Payment Systems (SWIFT, CHAPS, CREST, BACS)	Issuing Bank, Clearing Bank, Investment Bank, Settlement service, Exchanges

From the prior discussions about various forms of information management found in banks, the notion that banking is not a supply traditional chain-focused industry, can be said to be generally incorrect. On the face of it, banking routinely and regularly, involves operations which are not just confined to stocks, shares, foreign exchange, asset backed securities, futures, derivatives, corporate finance and wealth/ asset management.

Rather, the most visible aspect of capital market operations, is the supply and trade of finance-related information. This information, describes, upholds, authenticates and delivers such instruments between institutions and their clients. Therefore, it is imperative, that such information is timely, accurate and a true representation of capital commodities (common stocks, shares and other derivative products). It follows, that such processes are in some way in the best auspices of supply chain management (SCM) definitions.

CHALLENGES WITH MAPPING THE ENTIRE SUPPLY CHAIN

While banks have greatly increased knowledge about their customer 'supply chains' the former remain baffled that these same customers increasingly view decades of back-office processing or the entire banking institution as a "utility" or service that adds little value.

As Fintech advancements push front and middle office solutions into successive iterations driven by pervasive mobility and robust data intelligence, consumer relationships with banks themselves has become one of commoditization, and customers will view the bank as "What unique value do you, as a bank, provide to me, customer?"

This creates a series of problems for banking institutions. In the past, challenges to their internal fulfillment or supply chain efficiencies were between competitors under the watch of regulators. Now, consumers are using P2P settlement solutions and fixating on a mobile platform rather than the iconic capabilities financial institutions built over decades.

Factor in tens of billion put into startups in the past three years designed to replace vast portions of our infrastructure, while shifting consumer touchpoints to third parties, and executives at banking organizations seemed surprised that more than one-third of customers would rather bank with Amazon than a bank itself.

Consumers increasingly have a retail mindset and approach finances the same way. Banks seemingly failed to notice the quantum shift especially among the largest demographic segment--the Millennials.

According to the American Banking Association, for this 75-million strong demographic, 77% always have their phone (and apps) with them, 53% don't think banks have anything to offer and 71% would rather go to the dentist than listen to a bank (Wilber, 2019).

For supply chains implicitly embedded within financial institution operations by the processes, directives and technologies selected, delivery chaos and organizational resistance can be severe. The realities facing financial institutions brought on by capability limits and pressures are no longer about an organization adapting to one or two hazards to their operating models--there are many threats at once.

Banking institutions face a fundamental and comprehensive redesign of their supply chains starting with the customer and working back into every process and procedure.

It is this approach of moving through the supply or delivery chain, assessing existing and future capabilities (i.e., existing, build, partner, acquire), which will provide greatest value not just for efficiencies, but a clear understand of "can we compete?" If the answer is yes, then the "how" booking positive results, coupled with "what we will provide" creates a map for expansion or redevelopment.

An example of complex data product improvement designed to delight the consumer, as McKinsey noted in its digitization of business process brief, is where a bank case study "cut the cost of a new mortgage by 70% and slashing time to preliminary approval from several days to just one minute."

Reworking and augmenting the entire supply chain were mandatory. The layers of components from operational intelligence to strategies and patterns to regulatory compliance to risk analysis and back office must be matched to markets, competition, partnerships, joint ventures, business delivery capabilities and clients' expectations.

And then, within each of those segments, they are further decomposed into additional functional categories that demand further scrutiny before a single line of code can be cast. It is precisely why IT during the past two decades has become so fragmented within and across business lines.

The challenge is that banks' cultures and reward structures are driven towards high-producers or those who can increase the top line, while corporation models are constructed around individual customers and how they acquire, cross-sell and up-sell to clients--a one-stop shop.

Yet, the model emerging is one where banking organizations are not, and likely not to be, the starting point for customer contact. The future banking business models need to be increasingly based upon layered collaboration (not just top performers), consumption not construction and information standardization with a virtual staffing model.

Whatever the circumstances facing a bank, the latter should examine and integrate these circumstances into its own complex supply chains--if these circumstances fit without the supply chain being materially reworked. For banks to remain relevant, traditional organizational approaches (i.e., not touching the internal supply chains) cannot be THE competitive response in the face of permanent and fundamental shifts in the way financial offerings are being used by diverse consumer and homeowner demographics. These commonalities of problem and opportunity solutions are precisely what has led to commoditization of the industry and consumer perceptions of what value banking institutions deliver in their lives.

Holistic Supply Chain and Competitive Advantage

Generally speaking, business processes (and the underlying flows) within a banking organization are very much reliant upon a distinctive team and operational strategy. This is vitally important to the business operations, as factors such as regional and global economic conditions can greatly affect the value of currencies, stocks and bonds and must be guarded against. Therefore, within each of these operational strategies there is always, and must be, some form of risk management.

FIGURE 31: BUSINESS FLOWS IN BANKING

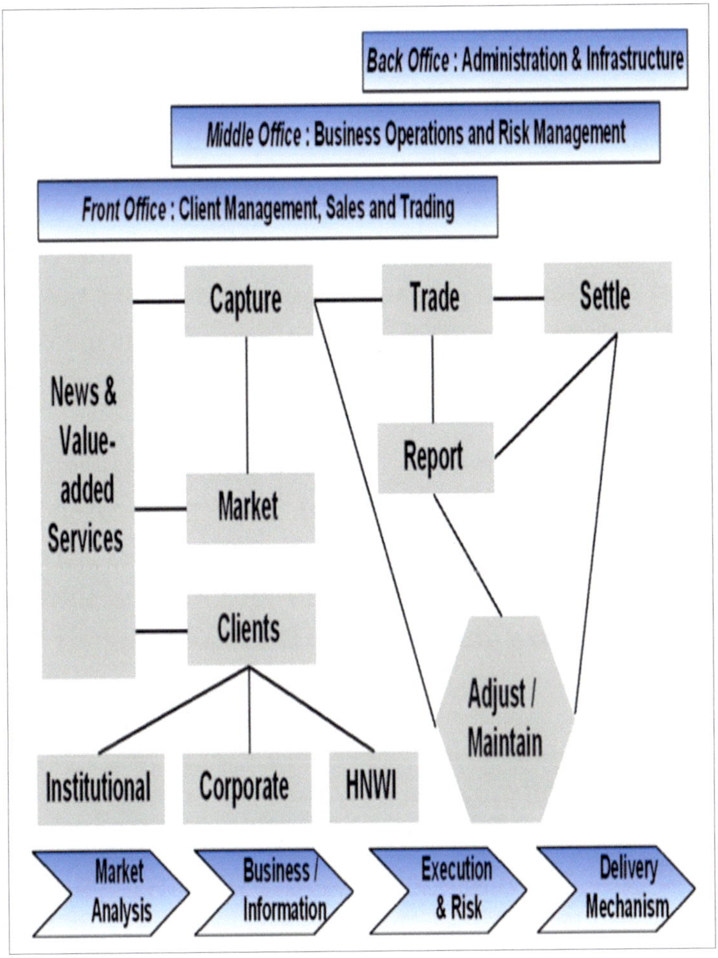

Source: American Banking Association

Another factor that defines the fluidity of each of these flows, is the extent to which a particular team has lines of communication both internally, and externally, to clients. This can be through a multitude of formats: telephone, fax, email, teleconferencing, and videoconferencing.

In order to transmit or deliver this information, there must be a distribution mechanism which supplies the information to the required stakeholders. This is usually defined as part of an information and technical architecture in the bank. Once again, this communication channel can be based upon the technologies previously mentioned, but is most often in the form of hard or soft-copy reports and articles which are emailed directly to the client. As such, each of these example flows show similarities to traditional supply chain management concepts (i.e. the make-source-move paradigm).

The underlying information flows are the subject of inter-related processes that can be and signify a high degree of interaction and integration between people, processes and technology. It is perhaps for this reason, that this industry sector has notably regularly embraced and adopted leading-edge technology and implemented it in order to derive the maximum benefit from the ensuing development.

The value-add of a holistic mapping of the entire supply chain within the bank is to be found not just in the execution of the processes in the chain itself. Rather, the way in which decisions about how the information is used to make trading decisions, is the key differentiator of this type of supply chain.

This differentiator, in terms of banking value-added knowledge, is in the form of, for instance, market and global economic news, as well as, for example, equity, credit and sector research analysis here.

These interdependencies show that there is a close relationship between the management and execution of the banking business. In order to maintain profitability, no single factor - client management, enabling technology or core business operations - can exist or provide benefit to the business in its own right and is part of a wider set of processes and information dependencies.

All of these constituent parts must be integrated and more importantly, synchronous, in order for rapid and dynamic business to be executed.

Information management is critical to a modern agile organization, especially in the banking sector. The understanding and modelling of supply chains can help to define and distinguish an organization in terms of their core values and operating behavior.

This is critical in terms of banking operations, where the margins for error and success are very fine, and have a direct consequence on the running of the business. For instance, the field of capital markets, is a vast and complex area, where the impact of technology to enable processes and day-to-day operations, has been seen to be of critical importance to sustaining competitive advantage.

Unequivocally, the field of banking is undergoing rapid change, supported by an increasing amount of change in terms of the underlying enabling technologies also. One needs to acknowledge the capabilities and characteristics of banking organizations in this arena; banks rely upon the key processes of lending and investment, deposit collection, trading and sales, financing and research, risk management, etc.

The supply chain of a bank is found to be equivalent in form to any other supply chain that can be found in the process or manufacture industries. The only exception with this particular type of chain, lies with the degree of direct visibility of the chain, visible through discrete sub-operations such as, for instance, stock trading, sales and research to specific client types. More importantly, it is found that supply chain concepts in this field, actively align and involve components of strategic management, delivery, execution and feedback as a matter of course.

The inclusion of strategic planning and client relationship feedback is further underpinned by technology. It is perhaps for this reason that the processes and information flows in banking are so vital to the fast moving and dynamic requirements of the business. This tight integration of planning, process and interlinked feedback, distinguishes this type of supply chain, from many others, not least because of its high information content.

The kinds of skills and capabilities needed to manage supply chains will evolve and may require much more collaboration with previously unrelated functions, such as treasury and IT systems management. As internal collaboration between, for instance, operations and finance takes place, banks need to dedicate continuous attention to all stakeholders at the foundation of supply chain collaboration.

By knowing these participants, banks can take advantage of the existing collaborative environment and play a vital role in ultimately supporting clients to achieve strategic objectives. It is a fact that every business decision has an impact on the supply chain and that supply chain executives see all stakeholders as strong contributors to overall bank success.

SECTION VIII: SLAs w/ 1st, 2nd, & 3rd PARTIES

Basics of a Service Level Agreement (SLA)

A service level agreement is a legal contract between a provider and the end user. Its primary purpose is to make sure that both parties involved agree on the services the provider is providing and the standards to which it will adhere.

If the provider does not have an SLA, it would be able to deliver the customer as little cloud storage space as the provider wanted to and they would not have any proof that the provider promised them more. A good SLA makes expectations between the client and contractor crystal clear.

It is focused on defining the service levels, availability and performance standards, as well as the company's performance goals. It also serves to help respond to dramatic changes and ensure the client's business operates smoothly and efficiently.

FIGURE 32: SERVICE LEVEL AGREEMENT

Source: The Lean Supply Chain, 2019

There are three main kinds of SLA's. Each one provides a different purpose that depends on the service provided.

- Single Service Agreement: Service Level Agreements cover a single service for each customer. For example, you might be providing IT services to a company's human resources department, administrative department, and marketing department. A service-level agreement would apply to all three offices, and they would all follow the same guidelines.
- Customer-level SLA's: Customer-level SLA's are individual agreements between the customer and the cloud service provider. These kinds of SLA's often cover several requests made by the same customer. For example, you would use it if a customer needed your company's cloud software, hosting capabilities, and IT support.
- Multi-level Agreements: Multi-level Agreements are comprised of service-level, customer-level, and corporate levels. They cover general service level issues for each customer in the organization.

WHY AVOIDING STANDARD SERVICE LEVEL AGREEMENTS (SLA)

Service-level agreement (SLA) contracts can drive the wrong business outcomes. Some technology leaders want to move away from those SLA-driven contracts. If you're like many risk management executives, the chances are your organization compensates third-party service providers for something they did not do, or pays them twice for something.

But executives need to move away from the typical SLA-driven contracts. A key objective for any executive is to make sure the organization is more responsive to business needs, doing the things that the business users care about and doing them in a reasonable time frame and cost point. In other words, the value equation at any organization need to be more focused, making it much more cost-effective, achieving results much faster and at the same time delivering higher quality and more reliable work. That's quite a formidable set of accomplishments. So, it's worth paying attention to her strategies for taking the organization to the next level.

A key component in the strategy is rethinking the role of service level agreements (SLAs) within an organization and with third-party service providers. When one has an SLA contract, the service providers just meet the service levels. That's what they do. But that's a problem. They don't meet the rapidly changing needs of the organization; they just meet the service levels, stipulated in the contracts.

As such, over time, SLAs drive behaviors that are focused on delivering a minimum level of service at minimum cost to the provider. This forces third party organizations (but also first parties within the organization) to become a commodity and not a strategic, value-added partner to the business. SLAs by their very nature are established as achievable contractual targets and can be static over time. Misused, they can be counter-intuitive to driving business agility and pace.

And, alas, there is little reason to innovate in an SLA arrangement. If it isn't broken, why fix it? For example, let's take a situation with an infrastructure managed-services provider: the SLA contract has metrics around uptime, performance and other metrics. Although the vendor can admirably be meeting the SLA standards today, there is little incentive to dramatically shift the IT organization to keep pace with rapidly changing business requirements.

The issue is paying a provider (third party, second party, or first party) based exclusively on meeting SLAs means paying for results that are sub-optimal and over time erode the benefit of a managed-services arrangement. And, in areas where the provider's services included also investing in stabilizing the environment, paying the provider for meeting SLAs means the provider, by design, is paid twice.

Meeting the SLAs is no longer a sufficient concern for a client getting services from a provider. Basically, an SLA contract says the provider's performance is good enough when meeting the SLAs. But good enough isn't what an organization wants to buy; it wants to stop the issues from happening in the first place; it wants to pay the provider for success in improving the environment.

But the criteria around "success" changes over time, especially with the pace of change in technologies and business models. The first struggle for success was stabilizing the environment. But once it's stabilized, that's no longer a measure of success. Any organization has to continuously drive towards right-sizing technology services to business need.

For example, the IT world is changing; and now the organization needs, and its business partners need, agreements with providers that help it evolve more than meeting basic performance requirements. SLAs around uptime and reliance do not matter when measuring for success where the focus is on speed and value.

Service level metrics are worthy targets. They set the bar for a provider's performance. But once the provider can consistently achieve those targets, the SLAs just represent yesterday's problems and their importance diminishes. This is especially the case in infrastructure services. SLA contracts just live on past successes and don't incentivize stretching forward to improve the environment or processes.

Service level metrics are usually time based (such as how quickly an agent can close an issue). But time-based metrics drive a different type of service behavior than a metric based on quality and business outcomes.

The typical SLA contracts are the wrong governance vehicle and should not drive a services relationship. Unless the organization keeps moving the SLA's bar to align with its current goals for "success," an SLA contract wrongly articulates what its business wants the provider to work on and achieve.

As a risk management executive, one needs to move your organization towards a defined business expectation model. These expectations allow the business to express targets that match delivery models to business outcomes.

It may not be unreasonable for a business-critical service to expect 24/7 or 100% availability 100% of the time; but there may be other services that need much less than the 99.9% availability level. Expectations and requirements can change often, so the provider must be in a position to adapt.

A model based on business expectation allows the provider (third party, second party, or first party) to focus on providing solutions that are the best fit for the business vs. a best-in-class technology team. In today's economic realities, best in class is often the most expensive option. A "best-for-business" expectation allows a balanced approach to performance and cost or value creation. These decisions are always made in partnership between business and IT.

SECTION IX: VALUE CHAIN MGMT & BANKS

Background

Nowadays, banks, just like any other firm, are guided by a need for competitiveness, and this implies not only vigilance over costs, but also a commitment, in conjunction with its customers to a procedure of creating value for both parties. Resorting to the value chain and the study of resources and associated competencies proves to be a useful means of understanding this procedure.

FIGURE 33A: TRENDS IN BANKING VALUE CHAIN

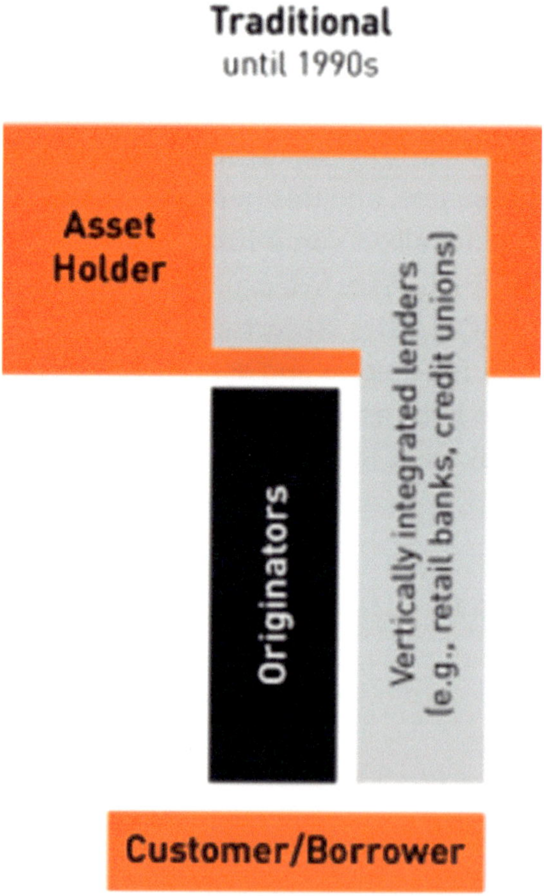

Source: Wallace & Herrick, 2009

FIGURE 33B: TRENDS IN BANKING VALUE CHAIN

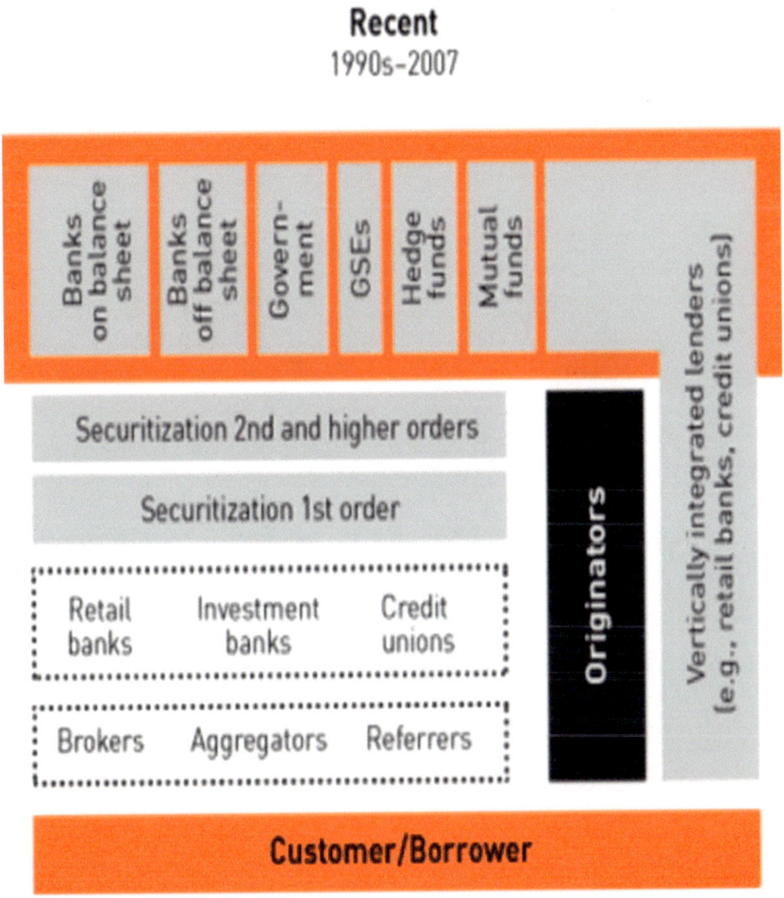

Source: Wallace & Herrick, 2009

FIGURE 33C: TRENDS IN BANKING VALUE CHAIN

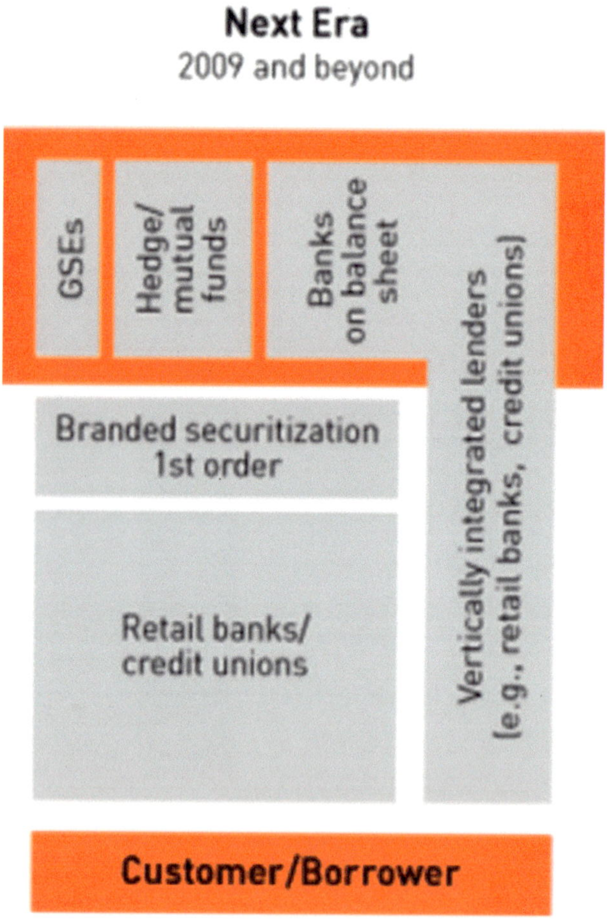

Source: Wallace & Herrick, 2009

In other words, there has been a constant evolution over the past two decades, in the banking business portfolio, due to economic globalization, deregulation and the advent of new technologies (Lamarque, 2005). This trend continues today and is even more marked by the emergence of production businesses, the latter being traditionally included in the value chain of banking services.

Thus, the reconfiguration would appear as the emergence of organizations dealing only with either distribution of products; other organizations may specialize in back-office activities such as bond holding or cheque processing. This strategy has been designed by a large number of operators in order to improve their competitiveness (Lamarque, 2000).

Faced with their low profitability, more and more banking institutions have evaluated the competitive strength of their production methods, as well as their economic performance relative to these processes. This operation is conveyed, amongst other methods, by value chain analysis on the different business undertaken by these institutions [M.E. Porter 1985].

In order to understand beyond these general remarks, one needs to comprehend the logical processes and the different aspects that have resulted to the re-engineering of the value chain. If this analysis tool was initially designed for the heavy industry, its application to the services sector, and, in particular the banking services, can prove invaluable for the analysis of evolution in the banking industry.

In order to do this, one needs to revert to Porter's initial idea, that of demonstrating at which level value is added to the product and thus identifying the sources of competitive advantage.

The quest for the origins of competitive strength in the value chain of different banking businesses is a first step in analyzing the key activities and the different possibilities for reconfiguring the value chain. These key activities are those identified as essential for the creation of the competitive advantage regardless of the type of business the institution offers. Their identification will be based on a general study of the nature of competencies associated to each type of business. The value chain and the notion of organizational competency appear complementary.

A series of surveys done by consulting cabinets [Deloitte Touche Tohmatsu, 1995], or by the organizations themselves, show the specialization of banking activities in either management or production, both traditionally included in the traditional value chain of the business.

Thus, the reshaping would appear as the emergence of institutions dealing only with either distribution of products or their elaboration. Others may specialize in back-office activities such as cheque processing or bond holding. This strategy has been developed by a large number of operators in order to improve their competitiveness.

In order to analyze beyond these general remarks, let us try and understand the logical processes and the different factors that have led to the redesign of the value chain. If this analysis tool was initially developed for heavy industry, its application to the services, and, in particular the financial services, can prove invaluable for the study of evolution in the banking industry.

In order to do this, one needs to revert to Porter's original idea, that of demonstrating at which level value is added to the product and thus identifying the origins of competitive advantage.

The search for the origins of competitive strength in the value chain of different banking businesses is a first step in analyzing the critical activities and the different possibilities for reconfiguring the value chain. These key activities are those identified as essential for the creation of the competitive advantage regardless of the type of business the institution offers.

Their identification will be based on a general study of the nature of competencies associated to each type of business. The value chain and the notion of organizational competency appear complementary. Each one offers an explanation of competitive advantage.

On the level of the different businesses, the description and the understanding of the primary and support activities, as well as the coordination of the chain as a whole, can be done by analyzing the nature of the competencies identified and by grouping these around the different activities. Given the proximity and the complementarity of the concepts used, it is necessary to clarify these before undergoing an in-depth study of the origins of the competitiveness and the essential activities of the chain.

Introduction of the notion of value chain

The distinction between a supply chain and a value chain is that the former is the process of all stakeholders engaged in fulfilling a client's request, while the latter is a set of interconnected activities an organization uses to establish a competitive advantage.

Another perspective on the use of value chain and supply chain is to take into account the point of view: a value chain is viewed from the customer side, so the relevant aspect is the value-for-money that it can provide customers with. On the other side supply chain emphasizes the supplier point of view, so it is about material and information flows, costs, service level, etc.

Activities in a supply chain emphasize more on timing, quality, and lower costs for delivering goods or service to customers both considering both short-term and long-term needs, while a value chain is the collection of activities (production, marketing, logistics, services) from a value-adding viewpoint, which may focus on all add-value processes, including both the delivery of goods/services and the improvement of goods/services.

Supply chain management originates from operations management, and the definition is "the integration of suppliers, manufacturers, warehouses and stores to that merchandise is produced and distributed to the right locations at the right time while containing costs and maintaining service levels." (Lambert et al., 1998)

Value chain originated from business management and was popularized by Michael Porter in his 1985 best-seller, 'Competitive Advantage: Creating and Sustaining Superior Performance'. A value chain is a chain of activities that a firm operating in a specific industry performs in order to deliver a valuable product or service for the market (Porter, 1985). So, supply chain can also fit the value chain definition in the case of creating and delivering physical products.

Value chain management is also concerned with the stream of goods to consumers but privileges s a distinct approach; you might say it's the complementary view of the process. The distinction between the two is that in supply chain management, the flux is downstream – from the source to the consumer. In value chain management, the flux is upstream – from the consumer to the source. The table below provides a succinct summary of these differences:

FIGURE 34: DIFFERENCES BETWEEN SUPPLY CHAIN AND VALUE CHAIN

Basis for comparison	Value chain	Supply chain
Objective	Gaining competitive advantage	Customer satisfaction
Focus	Creating value in the eyes of the customer	Costs and efficiencies of supply

Concept	Value addition	Conveyance
Originated from	Business management	Operations management
Meaning	Value Chain is defined as the series of activities, that adds value to the product.	The integration of all the activities involved in the procurement, conversion and logistics of the product is known as Supply Chain.
Sequence	Customer request – value chain - product	Product request – supply chain – customer

<u>Source</u>: SupplyChain247, 2015

In value chain management, the consumer is seen as the source of value. Consumers create value for manufacturers when they demand products. The focus is not on the cost of goods, as in supply chain management, but in creating value in the consumer's eyes (FloridaTech, 2019).

To correctly manage the value chain, companies often split operations into primary activities, such as logistics and production, and support activities, such as human resources, marketing and information technology. Creating a profitable value chain requires a connection between what customers value, or want, and what the company produces.

Supply Chain is described as a tool of business transformation, which minimizes costs and maximizes customer satisfaction by providing the right product at the right time at the right place and the right price.

Conversely, Value Chain is a way of getting a competitive advantage, through which a company can beat its competitors along with fulfilling customer requirements.

WHY VALUE CHAINS AS CONCEPT IT GAINING TRACTION

The growing interest in value chains in companies is because it helps provide the organization with a distinct competitive advantage over its rivals (M. Porter, 1985).

There are a number of trends that are now driving the need for operations orientated analysis from a value chain perspective. These trends are as follows:

- Globalization of supply and production: The huge growth in global sourcing and supply has begun the process of adding value worldwide (G. Gereffi et al, 2005). This leads to the need to model global value chains as the main mode of business in many industries.
- Many benefits already wrung out of manufacturing and the supply chain: The

Industrial Engineering and Operations Management together with management and operations improvement such as lean manufacturing and TQM have been improving the efficiency of manufacturing and supply chain operations for a long time. However, there is still a lot of work to be done, therefore many firms are turning to look at a broader view of the enterprise to continue improving its competitive advantage (A. Smith, 1937). Improving the operational and production capability of value-added activities in the manufacturing process require the firm to shift its perspective outlook from supply chain to value chain.

- Increasing competition and the primacy of strategy: The value chain is a strategic concept; companies struggle to compete in an environment of globalization and intense competition. This is when companies look to their value chain to formulate strategies to remain competitive in their respective industries.
- Evolving governance models for the extended enterprise: The information era led by the recent focus of capital investment on internet technologies has increased the research of

businesses to look for alternative value chains and business models to better their benchmarks as well as create a better competitive advantage. This new growth of business models has created significant interest in value chains and has made it a primary use to create new models of products.

- Trends in management discourse: A final reason for the growing interest in value chains is the nature of management fashion trends in academic and management discourse. Management trends have a life cycle and right now the fashion has shifted to value chains as this has become one of the best methods for a company to operate with to create a better competitive advantage as compared to any other. Value chains have ultimately led to a lack of interest in supply chain management, this is also due to the fact that organizations are in the information era that has given the value chain an upper hand in finding better alternatives for better production. Value chains have started since the 1980s this has given it a long time to grow and it has certainly been adopted as more important than supply chain and operations by management. Value chains is set to rise in popularity as it has been labeled as a dynamic differentiator (C.H. Fine et al, 2002).

'Service Concept' in Scope of Value Chain for Banks

A banking business can be defined as the capability to manage a supply system, that is all the tasks involved in order to offer a particular product or service to a specific clientele. This implies the possession, not only of the necessary competencies and resources needed to execute the task, but also the capacity to manage the linkages between these contributions from diverse origins (Koenig, 1993].

The definition of the banking activities relies thus on an internal analysis of the company and on the origins of its competitiveness. However, this concept goes further. When managers define their activity, they refer to the market (defined by the conditions of demand and consumer needs), to the industry (defined by the conditions of supply and often technology) and to their positioning (founded on their competencies and their positioning on the market).

The banking business is defined as the point at which supply and demand meet the intention to integrate internal and external analysis of the company [Drucker, 1994]. The supply system is required to answer market conditions and resources and competencies in the company must be able to satisfy the expectations and expressed needs.

In recent years, when discussing banking activities, publications by banking institutions or speeches by management, regularly talk in terms of banking business. This expresses a wish to clarify, out of a concern for transparency, an activity often misunderstood by the general public. Besides, this effort highlights the concern of organizations to present a coherent and controlled strategy and to publish the expertise and competencies which make up their business.

Analysis carried out on the banks' annual reports has shown different types of associate definitions to the concept of banking business. The majority of definitions are expressed in terms of target clientele or of families of products offered, and revolve around retail banking, commercial banks, private banking, and investment banks.

FIGURE 35: VALUE-CREATING POTENTIAL

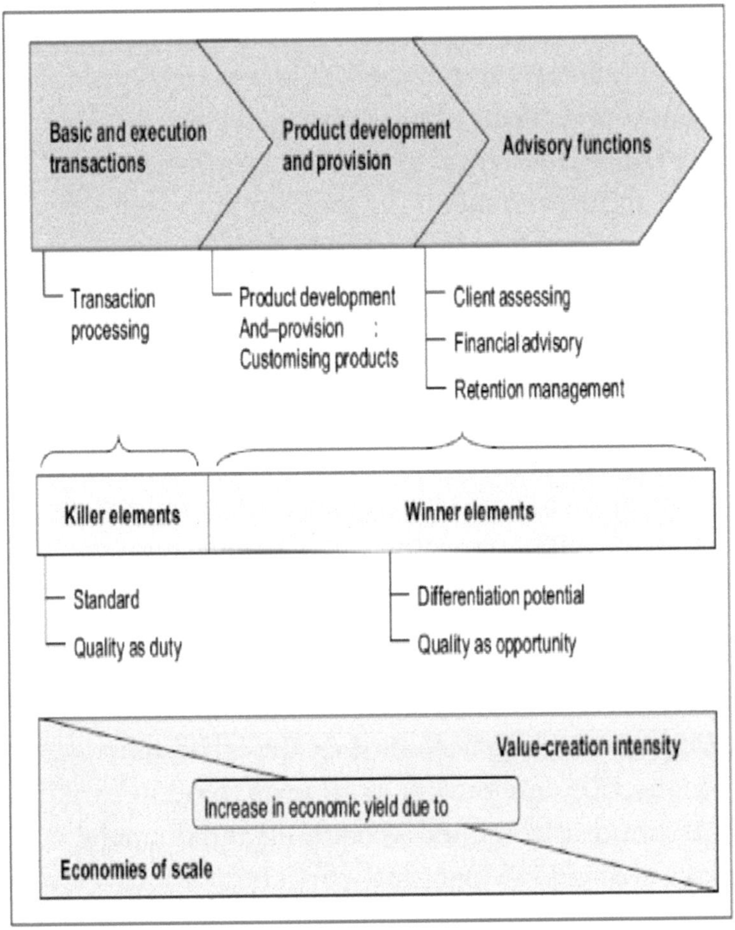

<u>Source</u>: Ebrary.net, 2019

Two formulations come out of this framework. Bankers define themselves sometimes as risk managers or distributors of financial products. Here it is a question of transversal formulations with respect to traditional formulations in terms of products/markets: they are founded on the essential functions in the exercise of banking unites, and justifying their emergence constitutes the primary aim of this procedure (Lamarque, 2000).

KEY ACTIVITIES VALUE CHAIN BANKS

COMMERCIAL BANK – RETAIL BANK – PRIVATE BANK

The value chain of the commercial bank corresponds to the description of retail banking activities for private investors or SMEs (financing, savings investment, services).

Retail banking deals with any banking services that are meant for everyday consumers (cf. this includes checking and savings accounts, credit cards, mortgages, auto loans, CDs, and more). Analogous to retail banking, private banking is defined as banking and financial services provided to high-net-worth individuals. Private bankers deliver financial and wealth management services on a much more individual level than traditional retail banks, which is why it can be viewed as a distinct type of banking.

If one takes a closer look at this schema:

- Raising funds: The aim is to find the cheapest way of raising funds for a sufficient length of time. The capital raised is from their funds, refinancing, savings or company and private deposits. The latter method constitutes a privileged means of finding inexpensive resources, but requires a means-of-payment management service. Savings-investment also implies a relationship follow-up.
- Product and service design for target markets: A distinction can be made between products depending directly or not on raising resources. Credit fits into the first category whereas some insurance products or relevant advice fits into the second. It is at this point that prices are fixed and decisions are made on the "dressing" of the product (offered alone or in a package) with regard to the adapted merchandising.
- Marketing and sales: This activity leads to identifying the definitive target market in terms of financial potential, risks, geographical situation... Marketing and conception must be in close collaboration in order to suggest and design the best deal for the consumer. Decisions must be taken concerning distribution methods (network of branches, direct banking, sales team) and also in the

policies for communication and image in order to promote the products.

- Service: This is the preferred direction in banking public relations. "Service" covers means-of-payment, back-office operations linked to administrative and accounts processing of operations, and especially the processing of incidents and risk management. After-sales service is often considered to be the crux of the bank-consumer relationship and is the principal cause of the break-up of this relationship.

The primary activities are very closely interlinked. Thus, the branches and sales teams are privileged sources for getting to know consumers' needs, and for conceiving new products. Price fixing also depends heavily on overheads linked to the back-office, evaluation of risk and cost of resources.

Apart from the emergence of risk management, the support activities stay within Porter's traditional formulation. One should note that risk management concerns every level of the chain. Whereas the traditional vision incorporates the risk factor only at the sales of financial product level (Default risk), the risk factor is now present at every level, just as much in the design as in the follow-up or even in the administrative and data processing of consumer files. In the same way, human risk is a non-negligible factor.

INVESTMENT BANK

In investment banking one notices differences with the previous chain at several levels. The more important ones are obvious at the conception, investment and associated services levels.

- Conception: All the banking activities of the investment bank are not directly affected by this function. It concerns mainly the financial products, sometimes very complex, linked to asset management and capital operations. The difference lies in the fact that here specialized advice is invoiced to the consumer whereas this service is free of charge in the commercial bank.
- Capital investment and holdings for its account or that of its customers: These activities require specific marketing for financial products. It implies a reinforced position on the capital markets in order to play the role of an efficient intermediary and to have the legitimacy of a prominent broker. Moreover, it is at this level that arbitration takes place over the extent of operations in which the client is to be involved or over the direct support that is to be brought.

- Position management: This includes all the back-office and after-sales operations. Position management concerns the follow-up of finished operations, covering decisions and risks.

Just as in commercial/ retail/ private banks, this is a crucial activity for professional recognition and consumer loyalty. Risk management also figures here as a support activity. However, the risks (not including risks linked to human error and technology), are of a different nature. The evaluation of a stock option or of complex financial products implies very different risks to those involved in credit operations.

FIGURE 36: VALUE CHAIN IN BANKING

Commercial banking	Investment banking
Retail banking	Merchant banking
- Raising funds	- Share capital operations
- Credit & Services	- Financial engineering
SMEs & professional banking	- Advice on M&A
- Financing	- Structured financing
- Payment & cash management	- Stock management
- Specialized services	Asset management
Insurance products	- Mutual funds management
- Life assurance	- Pension funds management
- Health	- Public funds management
- Damage	Stock market operator
Specialized financing	- Broker
- Financial leases	- Stock & derivatives broker
- Operating leases	- Custody

ORGANIZATIONAL COMPETENCY AND VALUE CHAIN

A competency is often defined as the capability to undertake a task or activity using resources (R.M. Grant, 1991). It designates a combination of the latter by using organizational procedures and collective know-how (R. Amit, P.J.H. Schoemaker 1993).

The concept of competency has therefore a dynamic dimension underlying an organizational know-how in action. Competitive advantage can be created from the basis of specific resources but mainly from the interaction between them. The competencies are generally distinguished by their ability to differentiate the firm from its competitors. Finally, specific competencies are considered to be key elements when they are able to support several different activities in the company.

Resources and competencies are entered in the value chain and various writers studying companies in the service industry have tried to put methods into practice which associate them to the activities of the chain.

They act as "differentiating inductors" allowing to make the service be perceived as unique and therefore, a bearer of value to the consumer. They also rationalize the cost structure, origin of profit margins for the company. The association of competencies and value chain conveys a desire to harmonize two concepts that ally the common aim of analyzing the origins and conditions of the competitive advantage. Such a proposition must undergo experimentation in order to measure its limits.

The difficulty resides in the identification of the competencies internal to the company, and in the allocation of the competencies to the activities in the value chain. The activities should be understood as the link between competencies and the position in terms of product/market.

The competencies must be put into action at the different stages of the value chain so as to answer market demand. If this answer is pertinent then the company is performing well and is creating value for itself and its consumers. The methodology chosen consists in defining different profiles of competencies for a specific business with respect to market demand.

SECTION X: SUSTAINABLE & RESILIENT SUPPLY CHAIN

INTRODUCTION

Supply chain sustainability refers to the management of social, economic, and environmental impacts, and the encouragement of good governance practices through the entire life cycle of goods and services. For banks, expanding efforts to include their supply chain gives institutions a way to integrate sustainability into their business further, minimizing risks and enhancing opportunities that can be derived from supplier relations.

While many banks do not face traditional supply chain risks, such as sourcing from factories in developing countries, they do have exposure to environmental, social, and governance issues on a variety of levels (BSR, 2015).

The banking sector does not traditionally get much coverage regarding supply chain sustainability. Focus, unsurprisingly, has geared toward industries with more severe and visible supply chain impacts, such as, for instance, the clothing industry. Still, sustainable supply chains are essential for the banking sector as well.

FIGURE 37: SUPPLY CHAIN RESILIENCE

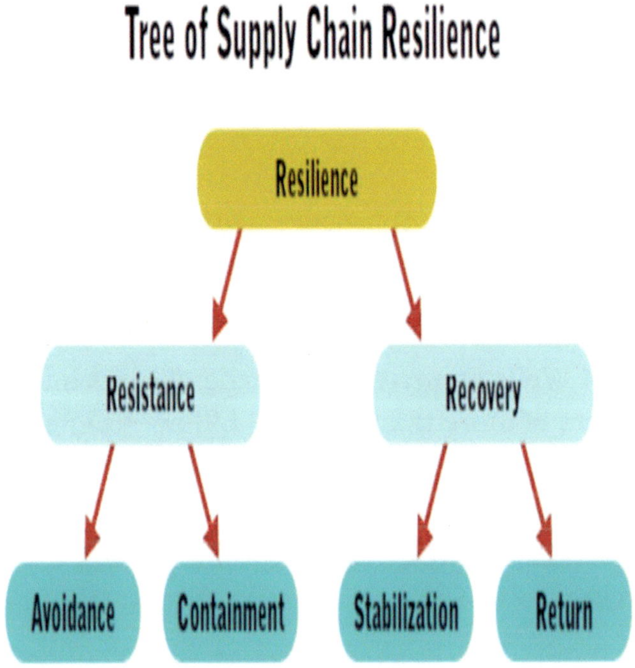

Source: SupplyChain247, 2015

The banking industry is complex and vast, and embeds various types of business models, players, and supply chains. For banking institutions, many social and environmental impacts stem not from direct activities, but rather from their respective supply chains.

Considering, for instance, the number of suppliers (i.e., vendors) and budgets (i.e., purchasing power) that many of these banks have, responsible choices can have profound impacts. Organizations in the sector can use their clout to drive sustainable development forward among their suppliers.

To get a sense of the scale of procurement spending in the banking sector, consider the following figures published five years ago (BSR, 2015):

- ⇒ In 2014 Wells Fargo reported expenditures on suppliers of more than USD14.7 billion[13], which constituted 30% of the company's total noninterest expense.
- ⇒ TD Bank, reported spending USD5.7 billion on sourcing in 2014.[14]

Notwithstanding the fact not all supply chains within the banking industry are similar, the

[13] Wells Fargo, 2014. This amount includes expenditures in equipment, net occupancy, outside professional services, outside data processing, contract services, travel and entertainment, postage and stationery supplies, advertising and promotion, insurance, and telecommunications.

[14] TD Bank, 2014

following central spend categories for the industry have been identified:

⇒ information technology, computers, printers, and scanners (office equipment), mobile banking software and related services, servers and networks for data storage, employment and professional services, consulting and training, call centers, cleaning services, temporary staffing, security, energy, transport and travel, facilities and real estate, marketing and advertising, branded products such as promotional items, and paper, postage, and office supplies[15].

Common business drivers for supply chain sustainability include an increased ability to manage business risks, fostering sustainability-driven productivity, cost cuts, and growth based on sustainability. Some of the risks that are traditionally connected with poor management of the supply chain are damage to reputation, reduced capacity to attract and retain employees, and loss of customers.

[15] While these categories were identified mostly by analyzing reports from Banks, we find that almost all of them are applicable to banking sector as a whole.

The banking industry is well positioned to address sustainability challenges and minimize risks in its supply chain. Rapidly changing circumstances have forced some industries, and sometimes by scandals, to take action and incorporate more sustainable procurement practices. In contrast, under the current landscape, banks have an opportunity to be proactive instead of reactive in implementing sustainability practices in their supply chain.

DEVELOPING TENDENCIES IN THE REALM OF BANKS

There are several interesting trends currently taking place in the industry that have an impact on banking sector supply chains. Below, one can highlight a few of these trends that have the most potent effect on the banking sector supply chain, raising new concerns as well as presenting new opportunities:

Firstly, there is this fashionable trend called “Big Data analytics”. In essence, the term also refers to a set of enabling technologies that allow these insights to be derived from diverse and extensive sources of data. An increasing number of digital transactions, the rise of new analytical tools, and enhanced computational power have all contributed to the growth of big data analytics. The notion ‘big data’ refers to a combined approach aimed at providing input for decision-making with analytical insights derived from data.

In 2018, the big data market was estimated at USD40 billion. More than any other sector, banks have worked to leverage the power of data analytics. Organizations in this sector can now gather and process more data than ever about their customers and the markets they operate in. Considering that many banks rely on third-party vendors for their big data related processes, this trend is very pertinent to supply chain management.

Also, when looking at the speed and magnitude of the growth of banking within the emerging markets, the following can be said: by 2023, some analysts estimate that China and India could have the world's first-and third-largest banking sectors, respectively, and by 2050, the banking sector in emerging economies is expected to surpass the assets and profits of the developed world greatly. (PwC, 2013)

The growth of emerging markets will likely lead to a geographic expansion of banking services, and subsequently this will increase the need for organizations in the industry to develop local supply chains. Whether it is construction organizations to build bank branches or IT service providers, institutions will need to understand and manage a new set of risks and navigate different (and often weaker) sets of regulations and standards, which will pose higher risks.

With today's technology, it's worth noting that the expansion of banks to emerging markets will be done differently from how it was done in developed nations. For example, there will probably be less need for physical bank branches, while digital banking will play a bigger role. This will undoubtedly create a different supply chain.

The move toward emerging markets also presents opportunities. Whenever possible, institutions can prioritize local sourcing alternatives to promote local development, foster diversity, engage with the community, and reduce greenhouse gas emissions associated with transport.

As it relates to the Western world, clearly banks have been faced with a heightened regulatory control. Indeed, in large part, as a response to the global financial crisis of 2007-2008, the banking industry has been subjected to major regulatory changes.

One of the most notable illustrations of this is the Dodd-Frank Act, which applies to both U.S. and non-U.S. financial institutions conducting business activities within the United States, and which aims to reinforce the accountability of banking organizations. The CFPB applies to any organization that provides a material service in connection with the provision or offering of a consumer financial service or product.

To shield consumers in transactions with banks in the United States, for instance, Dodd-Frank established the Consumer Finance Protection Bureau (CFPB). The law has determined that banks must uphold that all of their suppliers comply with CFPB regulations, and may be held accountable for breaches within their supply chain, potentially leading to penalties and fines. (BSR, 2015)

Another interesting trend revolves around online and mobile banking. More than five years ago in the United States, alone, more than 50% of the adult population utilizes online banking services (Statista, 2012), and now it is more than 70%.

Worldwide, global online banking penetrations are estimated to be nearly 40%. Within the overall digital banking trend, mobile banking has played a crucial role. In its research, EY (Ernst & Young, 2015) states that back in 2013 there were around 600 million users of mobile banking services. By 2020, that number is projected to grow to 2 billion. Novel mobile payment mechanisms are also a substantial component of technological transformation in the banking sector. Another anecdotal illustration: nearly twenty years ago, only one mobile payment system was available on the market; today, more than 200 such systems are being used, and approximately another 120 are being developed.

This trend is paramount to the banks' supply chain if one considers that two important components of the digital trend in this industry are (i) the reliance on cloud computing services, and (ii) the need for software development, for which banks commonly turn to specialized suppliers. Last but not least, one cannot escape the trend relating to contracting out services (aka outsourcing). Typical cases for outsourcing by the banking sector encompass data processing, IT management, data collection, and billing.

As services are being contracted out to other locations, risks are transferred as well, and it becomes more daunting to control them because they are further away from the organization's sphere of control. Drawn by reduced costs of labor in emerging markets and seeking to reinforce strategic advantage, banks have gradually turned to contract out their services. The global market for banks outsourcing is expected to continue its positive trajectory through 2019 with an average annual growth rate of around 8%.

Organizational Resilience And Supply Chain Risk Mgmt

Supply chain operations have become key to propelling growth, increasing value, and doing more with less. These operations enhance the ability to pursue nimble strategies for overall corporate growth, including globalization, accelerated product development cycles, and value chain ecosystem expansion, but they carry risks as well as opportunities.

FIGURE 38: RESISTANCE AND RECOVERY MIX

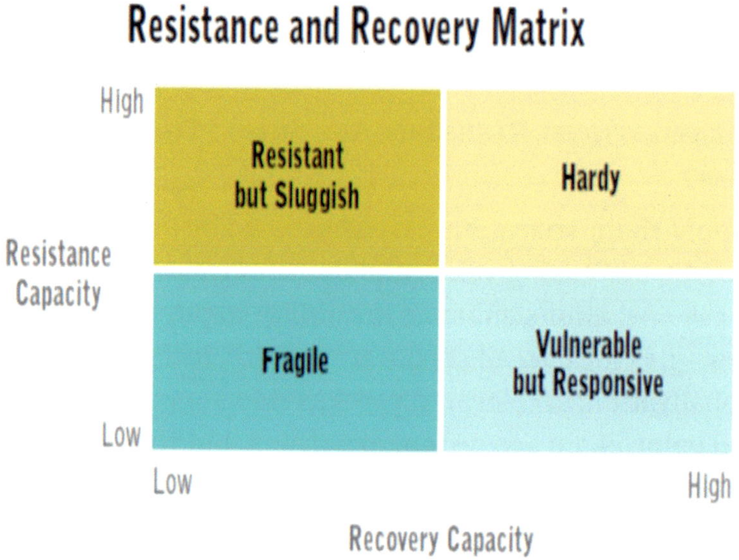

Source: SupplyChain247, 2015

Organizations understand that they need to adapt their supply chain management strategies to accommodate these new risks. To achieve this truly ¥resilient¦ state, organizations must constantly and proactively identify, measure, control, and monitor supply chain risk in real time, just as they already do for critical customer-facing and financial functions.

Supply chain resiliency is important to building a globally agile enterprise. Such a business consistently and efficiently executes to various global plans and service levels; effectively integrates across functions and geographies, and possesses the decision support and governance needed for an ongoing strategic decision-making process.

To achieve this, institutions must move beyond the traditional supply chain management goals of increasing operational efficiency or driving out excess costs.

Organizations are already beginning to take a risk-based approach to manage the supply chain. According to a January 2007 study by AMR Research (Dupras, 2014), 46% of organizations have plans to assess or deploy technology for risk management within 48 months; 33% have dedicated budgets for supply chain risk management activities, and 54% plan to increase risk management budgets over the next year.

Pressures On Supply Chain Operations

Four primary external risk factors are driving the need for improved supply chain resiliency: (i) the demand-driven nature of today's markets; (ii) environmental compliance; (iii) globalization; and (iv) increased market velocity:

Today's instant gratification and customer-centric culture are causing substantial supply chain volatility.

Precisely because customizing products for individual markets, or even individual customers, requires institutions to align specific supplier components to the right supply chain functions, failure to take a demand-driven approach to supply chain management can significantly erode customer satisfaction.

Although a handful of institutions have demonstrated strong leadership in supply chain risk management, those are the exception. Most institutions have a significant amount of work to do to achieve true resiliency.

As it relates to environmental compliance, the increasingly large body of environmental law, both domestic and international, requires institutions to track certain substances and report when they are used in products. Concomitantly, organizations are reaping significant benefits from globalization.

Some of these benefits include faster product delivery to geographically dispersed markets, shortened manufacturing lead times, more choices of suppliers, and overall reduced costs. But the risks organizations are exposed to, including tough trade and labor regulations; escalating legal, environmental, cultural and health concerns; and terrorism, as well as other security concerns, are also growing.

However, there is also increased market velocity, in the sense that customers expect ever-shorter product lead and delivery times. This puts pressure on institutions to accelerate product development life cycles. As margins continue to erode, due as much to increased competition as to rising costs, organizations¨ ability to increase profits depends on whether they align supply to global demand.

According to a relatively recent research study sponsored by BearingPoint (Coy & Bourke, 2013), 45% of senior executives named innovation in product and service offerings as a chief facilitator of competitive advantage. Almost one in three cited the ability to increase business with existing customers as a key growth initiative.

Enterprises also face a host of internal challenges to effective supply chain management, such as, for instance, the fact that many organizations face a limited visibility into internal operations. And, when institutions do not have insight into the product pipeline, they have trouble aligning operational capabilities, meeting regulatory requirements, and segmenting customers. Finally, in terms of outsourcing, organizations are exposed to the risk of not having direct control over partner institutions; therefore, they would benefit from putting in place the appropriate governance and performance measures to manage these types of risks.

Strategies To Achieve Supply Chain Resilience

Achieving resilience through better supply chain risk management does not mean avoiding risk. The ability of an organization to take on additional risk can be the key to its overall competitive edge. Organizations can weigh the relative trade-offs of risk versus opportunities so they can make decisions that directly lead to competitive advantage. Six possible strategies can be identified as already being implemented by leading institutions that are helping them become more resilient.

Firstly, organizations that proactively identify, track, and manage regulatory requirements and developments on a global scale can reap significant competitive advantage. Being reactive is no longer acceptable. Rather, organizations must implement supply chain risk management frameworks that streamline governance around business processes and mitigate risk across all value chain partners internationally. With recent product safety scares in North America due to reliance on third-party suppliers ¤including pet food contamination, E. coli-infected spinach and lead-based paint used on children's toys, a lack of visibility into supplier compliance can be a huge risk for retailers and consumer packaged goods (CPG) institutions. Moreover, the regulatory environment is volatile and in constant °ux. To meet growing pressure to comply with existing and new regulations, institutions must have sufficiently transparent supply chains in place to allow them to disclose their compliance records on demand to the public and shareholders alike.

Secondly, by putting contract management and compliance risk management procedures in place, leading organizations create safety nets in case strategic partner relationships falter. For example, in 2016, a global home goods retailer was having problems getting sufficient warehouse space.

FIGURE 39: ACHIEVING SUPPLY CHAIN RESILIENCE

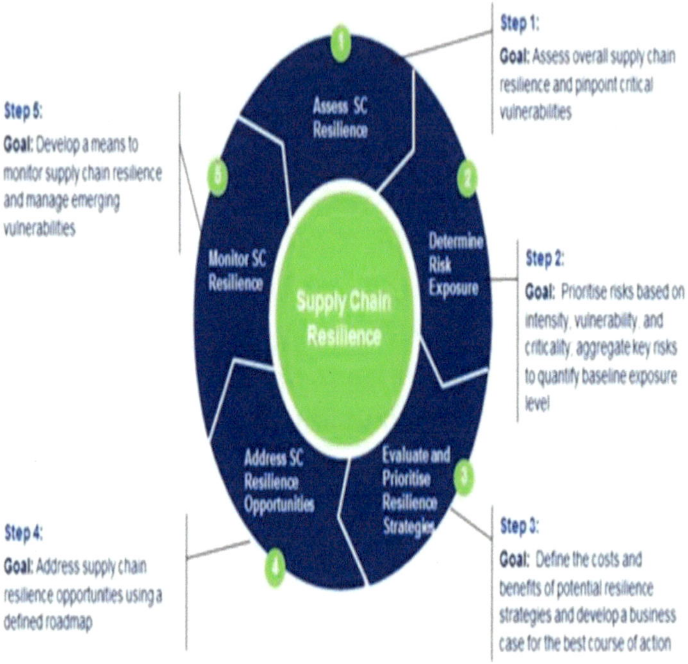

<u>Source</u>: Healy, 2019

Unless it collaborated more closely with suppliers, the company realized it would not be able to meet its business targets. By developing a single global integrated planning process using standard off-the-shelf software that could integrate easily with suppliers¨

systems, the company was able to reduce inventory by as much as 15% while simultaneously increasing customer service levels.

Thirdly, although currently being used only by a handful of industries, leading institutions are beginning to consider hedging as a viable way to mitigate risk. Organizations can perform hedging or contingency planning to avoid serious quality problems or disruptions in their supply chain operations.

By identifying the most critical risk factors in a supply chain and either hedging against them or purchasing the appropriate insurance, organizations can significantly reduce overall risks. As more organizations go global, hedging strategies will become increasingly useful as businesses seek to protect themselves from the risks arising from multiple currencies, supply fluctuations, and local trading practices.

Organizational transparency is equally important. With visibility into the supply chain, enterprises can continuously drive efficiency and process improvements, alleviate bottlenecks, and monitor previously identified risks. This increased transparency boosts institutions¨ ability to fix supply chain breakdowns promptly, while simultaneously collecting information they can use to improve the overall accuracy of their supply chain planning proactively. Organizations such as Nokia have learned through supply disruptions that developing or enhancing partner relationships with supply, manufacturing, and logistics providers to secure short-term supply chain capabilities can help mitigate disruptions.

Fourthly, ng this more advanced risk management strategy, supply chain managers look outside the enterprise at their global distribution networks, including their customers and their suppliers' suppliers. They constantly monitor performance and lead times and develop strategies for preventing disruptions.

This can include forging relationships with multiple suppliers; performing post-merger integration via network simulation modeling; establishing failover plans; or designing supplier networks that can survive natural or man-made disasters.

Fifthly, supply chain management is not just about mitigating risks arising from dependency on external suppliers. Organizations must look at the entire enterprise and align all internal functions, including marketing, sales, and operations activities. A robust S&OP (i.e. Sales and operations planning) process helps by providing management guidance on the most profitable ways to improve supply chain responsiveness, reliability, and asset utilization.

In 2004, a leading global manufacturer, specializing in valves and fluid handling components for heating, ventilating and air conditioning (HVAC) and industrial applications, implemented a supply chain risk management initiative that shifted its corporate focus from production to flexible customer fulfillment.

By tailoring its replenishment capabilities to specific market needs, the company was able to reduce stock keeping units (SKUs), enhance internal supply chain management capabilities, and collaborate with customers and suppliers more proactively. As a result of this strategic shift, the manufacturer managed to achieve 20% growth in 12 months at a time when its industry was growing at only 3% to 5%.

And, sixthly, using supply-base monitoring. Embracing this strategy, an organization carries more inventory than it needs. Maintaining ¥safety stock¦ has long been the accepted risk management approach for critical supply chain items. Despite the additional costs involved, this can still be a valid strategy.

For example, in the early 2000s, when the global market for cell phones was growing exponentially, a major supplier of a critical component for mobile phones made by electronics giant Nokia had a fire in a key factory that destroyed its inventory of components, as well as compromised its ability to continue production. Because Nokia already had strategic supply chain risk management measures in place that allowed it to monitor the supply of components in the pipeline continually, it immediately realized a major problem was developing that would disrupt its ability to get its phones to market (Dupras, 2014).

Central Sustainability Supply Chain in Banking

Below is a summary of the key issues that banks should address to manage the sustainability of their supply chains. While this is not a comprehensive list, it is illustrative of the areas that are most likely to have important repercussions, and where the greatest risks and opportunities can be found. The major issues found are data privacy and security, e-waste, GHG emissions, and human rights.

As it relates to data privacy and security, the following can be said: privacy is so fundamental that it is recognized in the Universal Declaration of Human

Rights, which states, "No one shall be subjected to arbitrary interference with his privacy."

As the movement to collect more and more data continues to grow, along with a tendency to outsource associated services such as data storage and processing, risks pertaining to data privacy are transferred to suppliers. A vendor's ability to protect sensitive or personal data to prevent issues such as privacy intrusions, cyber-attacks, and frauds should be a key criterion in the supplier selection process.

Although banks do not manufacture IT equipment, they do have substantial spend on IT, and their choices in selecting responsible suppliers can influence fostering more sustainable practices. Two of the main problems associated with IT are the proper management of waste from electronic equipment and the use of minerals that are commonly sourced in conflict zones.

E-waste is a problem because it contains hazardous substances and is often handled in crude, informal, and unsafe ways. Frequently, this waste ends up in landfills after being illegally exported to developing nations, and occurrences of forced and child labor are not uncommon.

Many scholars regard climate change as the most urgent challenge in today's world. Former U.S. President Barack Obama stated, "no challenge poses a greater threat to our future and future generations than a change in climate" (Geman, 2015). All business sectors have a role to play in addressing this issue.

In the banks' supply chain, the most relevant spend categories that have an impact on climate change are energy consumption, and transportation and travel. In terms of transport, business trips, courier services, armored vehicles, employee commutes, and business trips, all contribute to GHG emissions. Facilities' energy consumption and the power required for office IT equipment and server farms for data storage are also significant sources of emissions in this sector. In light of data provided by the CDP (formerly the Carbon Disclosure Project, a nonprofit that helps institutions manage the risks and opportunities associated with climate change on GHG reporting), there is significant room for improvement in the banking industry.

Although most financial institutions provide some disclosure on their scope 1 and 2 emissions, few of them report on their vendors' emissions, which may have a larger impact on climate change. The CDP observes that in terms of GHG in the banking sector, there is a general lack of understanding of the full impact of institutions' value chains.

Given that employment and professional services are one of the most important spending categories for banks, human rights are a fundamental issue in supply chain sustainability. Moreover, this is a topic that can be addressed across all spending categories because every supplier has a workforce and a responsibility to respect their rights.

Some of the main challenges related to human rights include providing a healthy and safe work environment; guaranteeing a diverse workplace and fostering non-discrimination; protecting employees from being overworked; eliminating the use of child and forced labor; ensuring that workers have the right to join or form unions or workers' association; and making sure all workers receive a fair wage.

Lastly, many banks need to employ security staff to protect branch offices and guard money that is being transported. Usually, this staffing requirement is met through the use of contractors. Using third-party labor introduces an additional component of risk because it is further away from internal company control mechanisms.

Sustainable practices in facilities and property management. Choosing the right suppliers to handle the design and construction of the facilities can have important repercussions on sustainability. For example, according to the International Energy Agency, buildings account for about 40% of the world's primary energy consumption. Consequently, selecting suppliers that follow green building standards can have significant impacts on energy consumption, as well as on other sustainability-related issues such as water use and GHG emissions.

Top of the Class Market Practices and Recommendations

Although supply chain sustainability in the banking sector is still relatively nascent, some institutions have been working on the matter and provide excellent illustrations on how responsible procurement can be applied to this industry.

Below, one will find a description of these practices as well as recommendations inspired by what has been done with other industries and that apply to banks. Good practices are applicable to all industries, and there are lessons to be learned for banks from leading organizations in other businesses. The practices and recommendations are framed around three key steps:

identifying priorities, taking action, and evaluating impacts:

In order to set up a platform for a responsible procurement program, it is initially necessary to have a clear understanding of the impacts that the organization's supply chain has. For example, in Australia - Westpac, which was ranked by the Dow Jones Sustainability Index as the most sustainable bank in 2014 - summarizes their process in the following way (BSR, 2015):

> "We can map our supply chain by tracing the key activities of organizations and people involved in bringing a product or service from raw material to market. This can help organizations gain a better understanding of the extent to which their supply chain impacts on their environmental and social footprint. This helps them to identify the most significant challenges that they and their suppliers face, and prioritize their efforts accordingly."

Large banks tend to have thousands of suppliers: In order to be most effective in addressing sustainability issues, organizations can benefit from prioritizing their efforts based on the potential impact that their suppliers can have.

UBS, for example, reports that they "identify high-impact suppliers of newly sourced goods or services based on their provision of goods and services that have either a substantial environmental and social impact or are sourced in markets with potentially high social risks."

TD Bank has a similar practice, assigning a risk rating to each of their sourced products and services and applying heightened due diligence to categories identified as having a higher risk. AXA (2015) is another banking organization that uses a risk assessment process for their supply chain, through which they identify high sustainability impact categories for their operations, such as "promotional items and gifts," and lower risk categories, such as "software."

Looking beyond the first tier and setting up traceability: In evaluating the impacts of the supply chain and implementing corrective actions, a good practice is to look beyond the first tier. Extending supply chain sustainability programs past first-tier suppliers allow institutions to enhance their positive impacts greatly. This is certainly relevant for banks because some of the most severe risks can be found with second- and third-tier vendors. Associated with the practice of analyzing impacts beyond the first tier is the practice of setting up traceability programs. Traceability is the capacity to identify and trace the history, distribution, location, and application of products to ensure the reliability of sustainability claims on issues such as human rights and environmental impacts.

Actions Speak Louder than Words

In managing the sustainability of the supply chain for this sector, one of the most widespread practices is the development of a supplier code of conduct. Many institutions have a publicly available code of conduct or set of standards for suppliers. However, the specific content of the codes varies, as does the way how they are implemented and monitored, illustrated as follows (BSR, 2015):

- Action #1: Leading institutions have been using digital platforms to track and measure impact. In addition to tracking individual supplier data, it is recommended to aggregate data in order to identify trends in regions and spend categories.
- Action #2: Collaboration among peers and other stakeholders has proven to generate positive impacts on supply chain sustainability. Examples of

supply chain collaborations that banks can engage with include the Electronics Industry Citizenship Coalition (EICC) and the Better Work program of the International Labor Organization (ILO). Leveraging the expertise of specialized organizations is an effective way to manage supply chain issues[16].

- Action #3: Banks seek to promote the development of traditionally vulnerable and minority communities, as well as expand their pool of talent, through the implementation of a diversity program specifically aimed at suppliers. In an industry in which one of the highest spend categories is professional and employment services, focus on this area is of significant importance. Since 1977, Citi (2015) has been implementing its Supplier Diversity program. To promote opportunities for diverse suppliers, Citi provides mentorship, training programs, and local supplier development councils. Bank of America (2015) is another institution that

[16] For instance, to enhance supplier diversity practices, several banking organizations have joined the National Minority Supplier Development Council. Council members from the financial sector include American Express, Bank of America, Capital One, Goldman Sachs, Citigroup, ING, Prudential Financial, JP Morgan Chase, and Wells Fargo

has a longstanding diversity program specifically aimed at their suppliers.

- Actions #4: Many banks have developed a code of ethics for their vendors. However, some institutions have taken this practice to a higher level by creating particular guidelines for each of their main procurement categories. This is a reasonable approach, considering that the vendors that service the banking industry are quite diverse, and the potential impacts they can have are very different. Deutsche Bank (2015), for instance, has developed Green Supply Chain frameworks for various sourcing categories, such as power from renewable energy, paper, multifunctional printers, and servers. Every framework establishes specific sustainability criteria for the goods or services in question. ANZ is another leader in this regard: They have also developed Sustainability Guidelines for Procurement of specific categories to help sourcing managers assess and reduce environmental and social impacts.
- Action #5: The consideration of sustainability criteria in procurement decisions is a fundamental direction forward in supply chain sustainability. Banking institutions that have incorporated sustainability criteria into their supplier selection

processes include AXA, Bloomberg, and Westpac (BSR, 2015). In the interest of institutionalizing this practice, these organizations have included specific corporate responsibility clauses in their service contracts and requests for proposals (RFPs). AXA (2015), for instance, has adopted a Corporate Responsibility section for each new contract, which outlines the need for compliance with the International Labor Organization's major principles.

- Action #6: To minimize the impact of e-waste, institutions can make sure that the supplier they work with has a good take-back program that can properly dispose of equipment after it reaches its end of life. Additionally, banking institutions can join e-Stewards, a third-party initiative that works to promote stricter standards for e-waste recycling. The e-Stewards program provides a certification to identify responsible recyclers of e-waste. Bloomberg, Wells Fargo, and Bank of America are institutions in this sector that have an e-Steward certification.
- Action #7: One of the ways that banks can help tackle the challenge of climate change is through their selection of energy vendors. For example, UBS (2014) stands out due to its procurement of alternative sources of energy. In the company's

Switzerland and Germany operations, 100% of its electricity comes from renewable energy sources such as hydroelectricity. Worldwide, UBS's use of renewable sources of energy accounts for 50% of its overall needs.

- Action #8: Giving employees access to technologies (e.g., mobile apps) that allow them to address issues such as personal safety and anonymously report violations. Leading institutions are also working with local governments to increase minimum wages and provide better working conditions.

EVALUATING IMPACT AND REPORTING

Banks can use a combination of mechanisms, including supplier self-assessments, evaluations carried out by internal teams, and auditing to monitor supply chain compliance. Westpac has made it obligatory for new suppliers to complete their Sustainable Supply Chain Management Code of Conduct. If areas of opportunity are detected, the company will require that the supplier provide a specific action plan to address the issue.

---

[17] AXA, for instance, has been implementing this practice since 2008. For 2015, AXA (2015) set up a target to have 90 % of its major suppliers assessed on their corporate responsibility performance by a third party.

To ensure expertise and independence, self-assessments can be complemented through third-party audits[17]. After evaluating supplier performance, the crucial next step is to take corrective actions and encourage supplier development. Leading institutions have acknowledged that in doing this, it is best to engage with suppliers to address problems and to invest in capacity building, engagement programs, and other tools to help their vendors to improve their sustainability performance[18].

---

[18] UBS (2014) offers an example of engaging with suppliers to improve their performance. Following an impact evaluation, if the company identifies instances of noncompliance with its Responsible Supply Chain Standard, it works with the vendor to define and agree on measures to tackle the issues.

Bank of America (2015) has worked with its suppliers since 2009 in responding to the CDP Supply Chain Survey in order to keep track of their GHG emissions. What makes Bank of America's practice noteworthy is not the fact that it asks suppliers to answer the survey—which is a good practice and relatively common—but rather the engagement it provides during the process to encourage improvement. The bank has established an open dialogue with its vendors, providing feedback on their transparency and performance, and assisting them in making improvements.

Reporting is an essential element to sustainability in business is transparency. It encourages institutions to analyze their practices formally and to document and learn from them. Transparency allows stakeholders to be aware of institutions' business practices, encourages feedback, establishes a relationship of openness and trust, and lays a foundation for accountability.

When it comes to disclosure of responsible procurement practices, the banking industry has already begun moving in the right direction. The institutions are reporting to some extent on their supply chain responsibility practices and how they align with their overall sustainability strategies. However, most banks have room to improve on their sustainability disclosure. For guidance on this issue, internationally recognized guidelines have been developed, with specific requirements for banks[19].

---

[19] Two of the most widely used standards are produced by the Global Reporting Initiative (GRI) and the Sustainability Accounting Standards Board (SASB). About supply chain issues of banks, GRI (2015) recommends reporting on the following aspects: percentage of suppliers that have been screened using labor practice and societal impacts criteria; negative impacts on society in the supply chain and actions taken, and the proportion of spending on local suppliers. Further guidance on ways to incorporate sustainable practices into the

A Framework For Enterprise Risk Management

To address the specific risks related to supply chain operations, organizations should establish supply chain risk management strategies that fit within their overall enterprise risk management strategies.

An organization's first step toward resiliency is to check its current capacity for managing supply chain risk exposure. Although such assessments can be comprehensive and involve considerable time, effort, and expense, a quick self-assessment diagnostic tool can help organizations understand where their supply chain risk management operations fit within their maturity model:

- Ability to identify risk: Exceptions occur at various nodes in the supply chain as a result of supplier, logistics, facilities, and demand fluctuations. Adequate risk management processes are in place to identify and assess these risk factors at regular intervals.
- Ability to measure risk: Key risk management vulnerability areas are well understood, and risk

---

supply chain can be found in Supply Chain Sustainability: A Practical Guide for Continuous Improvement developed jointly by the United Nations Global Compact and BSR.

exposure is measured in critical impact areas. These measurements are integrated with other critical management metrics in operational executive dashboards.

Risk management strategies are rule-based/metrics-oriented that translates itself in:

a) Ability to control risk: Supply chain risk management strategies today are categorized as being preventive by managing uncertainty through design of a robust supply chain. Contingency planning process includes collaboration with all critical trading partners whose operations, if disrupted, could significantly impact the business. The scope of risk management extends beyond the enterprise to consistently assess and mitigate risk from customer and supplier actions. Likewise, these collaborative risk management processes are defined and implemented.
b) Ability to monitor risk: Supply chain risk management strategy leverages supply chain management visibility-enhancing technologies such as enterprise resource planning, advanced planning, event management, radio frequency identification, the Internet, and environmental

monitoring tools. Supply chain risk management efforts are aligned to and integrated with enterprise risk management efforts. For instance, supply chain risk management personnel have dotted-line responsibility to the chief risk management officer and belong to enterprise risk management project teams. Supply chain risk management strategies include all value chain components, including manufacturing operations, purchasing, sales, and operations planning, customers, distribution and logistics, and financial markets. Once an organization determines where it fits within the maturity model, it can begin to take action to improve its organization's resiliency. The specific steps it takes will depend on the results of the self-assessment.

Putting Strategies Into Action

There are four steps involved in putting a comprehensive supply chain risk management framework in place. Organizations should understand these four steps, no matter what stage of maturity they have reached. Those currently in the first stage (ad hoc) will do so in a very rudimentary way and focus on early steps.

Alternatively, those currently in the fifth, most mature stage (optimized) will act very aggressively and invest significant resources in the actions of the later steps. Regardless of their current state of maturity, organizations can benefit from supporting their supply chain risk management efforts with a sustainable governance structure based on formal policies, procedures, and standards:

1. Risk identification. Risks can be either external or internal. External risks can include aspects of globalization, increased market velocity, environmental compliance and the nature of today's demand-driven environment; internal risks include aspects such as limited visibility into operations, outsourcing, new inventory management techniques and a lack of adequate process automation. Understanding what specific risks represent priority areas of focus as early as possible is essential.
2. Risk measurement. Risk can affect both revenues and costs. On the revenue side of the equation, supply chain disruptions can result in loss of sales and customers/market share and brand erosion. From a cost perspective, material and supply cost inefficiency, overhead cost increases, obsolescence, inventory, debts, fixed assets, and

litigation costs can all adversely affect an organization's finances. It is important to evaluate the likelihood of worst-case scenarios occurring across both internal and external risk factors.

3. Risk control. By putting in place an entire portfolio of risk management and mitigation strategies, processes and tools based on the results of the risk probability assessment, organizations can make significant strides toward strengthening the robustness of their supply chains.
4. Risk monitoring. This final step involves continuously monitoring the already identified risks and regularly reviewing the mitigation strategies in place to determine whether the strategy still satisfies an organization's needs amid ongoing market changes. For example, leading institutions are creating useful, succinct reporting tools that summarize in a dashboard format the current status of risk and related mitigation activity, allowing their executives to act swiftly if the risk profile of the organization changes.

Supply Chain Risk Mgmt & Organizational Resilience

Although tremendous opportunities exist within supply chain operations for increasing revenues and reducing costs, few institutions have achieved true organizational resilience that would allow them to make informed decisions about trade-offs between risks and opportunities.

By understanding where they are today, organizations can take the appropriate steps for achieving resiliency on their way to becoming globally agile enterprises. Organizations can benefit from the following:

- Gain senior managerial support. Day-to-day supply chain operations can take priority over longer-term risk assessments. Executives must buy into the need for a risk management strategy and prioritize planning and implementation of such a strategy even amid ongoing supply chain operational challenges. By integrating leading practices such as third-party reviews of risk procedures and business self-assessments, organizations can link line-of-business risk strategies and overall strategic goals.
- Link risk management with strategic execution. As institutions evolve from regional to global supply chains, they are naturally exposed to more risk. Organizations must evaluate the impact of entering new international markets and develop risk

mitigating activities where appropriate. By identifying, quantifying, controlling, and mitigating these risks, the enterprise becomes more efficient and capable of creating sustainable long-term shareholder value.

- Adapt systems to changes in risk. By integrating previously siloed applications, both internally and externally with suppliers¨ systems, institutions can more flexibly identify, measure, mitigate, and monitor risk.
- Communicate with and train staff. Strong lines of communication at the beginning of the risk management project, along with a concerted internal marketing effort on an ongoing basis, are critical. Everyone involved in identifying, assessing, mitigating, and monitoring risk should be properly trained to understand the elements of risk and the approach adopted by the organization.
- Invest in the technologies needed to measure and monitor risks. With the right automated tools, organizations can track the ongoing nature and severity of the risks they face during the normal course of doing business and determine what steps to take to mitigate those risks.
- Coordinate risk management across all stakeholders. Lines of business should collaborate

and coordinate supply chain management risk assessments across departmental boundaries. For example, for organizations that compete in highly cyclical markets, more effective workforce planning can lead to better agility when attempting to scale manufacturing up and down as demand dictates.

Supply Chain Risk Management In Systemic Crisis

Over the last decades, supply chain risk management has turned into a vital center point for organizations, whose focus has been even further acknowledged by the prevalent economic environment.

With this realm in mind, it is noteworthy to understand successful approaches and experiences by institutions in managing with this new reality, especially as it concerns the supply side. There is a differentiation dependent on whether organizations are prevalently focused on manufacturing or services, an aspect impacting how supply chain hazard is dealt with, and the economics revolving around transaction costs fills in as the primary hypothetical beacon.

Organizations that that have been coping with supply risks in a financial crisis environment are illustrative how their risk management methodologies have shifted, and delineate how they are associated to enterprise risk management.

The global financial crisis in 2007-2008 brought about a sharp increment of corporate bankruptcies, with an exceptionally large number of high-profile bankruptcies and insolvencies (e.g., Lehman Brothers, Washington Mutual, General Motors, CIT, Chrysler, Dexia, Wachovia, Northern Rock, Sears, Toys 'R Us, Thornburg Mortgage, Indymac). Pretty much every region and every sector has been impacted by the crisis in one way or the other, rendering the management of hazards related to the crisis an outright need for organizations[20].

Besides, with the trend towards outsourcing and institutions progressively concentrating on their core business skills, viable and efficient supply chain management has turned into a key feature of competitive advantage, corporate strategy, and success (Narasimhan and Talluri, 2009).

What's more, because of the scarcity of resources and the volatile environment, this importance is even

[20] This is particularly emphasized for institutions being tightly interlinked in a supply chain network comprised of multiple entities (most notably customers and suppliers) whom themselves may severely suffer under the financial crisis (Blome & Schoenherr, 2011).

heightened during economic distress. Within this setting, the sourcing of services, products, and capabilities can thus be imperiled by supplier defaults (Wagner et al., 2009). As a result of these realities, supply chain risk management is a vital focus point for the industry to be better able to anticipate, predict, prevent or reduce the impacts of supplier defaults and disruptions[21].

By and large, supply disruption represents today a much higher costs than any time in recent memory (Aydin et al., 2009), requiring the further understanding of supply chain risk management.

But, even without the financial crisis, supply chain risk management has become a necessity for many organizations. Globalization, improved infrastructure, and developments in information technology has resulted in supply chains becoming longer and more complex, exposing the organization to higher supply chain vulnerability (Aydin et al., 2009)[22].

---

[21] The negative effect of supplier defaults has been shown by Hendricks and Singhal (2005), who reported a median decrease in operating income of 31.28% for organizations that had experienced a supply chain glitch caused by suppliers.

[22] The importance of supply chain risk management was, for example,

Despite the fact it might be difficult to assess how well risk management systems would have been responding to the financial crisis, one needs to acknowledged that the financial crisis has deeply affected existing supply chain risk management approaches within the manufacturing and service-oriented organizations. While it has been judicious to implement supply chain risk management approaches all along, its significance has certainly been further put to the forefront as a result of the 2007-2008 financial crisis (Ariba, 2009). While enterprise risk management has been a significant aspect of all facets of business, its criticality is undoubtedly also acknowledged in the scope of the management of supply chain risks.

Since this aspect is beyond the scope of the internal control of the organization, selecting and monitoring vendors, while concomitantly overseeing its associated risks, becomes crucial (Blome & Schoenherr, 2011). This phenomenon, together with the growing reliance on the lean principle (i.e. minimal inventories and just-

illustrated by the results of a survey, which revealed that 90% of organizations felt threatened by supply-side risks (Snell, 2010). However, at the same time, respondents in 60% of the organizations noted that they were not confident or knowledgeable enough about supply risk issues.

in-time deliveries), heightens the need for a dynamic and proactive supply chain risk management[23]; and this causes for a major challenge for the entire industry.

Notwithstanding the fact that empirical research in supply chain risk management and enterprise risk management is at an early stage, it is concomitantly faced with an unprecedented environment of economic and financial turmoil.

Thus, supply chain risk management is considered as a crucial and foundational aspect of the broader notion of enterprise risk management that is addressing the supply side (i.e., even though supply chain risk management and enterprise risk management are often perceived as separate functions within the organization).

Most obvious are the changes in the manufacturing industry (i.e., especially the automotive sector), where new processes, teams, and information technology tools have been developed to address issues revolving around supply chain risk management. And, this has

[23] For example, while the global automotive industry faced approximately 70 major insolvencies in 2007, the financial crisis made this number rise to 225 insolvencies in 2009 (Berger, 2010).

also impacted the service driven industries, such as banking, for instance.

Subsequently, a high number of bankruptcies has impacted third parties. Many of those vendors are located overseas, such as in India and the Philippines. Basing supply chain risk management solely on monitoring financial data is, therefore, extremely risky; much more is needed in the increasingly complex environment.

Reputation-related issues on the supply side can serve as an illustrative example (e.g., the risk of vendors being involved in fraudulent schemes overseas, which is a very relevant topic in the financial services as it impact the compliance aspect of the business); these risks are not assessable based on the mere reactive monitoring of financial statements.

The Risk Management of Supply Chains

Organizations have at their disposal various strategic options as it related to supply chain risk management. Two of these options are, particularly prevalent in the financial crisis and appear to be focal in the risk mitigation approaches of organizations.

As such, institutions can either endeavor to prevent supply chain disruptions proactively, or they can embrace supply chain risk and be exposed to the detrimental impact if the risk materializes. For some organizations, their risk mitigation techniques have been affected more dramatically as a result of the financial crisis than for others.

To comprehend the effect of the systemic crisis on supply chain risk management, one needs to keep in mind the five building stones of risk management, namely: risk awareness, risk identification, risk analysis, risk acceptance, and risk monitoring (Lavanya and Malarvizhi, 2008):

- Risk awareness is paramount for risk management, and one can only be aware of and subsequently manage and try to mitigate hazards once one has acknowledged their existence. And, this awareness of supply chain risks has been increasing, especially due to insolvencies affecting vendors. As such, third party insolvencies as a result of the financial crisis has been acknowledged as one of the major or the most important corporate risk affecting organizations.

Consequently, some of these organizations decided to adapt their existing list of potential supply chain risks they track by adding, for instance, a financial dimension. However, some did not adjust, because they felt that their list of potential risks had already been exhaustive. Others introduced a new cross-functional process to map supply chain risks better, whereby there are now several players in a team assessing supplier risks, namely, risk management, procurement, and internal clients.

And sometimes the organizations get the help of the finance department to obtain financial ratings on the suppliers. Risk awareness efforts and comprehensiveness, thus, have increased in the financial crisis across organizations.

- Risk identification in supply chain risk management is focused on the structured and comprehensive recognition, determination, and mapping of potential supply risks associated with a particular supply chain aspect. This step allows for visibility of the potential risks and builds the bedrock for the ensuing supply chain risk management process.

In the current distressed environment, the focus of the supply risk identification phase has been improving, which seems to be due to the increasing risk awareness based on the growing number of vendors' insolvencies. For example, some organizations have established a very constricted corset of risk management measures to avoid third party insolvencies due to the heightened high-risk awareness of the organization as a whole.

- Once risks have been identified, the necessary next step is to analyze each risk individually and to determine its potential consequences for the entire supply chain of the organization. In the risk analysis stage, the probability of default and severity (loss given default) of each risk are assessed, in order to provide more detailed input to the subsequent decision as to which risks to mitigate.

  When analyzing the potential impact of risks, some organizations may explicitly determine the potential impact directly by using different scales or indicators (e.g., EBIT effect, procurement volumes). When assessing the likelihood of supply risks, organizations may use multiple criteria, like quality or delivery performance, to assess the probability indirectly or use a direct probability rating based on equidistant scales[24].

- Subsequent to the risk analysis, acceptable levels of risk need to be established (risk acceptance). Also, risk mitigation plans need to be developed, should a risk be evaluated above the determined threshold value. Some organizations may allow

[24] What changed during the financial crisis is the depth of analysis and the use of a multitude of indicators to predict supplier disruptions. Organizations show a heightened emphasis on the gathering of additional information and intelligence due to external threats, such as supplier disruptions. While some organizations consult external rating services, such as indexes from Dun & Bradstreet, others relied only on internal financial evaluations (e.g., using the Altman Z-score). Yet others may use a combination of both. In any case, proficiency in using financial indicators to examine the financial status of suppliers has increased significantly during the financial crisis. Before the financial crisis, many organizations did not have a very professional assessment of their suppliers' financials; now they have a very good system working.' The resources spent on risk assessment increased drastically. Even though organizations may make use of supplier financial analysis, some organizations have doubts about the usefulness of external, and, especially balance-sheet related indicators, since they are considered as lagging instead of leading indicators.

for the decentralized units in procurement – sometimes in combination with the internal clients – to decide on the appropriate risk measures and their acceptable levels.

Some organizations, however, posit some upfront normed strategies depending on the outcome of the risk analysis, such as a mandatory response plan including a report to executive or line management in case of a major and severe risk. The financial crisis had, due to the cash restrictions of the focal organizations, a disciplining effect on the risk mitigation strategies.

As such, managers have become much more compliant with existing risk mitigation processes, and risk mitigation measures are now determined jointly with top management. Overall, the financial crisis encouraged organizations to be more aware of their level of risk acceptance, as well as to plan their risk mitigation strategies.

- Risk monitoring includes monitoring developments in the supply chain that may increase or decrease risks on an on-going basis.

> In order to control risks, most organizations incorporate risk monitoring into their regular supplier monitoring activities, shorten the assessment cycle, and increase the monitoring depth during the financial crises (i.e., reducing the monitoring cycle form a half-yearly cycle to a weekly basis for all first-tier and also some second-tier suppliers).

The environmental uncertainty inherent in every exchange can be alleviated or at least mitigated by the identification and subsequent management of risk. The risk identification phase is, however, the most crucial since risks that are not identified cannot be managed. Due to the multitude of supply chain failures in the recent past, primarily based on the current economic downturn, the investment in risk identification processes may, therefore, be prudent and outweigh the imposed burden.

Doing business has become more complex and riskier, primarily due to increased dependency on suppliers; this risk needs to be managed carefully. Besides, transaction cost economics can provide a useful theoretical anchor to explain the heightened importance placed on supply risk analysis within supply chain risk management.

Higher transaction costs may very well be warranted in order to make sense of the collected risk information in the prior stage, and analyzed in the current one. Since the threat of supply disruptions has become even more real, it seems wise to invest in these initiatives necessary to ensure the successful transaction.

The observations related to risk mitigation and monitoring can also be explained from a transaction cost perspective: risk mitigation mainly addresses the safeguarding of the transaction to achieve the lowest overall transaction costs.

Especially in times of crisis, the cost for safeguarding the transaction (e.g., investing in a distressed supplier) can be substantial, and hence transaction cost analysis not only has to incorporate risk management costs but also the cost of damages in case of disruptions. Similarly, the increased costs for monitoring suppliers can lead to decreased overall transaction costs, as early detection of supply chain risks can enable risk mitigation, and hence lower overall transaction costs, especially as the likelihood of supply chain disruptions has been increasing in the financial crisis.

And, even though less money is available to help suppliers, the need to help distressed strategic suppliers is crucial. Helping suppliers must be more focused than before the financial crisis since the possibility to help has decreased. However, for organizations dealing primarily with indirect spend, it is still quite unusual to help suppliers financially; this has also not changed during the financial crisis.

And, the financial crisis has been used to consolidate suppliers. In the end, the supply chain risk management methods are very much based on the dependency level with the supplier. Overall, buying organizations primarily rely on monitoring suppliers instead of proactively avoiding supplier insolvencies, and hope that the suppliers will solve their problems independently.

Specifically, buyers try to be very reactive when a supplier becomes insolvent. In business, the most efficient and effective markets are used to conduct transactions. In the unexpected crisis that the world economy is struggling with at the moment, it may thus be more prudent for a buyer to accept the potential risk posed by financially weak suppliers. Rather than helping them out in the crisis, buyers tend to shift their production reactively to a secondary supplier[25].

---

[25] This shift has been observed, especially among organizations that

Besides detecting a greater focus on the five risk management process steps throughout, a further pattern has emerged, namely, the difference in supply chain risk management approaches taken by manufacturing versus service organizations.

Overall, the emphasis on the four risk management processes is greater among organizations procuring predominantly direct materials (manufacturing organizations) than for organizations producing primarily indirect items (service organizations).

As such, risk identification is of particular importance to manufacturing organizations dealing with primarily direct spend, due to the usually more immediate impact on the organization's operations in case of faulty direct supply. Similarly, risk analysis was pursued more rigorously by some of the direct spend (manufacturing) organizations, for example by extending their

focus on direct spend. It is less apparent for organizations with primarily indirect spend since they are usually already focusing on the more reactive and less strategic approach of risk acceptance (often due to the low significance or importance of indirect items). The current financial crisis fosters, especially a risk acceptance (as opposed to mitigation) approach in direct spend organizations. Indirect spend organizations are already more focused on risk acceptance approaches and have not changed their behavior.

probability rating as part of their risk analysis to almost every single possible factor that can be used to predict supplier insolvencies, mirroring the importance of this risk.

In contrast, financial services organizations which have historically already been using a comprehensive set of indicators – and have not changed the level of detail in analyzing supplier insolvency risk in the financial crisis[26].

Interaction Between Supply Chain Risk Management And Enterprise Risk Management

---

[26] The direct-spend organizations changed their supply chain risk monitoring to a larger extent as the service organizations (Blome & Schoenherr, 2011). For instance, some direct spend organizations assess suppliers at least half-yearly in workshops, in addition to separate audits, while others use a semi-annual approach predominantly; however, depending on the 'value at risk', also quarterly assessments are possible. However, indirect spend organizations tend to use a quarterly or semi-annual approach. These observations are also in line with transaction cost economics, which suggests that additional costs are especially then warranted when direct materials are involved, due to their increased potential to impact the proper operations of the company. As such, the additional focus on supply chain risk identification, risk analysis, risk mitigation, and risk monitoring are, especially prevalent for manufacturing organizations as opposed to service organizations.

There are two different approaches to the introduction of the supply chain risk management process.

- in some instances, enterprise risk management may request the procurement/supply chain department to implement such a process,
- And, in other cases the procurement/supply chain department initiates the supply chain risk management process, which is later aligned with the enterprise risk management process.

Interestingly, neither the origin of supply chain risk management implementation nor the nature of the organization (manufacturing versus service organization) seems to affect the relationship between enterprise risk management and supply chain risk management.

Enterprise risk management has gained importance over the last years and has been implemented in many organizations, even though in different organizational setups and with varying responsibilities.

In many cases, a separate enterprise risk management unit exists in the finance department of the organization, in which enterprise risk management was part of the general planning process and hence is mainly triggered by the managerial accounting department.

The alignment of supply chain risk management with the rules of enterprise risk management and its process compliance are assessed, on average, annually in many organizations.

For instance, organizations have a comprehensive enterprise risk management policy and procurement as part of that. Procurement has – like every other function – to prove that it complies with this enterprise risk management process. This compliance is ensured by a variety of measures. They can be audited yearly, or may report in more frequent intervals their assessments.

In other instances, procurement is using its methodology, to include also nonfinancial measures (financial measures have been the primary domain of enterprise risk management), since supply chain risk management suffers from unavailable or difficult-to-estimate data related to risk likelihood and severity (Blome & Schoenherr, 2011).

Many organizations do not possess common thresholds for risk reporting, an observation also prevalent for procurement. Only the risks above this threshold level are of interest to enterprise risk management and will be reported. Procurement seldom reaches these threshold levels and hence is of limited interest to enterprise risk management.

Overall, supply chain risk management and enterprise risk management are aligned in most organizations, even though supply chain risk management and enterprise risk management are two completely different events. Changes in the relationship between supply chain risk management and enterprise risk management have been observed among organizations, in addition to the generally increased level of risk awareness for organizations that are more severely affected by supplier insolvencies.

As such, the existence of an enterprise risk management system is a major antecedent for the implementation of a supply chain risk management process, and the financial crisis has not influenced the relationship between enterprise risk management and supply chain risk management.

Take-Away Message

In practice, supply chain risk management and enterprise risk management approaches must be adapted to the environment, in this case, the financial crisis; if there is no fit to the context, supply chain risk management is likely to fail. It seems that supply chain risk management and enterprise risk management require dynamic capabilities in order to be able to be managed in appropriate ways; hence organizations must invest in their human resources to enable employees to recognize changing environments and adapt quickly to trends.

Therefore, it is not only a question of developing the capability of reacting quickly to single risk incidents, but also on a larger scale, of adapting the entire risk management process to serve as a foundation for supply chain risk management; this will lead the latter to be most effective. For manufacturing organizations, the criticality of this point for their long-term sustainability was especially stressed.

Overall, developing a supply chain risk management process is not an easy task, and significant resources are required. Besides, developing a business case can pose a challenge, as severities of avoided risks are difficult to estimate. A proficient supply chain risk management is not only achieved by tools and resources but mainly by capabilities that must be dynamically adjusted.

Also, while the current crisis emphasizes on supply chain risk management, such monitoring and management must constantly be conducted, even in times of no crisis.

A systematic supply chain risk management approach is crucial for the effective prevention of disruptions on the supply side. Furthermore, changes in the different steps of supply chain risk management are interlinked, since all steps have been affected by the financial crisis in a similar fashion.

Hence it seems to be necessary to carry out all supply chain risk management process steps rigorously, otherwise, risk management cannot be successful (e.g., when an important risk has not been identified, or no appropriate measures have been taken to prevent such major risk).

Interestingly, even though enterprise risk management is a major antecedent for the introduction of supply chain risk management, it seems that supply chain risk management is reinventing the wheel of risk management, as there is very limited integration and knowledge transfer between supply chain risk management and enterprise risk management.

Even a major exogenous shock like the financial crisis seems to have no effect on the relationship between supply chain risk management and enterprise risk management, perhaps showing that these processes possess a nature that is too distinct, or that they have not found a common basis to profit from each other.

Supply chain risk management and enterprise risk management have become a key concern for organizations, which is even further emphasized by the current economic and financial crisis.

Manufacturing organizations have adjusted their supply chain risk management to a larger extent in the financial crisis. Even though both manufacturing and service organizations are affected by supplier insolvencies due to the financial crisis, service organizations seem to have higher strategic flexibility due to the lower level of dependence on a single supplier.

Hence, one can observe that service organizations are mainly influenced by the financial crisis on the demand side, whereas manufacturing organizations are affected by the demand and the supply side. Following this line of thought establishes supply chain risk management as a strategic capability in manufacturing organizations.

As such, manufacturing organizations should develop different supply chain risk management capabilities for strategic and nonstrategic suppliers. One could further argue that a supply chain risk management approach focusing on proactive risk mitigation might not be plausible for service organizations in case of existing sufficient substitutes.

In general, the financial crisis also had a positive effect on organizations in that supply chain risk management capabilities had been further developed, which may help organizations to be better prepared for a future crisis, but also 'usual' supply disruptions.

Another important contribution to practice is that while supply chain risk management and enterprise risk management are, to a large extent, well-aligned, they are not profiting from each other's expertise. It seems that a similar conflict of thoughts exist as one may envision for the integration between finance and purchasing/supply chain management departments.

A missing common language and different assumptions and value propositions appear to be complicating the knowledge exchange. However, due to the increased importance of purchasing and supply chain management for the organization, as illustrated above, both functions should work toward better integration with enterprise risk management.

This integration could enable more effective risk mitigation, ensuring the long-term sustainability of the organization.

SECTION XI: MEASURING RESILIENCE SUPPLY CHAIN

BACKGROUND

Resilience has been described as "the power of resuming the original shape or position after compression, bending..." (The Oxford English Dictionary, 1989). Following this initial definition, the notion of supply chain resilience has developed into the capacity to respond to unexpected events and to restore standard supply chain activities.

This being said, change in the business environment indicates that going back to the initial condition is not necessarily the strategic goal of an organization. Instead, very often, an affected organization aims to adjust to the new circumstances and evolve from the occurrence.

As noted repeatedly in the literature, resilience should seek to bounce back from chaos and disruptions, ideally doing more than merely surviving. Again, as already mentioned, the goal of resilience is for any organization to return to its original state or move to a new, more desirable state after being disturbed.

In today's organizational context, there has been an expansive analysis of hazards within organizations in numerous sectors. There has been significant development of the area of risk analysis and management leading to the design of several frameworks and models (Manuj & Mentzer, 2008) utilized to assess, predict, and discuss the various hazards an organization is exposed.

Nonetheless, there is a particular type of risk that has yet to be managed, as it requires a different type of understanding. This risk involves other results, known as high-impact, low-probability (HILP) events. These are a different set of difficulties, as they are difficult to predict due to the fact that very frequently these are impacts that an organization has rarely experienced.

It is similar to the case of the disappearance of the Titanic ship back in the early 1900s. due to the nature of these potential phenomena, their consequences could be not only serious for an organization, but as the literature has evidenced a phenomenon of this nature could mean the death of a profitable organization.

However, this implausibility should not be a driver to make its importance unnoted; on the contrary, these are the types of circumstances that an interconnected system should aim to anticipate to prevent a catastrophic effect.

DEFINITION OF SUPPLY CHAIN RESILIENCE

FIGURE 40: FOUR QUADRANTS OF RISK

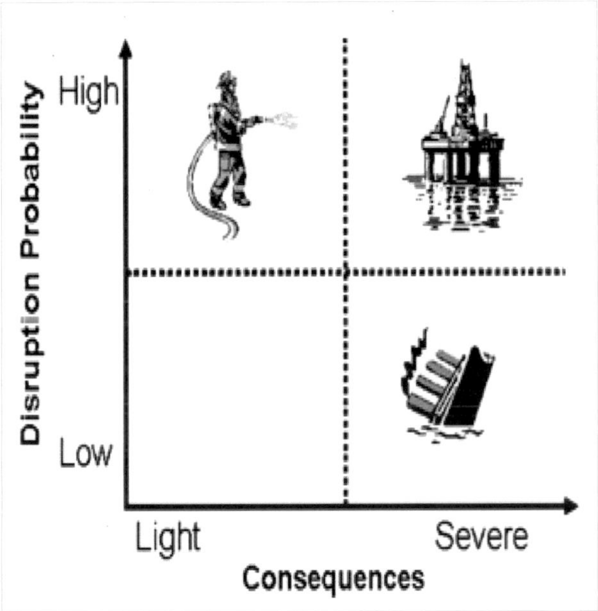

Source: Sheffi, Building a Resilient Organization, 2007)

As a notion that includes several aspects, the term 'resilience' is rooted in several disciplines. Flynn suggests that resilience is composed of the "four R's":

robustness, resourcefulness, recovery, review; however, these are but a portion of what supply chain resilience entitles (Flynn, 2007).

Although taking a strategic perspective, robustness is but one approach of addressing vulnerabilities, and despite the fact that recovery is a key point in determining resilience, not only is it mentioned as a general objective but also it lacks the depth to allow for a clear understanding and a potential manner of application. Concomitantly, risk management is but one of several disciplines from which resilience has emerged:

As the term 'resilience' is embraced by several distinct disciplines and domains, the evolution of the notion of resilience is ongoing. In the supply chain context, resilience has been characterized as the ability of a system to tolerate disruptions while retaining its function and structure.

Besides, resilience is a "critical feature" of a system; however, it is a modifiable aspect that will be continually affected both by the organization's experiences as by others. This strategic approach to supply chain resilience entails looking at the capacities of a system as a whole aiming at the continuation and permanence of the business activities in time. Although each supply chain has specific threats, it also faces mutual hazards to several different organizations. The concept of resilience refers to the ability of an organization to survive, adjust, and thrive in an ever changing and volatile environment.

Not being restricted to these disciplines, as vastly noted in the literature, it is important to note that the concept of resilience is separated from that of risk management. Generally, risk management will be framed by probability-based risks where the magnitude is also taken into account.

In the case of resilience, as the low occurrence probability means that the evaluation of importance will be completely different. The events covered within resilience are potentially catastrophic and, as such, require to be prioritized notwithstanding a low likelihood of materialization. That being said similar to risk management, resilience relies significantly on the identification of potential hazards.

Compelling business disruption may occur, not only because one of the organization's distribution channels, facilities, or workforce is put into disarray, but also when an aspect in its supply chain, its ecosystem, is jeopardized. There are various types of forces of change in the environment; these forces are the ones that cause for vulnerabilities within the supply chain.

With this assumption, the characterization of vulnerabilities is clarified in the business context: a factor leading an organization to become vulnerable to disturbances. Besides, disruptions refer to any occurrence with a significant severity and impact on operations, potentially leading to structural changes of the supply chain. Flynn also postulates that the component of urgency in terms of time is also a critical aspect of a disruption.

The ability of an organization to resist and address these vulnerabilities and, therefore, prevent, minimize, and overcome disruptions is given by a series of capacities a supply chain possesses. However, here, it is key to point out that an organization's abilities are not static.

Moreover, these capabilities are situational; as the environment for an organization changes, the adequateness of a current supply chain configuration will change as well. An organization "A" that is less resilient than organization "B" in the world of today might be more resilient than organization "B" in the world of tomorrow. Also, many of the actions aimed at a more resilient state will be in conflict with traditional business objectives.

This is the case given that the elements for a resilient system include agility, flexibility, adaptability, alignment, visibility, and collaboration, several of which not necessarily increase efficiency or reduce costs. Additionally, as already mentioned, it is vital to pinpoint that the relevance of each of these elements will change with the environment, and, therefore, the overall supply chain resilience will continually be changing as well.

This being said, on a tactical level, the improvement of one of these elements might seem justified, but it is global regard of all these that will define what is optimal.

Although several authors highlight the relevance of robustness, redundancy, safety, and many other solutions for becoming more "resilient", the focus when addressing this topic should be on broader characteristics that are aimed at a strategic level. Pettit et al. (2013) suggest in his list of capability factors fourteen specific capabilities that should be the focus of resilience, and, with that, his definition is supported.

Pettit's definition of resilience as the set of capabilities a supply chain possesses to bounce back from disturbances is very accurate. The grouping of these capabilities and analyzing them against the identified threats will give information on the competitiveness and future of the supply chain. However, given the fact that more than 80% of organizations are concerned about supply chain resilience today, the time has come to push the definition closer to the objective behind the word (Ubidia, 2014).

The topic of supply chain resilience has been debated primarily in a qualitative manner in the literature. However, currently, the focus of supply chain resilience is moving towards the improvement of the existent state of the system, and, therefore, a more quantitative and mathematical approach is required.

Nowadays, the focal point rests with the improvement of resilience, as the motion behind the word is fairly popularized. Nonetheless, you cannot improve what you cannot evaluate and measure. Even though the idea of measurement has been implicit in the definition of the concept, it is imperative to mention this as a necessary phase in order to foster the ongoing development of the discipline.

Furthermore, the measurement requires to be designed in order to include both qualitative measures referring to the configuration, management culture, supply chain design, and collaborative approaches as well as quantitative measures such as response time, efficiency, and forecast accuracy in line with Christopher and Peck's proposed six elements of supply chain resilience (2004): (i) supply chain understanding; (ii) supply base strategy; (iii) design principles; (iv) collaboration; (v) supply chain agility; and (vi) supply chain risk management culture.

These elements refer to a supply chain quantification and assessment, to be comparable to other organizations as that is the continuous way to evolve. Supply chain resilience is defined as the capacity of an organization to foresee, withstand, and adapt in the face of disturbances.

The main focus of the assessment is strategic, providing a view on allocation of efforts and development of capabilities in lieu of a current environment state. However, it is paramount to note that although measurement is a prerequisite, the granularity of the measure at this point is a secondary issue.

But more importantly, it is a measure, a constant reminder that a non-improving resilience means an increased risk of demise. Subsequently, supply chain resilience can be characterized as the metric of a system's capacity to bounce back from disruption or evolve towards a more desirable state after a disruption.

Measuring Supply Chain Resilience

The notion of risk has been the inception point for the evaluation of resiliency, and the idea of risk is embedded in resilience. Today the risks supply chains are facing are different in the sense that high impact/low probability risks exclude the use of predictive statistical tools and moreover the actual risk has been considered "unquantifiable." Resilience focuses on estimating the preparedness and ability to manage these low probability events.

Tools, such as the' Supply Chain Risk Radar'[27] developed by the World Economic Forum (2013), are continually striving to have a clearer view of the current hazards across industries by aiming to prioritize

[27] Supply Chain Risk Radar looks to prioritize aspects of supply chain disruptions, vulnerabilities and resilience as a basis for multi-stakeholder dialogue

aspects of supply chain disruptions, vulnerabilities, and resilience as a base for multi-stakeholder dialogue. As such, the tool provides input for understanding the up-to-date risks that appear across industries.

This, however, is, but the starting point in quantifying resilience, since each supply chain will have different competencies to respond to each risk and, therefore, will perceive each of them in a different fashion. An assessment of the current state of the supply chain is necessary to identify actual vulnerabilities based on the current risks.

The literature on supply chain resilience has gained importance in the managerial and supply chain context. However, the existence of models to measure the current status of an enterprise or supply chain resilience is very limited. As it has become clear from the existent articles on the subject, the measurement of resilience is not easy. Each organization presents specific vulnerabilities that need to be assessed on a case-by-case basis. Moreover, the impact of each potential disruption can vary greatly from industry to industry, organization to organization, and division to division.

In the same way, 'Vulnerability Maps' provide a compelling view of risks based on location. These are outstanding inputs for preparedness and mitigation of risks, as they provide information on the risks by region that a system should be concerned with. It is after identifying the risks that a system can compare its operations, structure, and measures to the current hazards.

The understanding of the existing risks is key in the assessment of the resilience of a supply chain. So far, most of the focus of the existent papers on the subject has been on the qualitative aspects of the resilient supply chain. More often than not, the analyzes of resilience have failed to reference the importance of the quantitative aspect.

Frameworks have targeted the evaluation of the organization under a limited view as they tend to focus on the operations of a particular business to aid tactical decision-making, but they fail to measure a global resilience for the extended enterprise. Therefore, the mentioned models are not sufficient for a supply chain wide evaluation.

The contribution of these studies, nonetheless, has been a reliable initial approach to the quantification of key subjects for supply chain resilience such as optimization of inventories for disaster-relief, supplier reliability, demand impact, amongst other things. However, the calculation has proven to be complicated and to require several large assumptions that limit the use of the models for strategic decision-making such as single product operations, fixed condition suppliers, and unlimited raw materials.

In the literature, there is also a series of measures and metrics that relate to supply chain resilience. Recovery time, level of recovery, and level of vulnerability to potential disruptions are just a few of several enterprise resilience indicators presented in different studies (Erol & al., 2010). These, although proven useful in the assessment of an organization, are limited to tactical policies within a supply chain.

An assessment of supply chain resilience means a global view not only of the vulnerabilities, and capacities of the focus organization but the combined vulnerabilities of its suppliers, manufacturers, and distributors. For these reasons, although tactical level measurements can be included in the assessment model, it is necessary to take a strategic approach in the measurement of supply chain resilience.

Vastly quoted frameworks and models in academia are highly conceptual and fail to provide a measurement scheme. Their focus, on the contrary, lies in the understanding of the capabilities, disruptions, and improvement actions.

Few models have been applied to serve as a strategic measure of supply chain resilience. Datta (2017) provides a model focused on the simulation of a supply chain as a complex system with the objective of proving the most appropriate set of solutions for a series of vulnerabilities.

This proposed model considers the flow of material, the information structure the supply chain manages, the decision-making structure, and the levels of strategic knowledge within the organization. Although the approach is instrumental in aiding decision making, it is not a measure of the current resilience state, but more a tool aimed at choosing the next step for a complex system. Nonetheless, it notes key considerations that should be accounted for in the measure of resilience.

The researcher, Datta, shows that resilience is not created only by the actions taken towards its improvement, but it depends on the complementary nature of these actions in the face of a disruptive environment. For this reason, she specifies that several good practices could end up canceling the positive effect if performance is not balanced with resilience.

Datta also makes a strong argument of the dynamic nature of supply chain resilience. As previously mentioned, resilience is to be measured under a given set of conditions and at a particular moment in time. As mentioned by Datta, "supply chain resilience is an ongoing process, which the agents have to work on through intelligent judgments continuously."

A well-known framework with a strategic approach to the assessment of a supply chain is the SCOR model developed by the Supply Chain Council (2012). This process-based model allows for a structured and straightforward assessment of different components in the adaptability, flexibility, and response capacity.

This allows the organization to focus on the identification, evaluation, and quantification of potential supply chain disruptions with the goal of reducing the impact and controlling the exposure to that risk. Five key phases are involved in SCOR's supply chain risk management : (1) establish context; (2) risk identification; (3) risk quantification; (4) risk evaluation; and (5) risk mitigation.

In the first phase, an understanding of the current situation of the supply chain is the main goal. This includes identifying and understanding the internal and external factors influencing the supply chain, figuring out relationships within the supply chain and defining the procedures, structure, and governance.

Once this is in place, for the second step, Risk Identification, the model seeks to identify risks from a series of different sources. At this point, there is no defined method for identification, but more of a suggestion of several ways. These include expert brainstorming, SC mapping, assessment surveys, amongst other things. A list is an expected output and the suggested categories of risks are fairly broad such as disruptions in supply, disruptions in demand, amongst other things.

For the quantification of risks phase, SCOR suggests an estimation of the importance of each risk. The standard calculation metric is the VaR (Value at Risk) = occurrence probability * monetary impact of occurrence (Supply Chain Council, 2012).

Moreover, SCOR evaluates each risk and, therefore, aims to decide the priority events to finalize the assessment by developing mitigation strategies aided by best practices.

FIGURE 41: SCOR RISK ASSESSMENT

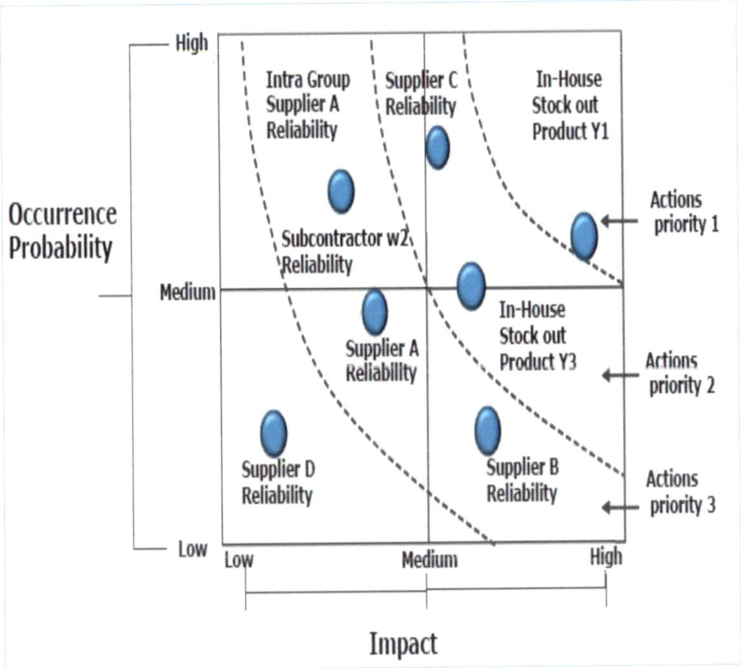

Source: Paul, 2010

Although the model is useful in the organization of the process, and the provision of a defined process flow for assessment, it is not effective for resilience calculation. The identification of risks is valuable as an input, but the calculation method and prioritization go back to the traditional definition of risk.

All those occurrences that are high impact - low probability are not prioritized or analyzed within the model. The best practices included in the model are useful and are even aligned with the improvement of resilience in certain cases; however, no linkages between the current supply chain characteristics (strengths/ weaknesses) and potential risks are explored to define vulnerabilities.

Additionally, for the HILP events identified during the initial steps, the analysis should be different, and the evaluation and mitigation itself will differ from the traditional way of approaching risks.

The SCRAM (Supply Chain Resilience Assessment Model)[28] is a proven framework aimed at identifying key capabilities, vulnerabilities and quantifying the

[28] The model assesses the supply chain on seven categories of vulnerabilities and fourteen different capabilities significant to resilience. Each of these has been validated for different industries and has been used by known global supply chains, such as Dow Chemicals.

supply chain resilience as a factor of these results. This framework developed by Pettit, Fiksel, and Croxton, (2008) makes use of the identified linkages between several vulnerabilities and supply chain capabilities to allow for useful analysis.

The tool is aimed at "...all business organizations, both for-profit and not-for-profit, global organizations and privately-owned small businesses, as well as corporations and government agencies..." (Pettit, Fiksel, and Croxton, 2008, p. 103).

FIGURE 42: TABLE VULNERABILITIES SCRAM

Variable	Vulnerability Factor
V1	Turbulence
V2	Deliberate threats
V3	External pressures
V4	Resource limits
V5	Sensitivity
V6	Connectivity
V7	Supplier/Customer disruptions

FIGURE 43: TABLE CAPABILITIES SCRAM

Variable	Capability Factor
C1	Flexibility in sourcing
C2	Flexibility in order fulfillment
C3	Capacity
C4	Efficiency
C5	Visibility
C6	Adaptability
C7	Anticipation
C8	Recovery
C9	Dispersion
C10	Collaboration
C11	Organization
C12	Market position
C13	Security
C14	Financial strength

The set of surveys delivered to a representative portion of the areas of the organization include a final question rating the relative importance of the factors to allow for a comparison between heterogeneous organizations and understand internal priorities (Lambert, 2006). The SCRAM is a straightforward and simplified method for the calculation of supply chain resilience. It details steps to follow and a proved set of linkages that are valuable in improving capability portfolio. Nonetheless, the model presents certain limitations that should be addressed.

The involvement of several different areas and levels of the supply chain enhance the subjective measure. Although the model provides an effective method for evaluation of resilience and the target of analysis and solutions is strategic in orientation, a clear strategic input is needed for more tailored results.

In a similar manner, the final resilience score presents a limitation. Since it is an aggregation of the entire factor scoring, it does not take into account the linkages between capabilities and vulnerabilities, finally resulting in a measure that focuses on averages and not on the actual state of the organization's group of key capabilities versus the key vulnerabilities.

Although still a useful indicator, a measure of the balance between actual capabilities in response to key vulnerabilities would be useful. Finally, an external view of the supply chain would be a valuable input, especially, for the vulnerabilities concerned.

This would allow for better information to use in prioritizing capabilities to develop. In spite of the mentioned limitations, SCRAM is today the main model addressing the issue of supply chain resilience measurement with a focus on strategy.

NON-FINANCIAL METRICS TO QUANTIFY SUPPLY CHAIN RESILIENCE

In operations management, resilience is characterized as a scope of organizational abilities to address prompt and sudden changes in the environment with proactive and reactive actions so as to envision, adjust, react, recoup, and gain from any disruptive event (Karl et al., 2018).

Consequently, developing capabilities to oversee organizational assets (tangible and intangible) is central to accomplish resilience in the supply chain, thereby achieving a competitive advantage. Supply chains are commonly known as a range of organizations which are associated through various processes and activities that yield value along the pipeline in the form of products and services to fulfill clients' expectations.

Under these circumstances, KPIs are utilized by organizations to address such processes and activities (local and worldwide). Nagyova & Pacaiova (2009) characterize KPIs as quantifiable metrics that mirror key factors that organizations must screen and oversee in order to make progress.

Acknowledging that KPIs from the supply chain perspective covers an expansive degree in the management area, and that any disturbances primarily affects the activities of any organization, it is worthwhile to explore also non-financial KPIs.

Moreover, financial KPIs are just as paramount to organizations as to the phenomenon of Supply Chain Resilience; however, it is mostly a result of non-financial KPIs (Ghalayini & Noble, 1996). According to Nudurupati et al. (2011, p. 281), non-financial indicators "[...] act as the leading indicators for the financial performance".

For this purpose, KPIs able to depict the present situation of an organization in combination with its supply chain should be set up, thus assisting management to oversee and assess processes (Maestrini et al., 2017).

To capture applicable metrics for needs and processes, each organization creates and determines its KPIs in terms of functional setting, obligations, and objectives (Chan, 2003; Cai et al., 2009). In the supply chain context, incorporating the goals at their various levels is a significant factor for the right selection of KPIs, which will give a more extensive perspective on the business.

According to the US Federal Emergency Management Agency (FEMA), around 40% of organizations that are seriously impacted by a disruption in the supply stream become insolvent (Federal Emergency Management Agency, 2016).

Notwithstanding the industry and size, supply chains face a horde of hazards in worldwide operations, which shift from digital risks to catastrophic events. As businesses enter a period of economic, geopolitical, societal, technological and environmental vulnerability (World Economic Forum, 2017), a wide range of unanticipated and unavoidable hazards may incur that may cause lead to major impacts to organizations throughout supply chains.

Acknowledging that market instability directly impacts supply chain activities, it is recognized that rivalry is no longer between individual organizations, yet instead between supply chains (Christopher, 2012). In this context, building versatility is an essential aspect for organizations, as well as for their supply chains.

Discussion Of The Non-Financial KPIs

Pre-disruption phase

The pre-disruption phase occurs before a possible disruption in the flow of goods or service in the supply chain. The constituent elements of resilience assigned to this phase is: security, knowledge management, visibility, information sharing, trust, risk management, and robustness.

- Agility: this refers to the organization's ability to respond rapidly to changes, which helps reduce the impacts of disruptions and enhances the response time. It is recommended that managers segment markets (based on volume, product variety, and demand uncertainty) to reduce costs and increase responsiveness to mitigate supply chain risks.

  Regarding this element, capacity utilization directly affects the speed of response to customers' demands. This is particularly important in times of disruption, considering that there might be available capacity to surplus the urgent requirements. It helps to gain flexibility and deliverability. Likewise, monitoring the stock level is a fundamental action during disruptions so as to guarantee that available stock will certainly cover urgent orders. A reduction in the order lead time leads to a reduction in the supply chain response time. In other words, it decreases the lead time from end to end of the pipeline and increases customer satisfaction.

This is also true for delivery lead time. Thus, measuring these KPIs can help managers act during disruption, and consequently in establishing creating supply chain resilience. Time is a very important element anywhere in the world. Thus, if the organization, as well as its supply chain, can deliver a product much faster than its competitors, customer satisfaction will undoubtedly increase. This is, especially, true in times of disruption.

- Information sharing: information sharing is also a widely recognized element for supply chain management under the effect of disruptions (Brandon-Jones et al., 2014). Sharing information in advance or in real time regarding organization assets or any events that might happen or have happened in a specific part of the supply chain can help managers to mitigate and overcome disruptions.

This is, therefore, the first step to achieve visibility. Supply chain KPIs must be linked to customer satisfaction, considering this information is needed to align customer requirement for product/service design. Additionally, monitoring stock level from suppliers and customers is also an important KPI to avoid or mitigate the bullwhip effect. To do so, information sharing about organizational assets is required among supply chain partners in order to allow upstream and downstream visibility (such as information on new project development or online order status).

It can consequently help managers to make better decisions to increase the supply chain profitability. To achieve this, information technology (IT) is typically used.

- Visibility: this is an essential element to achieve resilience, recognizing it is able to visualize conditions of inventories, demand, and supply from upstream to downstream of the supply chain (Christopher & Peck, 2004). It serves as a warning strategy that provides valuable time for organizations to align their capabilities to mitigate disruptive impacts. Due to this, this element is achieved and enhanced by using KPIs to monitor the organizational assets (tangible and intangible).

  Visibility helps to improve the supply chain performance, considering it can estimate the accuracy of supply/demand plan and assist managers to identify the key areas of improvement - whose impacts can be seen in the operating performance and, consequently, in the financial performance of the firm. Despite the fact that these authors do not point out a specific KPI for that, they affirm that a group of KPIs (financial and non-financial) can achieve an overall supply chain visibility.

- Trust: as previously highlighted, organizations that share information among each other throughout their supply chains increase their visibility, and consequently achieve better operational results than those who work isolated. For this to happen, they must trust each other, which promotes greater cooperation, conflict reduction, improved integration, and decision-making under conditions of uncertainty and ambiguity (Christopher & Peck, 2004).

Therefore, trust is considered a vital element to develop resilience due to the interdependence between organizations. Although trust is a conceptual idea, monitoring a set of KPIs can help develop it. Quality of delivered goods and On-time delivered products are KPIs that improve this element, considering it increases customers trust in the organization.

Supplier delivery efficiency is another related KPI as it aims to measure supplier's reliability in delivering materials. Thus, any failure on the supply side may simultaneously turn into a failure in service delivery performance. To avoid such an occurrence, trustworthy relationships should be built among supply chain partners. Inaccurate delivery greatly reduces the confidence of customers towards the organization.

It is a serious mistake that must be avoided. For this reason, Supplier rejection rate is also a KPI that can monitor trust.

- Robustness: this is characterized as the ability of the supply chain to support impacts arising from different disruptions or maintaining continuity of the process. Moreover, developing robustness helps organizations to sustain the operations' performance by being resistance to any major disruption. In this context, to assess the level of readiness robustness measures (e.g., inventory holding, redundancy, multiple sourcing) foster supply chain resilience proactively to absorb sudden shocks and reduce the potential disruption impact on performance.

  Therefore, monitoring the stock level is a way to prepare the organization for major and unavoidable breaks.

- Security: this is an essential element of any supply chain and should be designed in advance to mitigate the occurrence of disruptions. Developing security in operations means protecting organizations against different types of breakdowns related to the man-made disruptions - cyber-attacks or physical attacks (Scholten et al., 2014; Lam & Bai, 2016).

Taking this into account, security can be built and improved by creating partnerships or by monitoring KPIs among members of the supply chain (Hohenstein et al., 2015). On-time delivery is one of the KPIs that presented a co-occurrence to the security element in the literature. According to Chan (2003), it measures the product delivery performance by observing the percentage of orders delivered on or before the due date.

The same authors highlight that for delivery industries, customers rely on time delivery for key documents or goods transfer. Thus, monitoring this KPI can help predict future disruptions by observing the delay and promptly searching for the causes. Additionally, knowing that the result of this KPI influences the level of customer service (Katiyar et al., 2015), monitoring it can verify if customers feel secure and if they are satisfied, or if there is a need to develop practices to enhance security.

Ali et al. (2017) point out some security practices, such as security culture, cyber-security, layered defenses, creating public-private partnerships (PPP), and cooperative strategies with supply chain partners. By monitoring the on-time delivery of materials, supplier delivery efficiency is another metric that can help develop security by dynamically identifying if a specific supplier is not meeting the organizations' target (Chae, 2009).

This is vital because organizations typically expect their deliveries to be more important than pricing (Gunasekaran et al., 2004).

- Risk management: risk management is part of the supply chain resilience since many risks cannot be predicted or avoided. It can help reduce vulnerabilities through forecasting, monitoring, and mitigating risks. Thus, risk management culture must extend beyond the organization's boundaries in order to understand and share the risks among partners.

There is a special characteristic of cross-organization orientation in the supply chain risk management process that identifies and reduces risks not simply at the organization level, but rather focusing on supply chains. A lack of predictability and consistency in the flow of goods causes the effect of loading more inventories to avoid a lack of materials.

Thus, monitoring the stock level can help managers to mitigate risk and reduce inventory costs. Risks can also be mitigated by observing the level of order or delivery lead time, as it is vital in the context of customer service by serving as feedback to control the day-to-day operations.

Supplier delivery efficiency is also seen as a KPI to monitor risks since it can monitor and observe a drop-in supplier performance and consequent possible disruption in the flow of goods. Analyzing data from these KPIs can orientate managers to minimize the risk of supply disruptions.

- Knowledge management: understanding supply chain operations, needs and threats, as well as human and capital resources are key factors to creating a resilient supply chain (Scholten et al., 2014; Ali et al., 2017).

In addition, resilience must start being built in the pre-disruption phase through practices, such as education and training (Jüttner & Maklan, 2011) of knowledge acquired from past experiences (Pereira et al., 2014). Although all the identified KPIs can help build and enhance knowledge management by understanding the organization's environment, few KPIs presented a clear co-occurrence in the literature with this element.

Capacity utilization is a common non-financial KPI and plays a crucial role in determining the performance level in a supply chain by observing how well the capacity is used in the delivery of services (Katiyar et al., 2015). According to Cho et al. (2012), by understanding the capacity utilization throughout the months, it is possible to schedule better and use the resources to increase the efficiency of operations, and consequently reduce the product's final price with a view to increasing the market share.

Furthermore, the quality of delivered goods is also a key indicator since it affects customer satisfaction. By measuring the supplier delivery efficiency, it can be gauged if it is time to search for a more reliable or qualified supplier. Finally, there may be a relationship among different KPIs, such as capacity utilization, delivery lead time, and supplier delivery efficiency. Thus, building an understanding of the pattern of KPIs may help to develop knowledge management, and consequently supply chain resilience.

During-disruption phase

When the disruption has happened, KPIs can also be useful in monitoring the impacts and taking actions. The constituent elements of resilience in this phase are visibility, information sharing, collaboration, agility, flexibility, redundancy, and supply chain design.

Due to the fact that visibility and information sharing have already been discussed in the pre-disruption phase, their definition will not be mentioned in this subsection.

- Collaboration: this is the ability to respond to supply chain disruptions with partners through collaborative planning and information- and knowledge-sharing to coordinate the immediate response. Collaboration among all members of the supply chain is required, especially, in times of disruption.

Additionally, a high level of collaboration in supply chains can significantly help reduce risk, as the most significant challenge for managers is to create conditions in which collaborative work becomes possible.

- Quality of delivered goods and Supplier delivery efficiency are both KPIs that have clear co-occurrence in the literature. Collaboration is needed to increase the quality of delivered goods as customer satisfaction depends on the result of this KPI.

  It can also be observed that suppliers contribute directly to the production of services and are usually in direct contact with customers. Any mistake on the supply side might be replicated to the demand side. Hence supplier delivery efficiency is a KPI that should be monitored daily, especially, during the disruption time when the rate of this indicator drops typically.

  Damage return rate, as well as supplier rejection rate are additional KPIs that require collaboration between supply chain partners in order to reduce problems and improve its operational results for all of them.

- Visibility: knowing that even a simple supply chain consists of suppliers, manufacturers, distributors and customers, any requirement or change in the customer's order can take a long time to go through from one end to another. In this case, information might be distorted on the way, and many mistakes can occur. During a disruption, information must flow efficiently so as the supply chain has a great chance to succeed.

  Therefore, visibility for a supply chain is key for an accurate and fast delivery of information. Equally as in the pre-disruption phase, no co-occurrence has been found between a specific KPI and this element; nevertheless, it was affirmed in the literature that the management of a set of KPIs could undoubtedly generate visibility.

- Flexibility: this is the organization's ability to meet a growing variety of customer expectations without excessive costs, organizational disruptions, or performance losses. This element facilitates coordination processes and allows organizations to cope with high levels of uncertainties.

Thus, a resilient supply chain can deal with unexpected disruptions and disasters by reaching a relevant level of flexibility. Monitoring capacity utilization, on-time delivery of goods, and delivery lead time will help managers to 'flexibilize' operations to rapidly attend customers' needs.

Order lead time and delivery lead time also present an interesting co-occurrence for flexibility. They stated that once a customer gives an order to collect a package, a collector has to draw up a flexible route to collect the package within the established lead time.

- Information sharing: stock level and delivery lead times are vital KPIs to be measured and monitored. Being sure about the available stock and hence knowing the average time for deliveries, managers can better observe if the impacts from the disruption are increasing or decreasing.

By doing this, they keep up to date with the impacts, consequences, and supply chain partners' actions. Fast service and responding properly to customers' queries are crucial for keeping customers satisfied, and hence develop supply chain resilience.

- Redundancy: one alternative to overcome disruptions is to create redundancy of resources in the supply chain. This element is characterized by additional capacity (production, transportation, inventory, and storage facility) that can rapidly replace losses during unexpected events.

  Although additional stock is an opposite way of thinking to the Lean Management System, in which limited or no inventory is promoted, the redundancy may give time to managers to come up with an effective solution. During turbulent periods, holding extra resources is a key strategy for organizations to overcome critical and scarce situations caused by supply disruptions. Stock level is a KPI that helps managers to visualize how long the organization can maintain its operations in case a supply breakdown occurs.

  In this regard, safety stock is necessary, as there may be a sudden increase in orders or other interruptions can occur (which should be kept as low as possible) during manufacturing. However, it is crucial for the manager to determine the optimum resources necessary for every order. Redundancy can generate agility because customer orders can be placed immediately by means of available stock. It, therefore, reduces order lead time and hence increases customer satisfaction.

- Supply chain design: re-designing the supply chain is one of the elements that makes supply chains more robust, secure, and agile by focusing on location strategies. If this element is performed in real time, it is possible to mitigate risks and consequences of supply chain disruptions or even to avoid looming disruptive events.

Therefore, supply chains are mainly designed to achieve two objectives: cost optimization and customer satisfaction. As stated, security is an essential element of any supply chain and should be designed to mitigate the occurrence of disruptions. To build security, re-designing the supply chain is also required.

Thus, by monitoring the quality of delivered goods, failures can be identified from one source, and then actions can be taken to reallocate to another source. If the product is available from the warehouse, the order lead time can considerably decrease. However, if the slack of inventory is not possible (as discussed in the redundancy element), order lead time depends very much on the distribution network designed by the focal organization.

Therefore, during disruptions, this KPI can be kept as previously established if the supply chain is adaptable.

POST-DISRUPTION PHASE

After disruptions, KPIs should also be used to measure and monitor the recovery and lessons learned. The constituent elements of resilience in this phase are knowledge management, information sharing, visibility, and collaboration.

- Collaboration: to achieve a higher level of collaboration, order/delivery lead time and on-time delivery of goods should be controlled and optimized, considering that a collaborative supply chain is based on deadlines, including production and delivery times at all links in the chain (Scholten et al., 2014). Additionally, the supplier rejection rate can also be improved by increasing collaboration between supply chain members.

- Information sharing and visibility: following the same rationale in the prior phases, information sharing and visibility are the basis for achieving knowledge management. Therefore, the discussed KPIs (stock level, delivery lead time, and customer satisfaction) are also beneficial in the post-disruption phase.
- Knowledge management: knowledge management can be increased through optimization and control of the supplier delivery efficiency, considering that after disruptions, the identification of the supplier efficiency rate can help managers to make decisions about keeping the source or searching for another.

This rationale is also valid for the quality of delivered goods. Supply chain resilience is defined as the ability of the system to return to its original state or move to a new and more desirable state, after being disturbed". In this regard, monitoring the order or delivery lead time and on-time delivery of goods are ways to understand the supply chain behavior pre- and post-disruption, and thus develop strategies to achieve the more desirable state. Finally, customer satisfaction measurement, in which through after-sales monitoring, the assembler industry performs a diagnosis to check the critical points to be improved for future unexpected events.

SECTION XII: BANKS, SUPPLY CHAINS, WORKING CAPITAL

BACKGROUND

Working capital is considered as the nerve and lifeblood of any business concern; it is, therefore, crucial to accommodate the smooth operations of any business organization. A commonplace mistake when one is defining capital management is restricting its scope to portfolio management.

Capital management has a wider perspective, which includes portfolio management. However, business processes management is as vital for capital management as portfolio management. A particular opportunity for improvement in business processes applied to capital management is the management of physical hard currency.

Management of hard currency presents several challenges for banks (Yahaya & Bala, 2015):

- Availability of cash is a very sensitive matter, and, consequently, high safety stocks levels are required for guaranteeing customer satisfaction.

- Cost of opportunity for non-invested capital. Currency in branches and ATMs is not producing any profit, in times of high liquidity constraints, this is a very expensive resource that banks cannot afford wasting.
- Physical Currency demand can be modeled according to statistical patterns.
- Very high storage costs.
- Very high transportation costs.

And, the challenges above are very quasi identical as those confronted by other organizations with complex distribution channels (electronics, consumer, etc.). A particularly disturbing issue in supply chain management is the bullwhip effect; this refers to a trend of larger and larger swings in inventory in response to changes in demand.

Inefficient management of the supply chain with limited visibility increases variability of the client's demand one moves up the supply chain, as small changes in consumer demand can result in large variations in orders placed upstream.

As a consequence, the organization supports higher costs and offers poorer service. Unfortunately, it is not easy to find bankers who are aware of the potential improvements in applying supply chain management knowledge for capital optimization.

Many are aware of the opportunity that supply chain management represents for reducing transportation costs, but it is not obvious to the lion share of banks that this is also a component of working capital management.

CHALLENGES FOR BANKS

Working capital management is vital in the management of the bank's current account, which includes current assets and current liabilities. This explains the various forms of current assets and current liabilities adjustments, which a bank can make in order to meet its required working capital.

Working capital is of two types, gross type and net type. The gross type refers to the bank's investments in current assets, this means those assets can be converted into cash within accounting year, like short term securities, debtors' bills receivable, stock, and cash. The net type is the difference between current assets and current liabilities.

Current liabilities mean those claims of outsiders, which are expected to mature for payment within an accounting year, such as creditor, bank overdraft, and bills payable. Net working capital occurs when current assets exceed current liabilities. Working capital management is one of the important aspects of the bank's overall financial management.

This is because efficiency in this area is necessary in order to ensure the bank's long-term success, and achieve its overall goal, which is the maximization of owners' wealth.

The need for working capital to run the day to day activities of a bank business cannot be over-emphasized. We will hardly find banks or other organizations which does not require any amount of working capital.

Banks should earn enough return from their operations in order to be able to achieve their set goals, which of course includes the maximization of shareholders wealth, and, as such, to avoid the recent distress problems in today's banks which have its root basically from inadequate working capital caused by inefficient working capital management.

The banks have to invest enough in current assets for the success of their business. The need for working capital to run the day to day activities of a bank business cannot be over-emphasized. We will hardly find a bank or other firm which does not require any amount of working capital.

Banks should earn enough return from their operations in order to be able to achieve their set goals, which of course includes the maximization of shareholders wealth, and, as such, to avoid the recent distress problems in today's banks which has its root basically from inadequate working capital.

The inability of the bank to honor claims from individuals/customers demand may be the start a spiral of technical insolvent, and, therefore, it was for the avoidance of such embarrassing situation as liquidity, technical insolvency, high risk, and low profit that such theory, the liability management theory has been formulated in banking to guide bankers in their decision-making process.

There are many banks that are not able to meet the demands of their customers owing to their inability to manage their working capital efficiently and effectively. Their bank managers are consistently confronted with formidable challenges in striving to meet their level of working-owners investment in their banks.

The issue is related to the following:

- Abstaining from depositing money in the banks due to constant cases of banks distress by some would have been bank customers.
- Constant withdrawals of money deposited in the bank by their depositors owning to lack of confidence by customers.
- Inadequate cash reserves
- Non-compliance to rules and regulations in giving loans to their customers
- Non-payment of loans extended to customers on time, and sometimes not paying at all.
- Poor management of the available funds.

A certain level of working capital is required for operation in the banking industry. This level of working capital of a bank constitutes the cash holding or near cash holding or near cash assets required of a bank by a statue of the government or it should be noted however, that the level of working capital does not directly earn the bank any income when it is all allowed to be held in cash form, that is idle cash.

The main purpose of establishing commercial banks to operate is to generate profit for the shareholders. In that regards, banks as well as other profit-seeking enterprises strive to increase their net income and net present value of their assets. While recognizing this, the immediate concern of the bank manager is to provide satisfactory returns for the shareholders, and this requires holding a sufficient volume of safe and productive assets as well as sourcing for funds through the fast volatile and expensive available sources.

It should be noted however, that a bank does not possess full control over its assets, and, also, a greater part of its liabilities, the reality is that it possesses partial control on some current assets and current liabilities absolute control on some, and still lack total control over others. It is within this business environmental constraints and prospect that banks have to carry out their various adjustments to suit their long-run objectives. As already mentioned, there are two concepts of working capital (the gross and net working capital).

They have equal significance from the management viewpoint, the gross working capital concept focuses attention on the two aspects of current asset management:

- Financing current assets.
- Optimum investment in current assets

The consideration of the level of investment in current assets should avoid two danger points, the excessive and inadequate investment on assets. The investment in current assets should be in adequate form to enhance better performance. While the excessive investment in current assets should be avoided because it impairs a bank's profitability since idle investment earns nothing to the investor. On the other hand, inadequate availability of working capital can threaten the solvency of the bank when it fails to meet its current obligations.

Thus, the financial managers should have knowledge of the source of working capital funds as well as the investment avenues, where the idle funds may be temporally invested. The net working capital on the other hand has indicated liquidity position, and suggests that current assets should be sufficiently in excess of current liabilities in order to constitute a margin for maturing obligations within the ordinary operation cycle of a bank's business.

MANAGEMENT OF WORKING CAPITAL IS VITAL

Working capital management is an important component of corporate finance because it directly affects the liquidity and profitability of the organization. Indeed, interaction between working capital management practices and profitability should be a major area of research focus.

Any firm that puts inaccurate working capital management procedures into practice may likely face bankruptcy even though its profitability is constantly positive. Hence, it must be avoided to exceed from optimal working capital level by making an emphasis on the aim of profit maximization or just in direct contradiction, to focus only on liquidity, and, consequently, pass over to profitability.

In general, excessive levels of working capital will result in a substandard return on assets while an inadequate amount of it will lead to shortages and difficulties in maintaining day-to-day operations.

Today's competitive business setting demands economical use of resources, which underscores the importance of working capital management. It has been widely accepted that the profit margin of a business concern for the most part depends upon the manner in which its working capital is managed.

The inefficient management of working capital not solely reduces profitability but could ultimately result in distress and financial crises in an organization. An investigation regarding working capital practice in the banking sector is, therefore, of utmost importance. Working capital refers to the firm's investment in short-term assets.

The management of working capital is important to the financial health of businesses of all sizes. This importance is hinged on many reasons:

- First, the amounts invested in working capital are often high in proportion to the total assets employed, and so it is vital that these amounts are used in an efficient manner.
- Second, the management of working capital directly affects the liquidity and the profitability of a firm, and consequently its net worth (Smith, 1980).

Working capital management, therefore, aims at maintaining a balance between liquidity and profitability in conducting the day to day operations of a business concern.

The major concepts of working capital management are profitability and liquidity. They suggest that there exists a trade-off between profitability and liquidity. Thus, the association between profitability and working capital helps comprehend the link between profitability and liquidity, which represents the twin objectives of working capital management.

Although it seems that scholars who have written on this relationship have not completely synthesized their various hunches into a theory, there is noticeable consistency in the use of few guiding concepts in working capital management literature.

Also, working capital constitutes an important source of capital for small and medium scale enterprises as well as high flying organizations. In most developing countries, these categories of organizations face limited access to long term capital markets.

To overcome this constraint, these organizations tend to rely more heavily on owner financing, trade credit, and short-term capital bank loans. Hence, working capital position of such organizations is not only an internal firm-specific matter, but also an important indicator of risk for creditors.

Firms with high amount of working capital are able to meet their short-term obligations easily thereby decreasing the risk of default, and enhancing their borrowing capability. And, as an increase in borrowing capability is often perceived as an indication of a decrease in the cost of debt (and, also, in the cost of capital), it is possible to state that the efficiency in working capital management affects not just the short-term financial Performance (profitability) but also long-term financial performance.

A bank is the principal financial institution which assumes a significant role in the economic growth of a country. It is the spine as well as the foundation for the development of the country. Its principal operations are concerned with the accumulation of temporary idle money of the public for advancing to others for expenditures.

In other words, a bank is an institution that deals in money and its substitutes and, also, provides other financial services. Banks accept deposit and make loans, and derive a profit from the difference in the interest rates paid and charged, respectively. Depositors may be either individual or institutions.

These deposits may be current, saving or fixed, and the tenure depends upon the mutual agreements between the bank and with either an individual or institutions. The tenure of the loan may vary as per the demand, criteria, and the usefulness of the loan. Some banks also have the power to create money.

The principal types of banking in the contemporary industrial world are commercial banking and central banking. A commercial banker is a dealer in money and in substitutes for money, such as cheques or bills of exchange. The banker also provides a variety of other financial services. The basis of the banking business is borrowing from individuals and organizations, and, occasionally, receiving “deposits” from them.

With these resources and, also, with the bank’s capital, the banker makes loans or extends credit, and, also, invests in securities. The banker makes profit by borrowing at one rate of interest and lending at a higher rate, and by charging commissions for services rendered.

Working capital management is an important aspect of financial management. It is the lifeblood and controlling nerve center for any types of business organization because without the proper control of it, no business can run smoothly (Joshi, 2013).

The management of current assets and current liabilities is necessary for daily operations of any organizations. Thus, it plays a vital role in the success and failure of the organizations as it deals with the part of assets, which are transformed from one form to another during the course of the manufacturing cycle.

Therefore, the role of working capital management is more significant for every business organization irrespective of their nature.

Working capital management has to do with the administration of all aspects of current assets, namely cash, marketable securities, stock, and current liabilities. It is the functional area of finance that covers all the current accounts of the firm.

It is concerned with the adequacy of current assets as well as the level of risk posed by current liabilities. Working capital management is an aspect of financial management that seeks proper policies for managing current assets, liabilities, and, practically, for maximizing the benefits of managing working capital.

Commercial banks are the major financial institutions that play quite an important role in the economic development as well as in saving and investment sectors. Commercial banks are suppliers of finance for trade and industry, and play a vital role in the economic and financial life of the country.

They also provide an opportunity in the development of individual industries, trade, and business organization by investing savings and collected deposits. By investing the saving and collected deposits in the productive sectors, they help in the formation of capital. Besides, they also render numerous services to customers with a view to providing facilities to their economic and social life in the community.

A bank must always have cash balances in hand in order to pay its depositors upon demand or when the amounts credited to them becomes due. It must also keep a proportion of its assets in forms that can readily be converted into cash. Only in this way the confidence in the banking system can be maintained.

Working capital is the lifeblood of the organization. To sustain the confidence of the public, especially the customers, the organization should always get ready to meet its obligations.

Relevance Cash Flow Reporting by Banks

Banking operations are different than in most other organizations from a cash flow accounting perspective. One main operational activity in a bank, lending, leads to outflow of cash from the bank, and inflow when loans are paid back.

Another key function of banking is keeping deposits, which are assumed to flow into the bank, and can also flow out when demanded by customers. Interests received or paid on these loans and deposits are added to the cash flows. The accounting of these in- and outflows is problematic because the 'product' itself is cash.

From its start in August 2007 the financial crisis has been complicated to analyze and difficult to explain using the financial accounting information published in annual reports of financial organizations like banks.

Accounting is often said to be the language of business but something was missing in this communication. Most of the financial statements looked fine, even during the first year of the crisis until September 2008, when the world suddenly changed. The financial communication collapsed, and it became apparent that no common language for finance existed – the world's economy stopped.

To investigate why the global financial system almost melted down, multiple methods are required. The complexity of these events is large, and the unpreparedness of specialists in the fields of finance is perplexing. Emphasis in the debate has been on debt and the balance sheet of banks, but less focus has been put on banks' cash flow statements.

This is surprising because cash flow statements are prepared to illustrate the financial strength and the liquidity of a firm, by providing additional information about operations, investment, and financing activity.

Supply Chain Mgmt Affecting Cash Flow Bank

For organizations of all sizes and across all industries, cash is not only crucial—it is king. It sounds simple: In order to survive, businesses must ensure that payments are not going out faster than resources are coming in.

According to a recent study, however, not all businesses are following that formula: organizations that do monthly cash flow planning have an 80% survival rate—more than double the 36% survival rate for those only planning once a year (Huff, 2014). This discrepancy is partial because careful planning enables your organization to build up a solid cash reserve, and that reserve can serve as a life vest when you experience poor supplier performance, forecast errors, transportation breakdowns, weather disruptions, or other unexpected obstacles. And while cash is important for all businesses, cash flow management is especially vital for banks. They operate some of the largest, most complex and most secure supply chains in the world, transporting and storing cash across thousands of locations every day.

The cost of operating these supply chains extends to spending on all the equipment and services required to process, and distribute cash throughout the bank's network–from the central bank through to branches/ATMs and ultimately to customers.

These costs are high and growing due to two main drivers: the rising demand for cash, and the increasing use of more complex technology across the supply chain.

FIGURE 44: BANK AS USER OF SUPPLY CHAIN MANAGEMENT

Supply Chain Management

The Bank as User for SCM

4 Flows:

1. Material.	Money (Cash)	Banks are the solvency meter in societies. House of trust for several parties.
2. Capital.	Investments	Private Investments. Public Financial Needs.
3. Information.	Economic - Financial	Economic information to protect outside. Financial information to improve inside. Other Specific information (Legal, HR, ..etc.)
4. Man power	Employees	

2 Ends:

1. Suppliers.	Depositors
2. Customers.	Investors

Source: QNB

Relevance Banks Of Thriving Supply Chain Efficiencies

This reality—which many are calling the new normal—has changed the way organizations approach fundamental aspects of their business, such as cost structure, cash flow, and growth plans. Optimizing your supply chain—through better inventory management, increased automation and improved compliance controls—is one of the first steps toward achieving this leaner business structure and driving focused growth. Supply chain processes are the backbone of any organization's cash flow. Unfortunately, a supply chain can fail for a laundry list of reasons. Most organizations will face a supply chain crisis every four to five years. A crisis, in these instances, can easily cripple your business for weeks or even months, so facing one even every four to five years could be truly dangerous. Other common supply chain kinks include unavailable materials, changing government regulations, pricing pressures and natural disasters, and these obstacles also become increasingly more difficult to predict and prepare for as your supply chain gets more complex and global. As discussed earlier, having a solid cash reserve can help you stay afloat during supply chain crises.

However, optimizing and automating supply chain processes can also help prevent some failures, which can alleviate those cash crunches in the first place. And, that is just one reason why properly managing supply chain and cash flow via technology investments should be a priority to maintain health and stability across any organization. Investing in your supply chain can also be a growth avenue, given the current economic landscape. Despite being a few years removed from the depths of the recent Great Recession, businesses still face a relatively slow-growth economic environment. There is a new realism regarding economic growth, and the number of mid-market executives expecting moderate to robust economic growth has been steadily declining for several years.

FIGURE 45: BANK AS INITIATOR OF SUPPLY CHAIN MANAGEMENT

Supply Chain Management

The Bank as Initiator of SCM

Local Finance:

1. Cash Finance.	Overdrafts, Medium & Long Term Loans, Leasing, Factoring.
2. Contingent Finance.	Letters of Guarantees.

International Finance:

1. Direct Finance.	Direct Investments in foreign markets. Indirect Investments.
2. World Trade Finance.	Letters of Credit. International Documentary Collections.

Source: QNB

Manage Cash Cycle

The cash cycle is a highly interactive process and complex, where stakeholders with diverse incentives are compelled into cooperation while being closely monitored by a prudential authority. Banking institutions have to carefully balance cost management and cash availability in the tight framework given by the regulator.

Central banks around the world tend shift responsibility and cost to other players in the cash supply chain. For central banks security and integrity of the currency are key (Zink & Kemna, 2012). It is the central bank's role to monitor the resilience and efficiency of the payment system and ensure that banks and cash centers comply, even if this will result in increased cost and complicated processes on the part of the banks and cash centers.

Central banks have been delegating responsibilities and cost of the cash handling to other players in the cash cycle, such as cash centers, commercial banks and independent service providers (ISP), and even the end user. Today banks are more liable to secure the integrity of a currency, such as counterfeit identification and sorting out of unfit notes, than ever before.

Retail banks as well as regulators are pushing for payments by non-cash means to promote a cashless environment. As extensions of the government this push by regulators can be tricky, as they earn seigniorage on providing the economy with cash. Seigniorage can be seen as a de facto cash tax carried by the party holding the cash while it is not parked with the central bank. With tight sovereign budgets, governments will not readily give up this source of income or see it decrease.

Cash centers can create economies of scale when banks cooperate. Cash centers can either be run by a bank, a joint venture of banks, or independent service providers. The purpose of cash centers is twofold, firstly, to provide peripheral units such as branches, retailers and self-service terminals with the necessary cash, and secondly, to minimize the cost of unused cash in vaults by parking it with the central bank.

More than that, cash centers are often responsible for maintaining the quality of bank notes, with regard to counterfeit identification and currency fitness. Cash centers usually seek to optimize the cash supply chain as a logistics company would do–by minimizing the cost of storage while delivering goods on time. A major difference however is the security aspect in cash handling, which drives up cost through the need of armored transport, high cost for zero error tolerance machines and close regulatory supervision.

If cash centers are not well integrated in the cash cycle there are considerable double structures in banks, retailers and central banks, which slow down the flow of cash, cause high manual labor and thus drive cost.

Private cash centers can deliver value to banks by developing and managing the supply chain on lean principles, building on integrated logistics and optimizing efficiency through processing economies of scale by serving more than one bank. Cash centers and outsourcing companies with the necessary volume can invest in expensive counting and sorting machines.

However, it is clear that there is no "one size fits all" approach and service providers will have to customize their solutions to the individual bank's needs. Thus, cash centers and the supporting cash-in-transit (CIT) companies need to cater for banks' requirements, while maxing out synergies in the supply chain.

Retail banks carry the main risk for flaws in cash supply. Retail banks are the most vulnerable part of the value chain, because they carry the reputational risk as well as regulatory risk, e.g. for running out of cash, redistributing counterfeits, non-compliance, etc. As cash handling used to be a labor-intensive process with manual counting and sorting, retail banks benefit considerably from higher automation and from outsourcing labor-intensive work to cash centers and CIT operators.

Cash inflow, particularly cash deposits over the counter, is a key cost driver as it creates work duplication - it is processed at the counter, again in the back office to decide whether to dispatch surplus funds to the cash center, and again in the cash center itself. To date the cash deposit cycle has not been yet been fundamentally re-engineered. Automated deposit machines, teller assist terminals, etc. have helped to bring down cost.

However, many banks are still hesitant to fully outsource vital tasks, such as counting, forecasting, managing cash levels to ISPs and cash centers, as they are afraid to lose control over their funds and the risk of theft. But as long as the operations are kept in-branch they remain a cost factor.

While banks traditionally developed counting and sorting capabilities in-house, there is a strong trend to outsource those tasks today, or to at least centralize the operations and move it from the branch to an in-house cash operations center.

The latter though an improvement, results in a certain level of inefficiency due to the existence of double structures and the increased risk of transport and security.

Retail banks are now exploring new ways to manage the deposit process more efficiently, such as for example through cashless branches, where deposit collection is only executed via cash deposit machines and two-way ATMs. A number of retail bankers remain skeptical about the use of cash recycling machines which are able to sort deposited cash into separate cassettes according to currency fitness and potential counterfeits re-disbursing fit notes right away to the customer.

Although a wide range of retail banks are investing in those machines, many have not activated the recycling function but use it as combination of ATM and CDM.

Empowering customers with a choice can incentivize preferential behavior. In the end retail banks have to justify charges to the customer, who seeks convenience and accessibility, but is often not willing to pay for services that used to be free.

Retail banks for this reason need to balance the rising cost of cash with customer behavioral patterns, and offer alternatives and incentives to help customers adapt to change. We have seen the roll out of no-frills models, where customers only get basic services for free, and are charged extra for anything beyond. To this end, if customers are able to identify fees upfront, they can better select their preferred ways of banking.

Different supply chain models impact the speed and volume of cash in circulation. Basic supply chains, in which each bank deals directly with the central bank, result in long ways and require frequent secure transport. Long supply chains urge banks to hold more cash in stock in regional cash centers and branches, which increases the cost of interest, the risk of theft and the risk of delays.

Such a system will slow down the velocity of the cash cycle and thus force the central bank to print more bank notes. Velocity of cash refers to the speed at which cash circulates within the economy. A cash cycle with high velocity requires less cash in circulation, as inefficiencies such as unnecessary storage can be reduced.

As every bank works for itself, only larger banks will be able to stem the necessary infrastructure investments into the necessary technology and hardware. This will result in more manual intervention and duplication of processes.

In a more integrated supply chain, a joint venture of banks or an outsourcing company usually takes over the role of the cash center. With more banks using the same cash service provider, volumes increase, efficiency can be maximized and assets such as machines, better utilized.

Due to higher volumes integrated cash centers can invest in high quality machines, usually only deployed by central banks, in order to carry out the responsibilities according to central bank standards. An integrated cash center is able to balance the cash requirements of all clients and to minimize the cash in transport and storage. This increases the velocity of the cash cycle and (therefore) reduces excess cash, holding of expensive central bank cash, and transport.

Improving Cash Forecasting Accuracy

Cash forecasting has developed into a vital area for retail banks.

There are two approaches. One sees cash forecasting as too vital to be outsourced and wants to keep control over how much cash goes where. On the other hand, there are banks that feel comfortable in outsourcing cash forecasting to a service provider, simply giving the deliverables on how much cash should be in network and in the units.

Banks need to balance three factors to optimize forecasting:

- Manage the reorder levels for each and every ATM and branch
- Optimize the quantum of each reorder to avoid overstocking
- Balance this with the cost of transport

Cash demand forecasting models seek to balance the cost of transport, cash stocking and replenishment cost against interest rates, while guaranteeing the availability of cash in the channel network. Parameters of forecasting models are determined during the system implementation stage and should be held constant during the operation phase.

However, as business environment changes continually the model parameters must be flexible enough to be adapted quickly if necessary. The development of an accurate forecasting capability is a process of trial and error, usually with a safety buffer of excess cash. The latter should also be incorporated into the calculation, weighting it against cost and reputational damage.

The management of reorder levels is calculated along criteria such as user patterns, seasonality, special recurring events, and non-recurring events. Historical cash demand for every branch or ATM varies over time but usually follow weekly, monthly and annual cycles.

Other effects such as non-stationary behavior of users and additional factors, such as paydays, holidays, and seasonal demand in a specific area affect cash demand too. For example, people tend to draw relatively large sums of cash at the beginning of each month.

Before Christmas, Chinese New Year, and other holidays drawing rates rocket, whereas during other periods where people tend to take holidays, rates drop considerably. The location of ATMs is another key factor, while ATMs that are located in shopping centers, for example, are most frequented on Fridays and Saturdays, ATMs in the business district have low withdrawal volumes during the weekend.

Managing non-recurring events such as natural disasters provides the biggest challenge. Due to the earthquake and tsunami hitting the Japanese archipelago in March 2011, Japan's third largest banks experienced a week-long ATM and internet banking outage, as well as problems settling payments that created a backlog of 890,000 unsettled payments worth $10 billion (Zink & Kemna, 2012).

The bank was unable to meet the surge of demand for cash and money transfer orders by individuals and corporates who wanted to either withdraw cash for their immediate needs or send money to relatives or affected institutions in the disaster areas. In order to address the need for cash, the bank had to keep branches open over the weekend and a holiday, only allowing withdrawals of up to $1,200, for example. While such events cannot be forecasted, banks need to factor them into their cash planning and develop fast response mechanisms.

Above illustrations highlight that technology can help your organization with more than just inventory management; many organizations are installing solutions to automate their accounts payable and to facilitate purchase order collaboration.

Automating the accounts payable process enables business users to prioritize payments to suppliers that offer early payment bonuses - a practice called dynamic discounting. Similarly, software and systems upgrades can help reduce the processing time of purchase orders. In some cases, purchase orders are generated by the enterprise resource planning software and then shared collaboratively to ensure accurate information. This provides both sides with real-time visibility, creating fewer delays, minimizing over-ordering, enabling businesses to catch problems before they ship and helping them more quickly track change orders. Taking advantage of these efficiency opportunities is an easy step towards better managing a supply chain and improving cash flow.

Investing in the right technology can also help you plan ahead to reduce international shipping delays, as upgrading to a proper digital operating system - as opposed to manually re-keying data into several different systems - makes it easier to maintain compliance and regulation. Other software provides insight into the best inventory routes, your best-selling (and problematic) products and alternative vendors in order to minimize variety in your supply chain.

From building strong relationships to implementing new technology, there are a number of ways mid-market organizations can optimize and automate their supply chains to improve cash flow. Of course, it is important to note that making the decision to invest in automation technology or update a supply chain process is a cash flow decision in itself, and should thus be weighed carefully.

While it might be ideal for implementing all available functionality—automating as many processes as possible, for example—there are times when a simpler solution is the smartest. Software that is very complicated to integrate, for example, can require custom functionality and advanced training, which in turn means higher upfront costs and steeper support and upgrade costs.

It is also smart to spread out the technology costs when possible. Some software-as-a-service options are priced using a subscription model, as is the case with many cloud-computing solutions. Researching alternatives and carefully weighing all options can help ensure the solution investment is correctly configured.

Before making any decisions, however, a highly important recommendation for mid-market organizations is to perform a cost/benefit analysis to determine if the cost of failure is higher than the cost of prevention through tech investment. Still, supply chain solutions and automation technologies more often than not are worth the investment for growing mid-market organizations.

TAKE-AWAY LESSONS

Profitability is the ability to earn profit from all the activities of an enterprise. It indicates how well management of an enterprise generates earnings by using the resources at its disposal. It is composed of two words profit and ability. The word profit represents the absolute figure of profit but an absolute figure alone does not give an exact idea of the adequacy or otherwise of increase or change in performance as shown in the financial statement of the enterprise.

The word 'ability' reflects the power of an enterprise to earn profits, it is called earning performance. Earnings are essential requirements to continue the business. So, one can say that a healthy enterprise is that which has good profitability. Profitability may be defined as the net surplus of a large number of policies and decisions.

Under perfect capital market assumptions holding cash neither creates nor destroys value. The firm can always raise funds from capital markets when funds are needed without transaction cost. The trade-off theory suggests that organizations target an optimal level of liquidity to balance the benefit and cost of holding cash. The cost of holding cash includes a low rate of return of these assets because of liquidity premium and possibly tax disadvantage. The benefits of holding cash are in twofold:

- The organizations save transaction costs to raise funds and do not need to liquidate assets to make payments.
- The firm can use liquid assets to finance its activities and investment if other sources of funding are not available or are extremely expensive.

There is an agency problem associated with free-cash flow. Free cash flow problem can be somehow controlled by increasing the stake of managers in the business or by increasing debt in the capital structure, thereby reducing the amount of "free" cash available to managers.

As theory, the use of trade-off model cannot be ignored, as it explains that, organizations with high leverage attract a high cost of servicing the debt thereby affecting its profitability, and it becomes difficult for them to raise funds through other sources. Holding cash on that point is not only maintained by the smaller firm but also larger organizations.

So firm size does not matter when the question of bankruptcy interrupts the capital structure decision. Management of the banks should ensure as much as possible that (Yahaya & Bala, 2015):

a) the management should put more attention on their liquidity in order to maintain an adequate liquidity in the sector because the regression result of the study has empirically proved that the higher the current ratio the more the profitability of deposit money banks will increase, so, as a result of this, the listed deposit money banks should invest more in current assets because it will have a positive impact on the performance of listed deposit money banks.
b) the management should increase the quick ratio as the result revealed that the higher the quick ratio, then the higher the profitability of listed deposit money banks, therefore, the listed deposit money banks should try and maintain a higher quick ratio as it will have a positive impact on their profitability.
c) The management should reduce the amount held in cash as current assets and concentrate more

on investing them, so that it could yield a higher return rather than tie down the idle cash. If this is done, it will go a long way in enhancing the profitability of listed deposit money banks. The deposit money banks must develop necessary steps to utilize their idle cash and bank balances in order to meet their short-term debt obligations and operating cost thereby improving the current ratio. It is also shown from the analysis that the return on asset (ROA) is a better measure of profitability.

There are three major strategies for working capital management:

- Aggressive strategy: Profitability is the main focus of this strategy. Thus, it is characterized by high risk and high profitability (return) as the case may be. Aggressive strategies involve long-term funds, which are utilized only to finance fixed assets and part of permanent working capital, while short-term funds are utilized to finance temporary working capital. It saves the interest cost at the cost of high risk.

- Conservative strategy: This strategy involves low risk and profitability. In most cases, it is termed a risk-free approach to working capital financing. Working capital here is financed by long-term sources of funds such as term loans, equities, etc.

- Hedging/Marching strategy: This strategy can also be termed the hedging strategy and it involves an equal level of risk for the same level of return/profitability, i.e., in this strategy, each asset would be financed by a debt instrument of almost the same maturity.

SECTION XIII: SUPPLY CHAINS AND NETWORKS IN BANKING

CHAINS, STAKEHOLDERS, AND NETWORKS

Due to rapid technological advancement, organizations with a basic supply chain can develop this chain into a more complex structure involving a higher level of interdependence and connectivity between more organizations, this constitutes a supply-chain network. And, as such, a supply-chain network is an evolution of the basic supply chain. In practice, organizations, including banks, are often part of a larger network of organizations, a supply-chain network can be used to highlight interactions between organizations; they can also be used to show the flow of information and materials across organizations. In an effort to improve their competitive position in a rapidly changing marketplace, many organizations have replaced their traditional supply chains with extended supply chain networks built on a foundation of supply chain collaboration. These extended networks require the use of decision support tools and technologies to improve both operating efficiencies and customer service, but many organizations have struggled to realize the expected benefits of these tools and the increased collaboration. Organizations need to adopt an integrated strategy of people, processes, and technology to achieve their competitive supply chain goals. By introducing the term network in supply chains, it allows organizations to look at the bigger holistic picture; giving them a better understanding of the flow of materials and information (cf. and, in the case of banking organizations, data and cash). Often organizations focus only on their organization; what they manufacture or provide and not what the end customer receives. Looking at a supply chain as a network enables organizations to look at the overall movement of materials/information from start to end, allowing organizations to see the value in creating partnerships; and the value in working together to ensure the best possible value is provided to the end-customer. The notions of networks and supply chain management need to be associated with a systems approach, whereby the network is viewed as systems levels of supply chain management that are identified as the combination of internal supply chain, a dyadic (interactive) relationship, external supply chain, and an inter-business network. At the end of the day, supply chains and supply networks both describe the flow and movement of materials & information, by linking organizations together to serve the end-customer.

'Network' describes a more complex structure, where organizations can be cross-linked and there are two-way exchanges between them; 'chain' describes a simpler, sequential set of links (Harland et al., 1997). In order to understand a supply chain network; one needs to understand what a supply chain is. As already defined previously, a supply chain is a series of processes linked together to form a chain.

FIGURE 46: SUPPLY CHAIN EXAMPLE FOR APPLE JUICE

Orange farm	Orange juice plant	National distribution center	Regional distribution center	Shops, supermarkets, vending machines

The above diagram is an example of a simplified supply chain; the supply chain shows the movement of material flow from the orange farm right through the production process to the end users.

FIGURE 47: EXAMPLE SUPPLY CHAIN NETWORK ORANGE FARM

⇐Upstream						Downstream⇒
Inbound logistics			Internal logistics	Outbound logistics		
Oran. farm	Oran juice plant	Oran. juice bottling plant	Local firm	Nat. distrib. center	Region distr. center	Shops, superm. Vending mach.
Oil drill	Plastic manuf.	Label print				
Tree plantation	Paper manufacturer					

A supply chain network shows the links between organizations, and how information and materials flow between these links. The more detailed the supply chain network the more complex and web like the network becomes. The above example demonstrates a simplified version of a supply chain network of an Orange juice organization. The organization will have an upstream network and a downstream network.

Typically, organizations are linked via two types of flows:

- Material flow: Is the movement of goods from raw primary goods (such as Wool, Trees and Coal etc.) to complete goods (TV's, Radios and Computers) that are to be delivered to the final customer.

- Information flow: Is the demand from the end-customer to preceding organizations in the network.

To get a complete picture of an organizations supply chain network; information & material flow should be mapped; inefficiency can then be located and removed.

Supply Chain and Value Networks In Banking

All primary banking activity can be divided into three roles: supplier, producer and retailer. Currently, almost every bank performs all three roles. They supply resources, data and core competencies—such as risk management, KYC (know your customer) procedures and balance sheet.

Internally, they produce products, such as mortgages, personal loans and technical tools. And they retail through branch, telephony, online and mobile channels. To respond to the coming change, banks need to know for which of those roles they have significant competitive advantage and take a corresponding strategic approach. Similar to recognizing their strengths, banks must recognize their weaknesses and improve, or more likely outsource when necessary.

And, hundreds and thousands of funds are being regularly transferred from one region of the world to another within each day. Banks perform the necessary function of keeping money safe and secure for people and therefore, the processes in place require a lot of mediators.

The involvement of these mediators is what makes the industry more expensive. Moreover, with the involvement of too many people and manual processes, the chances of errors and frauds always increase.

As already alluded to in a previous section, here are some excellent chains that are mentioned in the banking industry:

- Bank Accounts - Saving Account, Current Account, etc.
- Plastic Cards - Debit Card, Credit Card, etc.
- Digital Banking - Enjoy secure access to your accounts 24/7.
- Money Transfer - Reliable options to transfer money on a global scale.
- Personalized Banking - Monitor and manage your working capital.
- Loans - Fast and flexible loans suits to you.

- Managing Bank Accounts- Enjoy real time access to all your bank accounts from anywhere in the world.
- SME Toolkit - How to get financing for your business.

FIGURE 48: PHYSICAL AND FINANCIAL SUPPLY CHAINS

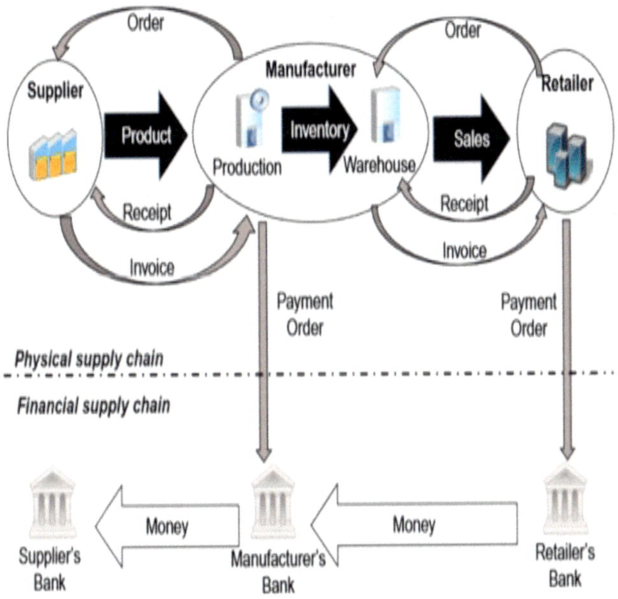

<u>Source</u>: International Journal of Operations & Production Management

Previous sections have in detail defined the contours of supply chains in banking. But, similar to many consumer-facing industries, banking has entered a new era. Changing customer attitudes and continued volatility are compounded by increased mobility and the relentless rise of FinTech ventures.

Technologies are now disruptive—no longer being applied to fix specific business demands, but must be integral to business strategy and exploited for maximum impact. The combination of these factors is creating a fundamental shift in the structure of the banking industry as it is known. And, banks need to incorporate in their supply chain mindset also a value network perspective.

A value network A set of interdependent connections (relationships) between multiple nodes (members) interacting with each other for mutual benefits (tangible and intangible). Products, services, technology as well as information and knowledge can be exchanged among members. Value networks can grow across adjacent or complimentary businesses and provide composite customer experiences that meet unfulfilled needs. Banks need to adopt a flexible, customer-centric strategy.

They must become more agile, so that they can be more responsive to cultural change, manage a digitally savvy workforce, keep pace with regulatory and security demands and explore the technologies that underpin the new wave of value networks. And, incumbent banks have three main limiting factors in tackling their changing landscape:

1. A gap in technology acumen and expertise in the "decision rooms" whereby board members lack professional experience in technology. Since technology is no longer an enabler of strategy, but serves as a critical competitive advantage, improved technology capabilities could help banking leaders make informed decisions, faster and more effectively.
2. A gap in the speed of change and time to act: Incumbents have strength in being large, well-structured organizations, but are weak in terms of agility and speed to change. Timing is crucial. Banks should evaluate their degree of "readiness" (in terms of technology, business, compliance and overall agility to change) and take action accordingly. Banks need to accelerate the pace of innovation and revitalize their businesses if they are to remain competitive.

3. A cultural attitude and aversion to change and risk: Start-ups may have the advantage of having less to lose, but being too conservative is risky in a fast-changing, digitally disruptive environment—culture must not be a barrier to the concept.

By developing value networks, banks can reconfigure each "business line"—and its value chain—to compete with the best disruptors by being focused, faster, better, and cheaper. Incumbents can take advantage of their unique scalability skills, capital availability and customer reach to unleash excellence and compete at the next level. Managing a portfolio of digital platforms that provide digital financial solutions is becoming a new strategic imperative. Banks seeking inspiration around value networks would do well to look to the East: (Machi et al., 2016)

> For example, Chinese banks and eCommerce players are already capturing customer data to drive increased sales and revenues through extended value networks. For example, the leading personal financial services provider in China, PingAn, has developed a value network to connect its various eCommerce and financial services businesses. The company now has 3,600 specific data elements related to a customer that

it can use to better segment and cross-sell products and services. PingAn is also using innovative technology platforms to connect its value network—such as P2P lending, enterprise-wide customer loyalty and connected payments across services through their wallet.

Design Of Supply Chain Network

Supply chain network design is a powerful modeling approach proven to deliver significant reduction in supply chain costs and improvements in service levels by better aligning supply chain strategies. It incorporates end-to-end supply chain cost, including purchase, production, warehousing, inventory and transportation. While this is considered a strategic supply chain planning initiative, organizations can gain competitive advantage by running supply chain network scenarios, evaluating and proactively implementing changes in response to dynamic business scenarios like new product introduction, changes in demand pattern, addition of new supply sources, changes in tax laws and so on.

The primary purpose of a supply chain network design is to assess organizational policies and programs and to meet targets to accomplish long-term strategic objectives, and most business units or functional areas within an organization are impacted by a network design project. It is paramount to recognize that an organization's network determines its supply chain efficiency and customer satisfaction.

Designing an optimal supply chain network means the network must be able to meet the long-term strategic objectives of the organization. Most business units or functional areas within a company are impacted by a network design project. When designing a supply chain, the following steps must be followed:

1) Define the business objectives,

2) The project scope must be defined,

3) The form of analyses to be done must be determined,

4) Determine what tools will be used,

5) Finally, Project completion, the best design. In practice, when transposed to the banking realm, there are five strategic questions that need to be answered by a banking organization:

1. What business is the bank in and why?
2. How should value be added to the business?
3. What are the target markets?

4. What are the products/ services and why will customers buy from the bank?
5. What capabilities are needed to assure that the bank adds value and differentiates?

Most banking institutions develop strategies for target markets and products #3 and #4. Some at least consider #1 and #2. Few banking organizations resolve #5 effectively. This is generally because operations strategies are not developed or implemented with the same scenario plan or rigor that is given to the more often seemingly interesting issues of markets and products.

The alignment of business and operations strategies is often weak or non-existent. Mission and vision statements, plans, goals, objectives, and performance measures while important for driving execution, most often do not ensure that capabilities will be built for scenarios from the business strategies.

Therefore, banking organizations do not always have carefully developed alternatives for customer demand, new channels, competition, supply risks, and product development. Hence, achieving clear and sustained alignment between operations execution and the plans derived from business strategies is challenging.

Leadership understands the complexities involved, but are concerned that 90% of business strategies are not implemented as intended. They are beginning to understand that supply chains are about more than logistics regarding the buying and selling of goods, they are about competitive differentiation and profitable business growth.

SECTION XIV: DIGITAL BANK, SUPPLY CHAIN RISK MGMT

INTRODUCTION

It is time to focus on the transformation of the whole supply chain process, not just in terms of increases in efficiency. The traditional linear nature is increasingly misaligned with the more networked nature of today's global production.

A digital supply chain can be described as "a customer-centric platform model that captures and maximizes utilization of real-time data coming from a variety of sources. It enables demand stimulation, matching, sensing and management to optimize performance and minimize risk." It doesn't matter whether the goods or services are digital or physical. "It refers to the way that the supply chain process is managed..." (DSCI, 2017).

The traditional supply chain has evolved over the years as a crucial process used by many organizations for the production, handling, or distribution of their products or services. Traditional supply chains generally comprise five separate back-office functions: transport, warehousing, purchasing, marketing and finance.

Their key objective has been to improve the efficiency of getting goods and services from suppliers to customers, through a series of intermediate steps including manufacturing, distributors and retailers. However, these supply chains were quite fragmented, with limited interactions and information sharing among their various functions and steps

Over the past couple of decades, the explosive growth of the Internet has made it much easier for organizations to transact with each other around the world. The connectivity and universal reach of the Internet has enabled organizations to integrate and better coordinate all their various processes, as well as to go beyond the boundaries of the firm and develop highly sophisticated global supply chains.

Vertically integrated organizations have evolved into virtual enterprises, increasingly relying on supply chain partners for many of the manufacturing and services functions once done in-house.

Successful organizations will need to take advantage of new management practices, a continuously expanding data reservoir, and new technologies relevant to digital supply chains if they are to achieve future competitive advantage and delight their customers.

The key element cited by all of the organizations involved with this initiative is the front side People running the global supply chain of the future [will have] to perform a front side flip. That is, they will have to flip their focus to the customer-facing side -- the front side -- of the business.

The evolution from traditional to digital supply chains is driven by five game changers (Wladawski-Berger, 2017):

I. Addressing Risks. Information sharing and transparency enhance the capacity to see and address risks in a digital supply chain, including cyber-attacks, IP theft, and compliance issues.

II. Blockchain. Blockchain technologies hold great promise for digital supply chains over time, increasing the speed, security and accuracy of financial and commercial settlements; tracking the supply chain lifecycle of any component or product; and securely protecting all the transactions and data moving through the supply chain.

III. Digital Manufacturing and Delivery. Several breakthrough technologies will have a major impact on manufacturing and delivery over the next several years. Foremost among them is the emerging robotics revolution. Robots are computers that have both a brain and a body. A robot's capabilities are defined by what its brains and body can jointly do. AI advances have greatly benefited the robot's brains, as they have those of all other computers. In addition, the electromechanical components used in robotic devices are also advancing rapidly. Innovations in their design and in the algorithms that guide their perception, reasoning, control, and coordination are driving the development of a wide variety of industrial and personal robots. 3D printing is another promising technology with the potential to significantly impact the supply chains of a growing number of industries, including medical devices, automotive and retail. So are drones, which are already being deployed in infrastructure maintenance, security, assets monitoring and other tasks across a number of industries.

IV. Purposeful Collaboration. Collaborative software or groupware, designed to help people work closely together to achieve a common goal, is critically important for an integrated supply chain to succeed. Purposeful collaborations are the only way to reconcile the competing goals and objectives of the various participants in a supply chain, both within the different departments of an organization, as well as across the external ecosystem of partners.

V. Real Time Big Data and Analytics. The most important factor enabling the ability to flip to the customer-facing front side is the massive amounts of data now at the disposal from a wide variety of sources, including mobile devices, sensors, IoT systems, and social media, along with the sophisticated tools being developed to collect, analyze and use the data. These data and tools will enable organizations to make better decisions across the overall supply chain, including product design, manufacturing, distribution and sales.

To help organizations in their evolution toward digital supply chains, the following framework based on four major imperatives can be proposed (DSCI, 2017):

1. Managing Demand -- Real-Time Continuous Engagement with Customers. Executing the front

side flip is difficult for supply chain organizations that have focused exclusively on procurement, manufacturing, shipping and logistics... Demand forecasting will improve as people manage new sources of data to create and make better DSC decisions. In many organizations, the demand forecast is developed by the sales team based on existing data and intuition. In the near future, winning organizations will use artificial intelligence to match demand and supply. Inventory will be reduced by as much as 30% as organizations build algorithms that automatically replenish based on observable demand signals.

2. Managing People -- Cultural and Organizational Shift. All organizational change is derived from people willing and capable of moving to the future. This is certainly true for the journey to a digital supply chain, which will require education, communication, organizational redesign, process redesign and bringing in new personnel... The crucial change for the supply chain division is to shift from being exclusively a support organization and instead realize

decision-making rights, similar to the line leaders that are running P&Ls.

3. Managing Risks -- Enhance Risk and Management Capability. The Digital Supply Chain will provide new, more sophisticated ways to identify risks. Big data will create early warning systems allowing organizations to become more proactive and preventative. Organizations will be able to mitigate risks more effectively. Organizations will also be able to go beyond risk mitigation and compliance to turn risk into a competitive advantage by outperforming other organizations in a targeted area... The management challenge is determining where to mitigate risks and where to excel and turn risk into a competitive advantage.

4. Managing Technology -- Enterprise/Platform Agility and Customer Visibility. As discussed earlier, data is growing at an unprecedented rate. "Much of this data will contribute to the DSC and help with everything from product design to shipping and delivery to sales and distribution.

The sub-story is that organizations today already have too much data and cannot readily integrate and use it to support management decisions... Almost all of the organizations report that they have trouble getting clean data today that is reliable for future Digital Supply Chain management and decisions. This has to be quickly fixed because it is the basis upon which the new sources of data will sit.

DISRUPTION OBJECTIVES

- Asset management and insurance are also on the disruption radar: although a high level of disruption triggered by FinTech is already beginning to reshape the nature of lending and payment practices, a second wave of disruption is making inroads in the asset management and insurance sectors.

  Nearly half of insurers and asset and wealth managers consider their respective industries to be the most disrupted.

  When asked which part of the banking sector is the most likely to be disrupted by FinTech over the next 5 years (PwC, 2016), 74% of insurance organizations identified their industry, while only 26% of players from other sectors agreed; 51% of asset managers said their industry would be disrupted, while only 31% of other players agreed. However, there seems to be a perception gap here; professionals from other industries do not see the same level of disruption in these areas.

The fact that only insiders are aware of this situation, while outsiders do not perceive it could indicate that the disruption is in its very early stages. Even so, venture capitalists are looking very closely at start-ups dedicated to reinventing the way money is invested and insurance is bought. The pace of change in the global insurance industry is accelerating more quickly than could have been envisaged.

The industry is at a pivotal juncture as it grapples with changing customer behavior, new technologies and new distribution and business models. The investment industry is also being pulled into the vortex of vast technological developments.

The emergence of data analytics in the investment space has enabled organizations to hone in on investors and deliver tailored products and automated investing. Additionally, innovations in lending and equity crowdfunding are providing access to asset classes formerly unavailable to individual investors, such as commercial real estate.

- Mostly consumer banking and payments: in keeping with changes already underway, the majority of the survey participants see consumer banking and fund transfer and payments as the sectors most likely to be disrupted over the next five years. In consumer and commercial lending, for example, the emergence of online platforms allows individuals and businesses to lend and borrow between each other.

- Lending innovation also manifests itself in alternative credit models, use of non-traditional data sources and powerful data analytics to price risks, rapid customer-centric lending processes, and lower operating costs. In recent years, the payments industry has also experienced a high level of disruption with the surge of new technology-driven payments processes, new digital applications that facilitate easier payments, alternative processing networks and the increased use of electronic devices to transfer money between accounts.

- Customer centricity Is fueling disruption: as clients are becoming accustomed to the digital experience offered by organizations such as Google, Amazon, Facebook and Apple, they expect the same level of customer experience from their financial services providers. FinTech is riding the waves of disruption with solutions that can better address customer needs by offering enhanced accessibility, convenience and tailored products. In this context, the pursuit of customer centricity has become the main priority and it will help to meet the needs of digital native clientele.

  Over the next decade, the average bank consumer profile will change dramatically as the Baby Boomer generation ages and Generations X and Y assume more significant roles in the global economy. The latter group, also known as "Millennials" (those born between 1980 and 2000), is bringing radical shifts to client demographics, behaviors and expectations.

Its preference for state-of-the-art customer experience, speed and convenience will further accelerate the adoption of FinTech solutions. Millennials seem to be bringing a higher degree of customer centricity to the entire financial system, a shift that is being crystallized in the DNA of FinTech organizations.

EMERGING FINTECH TRENDS ON THE RADAR

To help industry players navigate the changes in the banking, fund transfer and payments, insurance, and asset and wealth management sectors, the main emerging trends that will be most significant in the next five years in each area of the banking industry have been identified.

Overall, the key trends will enhance customer experience, self-directed services, sophisticated data analytics and cybersecurity. However, the focus will differ from one banking segment to another. The methodology is based on Neos[29] insights of emerging

---

[29] Neos is a next generation platform for strategy consulting that helps to understand the transformative ecosystem and technological potential of blockchain. The platform provides real-time content and insights to build proper strategy, business model and implementation. The solution delivers customized consulting and analysis based on

FinTech trends for each financial segment (PwC, 2016). Industry leaders assessed which trends in their segment will be important for their business over the next five years and indicated their likelihood to respond to each of them.

Renewed Digital Customer Experience

Banks are moving towards non-physical channels by implementing operational solutions and developing new methods to reach, engage and retain customers. As they pursue a renewed digital customer experience, many are engaging in FinTech to provide customer experiences on a par with large tech organizations and innovative start-ups.

The trends that financial institutions arc prioritizing in the banking industry are closely linked. Solutions that banks can easily integrate to improve and simplify operations are rated highest in terms of level of importance, whereas the move towards non-physical or virtual channels is ranked highest in terms of likelihood to respond.

---

such preferences as emerging technologies, business models, processes, and trends.

Banks are adopting new solutions to improve and simplify operations, which fosters a move away from physical channels and towards digital/mobile delivery. Open development and software-as-a-service (SaaS) solutions have been central to giving banks the ability to streamline operational capabilities.

The incorporation of application program interfaces (APIs) enables third parties to develop value-added solutions and features that can easily be integrated with bank platforms; and SaaS solutions assist banks in offering customers a wider array of options – which are constantly upgraded, without banks having to invest in the requisite research, design and development of new technologies.

The move towards virtual banking solutions is being driven, in large part, by consumer expectations. While some segments still prefer human interactions in certain parts of the process, a viable digital approach is now mandatory for lenders wishing to compete across all consumer segments.

Online banks rely on transparency, service quality and unlimited global access to attract Millennials, who are willing to access multiple service channels. In addition, new players in the banking market offer ease of use in product design and prioritize 24/7 customer service, often provided through non-traditional methods such as social media.

Traditional banks may already have many of the streamlined and digital/mobile-first capabilities, but they should look to integrate their multiple digital channels into an omni-channel customer experience and leverage their existing customer relationships and scale.

Banks can organize around customers, rather than a single product or channel, and refine their approach to provide holistic solutions by tailoring their offerings to customer expectations. These efforts can also be supported by using newfound digital channels to collect data from customers to help them better predict their needs, offer compelling value propositions, and generate new revenue streams.

Fund Transfer, Ease Of Payments, Security

The major trends for fund transfer and payments organizations are related to both increased ease and security of payments. Mobile smartphone adoption is one of the drivers of changing payments patterns. Today's mobile-first consumers expect immediacy, convenience and security to be integral to payments.

In the culture of on-demand streaming of digital products and services, archaic payment solutions that take days rather than seconds for settlement are considered unacceptable, motivating both incumbents and newcomers to develop solutions that enable the transfer of funds globally in real-time.

End users also expect a consistent omni-channel experience in banking and payments, making digital wallets key to streamlining the user experience and enabling reduced friction at the checkout.

Finally, end users expect all of this to be safe. Security and privacy are paramount to galvanizing support for nascent forms of digital transactions, and solutions that leverage biometrics for fast and robust authentication coupled with obfuscation technologies, such as tokenization, are critical components in creating an environment of trust for new payment paradigms.

Speed, security and digitization will be growing trends for the payments' ecosystem. In an environment, where traditional loyalty to financial institutions is being diminished and barriers to entry from third parties are lowered, the competitive landscape is fluid and potentially changeable, as newcomers like Apple Pay,

Venmo and Dwolla have demonstrated (Bank Innovation, 2018).

Incumbents that are slow to adapt to change could well find themselves losing market share to organizations that may not have a traditional payments pedigree, but that have a critical mass of users and the network connectivity to enable payment experiences that are considered at least equivalent to the status quo.

While most of these solutions "ride the rails" of traditional banking, in doing so they risk losing control of the customer experience and ceding ground to innovators, or "steers", who conduct transactions as they see fit.

Technology And Asset & Wealth Management

The main trend the asset and wealth management industries are focusing on at present is the increased sophistication of data analytics to identify better and quantify risk.

The proliferation of data, along with new methods to capture it and the declining cost of doing so, is reshaping the investment landscape. New uses of data analytics span the spectrum from institutional trading and risk management to small notional retail wealth management.

The increased sophistication of data analytics is reducing the asymmetry of information between small- and large-scale financial institutions and investors, with the latter taking advantage of automated bank solutions.

Sophisticated analytics also uses advanced trading and risk management approaches such as behavioral and predictive algorithms, enabling the analysis of all transactions in real time. Wealth managers are increasingly using analytics solutions at every stage of the customer relationship to increase client retention and reduce operational costs.

By incorporating broader and multi-source data sets, they are forming a more holistic view of customers to anticipate better and satisfy their needs.

Given that wealth managers have an upcoming multi-trillion- dollar opportunity in the transfer of wealth from Baby Boomers to Millennials, the incorporation of automated advisory capabilities – either in whole or in part – will be a prerequisite.

This fundamental change in the financial advisor's role empowers customers and can directly inform their financial decision-making process. Automated investment advice (i.e., robo-advisors) poses a significant competitive threat to operators in the execution-only and self-directed investment market as well as to traditional financial advisors.

Such robot and automatic advisory capabilities will put pressure on traditional advisory services and fees and will transform the delivery of advice. Many self-directed organizations have responded with in-house and proprietary solutions, and advisors are likely to adapt with hybrid high-tech/high- touch models.

A secondary by-product of automated customer analysis is the lower cost of customer onboarding, conversion and funding rates. This change in the financial advisory model has created a challenge for wealth managers, who have struggled for years to figure out how to create profitable relationships with clients in possession of fewer total assets.

Robo-advisors provide a viable solution for this segment and, if positioned correctly as part of a full-service offering, can serve as a segue to provide full-service advice for clients with specific needs or higher touch.

Leveraging Data And Analytics

The insurance sector sees usage-based risk models and new methods for capturing risk-related data as key trends, while the shift to more self-directed services remains a top priority in order to meet existing customer expectations efficiently.

As is the case in other industry segments, insurance organizations are investing in the design and implementation of more self-directed services for both customer acquisition and customer servicing. This allows organizations to improve their operational efficiency while enabling online/ mobile channels demanded by emerging segments such as Millennials.

There have been interesting cases where customer-centric designs create compelling user experiences (e.g., quotes obtained by sending a quick picture of the driving license and the car vehicle identification number (VIN)), and where new solutions bring the opportunity to mobilize core processes in a matter of hours (e.g., provide access to services by using "robots" to create a mobile layer on top of legacy systems) or augment current key processes (PwC, 2016).

Current trends also show an increasing interest in finding new underwriting approaches based on the generation of deep risk insights. In this respect, usage-based models – rated the second most important trend by survey participants are becoming more relevant even as initial challenges such as data privacy are being overcome.

Auto insurance pay-as-you-drive is now the most popular usage-based insurance (UBI) (Forbes, 2017), and the current focus is shifting from underwriting to the customer. Initially, incumbents viewed UBI as an opportunity to underwrite risk in a more granular way by using new driving/ behavioral variables, but new players see UBI as an opportunity to meet new customers' needs (e.g., low mileage or sporadic drivers).

Remote access and data capture was both ranked third by the survey respondents according to the level of importance. Deep risk (and loss) insights can be generated from new data sources that can be accessed remotely and in real-time if needed. This ability to capture huge amounts of data must be coupled with the ability to analyze it to generate the required insights.

This trend also includes the impact of the Internet of Things (IoT) (American Banker, 2018); for example, (1) drones offer the ability to access remote areas and assess loss by running advanced imagery analytics, and (2) integrated IoT platforms solutions include various types of sensors, such as telematics, wearables and those found in industrial sites, connected homes or any other facilities/ equipment.

Customers with new expectations and the need to build trusted relationships are forcing incumbents to seek value propositions where experience, transaction efficiency and transparency are key elements. As self-directed solutions emerge among competitors, the ability to differentiate will be a challenge.

Similarly, usage-based models are emerging in response to customer demands for personalized insurance solutions. The ability to access and capture remote risk data will help to develop a more granular view of the risk, thus enabling personalization.

The telematics-based solution that enables pay-as-you-drive is one of the first models to emerge and is gaining momentum; new approaches are also emerging in the life insurance market where the use of wearables to monitor the healthiness of lifestyles can bring rewards or premium discounts among other benefits.

Leveraging new data sources to obtain a more granular view of the risk will not only offer a key competitive advantage in a market where risk selection and pricing strategies can be augmented, but will also allow incumbents to explore unpenetrated segments.

In this line, new players that have generated deep risk insights are also expected to enter these unpenetrated segments of the market; for example, life insurance for individuals with specific diseases.

Finally, in addition to social changes, the driving force behind innovation in insurance can largely be attributed to technological advances outside the insurance sector that will bring new opportunities to understand and manage the risk (e.g., telematics, wearables, connected homes, industrial sensors, medical advances, etc.), but will also have a direct impact on some of the foundations.

BLOCKCHAIN & BANKS

Blockchain is a new technology that combines a number of mathematical, cryptographic and economic principles in order to maintain a database between multiple participants without the need for any third-party validator or reconciliation (Crypto Updates, 2019). In simple terms, it is a secure and distributed ledger.

The insight is that blockchain represents the next evolutionary jump in business process optimization technology. Just as Enterprise Resource Planning (ERP) software allowed functions and entities within a business to optimize business processes by sharing data and logic within the enterprise, blockchain will allow entire industries to optimize business processes further by sharing data between businesses that have different or competing economic objectives.

That said, although the technology shows a lot of promise, several challenges and barriers to adoption remain. Further, a deep understanding of blockchain and its commercial implications requires knowledge that intersects various disparate fields and this leads to some uncertainty regarding its potential applications.

Blockchain technology may result in a radically different competitive future in the banking industry, where current profit pools are disrupted and redistributed toward the owners of new, highly efficient blockchain platforms.

Not only could there be huge cost savings through its use in back-office operations but also large gains in transparency that could be very positive from an audit and regulatory point of view.

One particularly hot topic is that of 'smart contracts' – contracts that are translated into computer programs and, as such, have the ability to be self-executing and self-maintaining. This area is just starting to be explored, but its potential for automating and speeding up manual and costly processes is huge.

Innovation from start-ups in this space is frenetic, with the pace of change so rapid that by the time print materials go to press they could already be out of date. The use cases are coming thick and fast but usually center on increasing efficiency by removing the need for reconciliation between parties, speeding up the settlement of trades or completely revamping existing processes, including:

- Enhancing efficiency in loan origination and servicing;
- Improving clearinghouse functions used by banks;
- Facilitating access to securities. For example, a bond that could automatically pay the coupons to bondholders, and any additional provisions could be executed when the conditions are met, without any need for human maintenance;
- The application of smart contracts in relation to the Internet of Things (IoT). Imagine car insurance that is embedded in the car itself and changes the premium paid based on the driving habits of the owner. The car contract could also contact the nearest garages that have a contract

with the insurance organization in the event of an accident or a request for towing. All of this could happen with very limited human interaction.

When faced with disruptive technologies, the most effective organizations thrive by incorporating them into the way they do business. Distributed ledger technologies offer banks a once-in-a-generation opportunity to transform the industry to their benefit, or not.

However, as seen in the survey responses, the knowledge of and likelihood to react to the developments in blockchain technology are relatively low. We believe that a lack of understanding of the technology and its potential for disruption poses significant risks to the existing profit pools and business models.

A Sector Feeling the Pressure

Typically, disruption hits a tipping point at which just under 50% of the incumbent revenue is lost in about a five-year timeframe (Galvin et al., 2018). Recent disruptions that provide valuable insight include streaming video's impact on the video rental market.

When broadband in the home reached ubiquity and video compression technology matured, low cost streaming devices were developed and, within four years, the video rental business was completely transformed. The same pattern can be seen on the internet direct insurance model for car insurance. At present, 50% of the revenue from the traditional agent-based distribution model has been moved to direct insurance providers.

FinTech organizations are not just bringing concrete solutions to a morphing consumer base, they are also empowering customers by providing new services which can be delivered with the use of technological applications.

The rise of "digital finance" allows consumers to connect to information anywhere at any time, and digital services can address their needs in a more convenient way than traditional nine-to-five financial advisors can. One of the key ways in which FinTechs support the margin pressure point through innovation is step function improvements in operating costs.

For instance, the movement to cloud-based platforms decreases not only up-front costs but also reduces ongoing infrastructure costs. This may stem from two main scenarios.

First, standalone FinTech organizations might snatch business opportunities from incumbents, such as business-to-consumer (B2C) FinTech organizations selling their products and services directly to customers and positioning themselves as more dynamic and agile alternatives to traditional players.

Secondly, business-to-business (B2B) FinTech organizations might empower specific incumbents through strategic partnerships with the intent to provide better services.

FinTech also offers myriad possibilities for the banking industry. B2B FinTech organizations create real opportunities for incumbents to improve their traditional offerings. For example, white label robo-advisors can improve the customer experience of an independent financial advisor by providing software that helps clients to navigate better the investment world.

In the insurance industry, a telematics technology provider can help insurers to track risks and driving habits together with providing additional services such as pay-as-you-go solutions. Partnerships with FinTech organizations could increase the efficiency of incumbent businesses.

However, FinTech is not just about cutting costs. Incumbents partnering with FinTech organizations could deliver a differentiated offering, improve customer retention and bring additional revenues. In this regard, 74% of fund transfer and payment institutions consider additional revenues to be an opportunity coming from FinTech (Galvin et al., 2018).

This is already true in the payments industry, where FinTech generates additional revenues through faster and easier payments and digital wallet transactions. FinTech is more than technology. It is a cultural mindset.

Organizations hoping to flourish need to shift their thinking to meet better customer needs, constantly track technological developments, aggressively engage with external partners and integrate digitization into their corporate DNA. To fully leverage the potential of FinTech, banks should have a top-down approach, embracing new technologies in every aspect of their businesses.

Adopting a 'mobile-first' approach is the key to improving customer experience. The biggest trends in

FinTech will be the way banks engage with customers in various forms. Traditional providers are increasingly taking a 'mobile-first' approach to reach out to consumers, e.g., designing their products and services with the aim of enhancing customer engagement via mobile.

Banks, with a share of 81% offering mobile applications, are increasingly using these channels to deliver compelling value propositions, generate new revenue streams and collect data from customers. According to Bill Gates (2019), in the year 2030, two billion new customers will use their mobile phones to save, lend and make payments. Significant growth in clients using mobile applications is expected by 2020.

A More Collaborative Approach

Whether banks adopt digital or mobile strategies, integrating FinTech is essential. Traditional banks are not ready to go all in and invest fully in FinTech. Joint partnership is an easy and flexible way to get involved with a technology firm and harness its capabilities within a safe test environment.

By partnering with FinTech organizations, incumbents can strengthen their competitive position and bring solutions or products into the market more quickly.

Moreover, this is an effective way for both incumbents and FinTech organizations to identify challenges and opportunities as well as to gain a deeper understanding of how they complement one another.

Given the speed of technology development, incumbents cannot afford to ignore FinTech. Nevertheless, according to The Economist (2015), a significant minority rather than a non-negligible share (25%) of survey respondents do not liaise with FinTech organizations at all, which could lead to an underestimation of the potential benefits and threats they can bring.

The majority of bankers (54%) are either ignoring the challenge or talking about disruption without making any changes. FinTech executives confirm this view: 59% of FinTech organizations believe that banks are not reacting to the disruption by FinTech.

Challenges Integration FinTech

A common challenge FinTech organizations and incumbents face is regulatory uncertainty. FinTech represents a challenge to regulators, as there may be a risk of an uneven playing field between the banking and FinTech organizations. Some 85% of banks' CEOs (PwC, 2017) are concerned about the impact of over-regulation on their prospects for growth, making this the biggest threat to growth they face.

However, the problems do not correspond to specific regulations, but rather to ambiguity and confusion. Industry players are asking, which regulatory agencies govern FinTech organizations? Which rules do FinTech organizations have to abide by? And specifically, which FinTech organizations have to adhere to which regulations?

In particular, small players struggle to navigate a complex, ever-increasing regulatory compliance environment as they strive to define their compliance model. Recent years have brought an increase of regulations in the banking industry, where even long-standing players are struggling to keep up.

While most banking providers and FinTech organizations would agree that the regulatory environment poses serious challenges, there are differences of opinion on which are the most significant.

For incumbents, IT security is crucial. This highlights the genuine constraints traditional banking organizations face regarding the introduction of new technologies into existing systems. On the other hand, fund transfer and payments businesses see their biggest challenges in the differences in operational processes and business models.

The complexity of processes and emerging business models, which aim to lead the payments industry into a new era, have the potential to both disrupt and complement traditional fund transfer and payments institutions. Their challenge lies in refining old methods while pioneering new processes to compete in the long run.

As FinTech organizations are mainly smaller, they are more agile and flexible. And, because most are in the early stages of development, their structures and processes are not set in stone, allowing them to adapt more easily and quickly to challenges.

Surfing the FinTech wave – How to ensure an organization is ready to take advantage of the FinTech people opportunity (DSCI, 2017):

- Adopting a FinTech mindset: Big corporate structures are not necessarily the best fit for the success in the FinTech revolution. Established financial institutions will need to experiment with new business arrangements (such as partnerships and joint ventures) to gain access to the talent and the innovation needed to pinpoint game-changing products. This involves identifying promising profiles and developing incentives to attract entrepreneurial talent.

- Changing the way talent is developed: As new technologies enter the workplace, workers' skills and experience must evolve accordingly. Current employees need to keep abreast of new skills requirements and develop themselves to remain attractive to employers. Because new programming or digitally related skills cannot be taught formally, it is up to employees to build networks locally and embrace the emerging trends and technologies. Talent management frameworks should encourage and reward this attitude.

- Creating an agile enterprise: FinTech start-ups operate in a very different way than established banking businesses do. They move quickly, fail fast and are not afraid to take risks. Traditional players need to think about how this agile mindset dovetails with their current business processes and shareholder requirements.

- Digitizing the employee experience: Innovative start-ups attract youthful talent with very different career aspirations than those of the previous generation. This will necessitate a change in the way organizations interact with staff, e.g., by redesigning career paths, offering incentive arrangements, or outsourcing work to freelancers. HR departments will need to adapt to new talent acquisition methods and can learn a great deal from other industries that have gone through similar changes (e.g., some big pharma companies teaming up with biotech organizations).

- Encouraging and incubating innovation: financial institutions need to re-learn how to innovate and attract talent with the right mix of technical and commercial skills. This involves a mindset change from traditional leadership- down management to a model that encourages innovation.

- Fostering an attractive employer brand: Many FinTech start-ups have identified a specific niche or a purpose they are trying to achieve (for instance: global financial inclusion, or reducing the cost of money transfers to access developing markets). Established players need to take a similar approach to attract the right type of applicants and develop employer brands that appeal to aspiring talent.

They must also engage with the start-up environment and strive to develop corporate brands that are tech-friendly. Minimizing these challenges should be on the agendas of both FinTechs and traditional financial institutions, as well as governments, regulators and trade associations in order to create the best investment environment, regulatory framework and infrastructure for the development of FinTech within the banking industry.

Disruption of the banking industry is happening and FinTech is the driver as it reshapes the way organizations and consumers engage by altering how, when and where financial services and products are provided.

Success is driven by the ability to improve customer experience and meet changing customer needs. Information on FinTech is somewhat dispersed and obscure, which can make synthesizing the data challenging.

It is, therefore, critical to filter the noise around FinTech and focus on the most relevant trends, technologies and start-ups. In response to this rapidly changing environment, incumbent financial institutions have approached FinTech in various ways, such as through joint partnerships or start-up programs.

However, whatever strategy an organization pursues, it cannot afford to ignore FinTech. The main impact of FinTech will be the surge of new bank business models, which will create challenges for both regulators and market players.

Banking organizations should turn away from trying to control all parts of their value chain and customer experience through traditional business models, and instead move toward the center of the FinTech ecosystem by leveraging their trusted relationships with customers and their extensive access to client data.

For many traditional financial institutions, this approach will require a fundamental shift in identity and purpose. The new norm will involve turning away from a linear product push approach, to a customer-centric model in which bank providers are facilitators of a service that enables clients to acquire advice and interact with all relevant actors through multiple channels.

By focusing on incorporating new technologies into their architecture, traditional financial institutions can prepare themselves to play a central role in the new banking world in which they will operate at the center of customer activity and maintain strong positions even as innovations alter the marketplace.

Financial institutions should make the most of their position of trust with customers, brand recognition, access to data and knowledge of the regulatory environment to compete. banking players might not recognize the financial industry in the future, but they will be in the center of it.

SUMMARIES OF TRENDS

Preliminary remark: This is based on a 2017 PwC report (PwC, 2017 and Galvin et al., 2018)

Neo's Team is tracking emerging trends in FinTech to explain which start-ups, technologies, trends and new market entrants are relevant to you and, more importantly, why. The trends highlighted below are a snapshot in time of the most relevant ones for each banking segment:

1. The rise of peer-to-peer (P2P) lending

2. Services and solutions for underserved consumers
3. The enhancement of credit underwriting/decision making
4. Solutions that banks will integrate or incorporate to improve simplify operations
5. Sophistication in methods to reach, engage, and retain customers
6. The emergence of self-service tools
7. The move toward non-physical or virtual channels, including mobile channels
8. The digitalization of cash- and treasury-management functions
9. The democratization of banking and personal finance
10. The simplification and move toward streamlined product application processes to improve customer experience
11. The rise of crowdfunding/seed funding
12. Blockchain

Increased levels of technology have enabled an increase in lending without an intermediary. Lower cost of providing services to customers that are currently underbanked. More granular data enable banking providers to assess and price risks more accurately.

APIs enable third parties to develop value-added applications for organization platforms; artificial intelligence is enabling organizations to extract greater customer and insights, employees and intelligent machines are integrating to work as a team, banks are expediting the deployment of digital delivery. And there are many more ahead.

Engaging customers through gamification techniques in a collaborative environment is leading to better customer experience and reflecting in retention. Increase of customer autonomy in performing every service without human interaction.

Self-service tools, such as internet banking and apps, are becoming more popular. Virtual banking utilizes online and mobile platforms to integrate and simplify customer banking experience. Virtual banking platforms equip customers with on-demand access to manage bank accounts, pay bills, apply for loans, open new accounts, and perform other banking activities through a single portal.

Banks are using these channels to collect data from customers, generate new revenue streams and offer compelling value propositions.

Cash and treasury management includes the administration of external and internal funds, cash flow management, and corporate finance policies and procedures. The digitalization of cash and treasury management functions utilizes online platforms to disrupt the traditional models, creating new revenue streams and value propositions.

Cross-border payment transfers for businesses, foreign exchanges and invoice management are a few of the functions that are enabled primarily through the advent of online platforms. For example, organizations are developing new processes to perform international money transfers using mobile wallets and cryptocurrencies to improve speed and safety.

The democratization of banking and personal finance describes the shift in which customers take control of their financial health and seek new channels and solutions to assist in this process.

The consumer product application process (i.e., loan origination) has been streamlined with the emergence of cloud-based lending solutions and electronic bank account management systems which automate the loan origination process and increase overall transparency in the lending process. The move towards such solutions improves customer experience by reducing the amount of manual work, cutting down time and reducing errors.

New funding options have emerged in mid-market, such as P2P lending and marketplace lending platforms. Use of distributed and decentralized ledger technology in which transactions are recorded in order to improve payments, clearing and settlement, audit, or data management of assets.

There is also the possibility to create a so-called "smart contract" using blockchain technology. This is essentially a contract that is translated into a computer program and, as such, has the ability to be self-executing and self-maintaining.

SECTION XV: OPERAT. RISK & SUPPLY CHAIN RESILIENCE

BACKGROUND

Operational risks are the root cause for many of the (large scale) financial failures in the past decades. Operational risks are not new: human mistakes, fraud, theft, process failures, system errors and external hazards, such as fires and floods, have been around for decades.

However, the impact of operational risks was most often relatively insignificant. In contrast, recent trends such as globalization, global internet connectivity, and (value) chain dependencies, have made operational risks more significant than ever before. With increasing requirements, complexity and volume of risks, information systems are believed to provide benefits for risk management activities.

An increasing number of organizations, mainly in the financial sector, are required by regulatory authorities or by law to manage their operational risks. In the early 2000s the lion share of international banks was already allocating more financial reserves to account for operational risks than for market risks.

Operational risks tend to become more relevant in different types of organizations. For example, operational risks have been studied for years in the healthcare sector. Effective risk management influences the results in infrastructure contracts. Additionally, operational risks are becoming increasingly important in the energy sector. The importance of operational risks varies depending on industry and the markets that an organization operates in.

They found that financial organizations have the lowest expected returns on operational risk, and basic material producers have the highest return. Operational risk is different from other risks, such as credit risk or market risk, because operational risk is usually not taken to retrieve an expected return.

Operational risk exists in every organizational activity. Inappropriate management of operational risks can result in significant losses. With increasing requirements, complexity and volume of risks, information systems provide benefits for integrating risk management activities and optimizing risk management performance.

Information systems and technologies can support the improvement of operational risk management processes. Performance management systems is a set of technologies from the information systems domain suitable for application to support the operational risk management process. In recent years, this recognition is supported from practice by consulting firms, who state Business Performance Management and its supporting technologies could provide effective support for risk management processes.

Risk management should be part of the planning and control cycle, aligned with strategic goals of the organization. Integrated risk management and better collaboration lead to a more mature risk management. These benefits could only effectively be achieved by using appropriate software. However, many organizations do not appear to know what software features to use for effectively improving risk management.

Business Performance Management (BPM) related technologies such as workflow, centralized storage, and dashboarding, which could provide a solution for operational risk management issues.

However, it remains unclear whether the full spectrum of business performance management technologies is suitable for improving operational risk management processes and whether the same set of BPM technologies are applicable for all types of organizations.

Additionally, there appears to be no existing or specific guidance for organizations seeking to improve operational risk management processes using business performance management technologies.

Operational Risk Defined

The term "operations risk" first appeared in the early 1990s. When the Committee of Sponsoring Organizations of the Treadway Commission (COSO) officially introduced its first version of the integrated internal control framework in 1991.

The term "operations risk" did not gain full attention until 1999 when the Basel Committee introduced Basel II. Around the 2000s the Basel committee identified a need for a new type of risk appearing from fraud and human misbehaviors such as theft, mistakes or fraudulent actions, which were not covered by any other type of risk management.

Therefore, the Basel committee defined operational risk as: "the risk of loss resulting from inadequate or failed internal processes, people and systems or from external events. This definition includes legal risk, but excludes strategic and reputation risk".

The committee states organizations can adapt or modify the definition to their own specific context. The Basel committee detailed operational risks further into specific event type categories:

1. Business disruptions and system failures, loss from business disruptions and system failures;
2. Clients, products and business practices, losses arising from a failure to meet professional obligations to clients or from the nature or design of a product;
3. Damage to physical assets, losses or damage related to natural disasters or other events;
4. Employment practices and workplace safety, losses related to acts inconsistent with health, safety or employment laws or agreements;
5. Execution, delivery & process management, losses resulting from process management, transaction processing or external relations, such as trade counter parties and vendors.
6. External fraud, losses related to intentional or inappropriate acts regarding misappropriate property, information breaches (cyber-crime) or acts that circumvent the law by a third party;

7. Internal fraud, losses related to intentional or inappropriate acts. Circumventing laws, regulations or organization policy, involving at least one internal stakeholder;

Another definition states that operational risks refer to a company's reduced ability to produce and supply products and services as a consequence of a breakdown in a core operating, manufacturing, or processing capability (Sadgrove, 2005).

Operational risk, as defined by the Basel Committee, is a financial term, meaning the term operational risk is well known and understood by banking and insurance organizations. Within the financial services industry, operational risks are often part of COSO enterprise risk management activities and related to corporate governance activities.

Properly managing operational risks is described as a 'three lines of defense' model. Operational risk events and their consequences should be handled at the organization function in which they occur, however, severe consequences should be directly reported to the board and other stakeholders. Proper execution of the operational risk actions on the first lines should be managed and monitored by an (independent) function within the organization, called a second line of defense.

A third line of defense is formed by an (independent) audit committee assessing the complete operational risk management structure, process and implementation on a regular basis. An audit team can be internal, external or both.

Interaction Operational Risk Mgmt On Supply Chain Risk Mgmt

Additionally, the randomness of the business environment, variable consumer, demands, actions by competitors, along with market dynamics and continuous improvement initiatives within organizations imply that the supply chain never actually reaches a stable steady state condition.

These parameters of uncertainty and risk can promulgate through an ineffective supply chain design.

The consideration of the central role of business processes and the relevance of their effective and efficient management leads to the belief that operational risk and supply chain risk are connected. Risk management is the process devoted to protecting the organization and augmenting its capability to achieve its stated strategic objectives.

Operational processes represent the core business of most companies, and therefore the proper assessment of operational and supply chain risks is critical to effective and efficient prevention and protection of an organization. In fact, the successful assessment of these risks can represent an important competitive advantage for the organization.

Most banks are familiar with operational risks in the supply chain that arise from third parties. Indeed, as organizations increase their dependence on these networks, they become more vulnerable to their suppliers' operational risk profiles as well as other categories of risk associated with supply chains. Supplier operational risk profiles consist of risk events that can directly affect their internal operations.

Suppliers with a high probability of operational risk event occurrences can have a significant impact on the revenues realized by organizations that rely on their inputs. Thus, it is essential that supply chain network participants are capable of evaluating the operational risks associated with their supplier base.

But operational risk does not only arise from the interaction between the banking organization and a third party, but already also at the level of first party data providers (within the organization) (i.e., and, also, to some extent with second party data providers).

Alas, banks do not pay much attention to the operational risks arising from the interaction among first party data providers as they operational risk managers do not formalize the relationships between the various internal data providers. Granted, operational risk management will look at (Perez, 2014):

- People risk: Incompetency or wrong posting of personnel and misuse of powers
- Information technology risk: The failure of the information technology system, the hacking of the computer network by outsiders, and the programming errors that can take place any time and can cause loss to the bank
- Process-related risks: Possibilities of errors in information processing, data transmission, data retrieval, and inaccuracy of result or output

However, operational risk management as it is organized today within banking organization does not formalize by means of a mapping of the interrelationships and interactions between the various stakeholders that are part of a supply chain network, i.e., 1st, 2nd, 3rd, 4th, and 5th party data providers.

Operational risk managers do not sufficiently look in a holistic way at the entire chain as an integrated network constituted of the various data providers. In practice, operational risk managers do not have a say when SLAs are drafted among internal parties and with external data providers, even though a host of operational risks do arise in a supply chain:

Operational risks are stem from operations, i.e., from activities and resources. Any potential source that generates a negative impact on the information, goods, and cash in the operations is an operational risk.

The inclusion of cash owing through the operation implies that financial and operational risks are not mutually exclusive. Operational risks refer to a company's reduced ability to produce and supply products and services as a consequence of a breakdown in a core operating, manufacturing, or processing capability (Sadgrove, 2005).

This category also includes operational problems caused by human-resource problems, capacity constraints, logistics challenges, IT problems, and leadership issues. Operational risks include the everyday management of the supply chain whereas disruptions risks are associated with unexpected events including natural disasters.

And, with the ever-increasing push for efficiency, supply chains today are getting more and more risky. No matter how strong is the supply chain, risk and uncertainty come, risk and uncertainty come into the picture by disrupting the operational flow. Some of the operational risk factors have been described as follows (Chand et al. 2014): poor quality, utility failure, HR problems, IT system failure, loss of key equipment's, personnel and suppliers, theft of information, logistic route/mode disruption, and computer virus.

The symbiosis between supply chain management and operational risk management is yet to be formalized as associated risks with the operation in supply chain network have not sufficiently or inadequately been mapped.

Banking executives need to identify and measure the impact of operational risks on a supply chain network and develop suitable strategies to manage them. Both the Basel Committee as well as the regulators, and foremost the risk management executives within the bank, need to make this a priority in order to better comprehend the risks associated with a supply chain network.

Performance Management

Performance management is an abstract term that can be confusing because of its broad nature and the meaning of words, such as 'performance' and 'management'. It all depends on what kind of performance is intended to be managed. Performance is valued contribution to reach the goals of an organization.

In general, Performance Management can be seen as a way for organizations to become more successful and make sure they are delivering against their strategic priorities. The process of performance management starts at the highest level of the organization by translating a mission and vision statement into a strategy, composed of objectives and priorities.

These objectives and priorities should then be translated to high level measures and then by middle management into measures on operational levels. These high-level measures and operational measures express organizational performance. The performance should then be communicated by reporting the measured performance and managed to align people and culture with strategic goals.

- Performance can only be managed when the actual performance is known.
- Performance Measurement is the method of developing performance indicators and relating them to contextual factors to enable measurement of performance.
- Performance could then be actively improved by management.
- Performance measurement is a critical and inseparable component of performance management.
- Performance measurement systems assist managers in tracking the implementations of business strategy by comparing actual results against strategic goals and objectives.
- A performance measurement system typically comprises systematic methods of setting business goals together with periodic feedback reports that indicate progress against goals.

Business performance management evolved from decision support systems in the 1960s and developed throughout the following years into executive information systems. The development of aggregated data storage, known as data warehousing, led to the inception of business intelligence in the late 1980s.

Business performance management builds on the foundations of business intelligence, extending the latter with planning, consolidation and process automation. Business performance management is defined as the business processes, methodologies, metrics and technologies used by enterprises to measure, monitor and manage business performance.

Synonyms for business performance management are corporate performance management, enterprise performance management by Oracle and strategic enterprise management by SAP.

Business performance management is supported by a set of technologies for integrating and analyzing performance-relevant data, supporting decision making and facilitating the communication of decisions. Business performance management is a combination of technologies from the domains: business intelligence, business process modelling and enterprise application integration.

Combined with elements from process performance management, business process automation and real-time analytics.

The business performance management pyramid is intended to summarize the domain of business performance management. It is composed of three different layers:

- Strategy and objective setting at the top, because that is the ultimate goal related to (strategic) management, similar to the business intelligence pyramid.
- The middle layer is an important interface layer between organizational planning & control and supporting technologies. Data entry and workflow enable planning on the entry side. Dashboards and reporting interface the results and enable controlling on the output side. Proper implementation of this interface layer may also be facilitated by descriptive meta-algorithmic models as best practices process guides.
- The bottom layer is only technology related, facilitating input of clean source data on the entry side. Building on a Data Warehouse as central data storage, data mining and big data enhancing the data on the output side with analytics, as source for dashboards and reporting [58]. Business Performance Management technologies as described can

support any process with a continuous improvement cycle—using goal setting, performance measurement and reporting.

Integration of operational risk management practices appears to benefit from several business performance management technologies: workflow and data entry to support collaboration between the three lines of defense and other stakeholders, such as the board of directors and shareholders. Analysis, dashboarding and reporting could support communication and process monitoring activities.

Last but not Least About Operational Risk Management

Operational risks are seen as the alpha and omega for many of the (large scale) financial failures in the past decades. Operational Risk is defined by the Basel Committee from the Bank of International Settlements as risks resulting from: Internal Processes, Humans, Systems and External events.

In most organizations operational risk management is part of enterprise risk management. Business performance management technologies are believed to provide a solution for effective operational risk management by offering several combined technologies including: work flow, data warehousing, (advanced) analytics, reporting and dashboards.

Operational Risk Management was first placed into context by measuring the importance of the organizational process, before measuring the actual implementation level of operational risk management and the use of business performance management technologies.

There are some clear relations with specific sets of BPM technologies found to influence the maturity of operational risk management. Therefore, the maturity model as developed in this research could provide some useful guidelines on the applicability of certain technologies.

The maturity model as developed in this research provides a suitable path with six stages for organizations seeking to improve their operational risk management processes. The six stages provide an instrument to match appropriate technologies to the current stage of maturity and enables organizations to grow in maturity towards enterprise integration and continuous improvement.

As this research provides some answers to unanswered questions, all research leads to new research possibilities. Therefore, this section provides some future research directions. As this research explored a novel domain in a qualitative manner, larger samples are needed for further validation.

Operational risk management tooling in general is required for efficiency and structure. Only when using operational risk management tooling it will be possible to reach organization-wide integration. Especially business performance management technologies support organization wide integration and collaboration via workflow. Some participants suggested that maintainability of tooling for operational risk management is an issue.

This suggestion could be related to dissatisfaction, complaints about user-friendliness and mismatch between tooling and operational risk management.

SECTION XVI: CASE F/ SUPPLY CHAIN RISK MGMT BANKS

BACKGROUND

Most executives within procurement and supply chain management (and in other senior roles) understand that supply chain risk is an important issue. The topic has moved up the agenda in recent years, and many firms have made investments to support their activities.

Nevertheless, to bring the topic of supply chain risk management to the forefront of a banking organization, it may be necessary to present a compelling business case as to why management needs it. First, start by looking at the challenges that exist around making the convincing case for investment and consider how those can be overcome.

Then look at the five key steps in building a business case, and one notes how tools and technology can greatly assist in managing supply chain risk. Many organizations have invested in supply chain risk management, whether that is in the form of internal resources, training, tools or technology.

However, often executives who understand the need still struggle to create the business case and get approval for the appropriate levels of investment. Why is that?

Various steps to build a convincing case

In terms of procurement and how an organization looks at its suppliers and supply chain, value comes from two fundamental activities. Organizations look for opportunity: how their suppliers and supply chain can help generate value that ultimately leads to competitive advantage.

That can come from a low-cost strategy or even savings through cost avoidance, contributing to greater efficiency in the business. It can also come from driving revenue growth through innovation that originates with the supply chain; for example, via strategic sourcing to make better total value decisions by awarding business to a new, innovative supplier.

The other side of the value equation is risk management. Opportunities are important, but so is managing the risk inherent in any supply chain. Smart organizations and smart executives understand that in terms of the supply chain, both risk and opportunity management are critical to a sustainable success.

However, many companies and executives focus more on the obvious opportunities. A discussion about an acquisition, an exciting new product or a technical innovation is perhaps seen as more exciting for the board than an analysis of key strategic supplier risk.

Fundamentally, investment in risk management is designed to avoid something happening, rather than to make something happen. Investments in marketing, new branch equipment or even research and development generally have tangible outputs—a new banking product, more output, a social media campaign.

On the other hand, an investment in improved supply chain risk management means that something does not happen—the firm does not have a reputational risk crisis, branch shut-down or supply shortage.

While that is clearly important, it lacks the tangible nature of many other investment outcomes, which is one of the issues that must be overcome. Linking the improvements to risk management through to business outcomes or measurable benefits—such as better customer service or more efficient operations—can be challenging.

That means the business case has to be very explicit about the potential impact on the business arising from supply chain risk; it is not necessarily just a simple numerical return on investment calculation.

Nevertheless, the evidence for professionalizing supply chain risk management is overwhelming, and the growth of powerful and effective tools—often cloud-based and using the latest technology (such as artificial intelligence)— makes it easier than ever to create a persuasive business case.

But the case still needs to explain in appropriate business language the situation, the problem that needs addressing through the investment, and how the situation can and will be improved. It must be persuasive, robust and professional to motivate the organization to act and to invest.

So, how do you do it?

1. Explain the supply chain risk facing the banking organization: the goal of this step is to make sure that stakeholders understand exactly what supply chain risk is. This involves asking some key questions to highlight where risk lies, and can also involve bringing in past examples of risk incidents.
2. Explain the implications and the cost of the supply chain risk facing the banking organization: the goal of this step is to make sure that stakeholders

understand the need for supply chain risk management. This is when you create the burning platform that justifies the investment.

3. Explain what supply chain risk management should look like: the goal of this step is to describe the promised land of supply chain risk understanding: up-to-date market knowledge, rapid information and alerts and planned mitigation/ preventive actions—all of which will be in place after the investment.
4. Explain the plan: how to achieve the supply chain risk management vision: the goal of this step is to describe the proposed solution (presumably a technology solution) and what is required to establish it (in other words, a high-level adoption plan).
5. Explain the costs and benefits: The goal of this step is to explain the investment and the return on investment, with financial and non-financial costs and benefits explained, including the plan for tracking those benefits.

STEP 1: Explain Supply Chain Risk Facing a Banking Organization

The first job of the business case is this: Convince your stakeholders that they have a problem. The business case should start by laying out how supply chain risk is currently managed within the organization, highlighting strengths and—perhaps more importantly—weaknesses and areas for improvement. The aim should be to describe the situation honestly while being clear about the gaps and weaknesses. Here are some key questions that can help to structure that description:

- On a scale of 1-10 (10 being the best), how good is your visibility of suppliers?
- How many direct spend suppliers are monitored?
- Can you identify your suppliers and supply chains that generate the most significant risk?
- What supplier information is available?
- How is supplier information and data obtained and kept up to date?
- Do you know where your key services are developed?
- Do you have any processes to identify multi-tier supply chain risk; e.g., suppliers who are not first-tier but who could suffer risk events that would impact your organization?
- Do you analyze and segment suppliers based on their risk profiles?

- What is your process for being alerted to new and emerging risk, from supplier financial issues to natural disasters affecting supplier premises?
- What contingency plans are in place to respond if a potential risk becomes an actual risk event?
- Can your organization give assurances—relating to regulatory or reputational drivers—about issues such as GDPR (general data protection regulations) for example?
- Where and how has the organization experienced supply chain risk events in the past?

Answering these questions should give you a good understanding of what you're doing now, and where there are gaps in the processes that could be improved. In addition to asking these questions, it may also be helpful to highlight them with examples of past risk issues that had an impact on the business.

Step 2: Explain Implications and Cost of Supply Chain Risk Facing the Banking Organization

The business case must make a persuasive argument for investment to those who control the money. One problem is that individuals and organizations understand conceptually that supply chain risk is important, yet still do not consider it important enough to invest. Executives can learn here from successful sales techniques. The classic Huthwaite SPIN selling methodology (situation, problem, implications, need-payoff) suggests that to make the sale, it is not enough to highlight the problem to the buyer (or, in this case, stakeholder). Even if they understand that they have a real issue or problem, it is vital that they understand the implications of the problem.

And, so, it is with a supply chain risk management business case. In addition to communicating the problem, you must also communicate what the implications of the problem are—the "so what?" part of the story. And that needs to be expressed in terms of clear business outcomes, not just theoretical supply chain nice-to-haves. There are also regulatory and compliance issues in certain industries that increasingly require organizations to show they understand their supply chain, know who key suppliers are and manage risk proactively.

From modern slavery to GDPR to carbon reduction and environmental issues in the supply chain, both regulators and shareholders are taking an increasing interest in supply chain risk. Any current gaps here can be highlighted as part of the justification for investment.

Again, posing questions to the organization can be a useful way of highlighting the implications of risk problems. For example:

- What would happen if a major data source could not be delivered for days or weeks?
- What would you do if a major supplier went out of business?
- How would you respond if one of your key partners or suppliers experienced a major cyber risk event or were found to be breaching human rights or environmental regulations?

Step 3: Explain What Supply Chain Risk Management Should Look Like.

Having laid out the current situation and the implications of current weaknesses, your next step is to describe the vision for future supply chain risk management. What will the improved processes, performance and outcomes look like? How will technology support those changes and improvements?

Compared to the current situation, what will the tangible differences be? Starting from the weaknesses identified, lay out how your brave new world of supply chain risk management will work. This needs to work though the end-to-end risk management process. It is also key that proposed solutions don't focus just on having access to risk event information.

It is just as important and increasingly vital that organizations have a way to sort the signal from the noise. With the huge amount of data and information available today, the key point is having a way of establishing what really matters to your specific organization. Increasingly, that means using smart technology that relies on artificial intelligence and machine learning to help sift what is really relevant from the rest.

In defining the vision for supply chain risk management, the following might be part of the post- investment picture (although, of course, the exact details here will depend to a certain extent on your individual organization):

- Relevant staff will be in place, with an appropriate level of designated resources, who are tasked with managing risk.
- Your critical risks will be identified, and plans put in place to address and mitigate the most serious ones.

- The board or other senior group will regularly review supply chain risk based on appropriate reporting.
- A process and tools will be put in place to provide risk alerts and notifications, so that you are aware of risk and know quickly when and where risk events need addressing.
- Technology will help to identify the specific and relevant information that really matters to the banking organization and thus will help the banks to manage risk better.
- You will avoid the direct consequences of risk events; e.g., data shortages, fee increases, lost sales or higher refinancing costs.

One of the ways to present this information is to lay out a before-and- after comparison between the current practices and the post-investment practices.

Step 4: Explain the Plan: How to Achieve the Supply Chain Risk Management Vision

Next, you should provide a description of exactly what is proposed in terms of the investment, and how it will be implemented. In most cases, this will involve the introduction of a tool, platform or system to support better supply chain risk management.

There are four significant issues that need to be considered here as part of the overall change and investment program: people, tools, process and governance. Obviously, this is driven by the specific nature of the business case. If it is focused purely on investment in a risk management tool, then all of these areas may not need to be covered.

However, even in this case, there will usually be some implications, in terms of process at least, if as much value as possible is to be gained from the investment. In other cases, if the organization is looking to completely transform the way it approaches supply chain risk, then all four of these areas may need addressing.

- People: Is there a need for additional staff, or for structured staff training and development in order to become more competent supply chain risk managers? This may require detailed training for some staff, while in other cases it may be more about increasing general awareness of the issues without trying to create deep expertise. If this is required, what will be provided to make that happen, how will it be delivered, by whom and when?

- Tools: It's difficult to see any business case today for improved risk management that does not have an element of technology. The vast amount of data and information available relating to the supply chains for any organization of a reasonable size is virtually unmanageable without appropriate automation and systemization. So, assuming you propose to buy risk management tools, what will they provide in terms of better risk management, how will they be implemented and what integration issues (with existing systems) need to be addressed? Some risk platforms are relatively quick and easy to implement; other options may require considerable amounts of effort, meaning time-to-value will be longer.
- Process: Are any changes in procurement processes needed to assist in risk management changes? For instance, does your supplier onboarding process need to be reviewed or tightened up? Is a process needed to identify critical suppliers, or to ensure that appropriate information (which contributes towards

effective risk management) is obtained from suppliers?

- Governance: Will you need to change the governance around supply chain risk? This might mean new or revised policies (to support process change) or reporting and review requirements. Some organizations produce a quarterly supply chain risk report that may be formally reviewed at senior levels, for example.

Some business cases also provide a detailed project plan for the investment being proposed. Other organizations prefer a full plan to follow approval of the business case. There is no right or wrong here; the best approach depends on how the organization prefers to handle the process for investment.

The downside of a detailed plan at this stage is that the work will be wasted if the investment is not approved. However, a business case that does not include any real detail on the plan might leave those who have to approve it wondering if the appropriate level of thought has gone into the process.

It may leave open the suspicion that all the costs have not been assessed, or that the proposers do not understand the effort that might be needed to implement the recommendation. Often, the best solution will be a middle-of-the-road approach. The business case should have enough detail to demonstrate that it has been well-considered and is very likely to work, and that there will be no unpleasant cost surprises.

This means including a clear outline of what is going to be done, the timelines, the resource implications and who will execute the work. An outline of the key risks to the business case (i.e., what could stop the investment return being achieved) can also be included. It does not mean that a full project plan, with resource allocation and identification, day-by-day activity and even risk issues should be necessary. But the exact balance will depend on your organization's own expectations and ways of working in terms of business case development and presentation.

Step 5: Explain Costs and Benefits

No business case is complete without an analysis of the costs and benefits. This is your last step in making the case for supply chain risk management. Make sure you use the organization's internal policies for financial business cases—such as how issues like net present value should be handled.

Describe the costs: although there may be soft costs associated with a supply chain risk management program, it's usually the case that the biggest hurdle for approval is getting new technology approved. Assuming there is a technology component to the investment, categories of cost that should be included are:

- Core technology cost, up front license fees or annual/monthly subscriptions (particularly with cloud-based platforms)
- Other technology-related costs, if relevant (e.g., maintenance, upgrades)
- Training costs: formal or informal; may be linked to a system implementation or could be a core part of the program
- Integration: costs of developing links and feeds between the new system and any existing systems
- Communication: any costs associated with the launch of a new system
- Recruitment costs: if any additional staff required

Organizations have their own guidelines on how to calculate and present the financial elements of the business case.

Future costs and benefits will usually be discounted to a present value—that reflects the view that money spent or gained in the short-term matters more than that saved or spent in the distant future. Organizational policies on aspects such as the discount rate to be used need to be understood and followed.

Focus on the benefits: historically, many capital investment programs considered a lengthy timeframe, mainly in order to show many years of benefits to compensate for a major up-front year-one investment cost.

That was true for capital equipment but also many more software-based products that came with a major up-front license purchase cost (followed often by ongoing maintenance fees every year). The growth of cloud-based options, which generally don't have that year-one hit, has made many business cases more attractive.

There will still be some year-one costs such as training and perhaps some integration costs, but generally the business case can be made over a shorter time period.

Laying out the benefits clearly and convincingly is perhaps the most critical element of the business case. What are the key areas where you will expect to see benefits in terms of supply chain risk management? Benefits can be divided into three main types:

1. Quantified cost benefits

   - Improved working capital and return on capital: Reduced stock holding arising from better risk management can lead to less money tied up in stock and a consequent reduction in working capital.
   - Less manual work for buyers: Reduction in workload from information gathering, supplier liaison, data handling—even an hour or two a week—can add up to substantial savings across a large organization and multiple people.
   - Reduced or avoided costs for existing data providers where new technology is introduced.

2. Cost avoidance

   - Operating efficiencies: Better risk management means more branch up-time and productivity and lower chances of stoppages or slowdown.

- Staff time and effort: A coordinated response to a risk event mean costs are avoided in terms of staff and management effort.
- Avoidance of price increases: Early knowledge of a risk event enables faster action, which reduces the chance of the buyer being subject to higher prices in the market.

3. Revenue and reputation

- Reduced risk of reputational damage through product issues, shortages, etc. This can also have a direct cost effect; e.g., the operational cost of product recalls or advertising aimed at reassuring customers.
- Reduced risk of lost revenue; e.g., major risk events leading to outages or even product withdrawals or recalls.

The case for benefits is only half-made if you don't explain how to track them. Put simply, make sure to explain how you will know if the investment has been successful. Your business case should identify the KPIs (key performance indicators) or metrics that will help to identify the outcome from the investment and track whether it has met its goals.

As much as possible, hard numbers should be used, although it is important to recognize that in some areas (such as avoidance of catastrophic risk events or consequences), we are inevitably measuring something that did not happen. But in other cases, there will be numbers available to support both specific and ongoing investment in risk management capability and tools.

Conclusion

The nature of risk management is such that we are often looking to stop things from happening, which means the business case may need more thought than one that is looking at increasing sales or generating new products.

But by highlighting any weaknesses in the current situation, identifying the potential implications of supply chain risk events, laying out the vision for an improved situation, proposing a plan and analyzing the costs and benefits, a persuasive business case can be constructed.

When the benefits of a high-performance supply chain risk management program are laid out, it is clear that they are wide-ranging, varied and substantial. A business case that combines as much rigor and as many hard numbers as possible, with some narrative to support that (such as stories of past problems or failures), can prove effective in gaining approval for the investment needed.

SECTION XVII: FINAL NOTES SUPPLY CHAIN RISK MGMT

SUPPLY CHAIN MGMT OR SERVICES SUPPLY CHAIN MGMT?

Nowadays, and increasingly for the years to come, service industries (but also the service operations of manufacturing companies) are adjusting their delivery systems as data driven technology is shaping the business world.

Within the banking industry, self-services – aka online services - are replacing many of the traditional channels dominated by brick and mortar branches and the personnel that services these platforms. New types of channels for delivering financial and other services (credit reports, ID protection, etc.) are being created at a faster pace.

This restructuring is forcing financial institutions to re-evaluate their current customer service strategies, and already banks are increasingly embracing automation as the way to cut costs and to provide quick response for the large self-service markets while specialization allows organizations to focus on the needs of small custom-service segments.

Few organizations can achieve both economies of scale and scope in a competitive way. The application of new information technology has created opportunities to re-engineer the service processes in innovative ways.

And, while the concept of supply chain management is widely used in the manufacturing and distribution industry, not much has been written or researched on how supply chain management would apply to the services industry, and in particular the banking industry.

Concomitantly, much has been said about the use of information technology and its impact on an organization, and this is nowhere more apparent than in many services, particularly the banking industry.

Technology has revolutionized the way that companies perform service, enabling the development of long-term individualized relationships with customers. Advancements in computing have allowed companies to improve both profits and financial accountability by providing high quality, personalized service more easily and affordably than ever before.

Information Technology has been shown to not only lower the cost of service, but create avenues to enhance service revenues.

Still, with all of this research on information technology's influence on services, much is still to be learned of its impact in supply chain networks, and even more so when the aspect of resilience of a financial organization comes into play.

Similar to the manufacturing and logistics industries, financial institutions too need to begin to realize that it is not enough to improve efficiencies within an organization, but their entire supply chain from back to front needs to be made competitive.

They now realize that understanding and implementing effective supply chain risk management practices is an essential prerequisite not only to profitably competing in a global marketplace, but foremost to help develop a more resilient and thus competitive business organization.

Individual departments in financial organizations no longer operate as solely autonomous units, but rather as supply chains. Therefore, it is an integrated approach to the planning and control of resources, services and information flows that adds value for customers through collaborative relationships among supply chain members.

And, as already mentioned, while bridges and co-operations exist among departments, there is usually a lack of unified vision on the entire chain. For example, front office and middle office will work together in terms of working with high quality data on transactions and clients, but do they think a step further how a disruption of their service would impact Accounting/ Finance, HR, Risk Management, etc.?

One may state that supply chain management should be conducted in the same manner in both manufacturing and service organizations. It is true, is it not, that both industries are attempting to procure inputs that can be utilized to provide value to the end customer.

And, while much work has been done to analyze the supply chain management construct in a manufacturing (goods-producing) environment, the same cannot be said in the services arena. As explained throughout this document, the service industries are unique with their own set of defining factors, characteristics and measurements.

Now, how does a 'merchandize' differs from a 'service'? Services are distinct from merchandises in terms of intangibility, heterogeneity, simultaneity (inseparability), perishability, and customer participation (Ahlstrom and Nordin, 2006; Sampson and Froehle, 2006).

Yet, despite these differences, there is tendency in attempting to apply existing product-based supply chain management frameworks toward services to gain understanding. However, the problem with utilizing traditional supply chain management frameworks is that they all focus on the physical flow of goods among members of a supply chain. Though the number of supplier levels (and thus the inherent complexity) may vary by supply chain, manufacturing is still principally ordered around tracking the physical movements that take place among channel members.

Yet, this common link is missing in services supply chains. In services, there is no overarching focus because the output is different depending upon the services delivered. Services focus upon many different deliverables. For example, in the professional services, it is the transfer of the service firm's capacity to the customer that is most important. While in maintenance and repair services, the focus is upon a physical change to the equipment brought in for servicing. Yet even in these cases, differences will apply depending upon the final customer's needs and requirements.

That's why one should acknowledge the difference between 'core services' and 'supporting services'. Core services are the products that are actually delivered to the customer for their benefit. While supporting services are additional services that may be provided to the customer in addition to the core service, they become part of the deliverable that makes up the total service experience. Supporting services may be produced by the service provider organization or by one of its suppliers (Baltacioglu et al., 2007). However, these services should still be managed by the principle service provider. This is substantiated by research that has shown how customer satisfaction is affected by supporting services even if sold separately by the external supplier (Vandaele and Gemmel, 2007).

With services it is important to focus on the "service performance" (i.e. providing to the customer what they believe they contracted the service firm to deliver). Thus, services are more of a transfer of capacity than a transfer of goods. In a services supply chain, human labor usually forms a significant component of the value delivered to the end customer. This includes finding the optimal mix of permanent versus temporary, seasonal or subcontracted labor, developing strategies for managing demand and controlling supply, and managing the degree of outsourcing and franchising, among others. These capacity choices are especially important in high-customer-contact services because of the inherent characteristics of services and the variation caused by customers in the process (Roth and Menor, 2003). Because of the human involvement in services, the variability and uncertainties in outputs are higher.

Supply Chain Risk Mgmt & 3rd Party Risk Mgmt

Whenever an external supply chain is flagged third party risk comes to the forefront. A third party, per the OCC, is "any business arrangement between a bank and another entity (that is not a customer), by contract or otherwise." So, while vendors and IT providers fall into that category, "third party" must also include any contractor, broker, sales agent, franchisee, networking arrangement, joint venture, correspondent bank, marketing partner affiliate, or subsidiary as examples. Historically, banks have focused on their "supply chain"—vendors providing goods and services to support a bank's operations. Recent guidance and reports from different banking regulators have made it very clear that they're concerned with a bank or regulated entity's ability to understand and manage the risk across their ecosystem. OCC Bulletin 2013-29 issued in October 2013 is very explicit that the entire risk management framework applies not only to vendor relationships but to all third-party relationships within the value chain.

And, the driving force behind this deeper focus on third-party management in the financial services sector is mainly the introduction of OCC 2013-29. The comptroller of the currency summed it up stating that the regulators have concerns regarding the quality of risk management on the growing volume, diversity, and complexity of banks' third-party relationships, both foreign and domestic." Use of a third party does not absolve the institutions of obligations to ensure prudent conduct of operations, including business continuity, disaster recovery, and termination strategies. There also is concern about data protection. Whether it is protection of personal information of employees or consumers, or confidential information of customers or the bank itself, it is imperative that the bank ensures the third party has sufficient controls in place to protect the data it will access.

Finally, it's about ensuring protection of the consumer. If a third party utilizes inappropriate marketing techniques or coercion on a consumer and misrepresents the facts to induce a consumer to take action, the bank for whom they are doing so will be held liable. One key issue is the need to address so called fourth parties—those entities that your own third parties may outsource to or use for certain tasks. How do you address this issue and keep it from becoming a rabbit hole? If the third party is going to sub-contract work, the bank needs to ensure that the third party has adequate controls in place to assess and manage their sub-contractor risk, and that the bank has the ability to terminate their relationship with the third party in the event there is an issue with the fourth party (or even a fifth party). The regulators do not expect banks to perform the same level of due diligence on fourth parties, but if a problem occurs with a fourth party, the bank will be held responsible. So, they need to have sufficient visibility to ensure compliance.

FIGURE 49: DESCRIPTION OF A BANK'S BUSINESS LINES

CONSUMER BANKING	INVESTMENT BANKING	COMMERCIAL BANKING
Branch, ATM, telephone and online banking	Investment bank	Middle market
Credit cards	Asset management	Mid-corporate
Small business	Treasury services	Commercial real estate
Home finance and home equity loans	Worldwide securities services	Business credit
Auto finance	Private banking	Equipment finance
Education finance	Private client services	
Retirement and investing	Equity partners	

Source: Oracle, 2015

The group within the bank that is focused on the supply chain involving these business lines is typically operational risk management, and among the responsibilities for managing these risks is establishing a corporate wide contingency planning program. This department propagates a corporate-wide focus on operational risks.

Among these efforts were projects aimed at identifying and managing supply chain risk in financial services. This involves managing the risk in a complex supply chain ranging from its suppliers to its customers, and also includes institutional entities and competitors. The firm's suppliers include traditional suppliers of goods and services, direct and indirect supplies, hardware, telecommunications, software, consulting services, and so on.

In addition, the firm's operations depend upon third party networks operated by the Federal Reserve and local Clearinghouses. The growing importance of the Internet, ongoing increases in customer expectations for immediate service, and plans of both customer and competitors all has to be factored into a supply chain risk assessment.

What is needed is a program that encompasses not only data processing, but also critical functions and subfunctions to ensure service to critical customers would continue. Identifying the critical customers is a challenge, as is determining what functions are critical.

All business components must have documented and tested business continuity plans for the full range of operational and data processing resources required for service delivery. The level of service to be provided in the event of a disaster is a business-driven decision based on the cost of providing that level of service, potential losses, and vulnerability to disasters.

The level of detail of the documentation is to be consistent with the business addressed, the complexity of the operating environment, service requirements, and is based on established risk management principles.

Risk management decisions are among the most conceptually difficult decisions managers face because, by their very nature, such decisions must come to grips with uncertainties surrounding highly unlikely events with major potential adverse impact upon the operation of a business. Ideally a control is both affordable and effective.

To address this complexity, the planning group develops and applies a risk management methodology for business continuity management that is implemented for all business units and geographic locations. The few implementation problems that arise need to be overcome by presenting the approach in an intuitively appealing way and by providing the means to incorporate subjective judgment.

Managers proved to be surprisingly receptive to such concepts as events, probability, expected value, and utility—as long as these concepts are presented in an intuitive rather than a mathematical framework. The approach increases managers' risk awareness and provides them with a structured way of addressing risk issues, which they also apply to other problems.

As a result of the initial project and resulting methodology, the planning group is charged with worldwide functional responsibility for business continuity and information security.

A wide range of potential risks can impact service delivery in any organization. The firm's business continuity methodology includes steps to identify disasters that may lead to events that cause losses, and also procedures for selecting cost justifies control alternatives that reduce the probability of events and mitigated losses. Services are disrupted when the resources required to deliver the services are unavailable.

Some typical threats include fire, flood, power outage, strike, civil disturbances, terrorism, acts of war, pandemics, and acts of nature. The relevance of these threats depends upon the geographic location, the structure of the buildings, and the political/economic conditions. For example, hurricanes may be a threat in Puerto Rico, but not in Switzerland.

The occurrence of a disaster event may create a service disruption for a specific length of time, for example, a three-day outage disabling processing for a floor of a building. The same event could result from any one of several disruptions and disasters. For example, loss of data processing support for three days could result from flooding of a data center, lack of power, or a small fire.

Business continuity planning focuses on those events that could result in significant losses. Alternatives are developed to reduce the risk or impact of an event. An alternative may provide protection against only one event or against several. Some alternatives reduce the probability that an event will occur; other alternatives reduce losses by providing some continuation of customer service during a disaster.

Earnings are affected by these alternatives, just as they are by insurance. Annualized costs of the alternatives are developed and compared to the reduction in the expected annualized risk exposure. To identify potential disasters, it is necessary to clearly understand the service delivery mechanism. Information common to all services and other information that is specific to each particular service is collected.

Specific events that could impact the functions and disrupt service are identified. Control alternatives are developed to reduce the probability of the event occurring or to mitigate the impact of the event on the delivery of service.

For the initial implementation of the program, operations managers are responsible for developing and implementing the continuity plans in accordance with business needs and the business managers are accountable for overall business continuity planning.

This framework is not intended to replace management's intuitive judgment on occasions when and the results of an analysis disagree with the manager's intuitive judgment, the source of the disagreement is isolated and resolved in order to provide proper implementation. Business managers review all services provided by their units to identify the critical services for which disruption would result in significant losses.

Business continuity plans for critical services (for example, money transfer) address the full range of resources required to deliver the services. The important role of computer sources and data make business continuity planning for data centers and telecommunications links critical elements. Business managers determine when the services needed to resume and what priority transactions need to be processed to avoid incurring significant losses.

Data collection is an important element of this process and is conducted via interviews, workshops and questionnaires. The result of this initial identification process indicates what areas require more detailed analyzes. Since an objective of business continuity planning is to limit the impact and risk of major disruptions to an acceptable level, determining how long services could be deferred before unacceptable losses are incurred was an essential element of the process.

For each service, business managers specify the minimum level of service required and how soon service should be provided to avoid such losses. Management then determines recovery time objectives (RTO) and recovery point objectives (RPO) from the solicited information.

Given the upstream and downstream nature of the supply chain, businesses with given RTOs and RPOs, at times, require other business units to raise their respective RTO/ RPO values. Business managers help estimate financial losses including lost fees, compensation and interest losses, penalties, and consequential damages.

Management also estimates the impact on future business, including which customers would be lost to competition, how long it would take to reestablish lost business and the cost of regaining lost business. The impact on projected growth and the impact on other services also are evaluated. Finally, if business could be redirected, or if a service bureau provided a service, the magnitude of these costs is estimated.

Business impact costs involve determining direct and indirect losses. Direct losses include those losses related to the service or services for which the business continuity plan is being developed, such as loss of assets, loss of documents, personnel costs, and financial costs. Indirect losses included loss of future business and consequential damages, for example, payments that are made to offset losses resulting from failure to provide service on a timely basis.

Developing a strategy involves selecting from a set of preferred alternatives that meet business continuity management objectives. For each critical business function, the available recovery alternatives are evaluated according to their costs and benefits.

These include selecting from cold, warm, and hot sites; manual procedures; reciprocal agreements; work from home; quick ship; and other alternatives.

Sometimes the decision is obvious—for example, when an alternative provided protection for most events and was relatively inexpensive. Occasionally, an alternative is the only one that would provide the continuation of a service in case of all major events, and the service is so vital that management could not accept its disruption.

Also, the additional expenditure is small because it is combined with other plans, such as when the decision to place operations at two or more locations is made at the same time as additional space is being acquired for expansion.

Because a business continuity management strategy must provide backup for all major events, a primary focus was to include off-site alternatives. Some events that result in unacceptable consequences (such as the loss of key markets, restrictions from regulatory agencies, or very high losses) are reviewed and are selected, even when their costs seem excessive.

Each combination of alternatives and events is evaluated by assigning relative ratings (excellent, good, fair, poor) with respect to each criterion. These ratings provide a qualitative evaluation useful in comparing strategies.

Management judgment is used in both assigning the ratings and selecting the strategy. When the selection of a set of alternatives is not obvious, a more detailed cost-benefit analysis is done. The benefit of an alternative is the reduction in potential losses compared to a base case.

Quantifying benefits require reviewing all the events for which the alternative provides some protection, and estimating how it reduces the expected loss for each of these events. All losses are considered in conjunction with insurance coverage, including self-insurance. The net benefit of an alternative is obtained by subtracting the total annual cost of the alternative from its annual benefit.

The alternative with the largest positive net benefit is selected as part of the overall strategy. Sensitivity analysis is performed to determine how changes in the estimates of costs, losses, and probabilities would affect the selection of a strategy.

SERVICES SUPPLY CHAIN MANAGEMENT - PRIME OPPORTUNITY

According to the U.S. Bureau of Economic Analysis (BEA) the service sector business currently accounts for about 80% of the U.S. Gross Domestic Product. About 69% of the supply chain management professionals surveyed indicated that measuring flows of services is more difficult than mapping flows of goods.

In light of the increasing trend towards outsourcing business processes and also the likelihood of moving these business processes to offshore locations, it is prudent for organizations to focus on improving the means for obtaining these services.

First, there are a number of barriers to address if service purchasing is to be improved (Tate, Ellram, and Billington, 2008).

- Growing supply base -- In the CAPS study, 58% reported an increase in the number of offshore services suppliers, while only 4% reported a decrease. The supply base is growing larger, and the suppliers now are more difficult to manage with differing cultural nuances.

- Knowing when to outsource -- Overdependence on service providers because of reliance on supplier-specific assets, such as ordering and information systems, decreases the power that the buyer has over the supplier. This opens the door for opportunistic supplier behavior.

- Absence of a holistic view of services spending -- In the CAPS study, less than 60% of services spending flows through formal systems and processes. The spending on services is fragmented across many functions and locations, and often flows through decentralized structures. In addition, it frequently involves non-standard services unlike the more refined processes for purchasing goods.

- Gap in information technology support -- Services buyers are less likely to be supported by technology and information systems, and often have to use software provided by the service suppliers for making services purchases and tracking services spending and supplier performance.

- Lack of resources focused on services -- The CAPS survey mentioned above found that the average buyer of direct material is responsible for 36 active suppliers. The average buyer of direct services is responsible for about 105 active suppliers. These buyers are responsible for approximately the same level of total spending. The dilution of the services buyers' time makes it difficult for the buyers to be proactive with their suppliers.

- Understanding of cost drivers and structures -- There is limited understanding of the cost drivers and underlying cost structures of the services supplied. Part of the problem with this lack of understanding is that it can create misaligned incentives, as the buyer might think that the supplier wants higher volume when the supplier really desires more certainty in its volume.

These barriers are critical because services spending is growing as a percentage of total spending as firms outsource more activities, such as back-office operations, that used to be performed entirely in-house.

In addition, because services have not been managed as closely, services now present a greater opportunity for potential cost savings than does the purchase of materials and components. The latter areas of spending have been closely scrutinized by most firms over the past decade or more so that the low-hanging fruit has already been harvested.

In light of the potential positive contribution of improved management of purchasing spending to the bottom line, we are providing a number of ideas for organizations to address the weaknesses in their services purchasing practices. These suggestions include:

- Allocate appropriate resources relative to economic return to the area of services supply management. If there is a big opportunity, it is sensible to dedicate more resources.

- Increase the professionalism of the services purchasing area. A professionally trained service buyer can help control both overbuying and overspending. Services supply managers should have either focused college degrees or additional training on buying, negotiations, cost management, and the particular type of services that they are buying.

- Measure effectiveness and ensure proper business controls. This can help reduce risk and improve compliance to Sarbanes Oxley. What gets measured gets done.
- Put the best people in services supply management. This will help to increase the level of accountability for services spending. In addition, this is where the greatest area of opportunity lies for most organizations. Materials and components supplier management and spending is already largely under control.
- Segment the purchasing spending based on value and risk. This will allow you to set priorities, and allocate time so as to reduce the risk while maximizing potential rewards.
- Understand the magnitude of the services purchasing spending. Without an understanding of the total spending, it is difficult to assess the potential for savings and difficult to make a business case for pursuing services-purchasing improvement.

Even though the purchasing of services is growing in importance and magnitude, the resources to manage it are not. Because of the current state of services purchasing, it appears that there are untapped opportunities for organizations to improve their services purchasing in terms of both cost and value by dedicating more, and perhaps different, resources to services purchasing.

Some companies realize the importance of involving supply management in the purchase of services, and that supply management involvement in services may not mirror their involvement in the purchase of direct materials.

For example, Bank of America (BofA) has put effort into developing an understanding of its total services spending. It reports that Supply Management is involved in 100% of its service purchases and views supply management as performing an essential, value-added service.

It has increased the resources dedicated to and the professionalism of services supply management through training and hiring people with skills in purchasing goods, or specific backgrounds in the services being purchased. The supply management personnel, in turn, train the users of the services to better measure and manage the service providers.

Thus, BofA is better matching resources with the opportunities it perceives and improving services spending visibility, control, and measurement. Yet, much of the responsibility is placed in the hands of the "users" of services rather than having supply management take control. The user involvement is appropriate in this case because the users specify the needs and are most aware of whether the service supplier is performing to expectations.

Dedicating skilled resources to establishing new systems for better managing the purchase of services could result in a tremendous return on investment and improvement in value of services for the dollars spent. Developing an outstanding capability to purchase, and manage the purchase of, services could truly be the next frontier for improved supply chain and organizational performance.

SUPPLY CHAIN RISK MGMT IMPROVING RESILIENCE

Whereas in the past the principal objective of supply chain design was cost minimization or service optimization, the emphasis today has to be upon resilience (Blackhurst et al., 2011). There are still fundamental issues that researchers need to address to offer managers a prescriptive model of how to create resilient supply chains. First, much of the existing research focuses on the question why the companies are vulnerable to supply chain disruptions (Blackhurst et al., 2011).

There are evidences that the tendencies of many companies to seek out low-cost solutions may have led to leaner but also more vulnerable supply chains (Svensson, 2000). The Japan earthquake in March 2011 is a perfect example of how an unexpected event can affect global supply chains. Second, the development of the field tends to focus on anecdotal studies and there is lack of empirical evidences of how companies improve the supply chain resilience.

Blackhurst et al. (2011) state that there is a limited amount of information on how to deal with supply chain disturbances from a practical perspective in both the short and the long-term. While the existing research is valuable, no coherent set of practices in supply chain resilience has emerged. The main objective of this book is to propose a model for supply chain resilience management using inductive theory building approach.

A number of unexpected events or disturbances are continuously appearing leading to supply chain failure. To sustain, or even to improve, the companies and respective supply chain performance after a disturbance occurrence, supply chain should be resilient to these events.

The identification of supply chain failure modes and resilience practices using multiple companies instead of single case studies was the base of this study. From the cross-case analysis, it was possible to get a wider picture of the companies' behavior when a disruptive event happens. Secondary data was collected from a sample of 77 companies affected by the Japan earthquake in 2011.

The sample provides evidence that despite the several negative effects provoked by earthquake, the companies failed to sustain their operations because of capacity shortages and material shortages.

These failures modes characterize the negative effects of SC disturbances and makes possible to respond to the first research question 'How do supply chain disturbances affect companies? Which are the main negative consequences of supply chain disturbances?'.

The sample also provides empirical evidences of the following 13x resilience practices that can be deployed to reduce the disturbance severity and the recovery time: use alternative production path, use alternative delivery path; change production schedule; recovery production capacity; reallocate resources; use materials buffers; alternative suppliers/strategic sourcing; change delivery schedule; find new suppliers; redesign products to include alternative materials; create supply chain visibility, supply chain common response; demand management.

This makes possible to respond to the second research question 'How do companies overcome the negative consequences of supply chain disturbances? Which are the practices deployed?'. Using an inductive theory building approach, eight propositions and one conceptual model are proposed to support the development of supply chain resilience.

The proposed model intends to offer a holistic perspective towards supply chain resilience improvement, which decision makings should be considered in supply chain design and implementation of resilient practices. From the managerial point of view the proposed model provides managers with a deeper understanding on how disturbances can affect the supply chain behavior and which practices are more appropriate to reduce the occurrence of failure modes. (H. Carvalho et al., 2012)

Also, this research contributes to highlight the importance of supply chain management in order to make the individual companies and corresponding supply chains more resilient. The occurrence of a capacity or material shortage in an individual company could have a negative impact on a set of upstream and downstream companies belonging to the same supply chain.

This makes more demanding the suppliers' selection process and leads companies to work with contingency plans. Despite the paper achievements some limitations to the study remain. The model was developed with secondary data extracted from a sample constituted by 62 documents containing information related to 77 companies.

Therefore, its validity is limited to the studied sample, for that reason the model is biased by the available information in documents. Moreover, only the following two sources to collect secondary data were used: 'Google news' and 'Reuters global news agency'.

Future researches should include the model validation by performing in-depth case studies to identify disturbances, failures and practices that maybe are not referred in the sample. Also, using a larger sample, it will be interesting to study if the practices deployed to reduce the disturbance severity that result from the failure modes depends on the size or the sector of the companies.

Supply Chain (Risk) Mgmt & 3rd Party Risk Mgmt

Generally speaking, one could define internal supply chain as the chain of activities within a company that concludes with providing a product to the customer. This process involves multiple functions within companies such as sales, production, and distribution. It is obvious that a company's performance would be enhanced by the integration of these functions.

When transposing this notion to the financial services industry, and the banking sector in particular, one good way is to adopt a fresh perspective on what banking is really about. By thinking of cash as goods, banks can apply proven supply chain risk management strategies to reduce excess inventory, lower handling and processing costs, improve operating efficiency and optimize their network.

More critically, banks that manage their cash supply chain more effectively can also improve productivity and better position themselves to compete in the marketplace.

It is equally important to pinpoint that services supply chain management relates to much more than solely the sourcing of any service by a firm or only certain types of services. A lot of information flow and human involvement come also to play within the operations of a services organization.

Traditionally supply chain risk management in the services industry is associated with third party risk management involving contractors, vendors and consultants that act as third party with the business organization.

But, a services organization has also first party and second party risk. Indeed, companies in the services industry rely on, for example, the collection of data, and with the increasing importance of the digital economy this is becoming even more paramount.

There are different data types with different meanings, which must be handled differently. Often, however, there is confusion, so we want to clarify the difference between first party, second party and third-party risk.

First party risk relates to data that the company itself collects from its audience and customers, such as the identification of customers or social data, for example. For instance, a bank will collect data such as the name, date of birth, address, contact details, gender, product preferences, credit history, transaction statements, etc.

These data are collected by, for example, the front office or portfolio managers which are the points of contact with the client, and in turn they will pass on these data points to other departments within the bank (Risk Management, Accounting, Middle Office, Back Office, Data Analytics, etc.).

The financial institution has access to the respective data set at any time (cf. easy access) and at no cost (cf. cost-effective), and can use the data as approved by the user. Direct control and the independence from third parties are the main advantages of being a first party. It is thanks to the sequence of information that ultimately a service can be rendered to the client, and as such the final delivery (the service) is the result of the chain that is being fed by various suppliers.

In order to enrich and extend their own data, a company sometimes has to resort to data that it has not collected by itself, such as in the case of a bank, the interest rates, the exchange rates, the asset prices (stocks, bonds, derivatives, etc.), or an external credit rating.

Therefore, companies often integrate data from other companies (Bloomberg, Reuters, rating agencies, etc.). This form of data is called second party data, or someone else's first party data. The organization purchases 2nd party data directly from the company that owns it; there's no middle-man in such a transaction. Thus, it requires the organization to seek out companies with data you need and form a relationship with them. However, a company has to pay caution when using the data.

There is always a dependency on the provider of this data. Are the data correct? Can I rely on the fact that the provider will not modify its terms and conditions any time soon and prohibit certain types of data usage? Can I use the data legally safe? This applies in particular to personal data, e.g. address data in email marketing. In case of doubt, the liability here is not with the provider, but with the user of the data.

FIGURE 50: DISTINCTION BETWEEN THE DIFFERENT DATA PARTIES

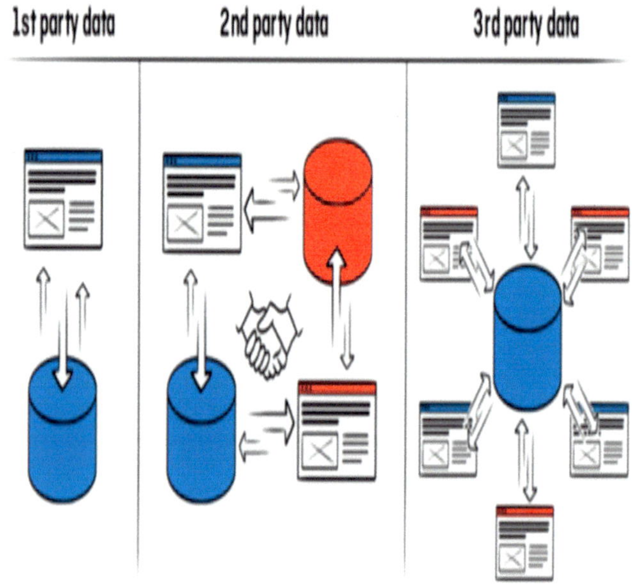

First, Second and Third Party Data (Source: Clearcode)

Source: IAB SEA+India, 2016

Second party data refers to data obtained from another provider. It can be either a one-time purchase or a lasting partnership in which the partners exchange data. For example, company A would like to buy data set X from company B. For company B, the data set X is first party data, since they collected the data by themselves. For enterprise A, the data set X becomes second party data, since A did not generate the data, but only company B. Company A is thus the “second party”.

In general, such an exchange or purchase is usually not a problem when it comes to anonymous market research data. In the case of personal data, the case is different since it is usually not possible to assume sufficient opt-ins to use this data. If a company buys data, it can always lead to dependencies or complications with the other company, so trustworthy partnerships are even more important.

If a company needs very specific records or a large amount of particular data, it may be helpful to access third party data. Third party data is data that the organization buys from outside sources that are not the original collectors of that data. Instead, organizations buy it from large data aggregators that pull it from various other platforms and websites where it was generated.

These aggregators pay publishers and other data owners for their 1st party data. Organizations can purchase this kind of data from external sources, which have also acquired the data or collected it themselves.

The business model of these external service providers is to collect, aggregate, and sell data from different sources.

A great advantage of third-party data is the fast availability and the large amount of available data. Negative is not only the cost. In addition, the use of this data is often questionable and risky, not only in terms of quality, but in terms of privacy regulations. For this reason, it is necessary to keep in mind the usage rights

Overall, one can identify basically several types of supply chain relationships within a financial institution. The one that was described as first and second party whereby on the one hand an internal supply chain is feeding an internal supply chain (i.e., aka: first party (a service provided by and to the benefit of the internal data supplier) and on the other hand a second party (a service provided by one data supplier to the benefit of another internal party) is supplying data to an internal agent.

However, there can also be instances where an internal agent will supply data and performs a service to the benefit of an external agent, who in turn will use the compounded information to yield a service to the company (for example, the bank will provide a third party a database will the outstanding risk exposures on a bond portfolios composed of asset backed securities; in turn this third party will analyze these portfolio data and use the analytics to deliver a particular service to the bank (for example a calculation of the actual risk appetite of the bank).

GENERAL CONCLUSION

In almost every respect, both banking organizations as well as manufacturers of finished goods, not to mention firms active in logistics, operate in an analogous business environment.

Banks transform commodities embodied by investor-supplied capital into the added-value financial services and products we know as savings accounts, residential mortgage loans, business loans or credit card accounts.

Concomitantly, these same banks rely on a variety of specialty suppliers (market data firms, scoring and credit ratings agencies, title and appraisal companies, data analytics vendors), loan servicers, secondary marketers, investors, and brokers.

Together, these relationships constitute a supply chain network as diversified, sophisticated and complex as anything found in logistics or manufacturing. As primary owners of the customer relationship and originators of most financial transactions, banking organizations are the core locomotives that drive supply chains within the financial services industry. With competition globalizing and hence intensifying, these same banking institutions are feeling the strain of the need to offer more competitive products that are highly desirable with the lowest possible price.

Similar to logistics companies and manufacturers, their endeavor in delivering better and more economical products to consumer markets relies in large measure on their ability to procure materials and services from business partners in the supply chain faster and at a lower cost.

In today's technological environment, business interactions with supply chain partners (whether internal (first party suppliers) or external (second/ third/ fourth/ fifth party suppliers) are conducted increasingly through efficient, low-cost e-business systems. As the efficiency and speed of these online systems increase, the individual firms' business activity becomes an increasingly collaborative and interactive process.

To respond optimally, all supply chain partners need greater holistic visibility into one another's operations and greater connectivity with one another's information and transaction processing systems. The entire supply chain must become one extended electronic network in which each participant has an increasing stake in the success of its trading partners.

And every link in the supply chain network has a major stake in the success of the originator. If banking institutions cannot correctly perceive and satisfy the needs of the customer, then the whole supply chain withers.

As a supply chain is looked upon as a network, such perspective enables banking organizations to look at the overall movement of data, materials, and cash from start to end, in turn allowing banks to see the value in creating partnerships; and the value in collaborating to ensure the best possible value is delivered to the end-customer. In other words, introducing the term network in supply chains allows banking organizations to look at the bigger holistic picture; giving them a better understanding of the flow of materials, cash, and information. Often banking institutions tend to focus solely on their organization; what they deliver or provide and not what the end-customer receives. Effective customer relationship management (CRM) probably represents the quest for the Holy Grail of supply chain management within the banking industry, since genuine CRM necessitates the integration of applications, as diverse as:

- exposure management system
- customer profitability analysis
- marketing
- demographics
- credit rating & scoring
- desktop underwriting
- contact center management systems

The more and sooner that banking organizations embrace the various stakeholders and contributors to the (internal & external) supply chain networks as partners and prime movers, the more readily they can adopt and exploit the take-away lessons that others have learned about the difficult and arduous task of integrating the supply chain. What are the key lessons for integrating a banking organization within the entire supply chain network, i.e., not just the typical third party or vendor risk, but foremost also the first party suppliers (cf. those that are part of the internal supply chain) as well as the second party suppliers (data that you buy directly from first party data owners)? What steps need banking organizations to take to design a supply chain network whose primary purpose is to assess organizational policies and programs and to meet targets to accomplish long-term strategic objectives?

Given that most functional areas or business units within an organization are impacted by a network design project, it is critical to acknowledge that a proper design of an organization's network helps determine its supply chain efficiency and customer satisfaction.

First Take Away Lesson: Map a Supply Chain that connects 1st, 2nd, 3rd, 4th, and 5th party data providers

Although in the corporate world supply chain management has been characterized as the integrated management of the flow of goods and services that includes both movement and storage of goods within a company as those outside the walls of the company (by relying on contractors and third parties, for example), interestingly enough, within the financial services industry, nothing comparable exists.

FIGURE 51: DIFFERENCE BETWEEN VARIOUS PARTIES

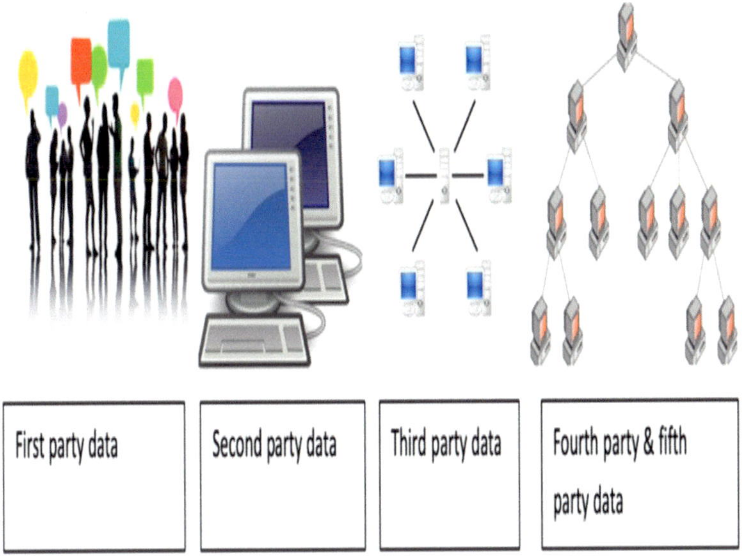

Source: SupplyChain247, 2015

Banking institutions do not possess a combined approach in managing the different phases aimed at delivering an end-product/service to a customer, and where they view, for example, the lending process as a supply chain. As such, banking organizations do not map a streamlined fully integrated chain of supply of services that involves internal units (i.e., back office, middle office, risk management, business developers, finance, and IT, f. ex.) in connection with second, third, fourth and even fifth party data suppliers.

That is, they do not view their supply chains as a vast network of intertwined supply chains, while they should. All these units within the organization operate in silo with, yes, bridges between themselves, but without really thinking about their service as being part of an integrated chain encompassing the entire organization.

Strictly speaking, while banks manage third party risks, they do not have at their disposal a mapping that reflects and connects the dots between, for instance, first party and second party as well as third party data providers; thus, banks are lacking in the risk management of a front-to-back processing for all banking activities.

They need an all-inclusive and exhaustive holistic picture of the entire supply chain (network). As a reminder, supply chain risk management aims at reducing supply-chain vulnerability via a coordinated holistic approach, involving all supply-chain stakeholders, which identifies and analyzes the risk of failure points within the supply chain. Risks to the supply chain range from unpredictable natural threats to counterfeit products, and reach across quality, security, to resiliency and product integrity.

Mitigation plans to manage these risks can involve logistics, cybersecurity, finance and risk management disciplines; the ultimate goal being to ensure supply chain continuity in the event of a scenario which otherwise would have interrupted normal business and so profitability.

SECOND TAKE AWAY LESSON: SUPPLY CHAIN AS A NETWORK

Organizations, including banks, are often part of a larger network of organizations, a supply-chain network can be used to highlight interactions between organizations; they can also be used to show the flow of information and materials across organizations.

In an effort to improve their competitive position in a rapidly changing marketplace, many organizations have replaced their traditional supply chains with extended supply chain networks built on a foundation of supply chain collaboration.

FIGURE 52: CASH SUPPLY CHAIN NETWORK

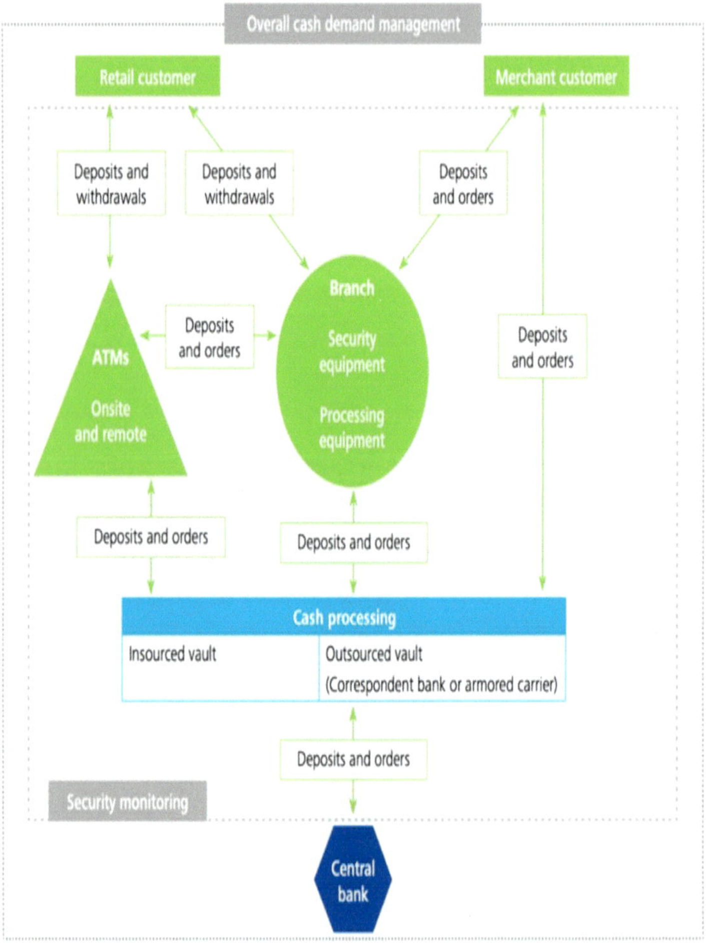

<u>Source</u>: Deloitte, 2013

By introducing the term network in supply chains, it allows organizations to look at the bigger holistic picture; giving them a better understanding of the flow of materials and information (cf. and, in the case of banking organizations, data and cash).

Often organizations focus only on their organization; what they manufacture or provide and not what the end customer receives. Looking at a supply chain as a network enables organizations to look at the overall movement of materials/information from start to end, allowing organizations to see the value in creating partnerships; and the value in working together to ensure the best possible value is provided to the end-customer.

Overall, supply chain network integration can seem a daunting task, and it can be a time-consuming process. However, the rewards, such as simplification of the entire lending transaction, lower operating costs, enhanced interest margins, and improved customer service, and foremost a holistic view on the entire supply chain network make the process well worth the effort.

THIRD TAKE AWAY LESSON: CUSTOMER EXPERIENCE

Process management embodied by workflow systems, as their name implies, automate the way work moves through an organization. Many workflow systems are established with an eye toward decreasing costs while concomitantly improving employee productivity.

FIGURE 53: EXAMPLE OF APPROVAL WORKFLOW

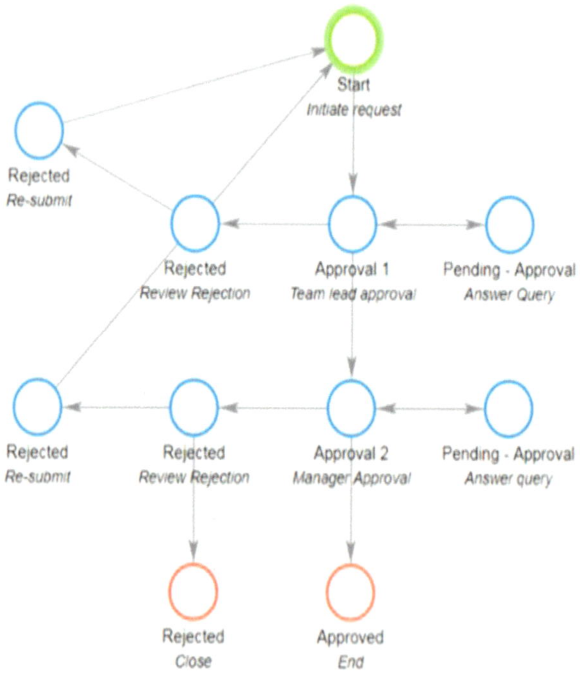

Source: Comindware, 2018

This internal focus on process management neglects the most important part of the entire transaction: the customer. Whether the workflow system is automating consumer loan origination and underwriting, or the purchase of products off the worldwide web, the end result of the workflow initiative should be improved customer service.

Improved customer service does not naturally occur once a workflow system is in place. Consider the consumer loan origination process; for most consumers, the entire processing of the loan, from taking the application to signing the closing documents, is uncomfortable. The very nature of the loan transaction, with its complexity and relative high dollar amount, causes consumer anxiety and unnecessary stress.

However, much more can and need to be done to improve the whole customer experience. For instance, automating the process of assembling consumer loan packages - including ordering and evaluating credit scoring searches, income statements and tax returns, and the like - would enable consumer lenders to spend more time on the personal aspects of the customer relationship and less on the logistics.

In addition, a system that automates the receiving and sending of data between supply chain partners would enable customers to view online a detailed status of their consumer loan. Does the underwriter require additional information of the income and assets of the loan applicant? Is loan applicant credit clouded by a lien that was actually satisfied two years ago?

Giving customers timely information about their loan can help ease their anxiety and provide them with a sense of control over the lending process, and hence an enhanced customer experience.

Fourth Take-Away Lesson: Expected Business Return

As fashionable acronyms feed the "alphabet soup" that characterizes the digital business integration arena, where mean different things to different people and new sets of letters are coined daily.

The same project may be described variously as workflow management, business process management, EAI or SCM, depending on the scope and extent of the project and the systems manager, consultant or technology provider involved.

The technology effort required to implement an EAI project may vary enormously. It could run from coding a simple interface between two legacy systems to installing a comprehensive new IT backbone, complete with message brokers and Web applications servers that can cost millions of dollars.

FIGURE 54: EXAMPLE OF PROCESS IMPROVEMENT IN BANKING

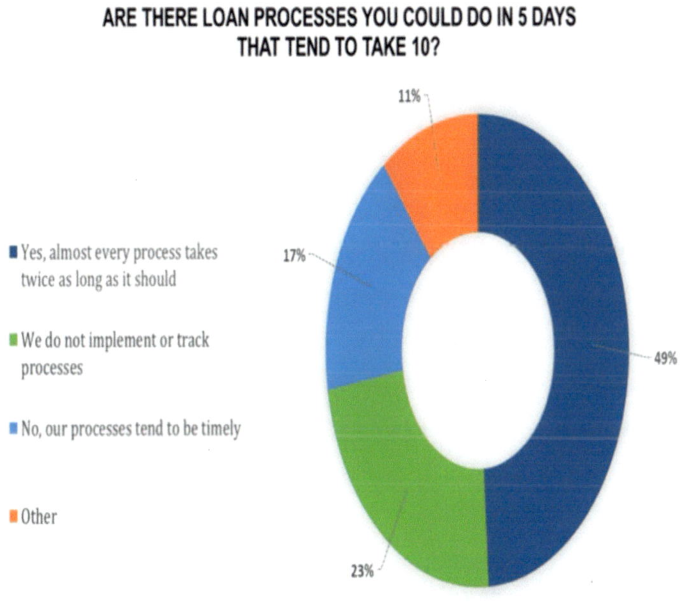

Source: Abrigo, 2019

Regardless of the scope, the focus should be not on connectivity but on process improvement. The danger here is that the use of murky terminology to characterize the project can confuse and distort the basic scope and objectives.

The resulting confusion can influence the choice of technology required to implement the project, with dire consequences for budgets, schedules and user satisfaction. Thus, banks need to be mindful when defining their projects carefully and specifically, in the terms appropriate to each and every business line within the bank.

For instance, if the banks want to "automate the application and approval processes for consumer loans under $25,000, which will enable the bank to double its volume with the same number of people" defines the project scope much better than "We want to do EAI for consumer loans." And a more precise definition ultimately helps the bank sell the project to others in an organization more easily.

Fifth Take Away Lesson: Two-Way Communication

Any relationship improves with two-way communication and true interaction, and the same is true for banking product flows, such as loan origination or credit card process. At first glance, the banking supply chain may seem linear: one step in the process triggers the next step, and so on.

FIGURE 55: COMMUNICATION IN SUPPLY CHAINS

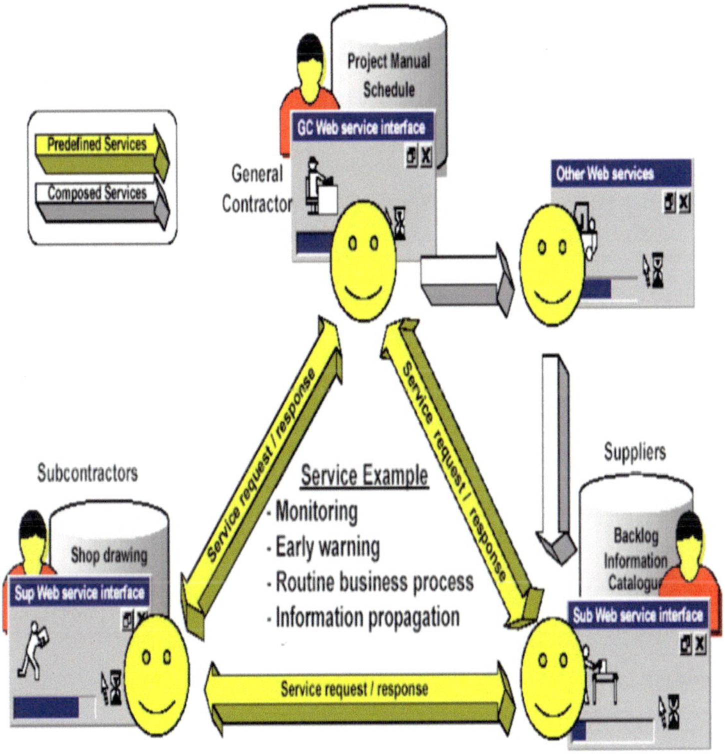

Source: Cutting-Decelle et al., 2007

For example, with some lenders, the completion of the underwriting typically means it's time to request a credit score search. But the banking origination process is not linear; instead, multiple actions can be occurring simultaneously. Try mapping out the steps for originating and booking, for example, a loan, and you will be amazed at the amount of back-and-forth that happens between supply chain participants, hence the term supply chain network.

Let's say the appraisal in the scope of a mortgage loan comes in at $15k below the sales price. Such a finding could trigger multiple tasks that could be automated, including advising sellers, borrowers, and real estate agents that they need to renegotiate, notifying the closing entity of the need for additional documentation and verifying that the LTV (loan-to-value) ratio is still within the accepted range. Once the partners negotiate a new sales price, the lender can automatically launch a title search and order the proper amount of title insurance. Recognizing the amount of collaboration that goes on among supply chain network participants is the first step in automating the process. Until one understands where all the data comes from, who uses it and what they use it for, one will not be able to make valid decisions about what you need to change.

SIXTH TAKE AWAY LESSON: INDEPENDENT "RULES ENGINE"

In the past, stand-alone applications were the norm, and programmers coded business rules directly into applications. For instance, in a mortgage processing system there might be a set of rules to determine who can approve a loan booking, in what amounts and within what price ranges or geographic areas. Other rules might specify what type of documentation is required before a cash disbursement can be made. Still others might mandate steps for compliance with regulatory requirements.

FIGURE 56: BUSINESS RULES AND PROCESSES ENGINE

Source: SupplyChain247, 2015

The problem, of course, is that business rules change, and, so do banking regulatory requirements. Likewise, so do organizations, especially in the banking arena, where mergers and acquisitions continue to be regular occurrences.

When banking institutions merge and consolidate, each party brings along its existing supply chain relationships and supply chain management systems. If the expectations that drove the merger are to be realized, the merged organization must reconstitute these existing supply chain applications and business relationships into a new supply chain network. If business rules are coded within individual applications, then the continuing changes to business rules will require constant recoding--an expensive and time-consuming prospect. (Remember that some legacy systems go back, for instance, some 30 years and require programming skills that may no longer be easy to find.)

A far better solution is to incorporate business process rules into a separate rules engine that can be readily accessed. Ideally, business line managers and business analysts will be able to modify these rules without calling in the programmers. Such rules engines already exist, and some feature graphical interfaces that make it easy for nonprogrammers to modify existing rules and establish new ones.

Seventh Take Away Lesson: Supply Chain Network

Operational risks are stemmed from operations, i.e., from activities and resources. Any potential source that generates a negative impact on the information, goods, and cash in the operations is an operational risk.

FIGURE 57: OPERATIONAL RISK IN SUPPLY CHAINS

Source: Supplychain247, 2015

The inclusion of cash owing through the operation implies that financial and operational risks are not mutually exclusive. Operational risks refer to a company's reduced ability to produce and supply products and services as a consequence of a breakdown in a core operating, manufacturing, or processing capability (Sadgrove, 2005).

This category also includes operational problems caused by human-resource problems, capacity constraints, logistics challenges, IT problems, and leadership issues. Operational risks include the everyday management of the supply chain whereas disruptions risks are associated with unexpected events including natural disasters.

And, with the ever-increasing push for efficiency, supply chains today are getting more and more risky. No matter how strong is the supply chain, risk and uncertainty come, risk and uncertainty come into the picture by disrupting the operational flow.

Some of the operational risk factors have been described as follows, such as poor quality, utility failure, HR problems, IT system failure, loss of key equipment's, personnel and suppliers, theft of information, logistic route/mode disruption, and computer virus.

Alas, operational risk management as it is organized today within banking organization does not formalize by means of a mapping of the interrelationships and interactions between the various stakeholders that are part of a supply chain network, i.e., 1st, 2nd, 3rd, 4th, and 5th party data providers.

Operational risk managers do not sufficiently look in a holistic way at the entire chain as an integrated network constituted of the various data providers. In practice, operational risk managers do not have a say when SLAs are drafted among internal parties and with external data providers, even though a host of operational risks do arise in a supply chain:

The symbiosis between supply chain management and operational risk management is yet to be formalized as associated risks with the operation in supply chain network have not sufficiently or inadequately been mapped.

Banking executives need to identify and measure the impact of operational risks on a supply chain network and develop suitable strategies to manage them.

Both the Basel Committee as well as the regulators, and foremost the risk management executives within the bank, need to make this a priority in order to better comprehend the risks associated with a supply chain network.

Eight Take Away Lesson: Enterprise Risk Mgmt

The goal of supply chain risk management is to acknowledge activities across and within organizations with the aim to deliver better customer value and foster a stronger resilience. Achieving resilience through better supply chain risk management does not mean avoiding risk.

The ability of an organization to take on additional risk can be the key to its overall competitive edge. Organizations can weigh the relative trade-offs of risk versus opportunities so they can make decisions that directly lead to competitive advantage.

FIGURE 58: ENTERPRISE RISK MANAGEMENT AND SUPPLY CHAINS

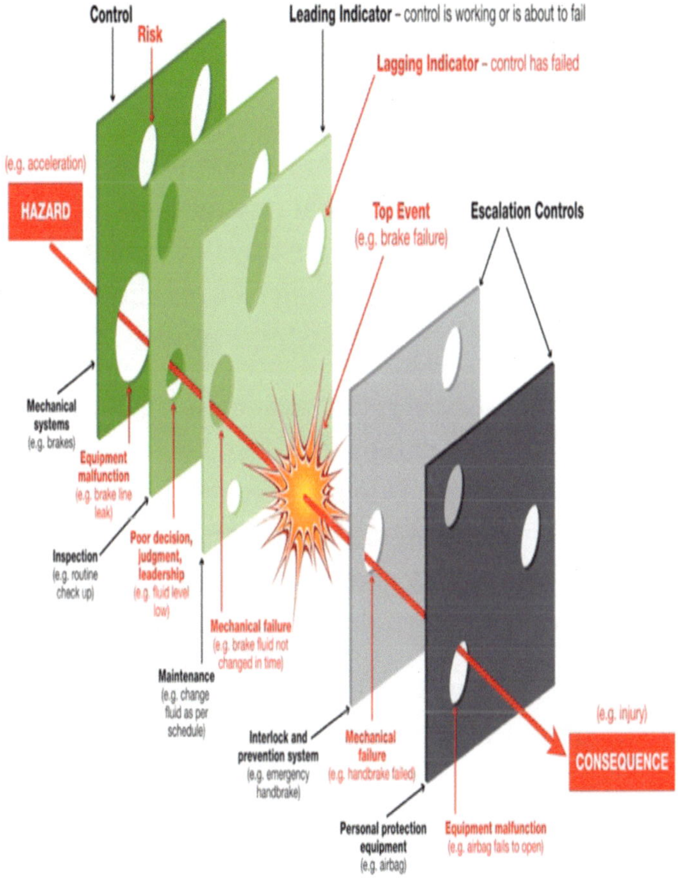

Source: Operational Sustainability, 2019

Complex, multi-stakeholder, outsourced and even cross-border delivery schedules mean that few banks (and businesses overall) can claim accurate visibility to any significant depth in the supply chains of their various business lines.

Supply chain risk management and supply chain resilience are therefore essential risk mitigation approaches that should underpin any decision to optimize supply chains in the long run, and hence help build more resilient banking business models.

Alas, today's operational risk management within banks does not embrace nor comprehend that view of supply chain risk management. Due to those facts, resilience is becoming the primary concern of any banking organization, and supply chain risk management can be one of the tools to achieve this resilience.

The good news is that the theories of supply chain risk management and supply chain resilience have been studied in relation to the use of qualitative risk tools to help the banking industry (and in particular the U.S. Global Systemically Important Banks (G-SIBs)) become more resilient when facing tail events.

Though, as a result of the increasing complexity of many supply chains and their environments, the mapping processes revolving around the formalization and acknowledgement of supply chains affecting also the banking industry might not suffice to warrant that for all eventualities a contingency plan exists.

That is why supply chain risk management needs to be combined with the concept of supply chain resilience as the latter which aims to ensure that the supply chain can bounce back from risks irrespective of their cause.

WORKS CITED

Abdou, K. And Kathawala, U., 2003, Supply Chain Evaluation In The Service Industry; Eastern Illinois University. Available At Https://Www.Emeraldinsight.Com/Doi/Abs/10.1108/02686900310455137

Abilla, P., 2010, Difference Between Manufacturing And Service, December 20, Available At Http://Www.Shmula.Com/Lean-Difference-Between-Manufacturing-Service/7773/

Åhlström, P. And Nordin, F., 2006, Problems Of Establishing Service Supply Relationships: Evidence From A High-Tech Manufacturing Company. Journal Of Purchasing & Supply Management, 12(2), 75-89.

Amit, Raphael, And Schoemaker, P., 1993, Strategic Assets And Organizational Rent Strategic Management 14(1), Pp. 33-46. Available At Http://Www.Jstor.Org/Stable/2486548.

Apics - Association For Operations Management Http://Www.Apics.Org/?Gclid=Eaiaiqobchmitofyl_A-4givxrjach2q9gyjeaayasaaegimlfd_Bwe

Appel, F., 2012, New Models For Addressing Supply Chain And Transport Risk, World Economic Forum. Available At

Https://Www.Weforum.Org/Reports/New-Models-Addressing-Supply-Chain-And-Transport-Risk

Ariba, 2009. Lessons Learned From The Recession: Supply Risk, Ariba Resource Library. Available At /Www.Ariba.Com/Resourcelibrarys.

Arkieva, 2018, Demand Driven Supply Chain Management. Available At: Https://Blog.Arkieva.Com/Demand-Driven-Supply-Chain/

Armerding, T., 2018, The 18 Biggest Data Breaches Of The 21st Century, Cso, December 20. Available At Https://Www.Csoonline.Com/Article/2130877/The-Biggest-Data-Breaches-Of-The-21st-Century.Html

Aydin, G., Babich, V., Beil, D., Yang, Z., 2009. Decentralized Supply Risk Management. Working Paper, Georgetown University.

Ayers, J.B., 2001. Handbook Of Supply Chain Management. Boca Raton: The St. Lucie Press/Apics Series.

Axa, 2015, Annual Report 2014. Available At Http://Annualreport.Axa/

Axa, 2015, Strategy And Commitments. Available At Http://Www.Axa.Com/En/Responsibility/Strategy-Commitments/.

Ballou, R., Gilbert, S. And Mukherjee, A., 2000. New Managerial Challenges From Supply Chain Opportunities. Industrial Marketing Management, 29 (1), Pp.7-18.

Baltacioglu, T., Ada, E., Kaplan, M. D., Yurt, O. And Kaplan, Y. C., 2007, A New Framework For Service Supply Chains, The Service Industries Journal, Vol. 27, No 2, Pp. 105-24.

Bank Of America, 2015, Corporate Social Responsibility In 2014, July 6. Available At Http://About.Bankofamerica.Com/Assets/Pdf/Bank-Of-America-2014-Corporate-Social- Responsibility-Report.Pdf.

Bea Studies - Https://Www.Bea.Gov/Industry/Industry-Economic-Accounts-Information-Guide

Blackhurst, J., Dunn, K. S., & Craighead, C. W., 2011, An Empirically Derived Framework Of Global Supply Resiliency. Journal Of Business Logistics, 32(4), Pp. 374-391. Available At Http://Dx.Doi.Org/10.1111/J.0000-0000.2011.01032.X.

Blome, C. And Schoenherr, T., 2011, Supply Chain Risk Management In Financial Crisis, International Journal Of Production Economics, 134(1), November, Pp. 43-57.

Blos, M. F., Wee, H. M., And Yang, W-H., 2012, Supply Chain Risk Management: Resilience And Business

Continuity, Intelligent Systems Reference Library. Available At Https://Link.Springer.Com/Chapter/10.1007/978-3-642-25755-1_12.

Borghesi, A. And Gaudenzi, B., 2012, Operational Risk And Supply Chain Risk Management, Risk Management. Perspectives In Business Culture. Available At Https://Link.Springer.Com/Chapter/10.1007/978-88-470-2531-8_8#Citeas.

Bowersox, D., Closs, D. And Cooper, B., 2002, Supply Chain Logistics Management. New York: Mcgraw-Hill/Irwin.

Bozarth, C. And Handfield, R.B., 2008, Introduction To Operations And Supply Chain Management. 2nd Edition. Upper Saddle River: Pearson Prentice Hall.

Brindley, Cl., 2004, Supply Chain Risk. England: Ashgate Publishing Ltd

Bsr, Supply Chain Sustainability In The Financial Sector, August 2015. Available At Https://Www.Bsr.Org/Reports/Bsr_Financial_Sector_Supply_Chain_Sustainability_2015.Pdf

Bsr And United Nations Global Compact, 2015, Supply Chain Sustainability / A Practical Guide For Continuous Improvement, Second Edition, June. Available At Https://Www.Unglobalcompact.Org/Docs/Issues_Doc/Supply_Chain/Supplychainrep_Spre Ad.Pdf.

Caddick, M. And Buchanan, T., 2011, Business Continuity And Supply Chain Risk, Pwc. Available At Https://Www.Pwc.Co.Uk/Assets/Pdf/Business-Continuity-And-Supply-Chain-Risk-April-2011.Pdf

Căescu, Ş.C. And Dumitru, I., 2011, Particularities Of The Competitive Environment In The Business To Business Field. Management & Marketing, 6 (2), Pp. 273-284.

Camerinelli, E., 2017, Supply Chain Collaboration: Why Banks Should Care, Finextra. Available At Https://Www.Finextra.Com/Blogposting/14219/Supply-Chain-Collaboration-Why-Banks-Should-Care.

Cassivi, L., 2006, Collaboration Planning In A Supply Chain, Supply Chain Management: An International Journal, Vol. 11, No. 3, Pp. 249–258.

Chae, B., 2009, Developing Key Performance Indicators For Supply Chain: An Industry Perspective. Supply Chain Management, 14(6), Pp. 422-428. Available At Http://Dx.Doi.Org/10.1108/13598540910995192.

Chandra, C. And Kumar, S., 2000, Supply Chain Management In Theory And Practice: A Passing Fad Or A Fundamental Change?, Industrial Management And Data Systems, Vol. 100, No. 3, Pp.100–114.

Chartered Institute Of Purchasing & Supply, 2012, Purchasing & Supply Management Jargon Buster. [Online] Chartered Institute Of Purchasing & Supply. Available At

<Http://Www.Cips.Org/Pagefiles/54881/Cips%20psmjargonbuster_V2.Pdf> [

Chen, I. J. And Paulraj, A., 2004, Towards A Theory Of Supply Chain Management: The Constructs And Measurements. Journal Of Operations Management, 22 (2), Pp. 119-150.

Cho, D. W., Young, H. L., Sung, H. A., And Swang, M. K., 2012, A Framework For Measuring The Performance Of Service Supply Chain Management, Computers And Industrial Engineering, Vol. 62, Pp. 801-818.

Chopra, S. And Meindl, P., 2007, Supply Chain Management: Strategy, Planning, And Operation. 3rd Edition. Upper Saddle River: Pearson Prentice Hall.

Christopher, M. And Peck, H., 2004, Building The Resilient Supply Chain - The Five Principles Of Supply Chain Resilience, Logistics Europe, Vol. 12 No. 1, Pp.16-21. Available At Https://Theicor.Org/Art/Present/Art/Arsc00038.Pdf

Christopher, M., & Peck, H., 2004, Building The Resilient Supply Chain. International Journal Of Logistics Management, 15(2), 1-14. Available At Http://Dx.Doi.Org/10.1108/09574090410700275.

Cia, 2018, The World Factbook. Available At Https://Www.Cia.Gov/Library/Publications/The-World- Factbook/Fields/2018.Html

Citigroup Inc., 2015, Citi Global Citizenship Report, July 4, Available At Http://Www.Citigroup.Com/Citi/About/Data/Corp_Citizenship/2014-Citi-Global-Citizenship- Report-En.Pdf.

Commission, U. S., 2018),Recent Trends In U.S. Services Trade. Washington Dc: Usitc. Available At Https://Www.Usitc.Gov/Publications/332/Pub4789.Pdf

Cooke, J. A., 2010, At Kraft Cash Is King, Supply Chain Quarterly. Available At Https://Www.Supplychainquarterly.Com/Topics/Finance/Scq201001kraft/

Cooper, M. C. And Ellram, L. M., 1993. Characteristics Of Supply Chain Management And The Implications For Purchasing And Logistics Strategy. The International Journal Of Logistics Management, 4 (2), Pp.13-24.

Coso, 2004, Enterprise Risk Management Comes From The Committee Of Sponsoring Organizations Of The Treadway Commission. Available At Https://Www.Coso.Org/Pages/Erm-Integratedframework.Aspx

Council Of Supply Chain Management Professionals, 2012, Cscmp Supply Chain Management Definitions. [Online] Council Of Supply Chain Management Professionals. Available At: <Http://Cscmp.Org/Aboutcscmp/Definitions.Asp> [Accessed 10 September 2012].

Davis, L., 2017, Mortgage Supply Chain Failure And Innovation, Boston College Journal Of Law & Social Justice , Vol. 37, No. 6. Available At Https://Lawdigitalcommons.Bc.Edu/Cgi/Viewcontent.Cgi?Referer=Https://Www.Google.Com/&Httpsredir=1&Article=1116&Context=Jlsj

Deutsche Bank, 2015, Sustainable Supply Chain: Organizing The Procurement Process Responsibly, April 15. Available At Https://Www.Db.Com/Cr/En/Concrete- Supply-Chain.Htm.

Dost, M. K., Rehman, C., Gilaninia, S., Ismail, K., And Akram, M., 2018, The Impact Of Knowledge Management's Practices On Supply Chain Performance Of The Dairy Sector In Central Punjab: A Mediating Role Of Decentralization, Economic Research-Ekonomska Istraživanja, 31(1), Pp. 290-312.

Drucker P.F., 1994, The Theory Of The Business, Harvard Business Review, September - October.

Dsci, 2017, Case Study: Colgate Palmolive Transforms Supply Chain With Smart Manufacturing, October 12. Available At Https://Www.Dscinstitute.Org/Resources-And-Tools/Case-Studies/Case-Study-Colgate-Palmolive-Transforms-Supply-Chain-With-Smart-Manufacturing

Dsci, 2016, Digital Supply Chains: A Frontside Flip, October. Available At

Https://Www.Thecge.Netweb/Viewer.Html?File=/Wp-Content/Uploads/2016/09/Final-Dsciwhitepaper.Pdf

Dupras, L., 2014, Trading Off Risks For Competitive Advantage, Neturania, March 30. Available At Http://Www.Neturania.Com/In-The-News/Personsnameonfacethenation

Elgazzar, S. And Elzarka, S., 2017, Supply Chain Management In The Service Sector: An Applied Framework, College Of International Transport And Logistics, Arab Academy For Science, Technology And Maritime Transport Alexandria, May. Available At Http://Www.Abrmr.Com/Myfile/Conference_Proceedings/Con_Pro_37094/Conference_59434.Pdf

Ellegaard, C., 2008, Supply Risk Management In A Small Company Perspective. Supply Chain Management: An International Journal 13 (6), Pp. 425–434.

Ellram, L. M., Tate, W. L. And Billington, C., 2007, Understanding And Managing The Services Supply Chain, Journal Of Supply Chain Management, Vol. 40, No.4, Pp. 17-32.

Ey, 2015, Building The Bank Of 2030: Top Eight Global Trends, Availabkle At Http://Www.Ey.Com/Gl/En/Industries/Financial-Services/Banking---Capital-Markets/8- Trends-Shaping-The-Bank-Of-2030.

Faisal, M.N., Banwet, D.K. & Shankar, R., 2007, Management Of Risk In Supply Chains: Scor Approach And Analytic Network Process, Supply Chain Forum: An International Journal, Vol. 8 No. 2, Pp. 66-79.

Fdic, 2018, Rms Manual Of Examination Policies Federal Deposit Insurance Corporation, Federal Deposit Insurance Corporation, Section 3-2. Available At Https://Www.Fdic.Gov/Regulations/Safety/Manual/

Felea, M. And Albăstroiu, I., 2013, Defining The Concept Of Supply Chain Management And Its Relevance Toromaniann Academics And Practitioners, Academy Of Economic Studies, Supply Chain Management, Vol. Xv, No. 33. Available At Http://Www.Amfiteatrueconomic.Ro/Temp/Article_1176.Pdf

Fiksel, J., 2006, Sustainability And Resilience: Toward A Systems Approach, Sustainability: Science, Practice And Policy, 2:2, Pp. 14-21.

Filkins, B. L., Kim, J. K., Roberts,B. , Armstrong,W., Miller, M. A., Hultner, M. L., Castillo, A. P., Ducom, J-C., Topol, E. J., And Steinhubl, S. R., 2016, Privacy And Security In The Era Of Digital Health: What Should Translational Researchers Know And Do About It?, Ncbi, 8(3): 1560–1580, March 15. Available At Https://Www.Ncbi.Nlm.Nih.Gov/Pmc/Articles/Pmc4859641/

Fine, C.H., Vardan, R., Pethick, R. And El-Hout, J., 2002, Rapid-Response Capability In Value-Chain Design, Mit Management Sloan Review, Winter, January 15. Available At Https://Sloanreview.Mit.Edu/Article/Rapidresponse-Capability-In-Valuechain-Design/

Floridatech, 2019, Supply Chain Management Vs. Value Chain Management. Available At Https://Www.Floridatechonline.Com/Blog/Process-Improvement/Supply-Chain-Management-Vs-Value-Chain-Management/

Flynn, S. E., 2007, The Edge Of Disaster: Rebuilding A Resilient Nation. Random House, New York, Usa.

Galvin, J., Han, F., Hynes, S., Qu, J., Rajgopal, K. And Shek, A., 2018, Synergy And Disruption: Ten Trends Shaping Fintech, Mckinsey, December. Available At Https://Www.Mckinsey.Com/Industries/Financial-Services/Our-Insights/Synergy-And-Disruption-Ten-Trends-Shaping-Fintech

Gates, B., 2019, We Didn't See This Coming, Gates Notes. February. Available At Https://Www.Gatesnotes.Com/2019-Annual-Letter

Gell-Mann, M., 1995, The Quark And The Jaguar: Adventures In The Simple And The Complex, W. H. Freeman & Co. New York.

Geman, B., 2015, Obama: 'No Challenge Poses A Greater Threat To Future Generations Than Climate Change', The Atlantic, January 20. Available At Https://Www.Theatlantic.Com/Politics/Archive/2015/01/Obama-No-Challenge-Poses-A-Greater-Threat-To-Future-Generations-Than-Climate-Change/446841/

Gerald, E.S., 2016, Factors Affecting The Performance Of Supply Chain Financing In Kenya: A Case Study Of Commercial Bank Of Africa, Fall. Available At Http://Erepo.Usiu.Ac.Ke/Bitstream/Handle/11732/3103/Euster%20seghete%20gerald%20final%20project.Pdf?Sequence=1&Isallowed=Y

Gereffi, G., Humphrey, J., And Sturgeon, T., 2005, The Governance Of Global Value Chains, Review Of International Political Economy 12(1), February, Pp. 78–104. Available At Http://Www.Fao.Org/Fileadmin/User_Upload/Fisheries/Docs/Gvc_Governance.Pdf

Ghalayini, A. M., & Noble, J. S., 1996, The Changing Basis Of Performance Measurement. International Journal Of Operations & Production Management, 16(8), Pp. 63-80. Available At Http://Dx.Doi.Org/10.1108/01443579610125787.

Giorgio, K. M., 2018, Goals & Objectives Of Supply Management, Bizfluent, November 08. Available At Https://Bizfluent.Com/List-6865099-Goals-Objectives-Supply-Management.Html

Global Reporting Initiative, 2015, G4 Sustainability Reporting Guidelines: Reporting Principles And Standard Disclosures, August 5. Available At Https://Www.Globalreporting.Org/Resourcelibrary/Grig4-Part1-Reporting-Principles-And- Standard-Disclosures.Pdf.

Gorg, H., Geishecker, I., & Krieger-Boden, C., 2011, Services Offshoring Increases Wage Inequality. Centre For Economic Policy Research.

Grant, R.M., 1991, The Resource-Based Theory Of Competitive Advantage: Implications For Strategy Formulation, Sage Journals April 1 ,33(3), Pp. 114-135. Available At Https://Doi.Org/10.2307/41166664

Gray, A. And Jopson, B., 2018, Us Banks Clear First Round Of Fed Stress Tests, The Financial Times. Available At Https://Www.Ft.Com/Content/59d77520-758e-11e8-A8c4-408cfba4327c.

Griffin&Co, 2018, Supply Chain Management In The Service Industry, Supply Chain Management, Small Business, August 16. Available At: Https://Griffinandco.Marketing/Blog/2018/8/16/Supply-Chain-Management-In-The-Service-Industry.

Gunasekaran, A., Patel, C., And Mcgaughey, R. E., 2004, A Framework For Supply Chain Performance Measurement, International Journal Of Production Economics, 87(3), Pp. 333-347.

Hallikas, J., Karvonen, I., Pulkkinen, U., Virolainen, V.-M., Tuominen, M., 2004. Risk Management Process In Supplier Networks. International Journal Of Production Economics, 90 (1), Pp. 47–58.

Handfield, R. B. And Nichols, E. L., 2003. Introduction To Supply Chain Management. 2nd Edition. Upper Saddle River: Prentice Hall.

Hendricks, K.N., Singhal, V.R., 2005. Association Between Supply Chain Glitches And Operating Performance. Management Science, 51 (5), 695–711.

Hohenstein, N. O., Feisel, E., Hartmann, E., & Giunipero, L., 2015, Research On The Phenomenon Of Supply Chain Resilience: A Systematic Review And Paths For Further Investigation. International Journal Of Physical Distribution & Logistics Management, 45(1-2), Pp. 90-117. Available At Http://Dx.Doi.Org/10.1108/Ijpdlm-05-2013-0128.

Howard, C. S., & Irving, J. A., 2013, The Impact Of Obstacles And Developmental Experiences On Resilience In Leadership Formation. Proceedings Of The American Society For Business And Behavioral Sciences, 20(1). Available At Http://Asbbs. Org/Files/Asbbs2013v1/Pdf/H/Howard_Irving(679-687). Pdf

Hubbard, D., 2009, The Failure Of Risk Management: Why It's Broken And How To Fix It. John Wiley & Sons.

Huff, B., 2014, Cash Is King: How To Optimize Supply Chain Operations For Strong Cash Flow, Industry Week, August 8. Available At Https://Www.Industryweek.Com/Cash-Is-King.

Hugos, M.H., 2006. Essentials Of Supply Chain Management. 2nd Edition. Hoboken: John Willey & Sons.

Iab Sea+India, 2016, How Data Is Used In Advertising?, Iab Training Series #8 Part 2, October. Available At: Https://Iabseaindia.Com/Iab-Training-Series-8-Part-2-How-Data-Is-Used-In/

Ickovics, J. R., & Park, C. L., 1998, Thriving: Broadening The Paradigm Beyond Illness To Health: Published Quarterly For The Society For The Psychological Study Of Social Issues By Blackwell Publishers.

Ism, 2019, Non-Manufacturing Ism Report On Business, Institute For Supply Management, May. Available At Https://Www.Instituteforsupplymanagement.Org/Ismreport/Nonmfgrob.Cfm?Navitemnumber=31136

Jackson P., And Davis, P. O., 2015, Rethinking Risk Management, Risk Management Survey Of Major Financial Institutions, Banks Focus On Non-Financial Risks And Accountability, Ey. Available At Https://Webforms.Ey.Com/Publication/Vwluassets/Ey-Rethinking-Risk-Management/$File/Ey-Rethinking-Risk-Management.Pdf

Jackson, P. And Schlich, B., 2013, Remaking Financial Services, Risk Management Five Years After The Crisis, A Survey Of Major Financial Institutions, Ey And Iif. Available At Https://Www.Ey.Com/Publication/Vwluassets/Remaking_Financial_Services_-_Risk_Management_Five_Years_After_The_Crisis_-_Complete/$File/Ey-Remaking_Financial_Services_Risk_Management_Five_Years_After_The_Crisis.Pdf

Janas, M. (2002). Build Resiliency. Intervention In School And Clinic, 38, Pp. 117-122.

Jeremy, X., 2019, How Blockchain Is Boosting The Fintech Sector, April 9. Available At Https://Www.Thecryptoupdates.Com/How-Blockchain-Is-Boosting-The-Fintech-Sector/

Johnson, M. And Mena, C., 2008, Supply Chain Management For Servitised Products: A Multi-Industry Case Study, International Journal Of Production Economics, 114(1), Pp. 27-39.

Jüttner, U., & Maklan, S., 2011, Supply Chain Resilience In The Global Financial Crisis: An Empirical Study. Supply Chain Management, 16(4), Pp. 246-259. Available At Http://Dx.Doi.Org/10.1108/13598541111139062.

Katiyar, R., Barua, M. K., & Meena, P. L., 2015. Modelling The Measures Of Supply Chain Performance In The

Indian Automotive Industry. Benchmarking, 22(4), Pp. 665-696.Available At Http://Dx.Doi.Org/10.1108/Bij-09-2014-0091.

Kiger, D., 2016, How Supply Chain Works Out For A Service Industry?, David Kiger's Blog, November. Available At Https://Davidkigerinfo.Wordpress.Com/2016/11/10/How-Supply-Chain-Works-Out-For-A-Service-Industry/

Kim, M., Raghuvanshi, K., Bucciarelli, R., And Sodhi, V., 2016, Optimizing The Retail Bank Supply Chain: How Retail Banks Can Lower Costs, Reduce Inventory And Boost Productivity: Lessons From Consumer Business, Deloitte Canada. Available At Https://Www2.Deloitte.Com/Content/Dam/Deloitte/Global/Documents/Financial-Services/Gx-Fsi-Ca-Optimizing-The-Retail-Bank-Supply-Chain-2013-10.Pdf.

Koenig, G., 1993, Management Stratégique, Paris, Nathan.

Krajewski, L.J., Ritzman, L.P. And Malhotra, M.K., 2007. Operations Management: Processes And Value Chains. Upper Saddle River: Pearson Prentice Hall.

Krivin, D., Samandari, H., Walsh, J., And Yueh, E., 2013, Managing Third-Party Risk In A Changing Regulatory Environment, Mckinsey Working Papers On Risk, Number 46. Available At Https://Www.Mckinsey.Com/~/Media/Mckinsey/Dotc

om/Client_Service/Risk/Working%20papers/46_Third_Party_Risk.Ashx

Krištofík, P., Kok, J., De Vries, S., And Van Sten-Van 'T Hoff, J., 2012, Financial Supply Chain Management – Challenges And Oostacles. Acm Journal Of Entrepreneurship Perspectives, 1, Pp. 132-143.

Kull, T., Closs, D., 2008. The Risk Of Second-Tier Supplier Failures In Serial Supply Chains: Implications For Order Policies And Distributor Autonomy. European Journal Of Operational Research 186 (3), Pp. 1158–1174.

Lamarque, E., 2000, Key Activities In The Banking Industry: An Analysis By The Value Chain, Bordeaux Montesquieu State University. Available At Https://Www.Researchgate.Net/Publication/228224964_Key_Activities_In_The_Banking_Industry_An_Analysis_By_The_Value_Chain

Lamarque, E., 2005, Identifying Key Activities In Banking Firms: A Competence-Based Analysis, In Ron Sanchez, Aime Heene (Ed.) Competence Perspective On Managing Internal Process (Advances In Applied Business Strategy, Volume 7) Emerald Group Publishing Limited, Pp.29 – 47. Available At Https://Www.Emeraldinsight.Com/Doi/Abs/10.1016/S0749-6826%2804%2907002-7

Lambert, D.M., Cooper, M.C. And Pagh, J.D., 1998. Supply Chain Management Implementation Issues And

Research Opportunities. The International Journal Of Logistics Management, 11 (1), Pp. 1-17.

Lambert, D.M. And Cooper, M.C., 2000, Issues In Supply Chain Management, Industrial Marketing Management, 29, 65-83, Http://Www.Hatfieldandassociates.Com/Pdf/Issues_In_Scm.Pdf

Lambert, D.M., Stock, J.R. And Ellram, L. M., 1998. Fundamentals Of Logistics Management. Boston: Irwin/Mcgraw-Hill.

Larsson, P.D. And Halldorsson, A., 2004. Logistics Versus Supply Chain Management. An International Survey. International Journal Of Logistics. Research And Applications, 7 (1), Pp. 17-31.

Ledesma, J., 2014, Conceptual Frameworks And Research Models On Resilience In Leadership, Sage Journals, Volume: 4 Issue: 3, August 13, Https://Journals.Sagepub.Com/Doi/Full/10.1177/2158244014545464

Leończuk, D., 2016, Categories Of Supply Chain Performance Indicators: An Overview Of Approaches, Business, Management And Education, Vol. 14, No.1, Pp.103–115.

Li, X., Barnes, I., 2008. Proactive Supply Risk Management Methods For Building A Robust Supply Selection Process When Sourcing From Emerging

Markets. Strategic Outsourcing: An International Journal 1 (3), Pp. 252–267.

Liu, W, Bai, E., Liu, L. And Wei, W., 2017, A Framework Of Sustainable Service Supply Chain Management: A Literature Review And Research Agenda, Sustainability, Vol.9, P 421.

Logistics & Supply Chain Management Society, 2012. Scm Dictionary. [Online] Logistics & Supply Chain Management Society. Available At: Http://Lscms.Org/Scm-Dictionary/.

Lu, R. And Xia, D., 2014, Application Of Supply Chain Risk Management Through Visualization And Value-At-Risk Quantification, Mit. Available At: Https://Ctl.Mit.Edu/Sites/Ctl.Mit.Edu/Files/Library/Public/2014researchfest-Luxia.Pptx

Maestrini, V., Luzzini, D., Maccarrone, P., & Caniato, F., 2017, Supply Chain Performance Measurement Systems: A Systematic Review And Research Agenda. International Journal Of Production Economics, 183, Pp. 299-315. Available At Http://Dx.Doi.Org/10.1016/J.Ijpe.2016.11.005.

Manuj, I., Mentzer, J.T., 2008, Global Supply Chain Risk Management, Journal Of Business Logistics, 26 (1), Pp. 133–155.

Masten, A. S., 2005, Ordinary Magic: Resilience Processes In Development. Annual Progress In Child Psychiatry And Child Development, 56, Pp. 227-238.

Mayer, B., 2012, Supply Chain Metrics That Matter: The Cash-To-Cash Cycle, Supply Chain Insights. Available At: Http://Supplychaininsights.Com/Wp-Content/Uploads/2012/11/Supply_Chain_Metrics_That_Matter-The_Cash-To-Cash_Cycle-30_Nov_2012.Pdf

Mckinsey & Company, 2018, The Lending Revolution: How Digital Credit Is Changing Banks From The Inside, August. Available At Https://Www.Mckinsey.Com/Business-Functions/Risk/Our-Insights/The-Lending-Revolution-How-Digital-Credit-Is-Changing-Banks-From-The-Inside.

Mentzer, J.T., Dewitt, W., Keebler, J.S., Min, S., Nix, N.W., Smith, C.D. And Zacharia Z.G., 2001. Defining Supply Chain Management. Journal Of Business Logistics, 22 (2), Pp. 1-25.

Millsap, D., 2012, Wal-Mart's Use Of Rfid In Global Supply Chain Management, Daniel Millsap Mba School Research, Http://Www.Danielmillsap.Com/Research/Rfid-In-Wal-Mart-Global-Supply-Chain-Management.Html

Moeller, R.R., 2007, Coso Enterprise Risk Management: Understanding The New Integrated Erm Framework. John Wiley & Sons, Inc., Hoboken, New Jersey.

Moise, M., 2008. The Importance Of Reverse Logistics For Retail Activity. Amfiteatru Economic, X (24), Pp. 192-209.

Moody's Analytics Risk Perspectives, 2016, The Convergence Of Risk, Finance, And Accounting: Cecl, Volume Viii, November.

More, D. And Basu, P., 2013, Challenges Of Supply Chain Finance: A Detailed Study And A Hierarchical Model Based On The Experiences Of An Indian Firm, Business Process Management Journal, 19(4), Pp. 624-647.

Mukaddes, A.M.M., Rashed,C.A.A., Abdul Malek, A. B. M. And Kaiser, J., 2010, Developing An Information Model For Supply Chain Information Flow And Its Management, International Journal Of Innovation, Management And Technology, 1(2), Pp. 226-231.

Nagyova, A., & Pacaiova, H., 2009. How To Build Manual For Key Performance Indicators - Kpi. In B. Katalinic (Ed.), Daaam International Scientific Book, Pp. 135-143. Available At Http://Dx.Doi.Org/10.2507/Daaam.Scibook.2009.15.

Narasimhan, R., Talluri, S., 2009. Perspectives On Risk Management In Supply Chains. Journal Of Operations Management 27 (2), Pp. 114–118.

Neely, A., Mills, J., Platts, K., Richards, H., Gregory, M., Bourne, M., & Kennerley, M., 2000, Performance Measurement System Design: Developing And Testing A

Process-Based Approach. Performance Measurement System Design, 20(10), Pp. 1119-1145.

Nishikawa, Y., 2006, Thriving In The Face Of Adversity: Perceptions Of Elementary-School Principals. La Verne, Ca: University Of La Verne.

Nissen, M., 1999, Knowledge-Based Knowledge Management In The Reengineering Domain", Decision Support Systems, 27(1), Pp. 47- 65.

Nudurupati, S. S., Bititci, U. S., Kumar, V., & Chan, F. T. S. , 2011, State Of The Art Literature Review On Performance Measurement. Computers & Industrial Engineering, 60(2), Pp. 279-290. Available At Http://Dx.Doi.Org/10.1016/J.Cie.2010.11.010.

O'leary, V. E., 1998, Strength In The Face Of Adversity: Individual And Social Thriving. Journal Of Social Issues, 54, Pp. 425-446.

Occ, 2013, Occ Bulletin, October. Available At Https://Www.Occ.Gov/News-Issuances/Bulletins/2013/Bulletin-2013-29.Html

Oke, A., Gopalakrishnan, M., 2009. Managing Disruptions In Supply Chains: A Case Study Of A Retails Supply Chain. International Journal Of Production Economics 118 (1), Pp. 168–174.

Park, K., Sen, S., And Griffiths D., 2015, Third Party Governance & Risk Management: Turning Risk Into

Opportunity, Deloitte, Available At Https://Www2.Deloitte.Com/Content/Dam/Deloitte/Uk/Documents/Audit/Deloitte-Uk-Third-Party-Governance-Risk-Management-Report.Pdf

Patterson, J. L. And Kelleher, P., 2005, Resilient School Leaders: Strategies For Turning Adversity Into Achievement. Alexandria, Va: Association For Supervision And Curriculum Development.

Payne, A. And Frow, P., 2005, A Strategic Framework For Customer Relationship Management, Journal Of Marketing, Vol. 69, October 2005, Pp. 167-176.

Peck, H., 2006, Reconciling Supply Chain Vulnerability, Risk And Supply Chain Management, International Journal Of Logistics: Research And Applications, Vol. 9 No. 2, Pp.127-142. Available At Https://Www.Tandfonline.Com/Doi/Abs/10.1080/13675560600673578?Journalcode=Cjol20

Pereira, C. R., Christopher, M., & Lago Da Silva, A., 2014, Achieving Supply Chain Resilience: The Role Of Procurement. Supply Chain Management, 19(5/6), Pp. 626-642. Available At Http://Dx.Doi.Org/10.1108/Scm-09-2013-0346.

Perry, B., 2002, How Children Become Resilient. Scholastic Parent & Child, 10(2), October, Pp. 33-35.

Pettit, T. J., Croxton, K. L., & Fiksel, J., 2013, Ensuring Supply Chain Resilience: Development And

Implementation Of An Assessment Tool. Journal Of Business Logistics, 34(1), Pp. 46-76. Available At Http://Dx.Doi.Org/10.1111/Jbl.12009.

Ping, W. L., & Jia, F., 2010, Analysis On Supply Chain Manufacturing Enterprise Product Service System. Ieee Conference On Emergency Management And Management Sciences, Pp. 126-129.

Plessis, M. D., 2007, Knowledge Management: What Make Complex Implementations Successful?, Journal Of Knowledge Management, 11(2), Pp. 91–101.

Ponomarov, S.Y. And Holcomb, M. C., 2009, Understanding The Concept Of Supply Chain Resilience, International Journal Of Logistics Management. 20(1):, Pp.124-143. Available At Doi:10.1108/09574090910954873.

Porter, M., 1985, Competitive Advantage: Creating And Sustaining Superior Performance. C. Macmillan, Ed., New York, Ny: Free Press.

Pride, W. And Ferrel, O., 2003, Marketing Concepts And Strategies. Boston: Houghton Mifflin.

Pritchard, J., 2018, Letter Of Credit Example - How Money And Documents Move, The Balance, July 13. Available At Https://Www.Thebalance.Com/Letter-Of-Credit-Example-How-Money-And-Documents-Move-315042

Pwc, 2013, Where Have You Been All My Life? How The Financial Services Industry Can Unlock The Value In Big Data, October. Available At Http://Www.Pwc.Com/En_Us/Us/Financial-Services/Publications/Viewpoints/Assets/Pwc-Unlocking-Big-Data-Value.Pdf.

Qnb, 2014, Application Of Supply Chain Management In Banking Industry. Available At: Https://Www.Slideshare.Net/Ahmedmoustapha/Application-Of-Supply-Chain-Management-In-Banking-Industry

Rogers, D. L., 2004, The Product Development And Commercialization Process. The International Journal Of Logistics Management, 15(2), Pp. 43-46.

Sengupta, K., Heiser, D., & Cook, L., 2006, Manufacturing And Service Supply Chain Performance: A Comparative Analysis. The Journal Of Supply Chain Management, 4-15.

Roland Berger, 2010, Handbrake On Slow Progress Over Consolidation: Short Study On The Current Situation In The Supplier Industry. Supplier Industry Consolidation Study. Available At /Http://Static.Lecho.Be/Upload/Roland_Berger_Automotive_Supplier_Study_2010_Compatibiliteitsfmodus_4_2227679-551912.Pdfs

Roth, A.V., Menor, L.J., 2003, Insights Into Service Operations Management: A Research Agenda"

Production & Operations Management, Vol. 12, No. 2, Pp145-164.

Russel, R. S. And Taylor, B.W., 2009. Operations Management Along The Supply Chain. 6th Edition. Hoboken: John Wiley & Sons.

Rutter, M., 1979, Protective Factors In Children's Responses To Stress And Disadvantage. In M. W. Kent & J. E. Rolf (Eds.), Primary Prevention Of Psychopathology: Social Competence In Children Hanover, Nh: University Press Of New England, Vol. 3, Pp. 49-74.

Rutter, M., 1987, Psychosocial Resilience And Protective Mecha- Nisms. American Journal Of Orthopsychiatry, 57, 316-331.

Ryan, Ph., 2018, Pwc Shutters Denovo, Its 'Fintech Insights, Bank Innovation, June 26. Available At Https://Bankinnovation.Net/2018/06/Pwc-Shutters-Denovo-Its-Fintech-Insights-Platform/

Saakvitne, K. W., Tennen, H., & Affleck, G., 1998, Exploring Thriving In The Context Of Clinical Trauma Theory: Constructivist Self-Development Theory. Journal Of Social Issues, 54, Pp. 279- 299.

Samaranayake, P., 2005, A Conceptual Framework For Supply Chain Management: A Structural Integration, Supply Chain Management: An International Journal,

10(1), Pp.47-59, Https://Doi.Org/10.1108/13598540510578379

Sampson, S. E. And Froehle C.M., 2006, Foundations And Implications Of A Proposed Unified Services Theory, Production And Operations Management, 15 (2), Pp. 329–343.

Sarkar, A., Mohapatra, P.K.J., 2009, Determining The Optimal Size Of The Supply Base With The Consideration Of Risks Of Supply Disruptions. International Journal Of Production Economics 119 (1), Pp. 122–135.

Sarkisyan, A. And Casu, B., 2013, Retained Interest In Securitizations And Implications For Bank Solvency, Ecb Working Papers, No. 1538. Available At IIttps://Www.Ecb.Europa.Eu/Pub/Pdf/Scpwps/Ecbwp 1538.Pdf

Schoeman, D., 2016, Concert Interrupted - An Agenda For The Chief Supply Chain Officer To Develop Countermeasures For Supply Chain Risks And Disruptions, Sapics. Available At Https://Www.Slideshare.Net/Tristanwiggill/Concert-Interrupted-An-Agenda-For-The-Chief-Supply-Chain-Officer-To-Develop-Countermeasures-For-Supply-Chain-Risks-And-Disruptions

Scrlc , 2011, Supply Chain Risk Management: A Compilation Of Best Practices, Supply Chain Risk Leadership Council. Available At

Http://Www.Scrlc.Com/Articles/Supply_Chain_Risk_Management_A_Compilation_Of_Best_Practices_Final[1].Pdf.

Seifbarghy, M. And Gilkalayeh A.P., 2012, Supply Chain Integration Under Vendor Managed Inventory Mode Of Operation Considering Stockout. Economic Computation And Economic Cybernetics Studies And Research – Ececsr, 46 (1), Pp.197-219.

Sengupta, S., & J., T., 1996. Seamless Optimization Of The Entire Supply Chain. Iie Solutions, 28(10), Pp. 28-33.

Stevens, G. C., 1989, Integration Of The Supply Chain. International Journal Of Physical Distribution And Logistics Management, 19(8), Pp. 3-8.

Simchi-Levi, D., 2013, Operations Rules: Delivering Customer Value Through Flexible Operations, Cambridge: The Mit Press.

Simchi-Level, D., 2015, Find The Weak Link In Your Supply Chain, Harvard Business Review. Available At Https://Hbr.Org/2015/06/Find-The-Weak-Link-In-Your-Supply-Chain

Simchi-Levi, D., Kaminsky, P. And Simchi-Levi, E., 2008, Designing And Managing The Supply Chain: Concepts, Strategies, And Case Studies. 3rd Edition. New York: Mc Graw Hill.

Simchi-Levi, D., Schmidt, W. And Wei, Y., 2014, From Superstorms To Factory Fires: Managing Unpredictable Supply Chain Disruptions, Harvard Business Review. Available At Https://Hbr.Org/2014/01/From-Superstorms-To-Factory-Fires-Managing-Unpredictable-Supply-Chain-Disruptions.

Singh, S., 2017, The Future Of Car Insurance: Digital, Predictive And Usage-Based, Forbes, February. Available At Https://Www.Forbes.Com/Sites/Sarwantsingh/2017/02/24/The-Future-Of-Car-Insurance-Digital-Predictive-And-Usage-Based/#1cc1b1fb52fb

Sonnier, E.B., 2014, Understanding Your Risk Exposure Index, Dupre Logistics. Available At Https://Www.Duprelogistics.Com/Understanding-Your-Risk-Exposure-Index/

Springboard Home Loans, 2018, Loan Products, Springboard Cdfi. Available At Http://Www.Springboard.Org/Loan-Products/

Statista, 2015, Global Online Banking Penetration In April 2012 By Region. Available At Http://Www.Statista.Com/Statistics/233284/Development-Of-Global-Online-Banking- Penetration/.

Supplychain247, 2015, Understanding Supply Chain Resilience, Supply Chain News, November. Available At: Http://Www.Supplychain247.Com/Article/Understanding_Supply_Chain_Resilience/

Svensson, G., 2000, A Conceptual Framework For The Analysis Of Vulnerability In Supply Chains, International Journal Of Physical Distribution & Logistics Management, 30(9), Pp.731-750. Available At Https://Doi.Org/10.1108/09600030010351444

Sweeney, E., 2007, Perspectives On Supply Chain Management And Logistics, Dublin: Blackhall Publishing.

Tan, K.C., Kannan, V.R. And Handfield, R.B., 1998, Supply Chain Management: Supplier Performance And Firm Performance. International Journal Of Purchasing And Material Management, 34 (3), Pp. 2-9.

Tan, K.C., 2002, Supply Chain Management: Practices, Concerns, And Performance Issues. Journal Of Supply Chain Management. 38(42)

Tang, C., 2006, Perspectives In Supply Chain Risk Management. International Journal Of Production Economics 103 (2), Pp. 451–488.

Tang, C. And Tomlin, B., 2008, The Power Of Flexibility For Mitigating Supply Chain Risks. International Journal Of Production Economics 116 (1), Pp. 12–27.

Taylor, E., 2010, Differences In Supply Chain Designs For A Manufacturing Industry Vs. A Service Industry, Small Business. Available At Https://Smallbusiness.Chron.Com/Differences-Supply-

Chain-Designs-Manufacturing-Industry-Vs-Service-Industry-14610.Html

Td Bank, 2015, Corporate Responsibility Report: How We Are Building The Better Bank, May 5. Available At Http://Www.Td.Com/Document/Pdf/Corporaterespon sibility/2014-Final-Crr_En.Pdf.

Thomas, D. J. And Griffin P.M., 1996, Coordinated Supply Chain Management. European Journal Of Operational Research, 94 (1), Pp. 1-15.

Tichy, N. And Charan,R., 1989, Speed, Simplicity, Self-Confidence: An Interview With Jack Welch, Hbr, September – October. Available At Https://Hbr.Org/1989/09/Speed-Simplicity-Self-Confidence-An-Interview-With-Jack-Welch

The Economist, 2015, The Disruption Of Banking, Intelligence Unit, Https://Eiuperspectives.Economist.Com/Sites/Default/Files/Eiu-The%20disruption%20of%20banking_Pdf_1.Pdf

Trkman, P., Mccormack, K., 2009, Supply Chain Risk In Turbulent Environments—A Conceptual Model For Managing Supply Chain Network Risk. International Journal Of Production Economics 119 (2), Pp. 247–258.

Trowbridge, M., 2017, Five Techniques To Manage Supply Chain Risk, Supply Chain Management Review. Available At

Http://Www.Scmr.Com/Article/Five_Techniques_To_Manage_Supply_Chain_Risk

Trudgia, P., 2018, Five Objectives For Every Supply Chain Director, Paul Trudgian Ltd. - Supply Chain & Logistics Consultancy, January 24. Available At Https://Www.Paultrudgian.Co.Uk/Five-Objectives-Every-Supply-Chain-Director/

Turner, M.D., 2011, Be Prepared To Bounce Back: Building A Resilient Supply Chain, Strategy & Booz Company (Pwc). Available At Https://Www.Strategyand.Pwc.Com/Media/File/Strategyand_Be-Prepared-To-Bounce-Back.Pdf.

Ubs, 2014, Responsible Supply Chain Management, March 27, Available At Https://Www.Ubs.Com/Global/En/About_Ubs/Corporate_Responsibility/Cr_In_Operations/Chai N_Management.Html

Vandaele, D. And Gemmel, P., 2007, Purchased Business Services Influence Downstream Supply Chain Members, International Journal Of Service Industry Management, Vol. 18 Issue: 3, Pp.307-321. Available At Https://Doi.Org/10.1108/09564230710751505

Vander Straeten, P., 2016, How To Apply Supply Chain Management To The Financial Services Industry, Linkedin, Available At Https://Www.Linkedin.Com/Pulse/How-Apply-Supply-

Chain-Management-Financial-Services-Pascal/ (Accessed On 9 August 2018).

Wailgum T. And Worthen B., 2008. Cio Supply Chain Management Definition And Solutions.[Online] Cio International Data Group. Available At: <Http://Www.Cio.Com/Article/40940/Supply_Chain_Management_Definition_And_Solutions>

Walker, P.L. And Shenkir, W.G., 2008, Implementing Enterprise Risk Management. Journal Of Accountancy 205 (3).

Waters, D. 2008, Supply Chain Risk Management: Vulnerability And Resilience In Logistics, Kogan Page.

Wells Fargo, 2015, Wells Fargo & Company Annual Report 2014: Culture Counts: An Unwavering Focus On The Customer, March 4. Available At Https://Www08.Wellsfargomedia.Com/Assets/Pdf/About/Investor-Relations/Annual- Reports/2014-Annual-Report.Pdf

Tate, W. And Ellram, L., And Billington, C., 2008, Services Supply Chain Management: An Untapped Opportunity, Industry Week, March 18. Available At Https://Www.Industryweek.Com/Software-Amp-Systems/Services-Supply-Chain-Management-Untapped-Opportunity

Wieland, A. And Wallenburg, C.M., 2012, Dealing With Supply Chain Risks: Linking Risk Management Practices

And Strategies To Performance, International Journal Of Physical Distribution & Logistics Management, 42(10) Pp. 887-905. Available At
Doi: 10.1108/09600031211281411

Wilber, D., 2019, The Best Ways To Build Trust With New Generations, American Banking Association, June 4. Available At
Https://Bankingjournal.Aba.Com/2019/06/The-Best-Ways-To-Build-Trust-With-New-Generations/

Wisner, J., Tan, K.C. And Leong, G.K., 2012, Principles Of Supply Chain Management: A Balanced Approach. 3rd Edition. Mason: South-Western Cengage Learning. Research, Fourth Ed. Sage, Thousand Oaks.

Witkowski, R. 2018, Floodgates Open? De Novo Applications Surge At Fdic, American Banker, October 3. Available At
Https://Www.Americanbanker.Com/News/Floodgates-Open-De-Novo-Applications-Surge-At-Fdic

Wladawsky-Berger, I., 2017, Digital Supply Chains Of The Future Will Focus On The Customer, Wsj, October 27. Available At
Https://Blogs.Wsj.Com/Cio/2017/10/27/Digital-Supply-Chains-Of-The-Future-Will-Focus-On-The-Customer/

Wolfl, A., 2004, Productivity Growth In Services Industries: Is There A Role For Measurement?

Iinternational Productivity Monitor, 8(Spring), Pp. 68-80.

Wu, D.D. And Olson, D.L., 2008, Supply Chain Risk, Simulation, And Vendor Selection. International Journal Of Production Economics 114 (2), Pp. 646–655.

Wu, T. And Blackhurst, J., 2009, Managing Supply Chain Risk And Vulnerability, New York: Springer.

Yahaya, A. And Bala, H., 2015, Working Capital Management And Financial Performance Of Deposit Money Banks In Nigeria, Journal Of Finance And Accounting, 6(16), Pp. 57-72

Zhang, R. And Chen, H., 2015, A Review Of Service Supply Chain And Future Prospects, Journal Of Service Science And Management, Vol.8, Pp.485-495.

Zhou, H. And Benton, W. C., 2007, Supply Chain Practice And Information Sharing, Journal Of Operations Management, Vol. 25, No. 6, Pp. 1348- 1365.

Zink, T. And Kemna, K., 2012, Understanding The Cost Of Handling Cash In Asia Pacific, Asian Banking Research. Available At Http://Retailbanking.Theasianbanker.Com/Assets/Media/Dl/Whitepaper/Understandingthecostofhandlingcashinasiapacific.Pdf

Zsidisin G.A., Ellram L.M., Carter J.R. And Cavinato X., 2004, An Analysis Of Supply Risk Assessment

Techniques, International Journal Of Physical Distribution Logistical Management ,34(5), Pp.397-413. Available At Https://Www.Researchgate.Net/Publication/235264645_An_Analysis_Of_Supply_Risk_Assessment_Techniques

WORKS CONSULTED

Abrigo, 2019, Bankers: Almost Every Part Of The Loan Process Takes Too Long, Sageworks. Available At: Https://Www.Abrigo.Com/Blog/2018/04/24/Bankers-Almost-Every-Part-Of-The-Loan-Process-Takes-Too-Long/

Ackerman, R. H. And Maslin-Ostrowski, P., 2002, The Wounded Leader: How Real Leadership Emerges In Times Of Crisis. San Francisco, Ca: Jossey-Bass.

Adaptive Cash, 2019, Cash Supply Chain. Available At: Https://Adaptivecash.Com

Affleck, G. And Tennen, H., 1996, Construing Benefits From Adversity: Adaptational Significance And Dispositional Underpinnings, Journal Of Personality, 64, Pp. 899-922.

Afza, T, And Nazir, M.S., ,2007, Working Capital Management Policies Of Firms: Empirical Evidence From Pakistan, Conference Proceedings Of 9th South Asian Management Forum (Samf) On February 24- 25, North South University, Dhaka, Bangladesh.

Afza, T. And Nazir, M. S., 2008, Working Capital Approaches And Firm's Returns In Pakistan. Pakistan Journal Of Commerce And Social Sciences, 1(1), Pp. 25-36.

Alexander, C., 2003, Operational Risk: Regulation, Analysis And Management; Pearson Education: London, Uk.

Ali, A., Mahfouz, A., & Arisha, A., 2017, Analyzing Supply Chain Resilience: Integrating The Constructs In A Concept Mapping Framework Via A Systematic Literature Review. Supply Chain Management, 22(1), Pp. 16-39.

Altman, E.I., 1968, Financial Ratios, Discriminant Analysis And The Prediction Of Corporate Bankruptcy. Journal Of Finance 23 (4), Pp. 589–609.

Amancei, B., 2009, Managementul Lanțului De Aprovizionare - Noțiuni Teoretice, Viziuni Strategice Şi Abordări Practice, București: Editura Universitară.

Ambulkar, S., Blackhurst, J., & Grawe, S., 2015, Firm's Resilience To Supply Chain Disruptions: Scale Development And Empirical Examination. Journal Of Operations Management, 33, Pp. 111-122.

Amr's Business Intelligence/Performance Management Maturity Model. Available At: Http://Www. Webcitation.Org/6tjsca0p4.

Anand, N., & Grover, N., 2015, Measuring Retail Supply Chain Performance: Theoretical Model Using Key Performance Indicators (Pis). Benchmarking, 22(1), Pp. 135-166. Available At Http://Dx.Doi.Org/10.1108/Bij-05-2012-0034.

Aragão, A. B. D., Scavarda, L. F., Hamacher, S., & Pires, S. R. I., 2004, Supply Chain Management Analysis Model: Fundaments And Application To Nvg Cylinder Chains. Gestão & Produção, 11(3), Pp. 299-311. Available At Http://Dx.Doi.Org/10.1590/S0104-530x2004000300005.

Arbuckle, J.L., 2005, Amos 6.0 User's Guide. Amos Development Corporation, Usa.

Armistead, C., 1990, Service Operations Strategy: Framework For Matching The Service Operations Task And The Service Delivery System. International Journal Of Service Industry Management, Pp. 6-16.

Armistead, C., & Clark, G., 1993, Resource Activity Mapping: The Value Chain In Service Operations Strategy. The Services Industries Journal, 13(4), Pp. 221-239.

Arnold, V.; Benford, T.; Canada, J.; Sutton, S.G, 2015, Leveraging Integrated Information Systems To Enhance Strategic Flexibility And Performance: The Enabling Role Of Enterprise Risk Management. Int. J. Account. Inf. Syst, 19, Pp. 1–16.

Asgari, N., Nikbakhsh, E., Hill, A., & Farahani, R. Z., 2016, Supply Chain Management 1982-2015: A Review. Ima Journal Of Management Mathematics, 27(3), Pp. 353-379. Available At Http://Dx.Doi.Org/10.1093/Imaman/Dpw004.

Ashton, R.H., 1986, Combining The Judgment Of Experts: How Many And Which Ones? Organ. Behav. Hum. Decis. Process, 38, Pp. 405–414.

Assessment Framework For Information Security. Available At: Http://Www.Webcitation.Org/ 6tqgvv1ff.

Association For Operations Management, 2012. Apics Dictionary. [Online] Association For Operations Management. Available At: <Http://Www.Apics-Sd.Org/Education/Apics_Quickreference.Aspx>

Avelar-Sosa, L., García-Alcaraz, J. L., & Castrellón-Torres, J. P., 2014, The Effects Of Some Risk Factors In The Supply Chains Performance: A Case Of Study. Journal Of Applied Research And Technology, 12(5), Pp. 958-968. Available At Http://Dx.Doi.Org/10.1016/S1665-6423(14)70602-9.

Azam, M., & Haider, S. I., 2011, Impact Of Working Capital Management On Firms' Performance: Evidence From Non-Financial Institutions Of Kse-30 Index. Interdisciplinary Journal Of Contemporary Research In Business, 3(5), Pp. 481-492.

Azvine, B.; Cui, Z.; Majeed, B.; Spott, M., 2007, Operational Risk Management With Real-Time Business Intelligence. Bt Technol. J., 25, Pp. 154–167.

Baars, T.; Spruit, M., 2012, Designing A Secure Cloud Architecture: The Seca Model. Int. J. Inf. Secur. Priv., 6, Pp. 14–32.

Babich, V., Burnetas, A.N., Ritchken, P.H., 2007. Competition And Diversification Effects In Supply Chains With Supplier Default Risk. Manufacturing & Service Operations Management, 9 (2), Pp. 123–146.

Bai, C., & Sarkis, J., 2014, Determining And Applying Sustainable Supplier Key Performance Indicators. Supply Chain Management, 19(3), Pp. 275-291. Available At Http://Dx.Doi.Org/10.1108/Scm-12-2013-0441.

Bălan, C., 2007, Logistică, Bucureşti: Editura Uranus, 3rd Edition.

Ballou, R., Gilbert, S., & Mukherjee, A., 2000, New Managerial Challenges From Supply Chain Opportunities. Industrial Marketing Management, 29, Pp. 7-18.

Bardin, L., 2008, Análise De Conteúdo, Lisboa: Edições 70.

Bdo Operational Risk Management Maturity Model, 2017, Available At: Http://Www.Webcitation.Org/

Beamon, B., 1999, Measuring Supply Chain Performance. International Journal Of Operations And Production Management, 19(3), Pp. 275-292.

Beardslee, W. R., 1989, The Role Of Self-Understanding In Resilient Individuals. American Journal Of Orthopsychiatry, 59, Pp. 266-278.

Beasley, M.; Chen, A.; Nunez, K.; Wright, L., 2006, Working Hand In Hand: Balanced Scorecards And Enterprise Risk Management, Strateg. Financ., 87, Pp. 49–55.

Beasley, M.S., Pagach, D., Warr, R., 2008, Information Conveyed In Hiring Announcements Of Senior Executives Overseeing Enterprise-Wide Risk Management Processes, Journal Of Accounting, Auditing And Finance, 23(3), Pp. 311–332.

Beaumont, S.M. & Begemann, E., 1997, Measuring Association Between Working Capital And Return On Investment, South African Journal Of Business Management, 28(1)

Bentler, P.M., 1990, Comparative Fit Indexes In Structural Models. Psychological Bulletin, 107, Pp. 238-246. Available At Http://Dx.Doi.Org/10.1037/0033-2909.107.2.238

Bernstein, L. A., & Wild, J. J., 1998, Financial Statement Analysis, Theory, Application And Interpretation (6ed.), Irwin/Mc Graw Hill.

Bhagwat, R. And Sharma, M.K., 2007, Performance Measurement Of Supply Chain Management: A Balanced Scorecard Approach, Computers & Industrial Engineering, 53(1), Pp. 43–62.

Bhunia, A., 2010, A Trend Analysis Of Liquidity Management Efficiency In Selected Private Sector

Industry, Indian Steel; International Journal Of Research In Commerce And Management, 1(5), Pp. 9-21.

Big Data & Analytics Maturity Model. Available At: Http://Www.Webcitation.Org/6u4lxwzsh

Bilal, A. R., Naveed, M., & Taliv, N. A., 2011, Impact Of Working Capital On Profitability Of Cement Sector Of Pakistan, Contemporary Research In Business, 3, Pp. 661-666.

Binti Mohamad, N. E. A., & Mohd Saad, N. B., 2010, Working Capital Management: The Effect Of Market Valuation And Profitability In Malaysia, International Journal Of Business And Management, 5(11), P. 140.

Bitner, M., 1995, Building Service Relationships: It's All About Promises, Academy Of Marketing Science Journal, 23(4), Pp. 246-252.

Blaikie, N. W. H., 2010, Designing Social Research: The Logic Of Anticipation, Cambridge: Polity Press.

Blumenthal, R. A., 1994, Leverage Impact On Working Capital In Small Businesses, Tma Journal, 14, Pp. 46-46.

Bonanno, G. A., 2004, Loss, Trauma, And Human Resilience, American Psychologist, 59, Pp. 20-28.

Boon-Itt, S. And Pongpanarat, C., 2011, Measuring Service Supply Chain Management Processes: The Application Of The Q-Sort Technique, International

Journal Of Innovation, Management And Technology, 2(3), Pp.217 -221.

Boyes, H., 2015, Cybersecurity And Cyber-Resilient Supply Chains, Technology Innovation Management Review, 5(4), Pp. 28-34. Available At Http:// Dx.Doi.Org/10.22215/Timreview/888.

Brandon-Jones, E., Squire, B., Autry, C. W., & Petersen, K. J., 2014, A Contingent Resource-Based Perspective Of Supply Chain Resilience And Robustness, The Journal Of Supply Chain Management, 50(3), Pp. 55-73. Available At Http://Dx.Doi.Org/10.1111/Jscm.12050.

Braunscheidel, M.J., Suresh, C., 2009, The Organizational Antecedents Of A Firm's Supply Chain Agility For Risk Mitigation And Response. Journal Of Operations Management, 27 (2), Pp. 119–140.

Breden, D., 2017, Managing Operational Risk In A Continuously Changing Environment (Bank Of Finland). Available At: Http://Www.Webcitation.Org/6tjvvi1pv.

Brigham E.F & Houston J.F, 2003, Fundamentals Of Financial Management, Harcourt College Publishers, 10th Edition.

Brigham, E. F & Ehrhardt, M. C., 2004, Financial Management: Theory And Practice, 11thedition, South-Western College Publishing, New York.

Brindley, C., 2004, Supply Chain Risk, England: Ashgate Publishing Ltd.

Brock, B. L., & Grady, M. L., 2002, Avoiding Burnout: A Principal's Guide To Keeping The Fire Alive, Thousand Oaks, Ca: Corwin Press.

Brown, D. And Lepeak, S., 2017, Supply Chain And Logistics Services Delivery, Inbound Logistics, June 29. Available At: Https://Www.Inboundlogistics.Com/Cms/Article/The-Future-Of-Supply-Chain-And-Logistics-Services-Delivery/

Brusset, X., & Teller, C., 2017, Supply Chain Capabilities, Risks, And Resilience. International Journal Of Production Economics, 184, Pp. 59-68. Available At Http://Dx.Doi.Org/10.1016/J.Ijpe.2016.09.008.

Burda, A., 2009. Logistica Şi Distribuţia Mărfurilor. Bucureşti: Editura Prouniversitaria.

Bureau Of Labor Statistics. (N.D.). Retrieved From Occupational Employment Statistics: Http://Www.Bls.Gov/Oes/#Tables

Burgess, K., Singh, P. And Koroglu, R., 2006. Supply Chain Management: A Structured Literature Review And Implications For Future Research. International Journal Of Operations & Production Management, 26(7), Pp.703-729.

Butilc, D., Crişan, E., Salanţă, I. And Ilieş, L., 2011, The Adoption/Adaption Of The „Supply Chain" Concept In Romanian, The Annals Of The University Of Oradea, Tom Xx 2nd Issue December, Pp.657-668.

Cai, J., Liu, X., Xiao, Z., & Liu, J., 2009, Improving Supply Chain Performance Management: A Systematic Approach To Analyzing Iterative Kpi Accomplishment. Decision Support Systems, 46(2), Pp. 512-521. Available At Http://Dx.Doi.Org/10.1016/J.Dss.2008.09.004.

Capstone Logistics, Data Stream In Supply Chains, 2019. Available At: Https://Www.Capstonelogistics.Com/Supply-Chain-Solutions/

Carvalho, H., Barroso, A. P., Machado, V. H., Azevedo, S., & Cruz-Machado, V., 2012, Supply Chain Redesign For Resilience Using Simulation. Computers & Industrial Engineering, 62(1), Pp. 329-341. Available At Http://Dx.Doi.Org/10.1016/J.Cie.2011.10.003.

Carver, C. S., 1998, Resilience And Thriving: Issues, Models, And Linkages, Journal Of Social Issues, 54, Pp. 245-266.

Cash, D. W., 2001, In Order To Aid In Diffusing Useful And Practical Information: Agricultural Extension And Boundary Organizations, Science, Technology, & Human Values, 26, Pp. 431-453.

Cedillo-Campos, M. G., Pérez-Salas, G., Bueno-Solano, A., González-Ramírez, R. G., & Jímenez-Sánchez, E., 2014, Supply Chain Disruptions Propagation Caused By Criminal Acts. Journal Of Applied Research And Technology, 12(4), Pp. 684-694. Available At Http://Dx.Doi. Org/10.1016/S1665-6423(14)70085-9.

Chan, F. T., 2003, Performance Measurement In A Supply Chain. International Journal Of Advanced Manufacturing Technology, 21(7), Pp. 534-548. Available At Http://Dx.Doi.Org/10.1007/S001700300063.

Chand, M., Raj, T., And Shankar, R., 2014, Analysing The Operational Risks In Supply Chain By Using Weighted Interpretive Structure Modelling Technique, Int. J. Services And Operations Management, Vol. 18, No. 4, 2014

Chelariu, C., Kwame Asare, A., & Brashear-Alejandro, T., 2014, A Rose, By Any Other Name"...: Relationship Typology And Performance Measurement In Supply Chains. Journal Of Business And Industrial Marketing, 29(4), Pp. 332-343. Available At Http://Dx.Doi.Org/10.1108/Jbim-08- 2013-0178.

Chen, H.L., 2011, An Empirical Examination Of Project Contractors' Supply-Chain Cash Flow Performance And Owners' Payment Patterns, International Journal Of Project Management, 29(5), Pp. 604-614.

Chernobai, A.S.; Rachev, S.T.; Fabozzi, F.J., 2008, Operational Risk: A Guide To Basel Ii Capital Requirements, Models, And Analysis; Johnwiley & Sons: Hoboken

Cho, D. W., Lee, Y. H., Ahn, S. H., & Hwang, M. K., 2012, A Framework For Measuring The Performance Of Service Supply Chain Management. Computers & Industrial Engineering, 62(3), Pp. 801-818. Available At Http://Dx.Doi.Org/10.1016/J.Cie.2011.11.014.

Choi, T., Li, D., Yan, H., Chiu, C., 2008, Channel Coordination In Supply Chains With Agents Having Mean-Variance Objectives, Omega, 36 (4),Pp. 565–576.

Christopher, M., 2003, Understanding Supply Chain Risk: A Self-Assessment Workbook, Centre For Logistics And Supply Chain Management, Cranfield School Of Management.

Christopher, M., 2012, Logística E Gerenciamento Da Cadeia De Suprimentos: Criando Redes Que Agregam Valor, São Paulo: Cengage Learning.

Christopher, M., 2003, Understanding Supply Chain Risk: A Self-Assessment Workbook, Centre For Logistics And Supply Chain Management, Cranfield School Of Management, Uk.

Cigolini, R., Cozzi, M. And Perona, M., 2004, A New Framework For Supply Chain Management. International Journal Of Operations & Production

Management, 24, Pp. 7-41. Available At Http://Dx.Doi.Org/10.1108/01443570410510979

Closs, D., Jacobs, M., Swink, M., Webb, S., 2008, Competencies For Managing Product Portfolio Complexity: Six Case Studies, Journal Of Operations Management, 25 (6), Pp. 590–610.

Cnn, 2012, Money, June. Available At Http://Money.Cnn.Com/Data/Dow30/

Coase, R., 1960, The Problem Of Social Cost. Journal Of Law And Economics, 3, October, Pp. 1–44.

Coca, D.; De Blas, R.; Gallejones, C.; Moral, R.; Calvo, J.; Álvarez, J.; Del Canto, Á., 2014, Operational Risk Management In The Energy Industr. Available At: Http://Www.Webcitation.Org/6xa33zgeb (Accessed On 11 February 2018).

Colicchia, C., & Strozzi, F., 2012, Supply Chain Risk Management: A New Methodology For A Systematic Literature Review. Supply Chain Management, 17(4), Pp. 403-418. Available At Http://Dx.Doi.Org/10.1108/13598541211246558.

Comindware, 2018, Six Imperative Steps To A Better Banking Process Workflow. Available At: Https://Www.Comindware.Com/Blog-Six-Imperative-Steps-Better-Banking-Process-Workflow/

Conceição, S. V., & Quintão, R. T., (2004, Avaliação Do Desempenho Logístico Da Cadeia Brasileira De Suprimentos De Refrigerantes. Gestão & Produção, 11(3), Pp. 441-453. Available At Http://Dx.Doi.Org/10.1590/S0104-530x2004000300015.

Conner, D. R., 1993, Managing At The Speed Of Change: How Resilient Managers Succeed And Prosper Where Others Fail, New York, Ny: Villard Books.

Cook, J. S., 2001, From Raw Materials To Customers: Supply Chain Management In The Service Industry. Sam Advanced Management Journal, Autumn, Pp. 14-21.

Copland, M., 2001, The Myth Of The Superprincipal. Phi Delta Kappan, 82, Pp. 528-533.

Coso, 2004. Enterprise Risk Management—Integrated Framework Executive Summary. Committee Of Sponsoring Organizations Of The Treadway Commission. Available At /Www.Coso.Org/Publications/Erm/Coso_Erm_Executivesummary.Pdfs.

Council Of Supply Chain Management Professionals, 2012, Cscmp Supply Chain Management Definitions. [Online] Council Of Supply Chain Management Professionals. Available At: <Http://Cscmp.Org/Aboutcscmp/Definitions.Asp>.

Coy, S. And Bourke, G., 2013, Procurement Innovation Vital To Growth, Bearingpoint, Red Paper. Available At: Https://Www.Bearingpoint.Com/Files/Procurement_Innovation_Vital_To_Growth.Pdf

Craighead, C.W., Blackhurst, J., Rungtusanatham, M.J., Handfield, R.B., 2007, The Severity Of Supply Chain Disruptions: Design Characteristics And Mitigation Capabilities. Decision Sciences 38 (1), Pp. 131–156.

Croom, S., Romano, P., & Giannakis, M. (2000). Supply Chain Management: An Analytical Framework For Critical Literature Review. European Journal Of Purchasing & Supply Management, 6(1), 67-83.

Croxton, K., Dastague-Garcia, S., Lambert, D., & Rogers, D., 2001, The Supply Chain Management Proocess. International Journal Of Logistics Management, 12(2), Pp. 13-36.

Croxton, K.L., 2003, The Order Fulfillment Process, The International Journal Of Logistics Management, Vol. 14, No. 1, Pp. 19-32.

Cruz, C.O.; Marques, R.C., 2012, Risk-Sharing In Seaport Terminal Concessions. Transp. Rev., 32, Pp. 455–471.

Csi. (N.D.). Available At The Coalition Of Service Industries: Http://Uscsi.Org/Statistics/Trade-In-Services-Statistics

Culp, C.L., 2002, The Revolution In Corporate Risk Management: A Decade Of Innovations In Process And Products. J. Appl. Corp. Financ.,14, Pp. 8–26.

Curbow, B., 1996, Personal Changes, Dispositional Optimism, And Psychological Adjustment To Bone Marrow Transplantation. Journal Of Behavioral Medicine, 16, Pp. 423-443.

Cutting-Decelle, A-F., Young, B., Das, B., Case, K. , Rahimifard, S., Anumba, C., And Bouchlaghem, D., 2007, A Review Of Approaches To Supply Chain Communications: From Manufacturing To Construction, Itcom, 12, January. Available At: Https://Www.Itcon.Org/Papers/2007_5.Content.06399 .Pdf

Cybersecurity Capability Maturity Model (C2m2). Available At: Http://Www.Webcitation.Org/ 6u4kjw1pf

Danskin, P., Englis, B. G., Solomon, M. R., Goldsmith, M., & Davey, J., 2005, Knowledge Management As Competitive Advantage: Lessons From The Textile And Apparel Value Chain, Journal Of Knowledge Management, 9(2), Pp.91-102.

Danuletiu, A. E., 2010, Working Capital Management And Profitability: A Case Of Alba County Companies. Annales Universitatis Apulensis Series Oeconomica, 1(12).

Davis, C. G., Nolen-Hoeksema, S., & Larson, J., 1998, Making Sense Of Loss And Growing From The Experience: Two Construals Of Meaning. Journal Of Personality And Social Psychology, 75, Pp. 561-574.

De Felice, F., & Petrillo, A., 2015, Multidimensional Balanced Efficiency Decision Model, Journal Of Technology Management & Innovation, 10(3), Pp. 92-103. Available At Http://Dx.Doi.Org/10.4067/S0718-27242015000300011.

Deane, J.K., Ragsdale, C.T., Rakes, T.R., Rees, L.P., 2009, Managing Supply Chain Risk And Disruption From It Security Incidents, Operations Management Research, 2 (1–4), Pp. 4–12.

Deloof, M. & Jegers, M., 1996, Trade Credit, Product Quality And Intragroup Trade: Some European Evidence, Financial Management, 25(3), Pp. 33-43.

Deloof, M., 2003, Does Working Capital Management Affects Profitability Of Belgian Firms?, Journal Of Business Finance And Accounting, 3(34), Pp. 573 - 587

Denyer, D., & Tranfield, D., 2009, Producing A Systematic Review. In D. A. Buchanan & A. Bryman (Eds.), The Sage Handbook Of Organizational Research Methods, London: Sage Publications, Pp. 671-689.

Dougherty, C., 2011, Outlines & Highlights For Introduction To Econometrics By: Cram101.

Dwyer, K., 2010, Is Supply Chain Management A Discipline? A Comparative Content Analysis Of Academic And Practitioner Knowledge To Determine Disciplinary Identity, Ph.D. University Of Otago. Available At: <Http://Otago.Ourarchive.Ac.Nz/Bitstream/Handle/10523/627/Dwyer%20kirsty%20-%20%20phd%20thesis%202011.Pdf?Sequence=1>.

Ebrary.Net, 2019, The Value Chain In Banking. Available At: Https://Webcache.Googleusercontent.Com/Search?Q=Cache:Q_Gpjm92bvmj:Https://Ebrary.Net/11786/Business_Finance/Value_Chain_Banking+&Cd=5&Hl=En&Ct=Clnk&Gl=Us

Eisenhardt, K., Graebner, M., 2007, Theory Building From Cases: Opportunities And Challenges. Academy Of Management Journal, 50(1), Pp. 25–32.

Eisenhardt, K.M., 1989, Building Theories From Case Study Research. Academy Of Management Review, 14(4), Pp. 532–550.

Ellis, S., Henry, R., Shockley, J., 2010, Buyer Perceptions Of Supply Disruption Risk: A Behavioral View And Empirical Assessment, Journal Of Operations Management, 28(1), Pp. 34–46.

Ellram, L. M., Tate, W. L. And Billington, C., 2007, Understanding And Managing The Services Supply

Chain, Journal Of Supply Chain Management, 40(4), Pp. 17-32.

Ellram, L.M., 1996, The Use Of The Case Study Method In Logistics Research. Journal Of Business Logistics, 17(2), Pp. 93–138.

Ellram, L.M., Tate, W.L., Billington, C., 2008, Offshore Outsourcing Of Professional Services: A Transaction Cost Economics Perspective, Journal Of Operations Management, 26(2), Pp. 148–163.

Elzarka, Sara M., 2013, Supply Chain Risk Management: The Lessons Learned From The Egyptian Revolution 2011, International Journal Of Logistics Research And Applications, 16(6), Pp: 482-492.

Enterprise Risk Management A 'Risk-Intelligent' Approach (Deloitte). Available At: Http://Www. Webcitation.Org/6tqfnicol

Faisal, M.N., Banwet, D., Shankar, R., 2006, Supply Chain Risk Mitigation: Modeling The Enablers, Business Process Management Journal, 12 (4), Pp. 535–552.

Federal Emergency Management Agency – Fema, 2016, Ready Business: Quakesmart Toolkit. Washington: Fema. Available At Https://Www.Fema.Gov/Media-Library-Data/1510690321803-1e6c4874b251c3022ac4b57b0369e2da/Quakesmart_Ready_Business_Toolkit_Interactive_Final_508.Pdf

Fernandes, R., Gouveia, J. B., & Pinho, C., 2011, Medição Da Incerteza Da Procura Numa Cadeia De Abastecimento Com Múltiplos Pontos De Inventário. Revista De Gestão Dos Países De Língua Portuguesa, 10(4), Pp. 67-79. Available At Http://Www. Scielo.Mec.Pt/Scielo.Php?Pid=S1645-44642011000300007&Script=Sci_Arttext&Tlng=Pt

Ferreira, F. A. L., Scavarda, L. F., Ceryno, P. S., & Leiras, A., 2018, Supply Chain Risk Analysis: A Shipbuilding Industry Case. International Journal Of Logistics Research And Applications, 21(5), Pp. 542-556. Available At Http://Dx.Doi.Org/10.1080/13675567.2018.1472748.

Fisher, M., 1997, What Is The Right Supply Chain For Your Product?, Harvard Business Review, Mar-Apr, Pp. 105-116.

Fisk, R., Brown, S., & Bitner, M. J., 1996, Tracking The Evolution Of The Services Marketing Literature. Journal Of Retailing, 69, Pp. 61-103.

Flach, F., 1988, Resilience: Discovering A New Strength At Times Of Stress, New York, Ny: Fawcett Columbine.

Florea, N. And Clipa, C., 2005, Supply Chain Management - Introducere, Bazele, Edificiul Şi Istoricul Scm. [Online]. Available At: <Http://Www.Ecr-Uvt.Ro/Simpozion_Ecr_2005/Materiale_Simpozion/15.15-15.25_N.Florea.Doc>.

Florian, V., Mikulincer, M., & Taubman, O., 1995, Does Hardiness Contribute To Mental Health During A Stressful Real-Life Situation? The Roles Of Appraisal And Coping. Journal Of Personality And Social Psychology, 68, Pp. 687-695.

Foerstl, K., Reuter, C., Hartmann, E., Blome, C., 2010, Managing Supplier Sustainability Risks In A Dynamically Changing Environment: Sustainable Supplier Management In The Chemical Industry, Journal Of Purchasing And Supply Management, 16, Pp. 118–130.

Fontnouvelle, P.; Dejesus-Rueff, V.; Jordan, J.; Rosengren, E., 2003, Using Loss Data To Quantify Operational Risk; Federal Reserve Bank Of Boston: Boston, Ma, Usa.

Fotache, D. And Hurbean, L., 2006, Supply Chain Management: From Linear Interactions To Networked Processes, Informatică Economică, 4(10), Pp.73-77.

Fraser, J.; Simkins, B.; Narvaez, K., 2014, Implementing Enterprise Risk Management: Case Studies And Best Practices, John Wiley & Sons: Hoboken.

Fraser, J.; Simkins, B.J., 2008, Enterprise Risk Management; John Wiley & Sons: Hoboken, Pp. 19–29.

Fraser, P.; Moultrie, J.; Gregory, M. The Use Of Maturity Models/Grids As A Tool In Assessing Product Development Capability. In Proceedings Of The

Engineering Management Conference, Cambridge, Uk, 18–20 August 2002; Pp. 244–249.

Frei, F. X. And P. T. Harker, 1999, Measuring The Efficiency Of Service Delivery Processes: An Application To Retail Banking" Journal Of Service Research, 1(4), Pp.300-312.

Frolick, M.N.; Ariyachandra, T.R., 2006, Business Performance Management: One Truth. Is Manag. 23, Pp. 41–44.

Funo, K. A., Muniz R, J., & Marins, F. A. S., 2013, Fatores De Risco Em Cadeia De Suprimentos Do Setor Aeroespacial: Aspectos Qualitativos E Quantitativos. Revista Produção, 23(4), Pp. 832-845. Available At Http://Dx.Doi.Org/10.1590/S0103-65132013005000016.

Ganesan, V., 2007, An Analysis Of Working Capital Management Efficiency In Telecommunication Equipment, Industry Rivier Academic Joumal, 3(2).

Ganga, G. M. D., Carpinetti, L. C. R., & Politano, P. R., 2011, Gestão Do Desempenho Em Cadeias De Suprimentos Usando Lógica Fuzzy. Gestão & Produção, 18(4), Pp. 755-774. Available At Http://Dx.Doi.Org/10.1590/S0104-530x2011000400006.

Garmezy, N., & Masten, A. S., 1986, Stress, Competence, And Resilience: Common Frontiers For Therapist And Psychopatholo- Gist. Behavior Therapy, 17, Pp. 500-521.

Geocaris, C. M., 2004, The Evolving Role Of The Principalship: Critical Insights For A New Paradigm (Unpublished Doctoral Dissertation, Northern Illinois University, Dekalb). (Umi Proquest Digital Dissertations, Aat 3132422). Available At Http://Proquest.Umi.Com/Pqdweb?Did=766022421&Fmt= 7&Clientid=1898&Rqt=309&Vname=Pqd

Gerring, J., 2007, Case Study Research: Principles And Practices, Cambridge University Press, Cambridge.

Giannakis, M., 2007), Performance Measurement Of Supplier Relationships, Supply Chain Management: An International Journal, 12(6), Pp. 400-411.

Gibbert, M., Ruigrok, W., Wicki, B., 2008, What Passes As A Rigorous Case Study, Strategic Management Journal, 29(13), Pp. 1465–1474.

Glaser-Segura, D.,A. Anghel, L.D. And Tucci, J.E., 2006, Supply Chain Management And The Romanian Transition. Amfiteatru Economic, Viii (19), Pp.18-26.

Glaser, B.G., Strauss, A.L., 1967, The Discovery Of Grounded Theory. Strategies For Qualitative Research. The Sociology Press, Mill Valley.

Goldstein, J. C., 2003, Voices Of Catholic School Principals: A Phenomenological Study Of Catholic School Principals' Perceptions Of Efficacy And Resiliency. Dissertation Abstracts International, 64(3146), 09a. (Umi No. Aat3329731) Greene, L. (2003). More And More With Less And Less. Principal-Arlington-, 83(1), 5-5.

Goldstein, S.M., Johnston, R., Duffy, J. And Rao, J., 2002, The Service Concept: The Missing Link In Service Design Research?, Journal Of Operations Management, 20(2), Pp. 121-134.

Gordon, L.A., Loeb, M.P., Tseng, C.-Y., 2009, Enterprise Risk Management And Firm Performance: A Contingency Perspective, Journal Of Accounting And Public Policy, 28(4), Pp. 301–327.

Gordon, L.A.; Loeb, M.P.; Tseng, C.Y., 2009, Enterprise Risk Management And Firm Performance: A Contingency Perspective, J. Account. Public Policy,28, Pp. 301–327.

Gottfredson, M., Puryear, R., Phillips, S., 2005, Strategic Sourcing: From Periphery To The Core, Harvard Business Review, 83(2), Pp. 132–139.

Grc Defined (Oceg). Available At: Http://Www.Webcitation.Org/6u4efwkf. Sustainability 2018, 10, 640 19 Of 20

Greene, R. R. (Ed.)., 2002, Resiliency: An Integrated Approach To Practice, Policy, And Research, Washington, Dc: National Association Of Social Workers Press.

Greene, R. R., Conrad, A. P., Livingstone, N. C., Barton, W. H., Watkins, M. L., Blundo, R., & Riley, J. G. 2002, An Integrated Approach To Practice, Policy, And Research, Washington, Dc: National Association Of Social Workers Press.

Gunasekaran, A., & Ngai, E., 2005, Build-To-Order Supply Chain Management: A Literature Review And Framework For Development, Journal Of Operations Management, Pp. 423-451.

Gunasekaran, A., Irani, Z., Choy, K. L., Filippi, L., & Papadopoulos, T., 2015, Performance Measures And Metrics In Outsourcing Decisions: A Review For Research And Applications. International Journal Of Production Economics, 161, Pp. 153-166. Available At Http://Dx.Doi.Org/10.1016/J. Ijpe.2014.12.021.

Gunasekaran, A., Patel, C., & Mcgaughey, R. E., 2004, A Framework For Supply Chain Performance Measurement, International Journal Of Production Economics, 87(3), Pp. 333-347. Available At Http://Dx.Doi.Org/10.1016/J.Ijpe.2003.08.003.

Gunasekaran, A., Patel, C., & Tirtiroglu, E., 2001, Performance Measures And Metrics In A Supply Chain Environment, International Journal Of Operations &

Production Management, 21(1-2), Pp. 71-87. Available At Http://Dx.Doi.Org/10.1108/01443570110358468.

Habib, M., 2009, An Integrated Educational Supply Chain Management (Itescm). Ph.D. Dissertation, Graduate School Of Information Technology, Assumption University Of Thailand, December.

Habib, M. (2010) An Empirical Research Of Itescm (Integrated Tertiary Educational Supply Chain Management) Model. Management And Services.

Habib, M., 2010, Supply Chain Management For Academia, Lap Lambert Academic Publishing, Germany.

Habib, M. And Jungthirapanich, C., 2008, An Integrated Framework For Research And Education Supply Chain For The Universities, Ieee International Conference On Management Of Innovation And Technology, Thailand, September, Pp. 1027-1032.

Habib, M. And Jungthirapanich, C., 2009, Integrated Educational Management For The Universities, The Journal Of China-Usa Business Review, 8, Pp. 25-38.

Habib, M. And Jungthirapanich, C., 2009, Research Framework Of Educational Supply Chain Management For The Universities, Ieee International Conference On Engineering Management And Service Sciences Ems, China, September.

Habib, M. And Jungthirapanich, C., 2010, An Empirical Research Of Educational Supply Chain For The Universities, The 5th Ieee International Conference On Management Of Innovation And Technology.

Habib, M. And Jungthirapanich, C., 2010, An Empirical Research Of Integrated Educational Management For The Universities, The 2nd Ieee International Conference On Information Management And Engineering, China.

Habib, M. And Jungthirapanich, C., (2010, An Empirical Study Of Educational Supply Chain Management For The Universities, Informs International Conference On Industrial Engineering And Operations Management, Bangladesh.

Habib, M., 2010, Supply Chain Management: Theory And Its Future Perspectives. International Journal Of Business, Management And Social Sciences, 1(1), Pp. 79-87.

Habib, M.M., 2011, An Exploratory Analysis Of Educational Management For The Universities. International Journal Of Engineering, Business, Management (Ijebm), 3, Pp. 16-24.

Habib, M.M., 2011, An Exploratory Research On Educational Supply Chain Management, The Ieee International Conference On Industrial Engineering And Engineering Management (Ieem), Singapore, December.

Habib, M.M., 2011, An Exploratory Study Of Supply Chain Management For Tertiary Educational Institutions, Ieee International Technology Management Conference (Itmc), San Jose, 27-30 June, Pp. 957-963.

Habib, M.M., 2011, Supply Chain Management (Scm): Theory And Evolution. Supply Chain Management, Applications And Simulations, Intech Open Access, Croatia, September.

Habib, M.M. And Pathik, B.B., 2012, Academic Supply Chain Management For Tertiary Educational Institutions, The Ieee International Conference On Industrial Engineering And Engineering Management (Ieem), Hong Kong.

Harland, C., Slack, N., Chambers S., Harrison, A. And Johnston, R., 1997, Operations Management, 2nd Edn, Harlow: Ft/Prentice Hall.

Hauser, L.M., 2003, Risk-Adjusted Supply Chain Management, Supply Chain Management Review, 7(6), Pp. 64-71.

Healy, E., 2019, Improving Supply Chain Resilience, Kpmg. Available At: Https://Www2.Deloitte.Com/Ie/En/Pages/Deloitte-Private/Articles/Improving-Supply-Chain-Resilience.Html

Heifetz, R. A., & Linsky, M., 2004, When Leadership Spells Dan- Ger. Educational Leadership, 61(7), Pp. 33-37.

Henderson, N., & Milstein, M. M., 1996,. Management Of Organizational Behavior: Utilizing Human Resources (5th Ed.), Thousand Oaks, Ca: Corwin Press.

Hertzel, M.G., Li, Z., Officer, M.S., Rodgers, K.J., 2008, Inter-Firm Linkages And The Wealth Effects Of Financial Distress Along The Supply Chain. Journal Of Financial Economics, 87(2), Pp. 374–387.

Hevner, A.; March, S.T.; Park, J.; Ram, S., 2004, Design Science In Information Systems Research. Mis Q., 28, Pp. 75–105.

Hevner, A.R., 2007, A Three Cycle View Of Design Science Research, Scand. J. Inf. Syst., 11, Pp .87–92.

Hewitt, F., 1994, Supply Chain Redesign. The International Journal Of Logistics Management, 5(2), Pp. 1-9.

Higgins, G. O., 1994, Resilient Adults: Overcoming A Cruel Past. San Francisco, Ca: Jossey-Bass.

Hillman, M. And Keltz, H., 2007. "Managing Supply Chain Risk In The Supply Chain – A Quantitative Study." Amr Research Available At <Http://Www.Amrresearch.Com/Content/View.Aspx?Compuri=Tcm:7-13798>.

Hillson, D.A., 1997, Towards A Risk Maturity Model, Int. J. Proj. Bus. Risk Manag., 1, Pp. 35–45.

Hoffman, D.G., 2002, Managing Operational Risk: 20 Firmwide Best Practice Strategies, John Wiley & Sons: Hoboken.

Homan, T., 2012, Us Service Industry Growth Surges In January, February 3, Available At Fox News: Http://Www.Foxnews.Com/Us/2012/02/03/Us-Service-Firms-Growth-Hits-11-Month-High-In-Jan/

Johnson, M. , 2008, Supply Chain Management For Servitised Products: A Multi-Industry Case Study, International Journal Of Production Economics, Pp. 27-39.

Hoyle, R.H., 1999, Statistical Strategies For Small Sample Research; Sage: Newcastle Upon Tyne, Uk.

Hsu, C.C. And Sandford, B.A., 2007, The Delphi Technique: Making Sense Of Consensus, Pract. Assess. Res. Eval., 12, Pp. 1–8.

Huang, S. H., & Keskar, H., 2007, Comprehensive And Configurable Metrics For Supplier Selection, International Journal Of Production Economics, 105(2), Pp. 510-523. Available At Http://Dx.Doi.Org/10.1016/J.Ijpe.2006.04.020.

Hugos, M., 2006, Essentials Of Supply Chain Management, 2nd Edition, New Jersey: John Wiley & Sons.

Humphrey, W.S., 1988, Characterizing The Software Process: A Maturity Framework. Ieee Softw., 5, Pp. 73–79.

Ickovics, J. R., & Park, C. L., 1998, Thriving: Broadening The Paradigm Beyond Illness To Health, The Society For The Psychological Study Of Social Issues By Blackwell Publishers.

Ikram Ul Haq, Sohail, M., Zaman, K., &Alam, Z., 2011, The Relationship Between Working Capital Management And Profitability: A Case Study Of Cement Industry In Pakistan. Mediterranean Journal Of Social Sciences, 2.

Ilieş, L., 2006, Logistica – Sursă De Competitivitate. Management &Marketing, 1 (1), Pp. 93-101.

India Gdp Composition Sector Wise, 2012. Available At Http://Business.Mapsofindia.Com/India-Gdp/Sectorwise/

Isaacs, A., 2003,. An Investigation Of Attributes Of School Principals In Relation To Resilience And Leadership Practices (Unpublished Doctoral Dissertation), Florida State University, Tallahassee, Fl. Available At Http://Diginole.Lib.Fsu.Edu/Etd/3863/

Iso 31000 Risk Management—Principles And Guidelines. Available At: Http://Www.Webcitation.Org/6u4gjyz7w.

Ivanov, D., Dolgui, A., Sokolov, B., & Ivanova, M., 2016, Disruptions In Supply Chains And Recovery Policies: State-Of-The Art Review, Ifac-Papersonline, 49(12), Pp. 1436-1441.

Jalali, S., & Wohlin, C., 2012, Systematic Literature Studies: Database Searches Vs. Backward Snowballing. In Proceedings Of The International Conference On Empirical Software Engineering And Measurement. Sweden: Blekinge Institute Of Technology. Available At Http://Www.Wohlin.Eu/Esem12a.Pdf

Jensen, M. C., 1986, Agency Cost Of Free Cash Flow, Corporate Finance And Takeovers, The American Economic Review, 76(2), Pp. 323-329.

Jesson, J. K., Matheson, L., & Lacey, F. M, 2011, Doing Your Literature Review Traditional And Systematic Techniques, Singapore: Sage Publications.

Jones, P. S., 1991, Adaptability, A Personal Resource For Health: Scholarly Inquiry For Nursing Practice, An International Journal, 5, Pp. 95-108.

Jose, M. L., Lancaster, C. & Stevens, J. L., 1996, Corporate Returns And Cash Conversion Cycles, Journal Of Economics And Finance, 20(1), Pp. 33-46.

Joshi, P., 1995, Working Capital Management Under Inflation, Research Journal Of Finance And Accounting, 6(16).

Joshi, R., 2013, Working Capital Management Of Commercial Banks In Nepal: Being An M.Sc. Thesis Submitted To Faculty Of Management Tribhuvan University, Shankar Dev. Campus, Kathmadu. Kargar, J., &

Jüttner, U., 2005, Supply Chain Risk Management", International Journal Of Logistics Management, 16(1), Pp. 120-41.

Juttner, U. P., 2003, Supply Chain Risk Management: Outlining An Agenda For Future Research. International Journal Of Logistics: Research And Applications, 6(4), Pp. 197-210.

Kamalahmadi, M., & Parast, M. M., 2016, A Review Of The Literature On The Principles Of Enterprise And Supply Chain Resilience: Major Findings And Directions For Future Research, International Journal Of Production Economics, 171, Pp. 116-133. Available At Http://Dx.Doi.Org/10.1016/J. Ijpe.2015.10.023.

Kamalahmadi, M., & Parast, M. M., 2017, An Assessment Of Supply Chain Disruption Mitigation Strategies, International Journal Of Production Economics, 184, Pp. 210-230.
Http://Dx.Doi.Org/10.1016/J.Ijpe.2016.12.011.

Kaplan, R. S., & Norton, D. P., 1992, The Balanced Scorecard - Measures That Drive Performance, Harvard Business Review, Jan-Feb, Pp. 71-79.

Kathawaia, Y., & Abdou, K., 2003. Supply Chain Evaluation In The Service Industry: A Framework Development Compared To Manufacturing. Managerial Auditing Journal, 18(2), Pp. 140-149.

Kathawala, Y. And Abdou, K., 2003, Supply Chain Evaluation In The Service Industry: A Framework Development Compared To Manufacturing. Managerial Auditing Journal, 18(14), Pp. 1-149. Available At Http://Dx.Doi.Org/10.1108/02686900310455137

Kavakr, F.; Spiegel, A.D., 2004, Risk Management In Health Care Institutions A Strategic Approach. J. Healthc. Qual. 26, Pp. 56–58.

Kearns, G. S. And Lederer, A. L., 2003, A Resourced-Based View Of Strategic It Alignment: How Knowledge Sharing Creates Competitive Advantage, Decision Sciences, 34(1), Pp. 1-29.

Kelle, P., Miller, P.A., 2001, Stockout Risk And Order Splitting, International Journal Of Production Economics, 71(1–3), Pp. 407–415.

Kenett, R.S.; Raanan, Y., 2011, Operational Risk Management: A Practical Approach To Intelligent Data Analysis; John Wiley & Sons: Hoboken.

Khan, O., Christopher, M., & Creazza, A., 2012, Aligning Product Design With The Supply Chain: A Case Study. Supply Chain Management, 17(3), Pp. 323-336. Available At Http://Dx.Doi.Org/10.1108/13598541211227144.

Kim, J., And Suh, E., And Hwang, H., 2003, A Model For Evaluating The Effectiveness Of Crm Using The Balanced Scorecard, Journal Of Interactive Marketing, 17(2), Pp. 5-19.

Kuckartz, U., 1999, Computergestützte Analyze Qualitativer Daten: Eine Einführung In Die Methoden Und Arbeitstechniken. Opladen: Westdeutscher Verlag. Available At Http://Dx.Doi.Org/10.1007/978-3-322-86592-2.

Kumpfer, K. L., & Hopkins, R., 1993, Prevention: Current Research And Trends. Recent Advances In Addictive Disorders, 16(1).

Lam, J., 2014, Enterprise Risk Management: From Incentives To Controls, John Wiley & Sons: Hoboken.

Lam, J. S. L., & Bai, X., 2016, A Quality Function Deployment Approach To Improve Maritime Supply Chain Resilience. Transportation Research Part E, Logistics And Transportation Review, 92, Pp. 16-27. Available At Http://Dx.Doi.Org/10.1016/J.Tre.2016.01.012.

Lambert, D.M. And Cooper, M.C., 2000, Issues In Supply Chain Management, Industrial Marketing Management, 29(1(, Pp. 65-83.

Lau, A.K.W., 2007, Educational Supply Chain Management: A Case Study. On The Horizon, 15, Pp. 15-27. Available At Http://Dx.Doi.Org/10.1108/10748120710735239

Lavanya, N. And Malarvizhi, T., 2008, Risk Analysis And Management: A Vital Key To Effective Project Management. Paper Presented At Pmi Global Congress 2008—Asia Pacific, Sydney, New South Wales, Australia. Newtown Square, Pa: Project Management Institute.

Lawson, 2019, Lawson's Scm-Crm Model Is A Driving Engine. Available At: Http://Lawson.Jp/En/About/Message/Scm_Crm/

Lebas, M., 1995, Performance Measurement And Performance Management. Int. J. Prod. Econ., 41.

Ledesma, J., 2012, Narratives Of Longevity From The Perspective Of Seventh-Day Adventist School Administrators In North America: A Multiple Case Study. Andrews University.

Lee, H., & Billington, C., 1993, Material Management In Decentralized Supply Chains. Operations Research, 25(5), Pp. 42-63.

Leong, G., Snyder, D., & Ward, P., 1990, Research In The Process And Content Of Manufacturing Strategy, Omega International Journal Of Management Science, 18(2), Pp. 109-122.

Leukel, J., Kirn, S., & Schlegel, T., 2011, Supply Chain As A Service: A Cloud Perspective On Supply Chain Systems, Ieee Systems Journal, 5(1), Pp. 16-27.

Li, S. Ragu-Nathan, B., Ragu-Nathan, T.S. And Rao, S.S., 2006, The Impact Of Supply Chain Management Practices On Competitive Advantage And Organizational Performance, Omega, 34(2), Pp. 107-124.

Lima, F. R. P., Silva, A. L., Godinho Filho, M., & Dias, E. M., 2018, Systematic Review: Resilience Enablers To Combat Counterfeit Medicines, Supply Chain Management, 12(3), Pp. 117-135. Available At Http://Dx.Doi.Org/10.1108/Scm-04-2017-0155.

Linnenluecke, M. K., 2017, Resilience In Business And Management Research: A Review Of Influential Publications And A Research Agenda, International Journal Of Management Reviews, 19(1), Pp. 4-30. Available At Http://Dx.Doi.Org/10.1111/Ijmr.12076.

Linstone, H.A.; Turoff, M., 2002, The Delphi Method. Techniques And Applications, Addison-Wesley: Reading,.

Lo Nigro, G., Abbate, L., 2011, Risk Assessment And Profit Sharing In Supply Networks. International Journal Of Production Economics, 131(1), Pp. 234-241.

Logistics Bureau, 2016, Key Supply Chain Skills Needed. Available At Https://Www.Logisticsbureau.Com/6-Key-Supply-Chain-Leaders-Skills-And-Why-You-Need-Them/

Lovelock, C., & Gummesson, E., 2004, Whither Services Marketing? In Search Of A New Paradigm And Fresh Perspectives, Journal Of Service Research, 7(1).

Lupşe, V. And Cosma, O., 2006, Erp Extension - Supply Chain Management (Scm), Informatică Economică, 38(2), Pp.120-123.

Luthar, S. S., Cicchetti, D., & Becker, B., 2000, The Construct Of Resilience: A Critical Evaluation And Guidelines For Future Work, Child Development, 71, Pp. 543-562.

Lytras, M.; Raghavan, V.; Damiani, E., 2017, Big Data And Data Analytics Research: From Metaphors To Value Space For Collective Wisdom In Human Decision Making And Smart Machines, Int. J. Sem. Web Inf. Sys., 13, Pp. 1–10.

Macchi, M., Levi, D.J., And Westland, S. 2016, Banking Reinvented: Beyond Value Chains To Value Networks, Accenturestrategy. Available At: Https://Www.Accenture.Com/T20160628t211350__W_

_/Us-En/_Acnmedia/Pdf-24/Accenture-Strategy-Banking-Reinvented-Value-Chains-Networks.Pdf

Maddi, S. R., & Khoshaba, D. M., 2005, Resilience At Work: How To Succeed No Matter What Life Throws At You, Amacom Div American Mgmt Assn.

Maddi, S. R., & Kobasa, S. C., 1984, The Hardy Executive: Health Under Stress. Homewood, Il: Dow Jones-Irwin.

Makomaski, J., 2008, So What Exactly Is Erm? Risk Management 55 (4), Pp. 80–81.

Malik, S.A.; Holt, B., 2013, Factors That Affect The Adoption Of Enterprise Risk Management (Erm), Or Insight 26, Pp. 253–269.

Mallik, A., Sur, D., & Rakshit, D., 2005, Working Capital And Profitability: A Study On Their Relationship With Reference To Selected Companies In Indian Pharmaceutical Industry, Gitam Journal Of Management, 3(2).

Manuj, I., Dittmann, J. And Gaudenzi, B., 2007, Risk Management" In Mentzer, John T., Myers, Mathew B. And Stank, Theodore P. (Eds.), Handbook Of Global Supply Chain Management, Sage Publishing, Usa.

Marques, R.C.; Berg, S., 2011, Risks, Contracts, And Private-Sector Participation In Infrastructure, J. Constr. Eng. Manag., 137, Pp. 925–932.

Masten, A. S., 2001, Defining Resilience. American Psychologist, 56, Pp. 227-238.

Maturity Model For Business Intelligence And Performance Management. Available At: Http://Www. Webcitation.Org/6u4l6trsm.

Maturity Model For Operational Risk Management. Available At: Http://Www.Webcitation.Org/ 6u4ks5lsa.

Mccormack, K.;Willems, J.; Van Den Bergh, J.; Deschoolmeester, D.;Willaert, P.; Štemberger, M.; Vlahovic, N., 2009, A Global Investigation Of Key Turning Points In Business Process Maturity, Bus. Process Manag. J. 15, Pp. 792–815.

Melchert, F.; Winter, R.; Klesse, M., 2004, Aligning Process Automation And Business Intelligence To Support Corporate Performance Management. In Proceedings Of The Tenth Americas Conference On Information Systems, New York, 6–8 August, Pp. 4053–4063.

Meszek, W., & Polewski, M., 2006, Certain Aspects Of Working Capital In A Construction Company. Technological And Economic Development Of Economy, 12(3), Pp. 222-226.

Meulbroek, L.K., 2002, A Senior Manager's Guide To Integrated Risk Management, J. Appl. Corp. Financ., 14, Pp. 56–70.

Miller, K.D., 1992, A Framework For Integrated Risk Management In International Business, J. Int. Bus. Stud., 23, Pp. 311–331.

Mishra, A., And Mishra, D., 2009, Customer Relationship Management: Implementation Process Perspective, Acta Polytechnica Hungarica, 6(4), Pp. 83-99.

Mitra, S.; Karathanasopoulos, A.; Sermpinis, G.; Dunis, C.; Hood, J. 2015, Operational Risk: Emerging Markets, Sectors And Measurement. Eur. J. Oper. Res., 24, Pp. 122–132.

Mitroff, I.I., And Alpasan, M.C., 2003, Preparing For Evil, Harvard Business Review, April.

Mocuţa, G.E., 2009, Logistica – Instrument Şi Concept În Continuă Evoluţie, Buletinul Agir, 2-3, April-September Issue, Pp.88-93.

Mohamad, N. E. A. B., & Saad, N. B. M., 2010, Working Capital Management: The Effect Of Market Valuation And Profitability In Malaysia, International Journal Of Business And Management, 5(11), 140.

Mohr, L. A. And M. J. Bitner, 1995, The Role Of Employee Effort In Satisfaction With Service Transactions, Journal Of Business Research, 32(3), Pp. 239-252.

Monczka, R. M., Petersen, K. J., Handfield, R. B. And Ragatz, G. L., 1998, Success Factors In Strategic Supplier

Alliances: The Buying Company Perspective, Decision Sciences, 29(3), Pp. 553-77.

Moog, M., Giarrusso, M., Ritterbush, C., Seth, K., Lim, C., Deropp, H., And Hassan, H., 2018, Global Financial Services Third-Party Risk Management Survey: Is It Time To Shift Your Perspective Of Third-Party Risk?", Ey. Available At Https://Www.Ey.Com/Publication/Vwluassets/Ey-Global-Financial-Services-Third-Party-Risk-Management-Survey/%24file/Ey-Global-Financial-Services-Third-Party-Risk-Management-Survey.Pdf (Accessed: 10 August 2018).

Moosa, I.A., 2007, Operational Risk: A Survey, Financ. Mark. Inst. Instrum.,16, Pp. 167–200.

Morini, C., Inácio Júnior, E., Santa-Eulália, L. A., & Serafim, M. P., 2015, Indicadores De Desempenho Da Aduana Do Brasil: Em Busca De Uma Abordagem Equilibrada, Gestão & Produção, 22(3), Pp. 508-524. Available At Http://Dx.Doi.Org/10.1590/0104-530x1407-14.

Moseley, G.B., Iii, 2013, Managing Legal Compliance In The Health Care Industry; Jones And Bartlett Publishers: Burlington.

Moyer, R. C., Mcguigan, J. R., & Kretlow, W. J., 2005, Contemporary Financial Management,10th Edition, South-Western College Publishing, New York.

Murphy, P.R. And Poist, R.F., 2006, Skill Requirements Of Contemporary Senior And Entry Level Logistics Managers: A Comparative Analysis, Transportation Journal, 33, Pp. 36-48.

Murray, J.Y., Kotabe, M., 1999, Sourcing Strategies Of Us Service Companies: A Modified Transaction–Cost Analysis, Strategic Management Journal, 20(9), Pp. 791–809.

Neiger, D., Rotaru, K., Churilov, L., 2009, Supply Chain Risk Identification With Value-Focused Process Engineering, Journal Of Operations Management, 27(2), Pp. 154–168.

Nissen, V.; Marekfia, W., 2013, Towards A Research Agenda For Strategic Governance, Risk And Compliance (Grc) Management, In Proceedings Of The Conference Business Informatics (Cbi), Vienna, Austria, 15–18 July Pp. 1–6.

Nolan, R.L., 2018, Managing The Computer Resource: A Stage Hypothesis, Commun. Acm 1973, 16, Pp. 399–405.

Noordewier, T.G., John, G., Nevin, J.R., 1990, Performance Outcomes Of Purchasing Arrangements In Industrial Buyer-Vendor Relationships, Journal Of Marketing, 54(4), Pp. 80–93.

Norrman, A. And Lindroth, R., 2004, Categorization Of Supply Chain Risk And Risk Management, In Brindley, C. (Ed.), Supply Chain Risk, Ashgate, London, Pp. 14-28.

O'leary, V. E., & Ickovics, J. R., 1995, Resilience And Thriving In Response To Challenge: An Opportunity For A Paradigm Shift In Women's Health. Women's Health: Research On Gender, Behavior, And Policy, 1(2), Pp. 121-142.

Oke, A., & Gopalakrishnan, M., 2009, Managing Disruptions In Supply Chains: A Case Study Of A Retail Supply Chain. International Journal Of Production Economics, 118(1), Pp. 168-174. Available At Http://Dx.Doi.Org/10.1016/J.Ijpe.2008.08.045.

Oliver, K. And Webber, M., 1982, Supply-Chain Management: Logistics Catches Up With Strategy. 5.

Olson, D. And Wu, D.D., 2015, Enterprise Risk Management, World Scientific Publishing Co., Inc.: Singapore.

Operational Issues Of Risk Management (Pwc). Available At: Http://Www.Webcitation.Org/6xa3v6uxv

Operational Sustainability, 2019, Enterprise Risk Management System Overview. Available At: Https://Www.Osorm.Com/Services-Consulting/Erm.Php

Operational Risk (Bank Of International Settlements). Available At: Http://Www.Webcitation.Org/ 6tjuxt27o.

Oracle, 2015, Big Data In Financial Services And Banking: Architect's Guide And Reference Architecture

Introduction, Oracle Enterprise Architecture White Paper, February. Available At: Http://Www.Oracle.Com/Us/Technologies/Big-Data/Big-Data-In-Financial-Services-Wp-2415760.Pdf

Padachi, K., 2006, Trends In Working Capital Management And Its Impact On Firms' Performance: An Analysis Of Mauritian Small Manufacturing Firms. International Review Of Business Research Papers, 2(2), Pp. 45-58.

Pagell, M. And Krause, D.R., 2005, Determining When Multiple Respondents Are Needed In Supply Chain Management Research: The Case Of Purchasing And Operations. In: Weaver, K.A. (Ed.), A New Vision Of Management In The 21st Century. Proceedings Of The Academy Of Management Conference, 5–10 August.

Panjer, H.H., 2006, Operational Risk: Modeling Analytics; John Wiley & Sons: Hoboken.

Park, C. L., 1998, Stress-Related Growth And Thriving Through Coping: The Roles Of Personality And Cognitive Processes, Journal Of Social Issues, 54, Pp. 268-278.

Park, C. L., Cohen, H., & Murch, R., 1996, Assessment And Pre- Diction Of Stress-Related Growth, Journal Of Personality, 64, Pp. 71-105.

Pathik, B.B. And Habib, M.M., 2012, Redesigned Itescm Model: An Academic Scm For The Universities,

International Journal Of Supply Chain Management, Excelingtech Publisher, Uk.

Pathik, B.B., Habib, M.M. And Chowdhury, M.T., 2012, A Descriptive Study On Supply Chain Management Model For The Academia, The 6th Ieee Conference Of Management Of Innovation And Technology, Indonesia.

Pathik, B.B., Habib, M.M. And Chowdhury, M.T., 2012, Analysis Of Educational Supply Chain Management Model: A Case Study Approach. Proceedings Of The 2012 International Conference On Industrial Engineering And Operations Management, Turkey.

Patterson, J. L., Patterson, J., & Collins, L., 2002, Bouncing Back: How Your School Can Succeed In The Face Of Adversity. Larchmont, Ny: Eye On Education.

Patterson, J., & Patterson, J. H., 2001, Resilience In The Face Of Imposed Changes. Principal Leadership, 1(6), Pp. 50-55.

Paulk, M.C.; Curtis, B.; Chrissis, M.B.; Weber, C.V., 1993, Capability Maturity Model, Version 1.1. Ieee Softw., 10, Pp. 18–27.

Pearsall, P., 2003, The Beethoven Factor: The New Positive Psychology Of Hardiness, Happiness, Healing, And Hope, Charlottesville, Va: Hampton Roa

Pelău, C., 2007, Structuri Organizatorice La Nivel De Întreprindere Pentru Implementarea Marketing-

Controlling-Ului, Management & Marketing, 2(1), Pp.133-142.

Peng, M., Peng, Y., & Chen, H., 2014, Post-Seismic Supply Chain Risk Management: A System Dynamics Disruption Analysis Approach For Inventory And Logistics Planning, Computers & Operations Research, 42, Pp. 14-24. Available At Http://Dx.Doi.Org/10.1016/J.Cor.2013.03.003.

Pereira, J. V., 2009, The New Supply Chain's Frontier: Information Management, International Journal Of Information Management, 29(5), Pp. 372-379. Available At Http://Dx.Doi.Org/10.1016/J.Ijinfomgt.2009.02.001.

Perez, S., 2014, Operational Risk: The Risk In All Banking Transactions, Market Realist, September 1. Available At: Https://Articles2.Marketrealist.Com/2014/09/Operational-Risk-Risk-Banking-Transactions/

Pieket Weeserik, B.; Spruit, M. B4orm Assessment Instrument. Available At: Http://Bit.Ly/B4ormassessment.

Ponomarov, S. Y., & Holcomb, M. C., 2009, Understanding The Concept Of Supply Chain Resilience. International Journal Of Logistics Management, 20(1), Pp. 124-143. Available At Http://Dx.Doi.Org/10.1108/09574090910954873.

Ponomarov, Serhiy Y And Holcomb, Mary C., 2009, Understanding The Concept Of Supply Chain Resilience, The International Journal Of Logistics Management, 20(1), Pp. 124-143.

Popa, V., 2009, Managementul Lanţului De Distribuţie/Aprovizionare Pentru Un Răspuns Eficient Consumatorului, Târgovişte: Valahia University Press.

Power, M., 2005, The Invention Of Operational Risk, Rev. Int. Political Econ., 12, Pp. 577–599.

Power, M., 2009. The Risk Management Of Nothing. Accounting, Organizations And Society 34, 849–855.

Purdy, G., 2010, Iso 31000: 2009—Setting A New Standard For Risk Management. Risk Anal., 30, Pp. 881–886.

Putz, E. And Bîzoi, G., 2010, Managementul Lanţului Logistic, Timişoara: Editura Universităţii De Vest.

Pwc, 2016 Blurred Lines: How Fintech Is Shaping Financial Services, Global Fintech Report, 2016, Available At Https://Www.Pwc.Co.Uk/Financial-Services/Fintech/Assets/Fintech-Global-Report2016.Pdf

Racz, N.; Weippl, E.; Seufert, A., 2010, A Frame Of Reference For Research Of Integrated Grc. In Communications And Multimedia Security, Springer: Berlin, Pp. 106–117.

Racz, N.; Weippl, E.; Seufert, A., 2011, Governance, Risk & Compliance (Grc) Software-An Exploratory Study Of Software Vendor And Market Research Perspectives, In Proceedings Of The 44th Hawaii International Conference Of System Sciences (Hicss), Honolulu, 4–7 January, Pp. 1–10.

Raheman, A. & Nasr, M., 2007, Working Capital Management And Profitability –Case Of Pakistani Firms, International Review Of Business Research Papers, 3(2), Pp. 275-296.

Raheman, A., Qayyum, A., & Afza, T., 2011, Sector-Wise Performance Of Working Capital Management Measures And Profitability Using Ratio Analysis, Interdisciplinary Journal Of Contemporary Research In Business, 3(8).

Rajesh, R., 2016, Forecasting Supply Chain Resilience Performance Using Grey Prediction, Electronic Commerce Research And Applications, 20, Pp. 42-58. Available At Http://Dx.Doi.Org/10.1016/J.Elerap.2016.09.006.

Rajesh, R., & Ravi, V., 2015, Supplier Selection In Resilient Supply Chains: A Grey Relational Analysis Approach, Journal Of Cleaner Production, 86, Pp. 343-359. Available At Http://Dx.Doi.Org/10.1016/J.Jclepro.2014.08.054.

Ramanathan, U., 2011, Supply Chain Collaboration For Improved Forecast Accuracy Of Promotional Sales,

International Journal Of Operations & Production Management, 32(6), Pp. 676-695.

Reuter, C., Foerstl, K., Hartmann, E., And Blome, C., 2010. Sustainable Global Supplier Management: The Role Of Dynamic Capabilities In Achieving Competitive Advantage, Journal Of Supply Chain Management 46 (2), Pp. 45–63.

Rims Risk Maturity Model (Rmm) For Enterprise Risk Management. Available At: Http://Www. Webcitation.Org/6u4jnw9vu.

Ritchie, B., Brindley, C., 2007, Supply Chain Risk Management And Performance, International Journal Of Operations And Production Management 27(3), Pp. 303–322.

Roceanu, I., 2003, Compoziția Şi Gestionarea Lanțului De Distribuție, Computerworld Profesional, 7(7), Pp.,3-10.

Romano, P., 2003, Coordination And Integration Mechanisms To Manage Logistics Processes Across Supply Networks, Journal Of Purchasing And Supply Management, 9(3), Pp. 119-134.

Rosenberg, J.V.; Schuermann, T., 2006, A General Approach To Integrated Risk Management With Skewed, Fat-Tailed Risks, J. Financ. Econ., 79, Pp. 569–614.

Saccurato, F., 1994, The Study Of Working Capital, Business Credit, January; Pp. 36–37.

Sacomano Neto, M., & Pires, S. R. I., 2012, Medição De Desempenho Em Cadeias De Suprimentos: Um Estudo Na Indústria Automobilística, Gestão & Produção, 19(4), Pp. 733-746. Available At Http://Dx.Doi.Org/10.1590/S0104-530x2012000400006.

Sacu, C.; Spruit, M., 2010, Bidm: The Business Intelligence Development Model. In Proceedings Of The 12th International Conference On Enterprise Information Systems, Funchal, Madeira, Portugal, 8–12 June; Pp. 288–293.

Sadgrove, K., 2005, The Complete Guide To Business Risk Management, Gower: London.

Sadgrove, K., 2016, The Complete Guide To Business Risk Management; Routledge: Abingdon-On-Thames.

Sahin, F. And Robinson, E.P., 2002, Flow Coordination And Information Sharing In Supply Chains: Review, Implications, And Directions For Future Research, Decision Sciences, 33(4), Pp 1-32.

Sahu, A. K., Datta, S., & Mahapatra, S. S., 2017. Evaluation Of Performance Index In Resilient Supply Chain: A Fuzzy-Based Approach, Benchmarking, 24(1), Pp. 118-142. Available At Http://Dx.Doi.Org/10.1108/Bij-07-2015-0068.

Sampson, S.E., 2000, Customer-Supplier Duality And Bidirectional Supply Chains In Service Organization, International Journal Of Service Industry Management, 11, Pp. 348-364. Available At Http://Dx.Doi.Org/10.1108/09564230010355377

Samsonowa, T., 2011, Industrial Research Performance Management: Key Performance Indicators In The Ict Industry; Springer: Berlin.

Scavarda, L. F., Ceryno, P. S., Pires, S., & Klingebiel, K., 2015, Supply Chain Resilience Analysis: A Brazilian Automotive Case, Revista De Administração De Empresas, 55(3), Pp. 304-313. Available At Http://Dx.Doi.Org/10.1590/S0034-759020150306.

Schaid, T., 2005, The Impact Of Struggle On Spiritually-Centered Education Leaders And Their Leadership, Unpublished Doctoral Dissertation, University Of Wisconsin, Madison. (Umi No. 3200002)

Schoenherr, T., Tummala, V.M.R., Harrison, T.P., 2008, Assessing Supply Chain Risks With The Analytic Hierarchy Process: Providing Decision Support For The Offshoring Decision By A U.S. Manufacturing Company, Journal Of Purchasing And Supply Management, 14(2), Pp. 100–111.

Scholes, M.S., 2000, Crisis And Risk Management, The American Economic Review, 90(2), Pp. 17–21.

Scholten, K., & Schilder, S,.2015, The Role Of Collaboration In Supply Chain Resilience, Supply Chain Management, 20(4), Pp. 471-484. Available At Http://Dx.Doi.Org/10.1108/Scm-11-2014-0386.

Scholten, K., Sharkey Scott, P., & Fynes, B., 2014, Mitigation Processes-Antecedents For Building Supply Chain Resilience, Supply Chain Management, 19(2), Pp. 211-228. Available At Http://Dx.Doi.Org/10.1108/Scm-06-2013-0191.

Schurrab, H., 2013, The Design And Analysis Of Supply Chain Performance Measures In Industrial Production, Slidesharenet. Available At: Https://Www.Slideshare.Net/Hafezshurrab1/The-Design-And-Analysis-Of-Supply-Chain-Performance-Measures-In-Industrial-Production

Segal, J., 1986, Winning Life's Toughest Battles: Roots Of Human Resilience, New York, Ny: Mcgraw-Hill.

Sellitto, M. A., & Mendes, L. W., 2006, Avaliação Comparativa Do Desempenho De Três Cadeias De Suprimentos Em Manufatura, Revista Produção, 16(3), Pp. 552-568. Available At Http://Dx.Doi.Org/10.1590/S0103-65132006000300015.

Seuring, S., & Gold, S., 2012, Conducting Content-Analysis Based Literature Reviews In Supply Chain Management, Supply Chain Management, 17(5), Pp.

544-555. Available At Http://Dx.Doi.Org/10.1108/13598541211258609.

Shah, S. M. A., & Sana, A., 2006, Impact Of Working Capital Management On The Profitability Of Oil And Gas Sector Of Pakistan. European Journal Of Scientific Research, 15(3), Pp. 301-307

Sharda, R.; Delen, D.; Turban, E., 2014, Business Intelligence A Managerial Perspective On Analytics, Pearson Education Limited: London.

Shaw, N. C., Meixell, M. J., And Tuggle, F. D., 2003, A Case Study Of Integrating Knowledge Management Into The Supply Chain Management Process, In System Sciences, 2003, Proceedings Of The 36th Annual Hawaii International Conference On (Pp. 10-Pp).

Shin, H. H., & Soenen, L., 1998, Efficiency Of Working Capital Management And Corporate Profitability, Financial Practice And Education, 8, Pp. 37-45.

Simkins, B., 2008, Enterprise Risk Management: Current Initiatives And Issues, Journal Of Applied Finance 18(1), Pp. 115–132.

Simkins, B.; Ramirez, S.A., 2007, Enterprise-Wide Risk Management And Corporate Governance, Loyola Univ. Chic. Law J., 39.

Simons, R., 2002, Performance Measurement And Control Systems For Implementing Strategy, Prentice Hall: Upper Saddle River.

Sin, Leo Y.M, Tse, Alan C.B. And Yim, And Frederick H.K., 2005, Crm: Conceptualization And Scale Development, European Journal Of Marketing, 39(11/12). Pp. 1264-1290.

Sinha, P.R., Whitman, L.E., And Malzahn, D., 2004, Methodology To Mitigate Supplier Risk In An Aerospace Supply Chain, Supply Chain Management: An International Journal, 9(2), Pp. 154–168.

Sjøbakk, B., Bakås, O., Bondarenko, O., & Kamran, T., 2015, Designing A Performance Measurement System To Support Materials Management In Engineer-To-Order: A Case Study. Advances In Manufacturing, Available At Http://Dx.Doi.Org/10.1007/S40436- 015-0109-2.

Smeltzer, L.R., Siferd, P., 1998. Proactive Supply Management: The Management Of Risk, Journal Of Supply Chain Management 34(1), Pp. 38–45.

Snell, P., 2010, Beware Of The Risks, And Snap Up The Opportunities In 2010, Ifpsm Ezine Highlights, January 11. Available At Http://Www.Ifpsm-Ezine.Org/S.

Soenen, L. A., 1993, Cash Conversion Cycle And Corporate Profitability, Journal Of Cash Management, 13(4), Pp. 53-58.

Soni, U., Jain, V., & Kumar, S., 2014, Measuring Supply Chain Resilience Using A Deterministic Modeling Approach, Computers & Industrial Engineering, 74, Pp. 11-25. Available At Http://Dx.Doi.Org/10.1016/J.Cie.2014.04.019.

Sound Practices For The Management And Supervision Of Operational Risk (Bank Of International Settlements). Available At: Http://Www.Webcitation.Org/6tjugpqob.

Spruit, M.; Jagesar, R., 2016, Power To The People! Meta-Algorithmic Modelling In Applied Data Science. In Proceedings Of The 8th International Joint Conference On Knowledge Discovery, Knowledge Engineering And Knowledge Management, Porto, Portugal, 11–13 November; Pp. 400–406.

Spruit, M.; Pietzka, K. , 2015, 3m: The Master Data Management Maturity Model, Comput. Hum. Behav., 51, Pp. 1068–1076.

Spruit, M. And Roeling, M., 2014, Isfam: The Information Security Focus Area Maturity Model. In Proceedings Of The 22nd European Conference On Information Systems, Tel Aviv, Israel, 9–14 June.

Spruit, M. And Sacu, C., 2015, The Datawarehouse Capability Maturity Model, J. Univ. Comput. Sci., 21, Pp. 1508–1534.

Srikanthadath, T. N., Rajendran, C., And Narashiman, K., 2010, An Empirical Study On Supply Chain Management: The Perspective Of Logistics Service Providers, International Journal Of Logistics Systems And Management, 6(1), Pp. 1-22.

Srivastava, R.K., Shervani, T.A., And Fahey, L., 1999, Marketing, Business Processes, And Shareholder Value: An Embedded View Of Marketing Activities And The Discipline Of Marketing, Journal Of Marketing, 63(4), Pp. 168–179.

Stewart, G., 1995, Supply Chain Performance Benchmarking Study Reveals Keys To Supply Chain Excellence, Logistics Information Management, 8(2), Pp. 38-44.

Supply Chain Operations Reference Model. (N.D.). Available At Http://Supply-Chain.Org/Scor

Swinney, R., Netessine, S., 2009, Long-Term Contracts Under The Threat Of Supplier Default, Manufacturing & Service Operations Management 11(1), Pp. 109–127.

Talluri, S. S., Kull, T. J., Yildiz, H., & Yoon, J., 2013, Assessing The Efficiency Of Risk Mitigation Strategies In Supply Chains, Journal Of Business Logistics, 34(4), Pp. 253-269. Available At Http://Dx.Doi.Org/10.1111/Jbl.12025.

Tan, K. C., 2001, A Framework Of Supply Chain Management Literature, European Journal Of Purchasing And Supply Management, 7, Pp. 39-48.

Tang, C., 2006, Perspectives In Supply Chain Risk Management, International Journal Of Production Economics, 103(2), Pp. 451-488.

Tang, C., 2006. Robust Strategies For Mitigating Supply Chain Disruptions, International Journal Of Logistics: Research And Applications 9(1), Pp. 33–45.

Tarantino, A., 2008, Governance, Risk, And Compliance Handbook: Technology, Finance, Environmental, And International Guidance And Best Practices, Johnwiley & Sons: Hoboken.

Tattam, D., 2011, A Short Guide To Operational Risk, Gower Publishing: Farnham.

Taxonomy-Based Risk Identification (Carnegie-Mellon University). Available At: Http://Www. Webcitation.Org/6tjvlxoxf.

Tedeschi, R. G., & Calhoun, L. G., 1996, The Posttraumatic Growth Inventory: Measuring The Positive Legacy Of Trauma, Journal Of Traumatic Stress, 9, Pp. 455-471.

Thakkar, J., Kanda, A., And Deshmukh, S. G., 2009, Supply Chain Performance Measurement Framework For Small And Medium Scale Enterprises,

Benchmarking: An International Journal, 16(5), Pp. 702-723.

The 2015 Grc Maturity Survey Report (Oceg). Available At: Http://Www.Webcitation.Org/6tq1wnl8r.

The Lean Supply Machine, 2019, Service Level Agreements: Clarifying The Concept. Available At: Http://Theleansupplychain.Com/2015/05/Service-Level-Agreements-Clarifying-The-Concept/

Thomé, A. M. T., Scavarda, L. F., & Scavarda, A. J., 2016, Conducting Systematic Literature Review In Operations Management. Production Planning & Control, 27(5), Pp. 408-420. Available At Http://Dx.Doi.Org/10.1080/09537287.2015.1129464.

Thomé, A. M. T., Scavarda, L. F., Fernandez, N. S., & Scavarda, A. J., 2012, Sales And Operations Planning: A Research Synthesis, International Journal Of Production Economics, 138(1), Pp. 1-13. Available At Http://Dx.Doi.Org/10.1016/J.Ijpe.2011.11.027.

Tranfield, D., Denyer, D., & Smart, P., 2003, Towards A Methodology For Developing Evidence-Informed Management Knowledge By Means Of Systematic Review, British Journal Of Management, 14(3), Pp. 207-222. Available At Http://Dx.Doi.Org/10.1111/1467-8551.00375.

Tranfield, D., Denyer, D., Marcos, J., & Burr, M., 2004, Co-Producing Management Knowledge, Management

Decision, 42(3-4), Pp. 375-386. Available At Http://Dx.Doi.Org/10.1108/00251740410518895.

Tummala, V.M.R. And Schoenherr, T., 2011, Assessing And Managing Risk Using The Supply Chain Risk Management Process (Scrmp). Supply Chain Management, 16(6), Pp. 474-483.

Tweede Nationaal Onderzoek Risicomanagement In Nederland (Nyenrode Business University). Available At: Http://Www.Webcitation.Org/6u4nmanuk.

Ungar, M., 2004, A Constructionist Discourse On Resilience, Youth & Society, 35, Pp. 341-365.

Urciuoli, L., Mohanty, S., Hintsa, J., & Gerine Boekesteijn, E., 2014, The Resilience Of Energy Supply Chains: A Multiple Case Study Approach On Oil And Gas Supply Chains To Europe, Supply Chain Management, 19(1), Pp. 46-63. Available At Http://Dx.Doi.Org/10.1108/Scm-09-2012-0307.

Uyar, A.H., 2009, The Relationship Of Cash Conversion Cycle With Firm Size And Profitability: An Empirical Investigation In Turkey, International Research Journal Of Finance And Economics, 24, Pp.186-193.

Vanpoucke, E., Boyer, K. And Vereecke, A., 2009, Supply Chain Information Flow Strategies: An Empirical Taxonomy, Working Paper, Vlerick Leuven Gent Management School & Ghent University, Belgium. March.

Vasiliu, C., 2008, Warehousing - Activity Which Contribute To Supply Chain Performance, Amfiteatru Economic, X (24), Pp. 94-108.

Vasiliu, C., Felea, M., Mărunţelu (Albăstroiu), I. And Caraiani, G., 2008, Logistica Şi Distribuţia Mărfurilor, Note De Cursus, Bucureşti: Editura Ase.

Verweij, H. And Peek, L., 2013, Supplier Relationship Management, How Key Suppliers Drive Your Company's Competitive Advantage, Pwc. Available At: Https://Www.Pwc.Nl/Nl/Assets/Documents/Pwc-Supplier-Relationship-Management.Pdf

Wagner, S.M., Bode, C., 2006, An Empirical Investigation Into Supply Chain Vulnerability, Journal Of Purchasing And Supply Management, 12(6), Pp. 301–312.

Wagner, S.M., Bode, C., Koziol, P., 2009, Supplier Default Dependencies: Empirical Evidence From The Automotive Industry, European Journal Of Operational Research 199(1), Pp. 150–161.

Wallace, V. And Herrick, A., 2009, What Banking Needs To Become, Strategy, Winter. Available At: Https://Www.Strategy-Business.Com/Article/09405?Gko=213ea

Waller. D.L., 2003, Operations Management: A Supply Chain Approach, 2nd Edition. London: Thomson Learning.

Wang, X., Herty, M., & Zhao, L., 2016, Contingent Rerouting For Enhancing Supply Chain Resilience From Supplier Behavior Perspective, International Transactions In Operational Research, 23(4), Pp. 775-796. Available At Http://Dx.Doi.Org/10.1111/Itor.12151.

Wasmann, M. And Spruit, M..2012, Performance Management Within Social Network Sites: The Social Network Intelligence Process Method, Int. J. Bus. Intell. Res., 3, Pp. 49–63.

Waters, D., 2008, Supply Chain Risk Management: Vulnerability And Resilience In Logistics, London: Kogan Page.

Werner, E. E., & Smith, R. S., 2001, Journeys From Childhood To Midlife: Risk Resilience And Recovery, New York, Ny: Cornell University Press.

Weston J.F. & Brigham E.F., 1977, Essentials Of Managerial Finance, Illinois:The Dryde Press, Pp. 261-76

Wettstein, T. And Kueng, P., 2002, A Maturity Model For Performance Measurement Systems, Wit Trans. Inf. Commun. Technol., 26, Pp. 113–122.

Wieland, A., Wallenburg, C.M., 2012, Dealing With Supply-Chain Risks: Linking Risk Management Practices And Strategies To Performance, International Journal Of Physical Distribution & Logistics Management, 42(10).

Wild, J. J., 1998, Financial Statement Analysis, Theory, Application And Interpretation (6ed.): Irwin/Mc Graw Hill.

Williams, Z., Ponder, N., & Autry, C. W., 2009, Supply Chain Security Culture: Measure Development And Validation, International Journal Of Logistics Management, 20(2), Pp. 243-260. Available At Http://Dx.Doi.Org/10.1108/09574090910981323.

Williamson, O.E., 1979, Transaction-Cost Economics: The Governance Of Contractual Relations, Journal Of Law And Economics, 22 (October), Pp. 3–61.

Williamson, O.E., 1981. The Economics Of Organization: The Transaction Cost Approach. The American Journal Of Sociology 87 (3), 548–577.

Williamson, O.E., 1985, The Economic Institutions Of Capitalism, The Free Press, New York.

Williamson, O.E., 2008, Outsourcing: Transaction Cost Economics And Supply Chain Management, Journal Of Supply Chain Management, 44(2), Pp. 5–16.

Wisner, J.D., Keong, L.G., Keah-Choon, T., 2005, Supply Chain Management: A Balanced Approach, Thomson South–Western, Mason, Oh.

Wolin, S. J., & Wolin, S., 1993, The Resilient Self: How Survivors Of Troubled Families Rise Above Adversity. New York, Ny: Villard Books.

Wong, C. Y., And Karia, N., 2010, Explaining The Competitive Advantage Of Logistics Service Providers: A Resource-Based View Approach, International Journal Of Production Economics, 128(1), Pp. 51-67.

World Economic Forum, 2017, The Global Risks Report 2017 (12th Ed.). Geneva: World Economic Forum. Available At Http://Www3.Weforum.Org/Docs/Grr17_Report_Web.Pdf

Wu, D.D., Kefan, X., Gang, C., Ping, G., 2010, A Risk Analysis Model In Concurrent Engineering Product Development, Risk Analysis, 30(9), Pp. 1440–1453.

Wu, D.D., Olson, D., Birge, J., 2009, Call For Papers, International Journal Of Production Economics, Enterprise Risk Management In Operations. Available At /Www.Elsevier.Com/Framework_Products/Promis_Misc/Cfp_Enterpriserisk0509.Pdfs.

Wu, D.D., Olson, D.L., 2009, Enterprise Risk Management: Small Business Scorecard Analysis, Production Planning & Control, 20(4), Pp. 362–369.

Wu, D.D., Olson, D.L., 2009, Introduction To The Special Issue On 'Optimizing Risk Management Methods And Tools', Human And Ecological Risk Assessment, 15(2), Pp. 220–226.

Wu, D.D., Olson, D.L., 2010, Enterprise Risk Management: Coping With Model Risk In A Large Bank, Journal Of The Operational Research Society, 61(2), Pp. 179–190.

Wu, D.D., Olson, D.L., 2010, Enterprise Risk Management: A Dea Var Approach In Vendor Selection, International Journal Of Production Research, 48(16), Pp. 4919–4932.

Wyman, P., Sandler, I., Wolchik, S., Nelson, K., And Cicchetti, D. (Ed); Rappaport, Julian (Ed); Sandler, Irwin (Ed); Weissberg, Roger P. (Ed), 2000, The Promotion Of Wellness In Children And Adolescents., Pp. 133- 184.

Yang, C. C., Marlow, P. B., And Lu, C. S., 2009, Assessing Resources, Logistics Service Capabilities, Innovation Capabilities And The Performance Of Container Shipping Service In Taiwan, International Journal Of Production Economics, 122(1), Pp. 4–20.

Zhang, Z., & Sharifi, H., 2000, A Methodology For Achieving Agility In Manufacturing Organizations, International Journal Of Operations And Production Management, 20(4), Pp. 496-512.

Zhu, J., & Ruth, M., 2013, Exploring The Resilience Of Industrial Ecosystems. Journal Of Environmental Management, 122, Pp. 65-75. Available At Http:// Dx.Doi.Org/10.1016/J.Jenvman.2013.02.052. Pmid:23562949.

Zsidisin, G.A., 2003, A Grounded Definition Of Supply Risk, Journal Of Purchasing And Supply Management, 9(5–6), Pp. 217–224.

Zsidisin, G.A., 2003, Managerial Perceptions Of Supply Risk, Journal Of Supply Chain Management, 39(1), Pp. 14–26.

Zsidisin, G.A., Ellram, L.M., 2003, An Agency Theory Investigation Of Supply Risk Management, Journal Of Supply Chain Management, 39(3), Pp. 15–27.

Zsidisin, G.A., Melnyk, S.A., Ragatz, G.L., 2005, An Institutional Theory Perspective Of Business Continuity Planning For Purchasing And Supply Management, International Journal Of Production Research, 43(16), Pp. 3401–3420.

INDEX

A

B

C

D

M

O

P

R

S

T

V

W

Made in the USA
Las Vegas, NV
03 November 2026

57421607R00431